D0077077

ecent Titles from Quorum Books

he Management of Corporate Business Units: Portfolio Strategies for Turbulent
mes
ouis E. V. Nevaer and Steven A. Deck

ow to Write for the Professional Journals: A Guide for Technically Trained
anagers
le L. Miller, Jr.

fective Information Centers: Guidelines for MIS and IC Managers
bert J. Thierauf

ucation Incorporated: School-Business Cooperation for Economic Growth
rtheast-Midwest Institute, editor

cision Support Systems in Finance and Accounting
G. Heymann and Robert Bloom

eedom of Speech on Private Property
rren Freedman

uses of Failure in Performance Appraisal and Supervision: A Guide to Analysis
d Evaluation for Human Resources Professionals
Baker, Jr.

e Modern Economics of Housing: A Guide to Theory and Policy for Finance
d Real Estate Professionals
ndall Johnston Pozdena

oductivity and Quality Through Science and Technology
K. Shetty and Vernon M. Buehler, editors

eractive Corporate Compliance: An Alternative to Regulatory Compulsion
A. Sigler and Joseph E. Murphy

untary Corporate Liquidations
nald J. Kudla

iness-Government Relations and Interdependence: A Managerial and Analytic
spective
n M. Stevens, Steven L. Wartick, and John W. Bagby

Career Growth
and
Human Resource
Strategies

R
T
T
L
H
M
R
Ef
R
Ed
N
De
H.
Fr
W
Ca
an
Jo
Th
an
Ra
Pro
Y.
Int
Jay
Vo
Ro
Bu
Per
Joh

CAREER GROWTH AND HUMAN RESOURCE STRATEGIES

THE ROLE OF THE HUMAN RESOURCE PROFESSIONAL IN EMPLOYEE DEVELOPMENT

EDITED BY

Manuel London

AND

Edward M. Mone

QUORUM BOOKS

New York • Westport, Connecticut • London

Library of Congress Cataloging-in-Publication Data

Career growth and human resource strategies : the role of the human
  resource professional in employee development / edited by Manuel
  London and Edward M. Mone.
    p.   cm.
  Bibliography: p.
  Includes index.
  ISBN 0–89930–229–7 (lib. bdg. : alk. paper)
  1. Career development.   I. London, Manuel.   II. Mone, Edward M.
HF5549.5.C35C37 1988
658.3'124—dc19   87–32281

British Library Cataloguing in Publication Data is available.

Library of Congress Catalog Card Number: 87–32281
ISBN: 0–89930–229–7

First published in 1988 by Quorum Books

Greenwood Press, Inc.
88 Post Road West, Westport, Connecticut 06881

Printed in the United States of America

The paper used in this book complies with the
Permanent Paper Standard issued by the National
Information Standards Organization (Z39.48–1984).

10 9 8 7 6 5 4 3 2 1

Copyright Acknowledgments

Grateful acknowledgment is given to the following for permission to use:

Figure 2.1, from Exhibit 2.1, "A Model of Career Management," from Jeffrey H. Greenhaus, *Career Management*, p. 18. Copyright (c) 1987 by CBS College Publishing. Reprinted by Permission of Holt, Rinehart & Winston, Inc.

Exhibit 2.2, adapted from Table 5.4, "Five Stages of Career Development," in Jeffrey H. Greenhaus, *Career Management*, p. 87. Copyright (c) 1987 by CBS College Publishing. Reprinted by permission of Holt, Rinehart & Winston, Inc.

Figure 20.1, reprinted from the February (48–55) issue of *Personnel Administrator*, copyright, 1987, The American Society for Personnel Administration, 606 North Washington Street, Alexandria, VA 22314.

CONTENTS

FIGURES AND EXHIBITS   xi

PREFACE   xiii

Part I. Career Processes   1

Chapter 1.   Management Career Motivation: Life
              Changes and Social Vicissitudes
              Douglas W. Bray and Ann Howard   5

Chapter 2.   Career Exploration
              Jeffrey H. Greenhaus   17

Chapter 3.   The Socialization Process: Building
              Newcomer Commitment
              Georgia T. Chao   31

Chapter 4.   Promoting Career-Enhancing
              Relationships in Organizations: The
              Role of the Human Resource
              Professional
              David A. Thomas and Kathy E. Kram   49

Chapter 5.   Maintaining Employee Involvement in a
              Plateaued Career
              Douglas T. Hall and Samuel Rabinowitz   67

Chapter 6.   Career Success and Personal Failure:
                  Mid- to Late-Career Feelings and Events
                  Abraham K. Korman   81

Part II. Organizational Strategies for Career Development   95

Chapter 7.   Corporate Philosophies of Employee
                  Development
                  Mirian M. Graddick   99

Chapter 8.   How to Win Friends and Develop
                  Managers: An Approach to Setting
                  Management Development Policies
                  Lynn Summers   111

Chapter 9.   A Taxonomy for Managerial
                  Effectiveness
                  Edward R. Del Gaizo   125

Chapter 10.   Business Strategy, Staffing, and Career
                  Management Issues
                  *John W. Slocum, Jr., and William L.
                  Cron*   135

Part III. Career Development Tools, Techniques, and Programs   153

Chapter 11.   Designing and Facilitating a Self-
                  Assessment Experience
                  Cynthia B. Smith   157

Chapter 12.   Designing Developmental Assessment
                  Centers: Step by Step
                  Virginia R. Boehm   173

Chapter 13.   Stimulating High-Potential Career
                  Development through an Assessment
                  Center Process
                  Peter Cairo and Karen S. Lyness   183

Chapter 14.   Business Simulations for Skill Diagnosis
                  and Development
                  Stephen A. Stumpf   195

Chapter 15.   Training Managers to Be Developers
                 Edward M. Mone   207

Part IV. Career Experiences   223

Chapter 16.   Human Resources and the Extraordinary
                 Problems Minorities Face
                 John P. Fernandez   227

Chapter 17.   ✗ Women in Management
                 Ronald G. Downey and Mary Anne
                 Lahey   241

Chapter 18.   How Successful Executives Develop: The
                 Challenges of Leadership, Other People,
                 Hard Times, and the Classroom
                 Michael M. Lombardo   257

Chapter 19.   The Role of the Human Resource
                 Professional in Managing Other Salaried
                 Professionals
                 Joseph A. Raelin   271

Chapter 20.   ✗ Termination and Outplacement
                 Strategies
                 Janina C. Latack and Harold G.
                 Kaufman   289

Part V. Multiple Roles of Human Resource Professionals   315

Chapter 21.   ✗ The Future Role of HR Professionals in
                 Employee Career Development
                 Manuel London   317

INDEX   329

ABOUT THE CONTRIBUTORS   335

FIGURES AND EXHIBITS

FIGURES

Figure	1.1	Key Motivation Scores over Time for MPS College Graduates	9
Figure	1.2	Occupational Life Theme (Average Score over Time by MPS: 20 Level)	11
Figure	1.3	Key Motivation Scores for MPS versus MCS College Recruits	12
Figure	2.1	A Model of Career Management	19
Figure	3.1	Organizational Socialization Model for Newcomers	33
Figure	4.1	Typology of Career-Enhancing Relations	52
Figure	5.1	Grid for Analyzing Plateauing and Performance	70
Figure	5.2	Two-Path Career Model	74
Figure	9.1	Managerial Taxonomy	129
Figure	10.1	Organization Strategy and Its Consequences on Human Resources in Organizations	137
Figure	20.1	Stroh Transition Services Program Activity Flowchart	302

EXHIBITS

Exhibit	2.1	Vehicles for Career Exploration	22
Exhibit	2.2	Characteristics of Different Career Stages	24

Exhibit 8.1   Five Sticky Problems   113

Exhibit 8.2   Management Development Responsibilities   116

Exhibit 8.3   A Sampling of Skills Underlying the
               Leadership Dimension   119

Exhibit 9.1   Decision Points for Phases 2 and 3   127

Exhibit 9.2   Examples of Actions Required to Improve
               Proficiency in Each Role   133

Exhibit 10.1   Summary of Important Managerial
               Requirements for Defenders and Analyzers   138

Exhibit 10.2   Summary of Staffing Practices for Defenders
               and Analyzers   142

Exhibit 10.3   Career Issues for Employees Working in
               Defender and Analyzer Companies   144

Exhibit 10.4   Job Attitudes and Job Performance of
               Employees in Defender and Analyzer
               Companies   147

Exhibit 15.1   Criteria for Evaluating Goal
               Accomplishments: An Example   211

Exhibit 15.2   A Detailed Developmental Plan for One
               Goal   212

Exhibit 18.1   Skills and Perspectives Important for
               Executive Success   263

Exhibit 19.1   The Mediation Strategies for Integrating
               Professional and Management Values   276

Exhibit 20.1   Questions to Consider in Making
               Termination Decisions   297

Exhibit 20.2   Preparing and Conducting the Dismissal
               Meeting   299

Exhibit 20.3   Outplacement Program Components   301

Exhibit 20.4   A Sample of Severance Pay Agreements   304

PREFACE

This is a book of original papers on the roles and responsibilities of human resource professionals in career planning and development. The intended audience includes personnel program developers, personnel policy setters, trainers, training program developers, career counselors, and resource planners. Written by experienced practitioners, the papers present a picture of current issues and problems, with descriptions of programs and strategies for dealing with them.

The book is timely for several reasons. The field of career planning and development is reaching a level of maturity after its rise in popularity in the late 1970s. The concern has shifted from an emphasis on the individual—for example, self-help books and programs on "What are *my* interests?" "What do *I* want from *my* life and career?" and "How can *I* get what *I* want?"—to an emphasis on the individual's needs in relation to the organization's current and future position. That is, we are learning that career planning cannot be done fruitfully without attention to the corporation's philosophy of developing people, the expectations of different departments or its employees, and the opportunities that are available today and that are forecasted for the future.

A reason for this integration of organizational and individual needs and career planning and development programs is that organizations are experiencing tremendous pressures to be more competitive in the international marketplace. Moreover, corporate mergers lead to new organizational structures and often to the need for fewer people. All this has required increases in productivity with fewer resources. Trends include layoffs, often affecting middle management employees, and increased spans of control, which may mean more responsibility for those remaining. There is an emphasis on developing specialists in their fields (for example, marketing, finance, and so forth), in addition to developing generalist managers (people who have excellent managerial skills which can be applied in many different settings). Also, advances in technology, including new office technologies, often require retraining employees to meet new work demands. The topics in this book reflect this changing, highly pressured organizational environment and the resulting tie between career development and human resource strategy.

This book is divided into five parts. Part 1 focuses on career processes in early, middle, and late career. The chapters address changes in motivation during the course of one's career, career alternatives, the socialization processes organizations use to engender newcomer commitment, career enhancing relationships such as having a mentor, career plateauing, and the phenomenon of simultaneously experiencing career success and personal failure which may occur in mid- to late career. Part 2 describes organizational strategies for career development. The chapters review corporate philosophies of employee development and examples of management development policies. The types of managerial skills needed for today and the future are examined, and the link of business strategies and career opportunities is clarified. Part 3 focuses on tools, techniques, and programs for career development. Chapters cover self-assessment methods, designing assessment centers for career planning and development, a career development program for high potential managers, the use of simulations for assessment and development, and a program to train managers to develop their subordinates. Part 4 highlights various career experiences. Chapters examine career opportunities and barriers for minorities and women, executives' development experiences, the meaning of career development for salaried professionals, and job loss. Part 5 considers the experiences and roles of human resource professionals in career development for the future.

Ten major themes run through the chapters:

1. The importance of understanding one's strengths and weaknesses and using that knowledge to form career plans and take actions to achieve those plans is evident in chapters on career exploration, socialization, self-assessment, assessment centers, and simulations.

2. Corporate resources can be used in an effective way to enhance career development. Job experiences, communication about career opportunities, and training programs are some of the ways organizations use their resources to enhance both the organization's objectives and the individual's professional growth.

3. Social pressures lead to organizational inefficiencies and unwarranted career barriers. This is obvious in the chapters on race and sex discrimination.

4. A career is a life-long developmental process. While many of the chapters deal with discrete portions of a career (for example, socialization into an organization), other chapters deal with the career as a whole, emphasizing the continuity of development, how different experiences contribute to change in the

person over time, and the alternative career paths open to people (for example, professional versus managerial paths).

5. Discontinuities may disrupt or significantly alter the career development process. For instance, chapters discuss the feelings of personal failure that may accompany career success and the learning that can be derived from hard times (a tough job, demotion, or job loss).

6. Organizational experiences can be designed or controlled to systematically affect career development. Socialization experiences and the establishment of alternative career paths are examples. Leaders can be developed by placing managers in a sequence of assignments that require increasing responsibility. In addition, the business strategy of the organization influences the career opportunities that will be available to employees.

7. Interpersonal relationships are important to career development. Chapters discuss mentor-protégé relationships, the manager's role in developing subordinates, and the manager's role in creating an environment that engenders employee involvement and commitment, even for people whose careers have plateaued.

8. Several chapters note that the leadership role has been changing to meet current business demands, and this is reflected in management and leadership development programs. There is the need for different types of leadership skills to match different business environments. Moreover, leaders and managers at all organizational levels play critical roles in the development of people to ensure their contribution to the organization and to ensure their professional growth for the future.

9. Several chapters cover a variety of training methods for supporting career development. These tools include assessment centers, post-assessment development programs, and other methods that lead to self-awareness of strengths and weaknesses and suggest directions for career movement.

10. Human resource managers play several significant roles in the career development process. As evident throughout the book and summarized in the final chapter, human resource professionals are educators, facilitators, innovators, experimenters, leaders, and strategists.

We are grateful to the chapter authors for their enthusiasm and timely response. Their excitement and concern about career development is reflected in the quality of their contributions. Special thanks to Joseph L. Moses for his review of several chapters. We also appreciate the enthusiasm of Eric Valentine, our editor at Quorum Press.

Career Growth
and
Human Resource
Strategies

Part I

Career Processes

This first section of the book examines psychological and social processes throughout one's career. It focuses on the theme of career as a life-long developmental process and shows how other career development themes operate at different career stages—for instance, the importance of self-understanding through career exploration, the contribution of organizational experiences such as socialization to later development, the value of supportive interpersonal relationships, and ways to resolve career discontinuities, such as mid-career plateauing and the feeling of personal failure that may accompany career success.

Douglas Bray and Ann Howard write about changes in career motivation over time. Drawing on extensive data from a sample of managers followed for over thirty years and another sample of younger managers followed for ten years, Bray and Howard find that the motivation of young managers entering an organization is the foundation for future levels of motivation. However, motivation changes as a function of age, experience, and especially degree of success. A striking change found in the authors' research was the decline of advancement motivation for those who realize that they are unlikely to reach a higher level. This trend is evident five years into a person's career, suggesting that motivational growth or decline start early in management careers. Bray and Howard also find that prevailing social factors affect motivation. The younger group of managers was substantially lower in most aspects of motivation than those who started their careers twenty years earlier. However, the new generation resembles the previous one in wanting challenging work and financial return. Bray and Howard conclude with a discussion of ways organizations can provide assignments and an environment to enhance motivation.

Jeffrey Greenhaus's chapter on career exploration begins a discussion of early career issues that also have relevance to later career moves. He examines how career exploration contributes to meaningful self-understanding and to effective career decision-making. His career management model outlines a problem-solving process incorporating collecting career-related information, developing insight about oneself and the environment, setting goals, and developing and implementing a strategy to accomplish those goals. Obtaining feedback and evaluating one's goal accomplishments may lead to renewing the exploration process. Greenhaus then focuses on career exploration by outlining sources of information and describing ways to prepare for work (for example, by obtaining the necessary education). Obstacles to effective career exploration include getting incomplete information, being coerced, ignoring nonwork considerations, and not considering ways to improve one's present job. Finally, Greenhaus recommends actions to encourage career motivation, such as making it voluntary, providing opportunities and tools for self-analysis, encouraging peers to share insights about their careers, involving subordinates in providing feedback, incorporating nonwork aspirations into the exploration process, and providing up-to-date information about the organization.

Georgia Chao writes about socialization processes to build newcomer commitment. She recognizes that valid selection systems, when matched with appropriate socialization strategies, will ensure that the most qualified people are selected into an organization and that new hires will be properly taught to perform their jobs. Socialization refers to learning about the necessary knowledge, skills, and abilities to do the job, and learning about the way the organization functions. Socialization shapes the individual's general work values and attitudes and how important the job should be in relation to one's total life. Chao emphasizes the importance of maintaining a work force that represents a variety of knowledge, skills, and abilities. Formal socialization practices described in the chapter include orientation programs, training, development, and job assignments. Informal socialization forces include one's supervisors and mentors, professional colleagues, and subordinates. Disadvantages of socialization are information overload and inappropriate dysfunctional strategies, such as requiring job rotations when new, young employees do not wish to relocate. Advantages of paying attention to the socialization process are the efficiency of bringing a newcomer up to speed on work productivity, helping the newcomer focus on the most important features of the job, building self-confidence, and enhancing commitment to the organization. Chao covers how the human resource professional controls the organization's practices through recruitment and selection, orientation and training programs, the design of early job experiences, and training line managers to be aware of their influence over newcomer socialization.

David Thomas and Kathy Kram describe career-enhancing relations in organizations. They distinguish between temporary/instrumental relationships, sustained/career-support relationships, and mentor/protégé relationships. These relationships usually involve individuals with their immediate supervisor, but they may also be with persons two levels or more above the individual or with peers (people at the same level). Thomas and Kram point to the need for human resource professionals to develop an understanding of the range of career-enhancing relationships and the conditions which foster them. Organizations can develop incentive structures to encourage the formation of career-enhancing relationships. For instance, affirmative action requirements may influence white and male managers to sponsor minorities and women. The authors highlight the complexities and the development of cross-race and cross-gender career-enhancing relationships, for instance, in the ability to form a positive identification with an individual. The chapter concludes with alternatives for human resource managers to improving the quality of developmental relationships through formal mentor programs and training to help managers understand developmental relationships at all career stages.

The next chapter describes ways to maintain employee involvement in a plateaued career. Douglas T. Hall and Samuel Rabinowitz describe how career plateauing (reaching a stage where further advancement is unlikely) generally occurs in mid-career. This is usually accompanied by feelings of low marketability, dissatisfaction with advancement prospects, lower job involvement, and feeling that one's contribution to the organization is recognized less. The authors emphasize that plateaued employees who are good performers are valuable to the organization; so their motivation needs to be encouraged. Hall and Rabinowitz describe techniques for high-involvement management which generate employee motivation and involvement. One example is a gain-sharing plan which allows employees in a work group to share a monetary bonus because of the group's performance. Other examples include ways to involve employees in making important job decisions. Job rotations may keep employees fresh and engaged in the organization's activities. Another option is to find ways to help plateaued people manage their work so that their jobs are less involving. Rather then providing stimulation through job enrichment, the goal here is to make the job worthwhile as a vehicle for accomplishing nonwork goals by allowing more time off, a four-day workweek, and more focus on extrinsic rewards, such as pay and benefits.

Some organizations offer employees a choice of career track. One career track is advancing in level of management with increasing responsibility for running the organization. Another career track is advancing by gaining distinction as a professional (for instance, rewarding the contributions of a scientist to the firm's research and development by increasing the individual's rate of pay and benefits). A third career ladder may be project management involving increasing technical and managerial responsibilities. Hall and Rabinowitz conclude with creative ideas for developing the skills of plateauing employees through job switches downward and other ways to encourage the individual to acquire new skills.

The final chapter in this section discusses mid- to late-career feelings and events. Abraham Korman describes how career success and feelings of personal failure may go together. Korman begins by reviewing the evidence for this phenomenon. He describes reports of self-destructive behavior (for example, drug abuse, depression, divorce, feelings of stress, and loss of emotional ties with others). The author attributes these outcomes to what has been termed the mid-life crisis—the emotional trauma brought about by a number of factors that become salient as one reaches mid-life. These factors include realizing one's mortality, an increasing sense of personal obsolescence, the growth and maturity of one's children, and the emotions accompanying the aging of one's parents.

Loss of career opportunities and narrowing of opportunities, as discussed by Hall and Rabinowitz, are other mid-career problems noted by Korman. Even high income levels may make a person feel worse when money and career success become meaningless because there are no longer benefits from acquiring more wealth and recognition. Another cause of mid-life crisis is the sudden recognition that career success came at the price of personal sacrifice, such as less attention to one's family than one would have liked, or not having children. Korman notes that women are less apt to pay such "affiliative costs" because they are likely to maintain relationships during the course of their careers, although incurring other costs, such as exhaustion from juggling the roles of wife, mother, and executive.

There is a limit to what management can do about the phenomenon of career success and personal failure in middle age since the feelings are a function of facing reality. Korman recommends encouraging people to develop ways to achieve a greater sense of satisfaction—perhaps by becoming involved in more challenging work assignments. Ways to help people experience a greater sense of competence in their work and encourage them to pay more attention to family life and social relationships are also recommended. However, organizations may be reluctant to interfere in employees' personal lives, and male executives in particular are likely to ignore or postpone dealing with problems stemming from affiliative relationships.

CHAPTER 1

MANAGEMENT CAREER MOTIVATION: LIFE CHANGES AND SOCIAL VICISSITUDES

DOUGLAS W. BRAY AND ANN HOWARD

The quality of an organization's management depends on many factors, including the characteristics of those recruited and selected for employment, their development in management, and their advancement into positions of higher responsibility. Management ability and the potential to develop additional skills are of critical importance. So, too, are motivational characteristics: the desire to pursue a career in management and those underlying motives that will support and impel such a career.

Although abilities are often evaluated only loosely, they still are given more analytic attention than motivation. Motivations are often uncritically assumed. Nearly everyone in management may be thought eager for promotion, reasonably strongly identified with the organization, and desirous of participating in decision making. There is little appreciation of factors such as changes in motivation with age and experience, differences between those in various levels of management, or generational variations. Even when there is a vague awareness that not all managers are similarly motivated, action implications tend to be elusive.

A deeper understanding of management career motivation would be of great value to the human resource professional. Selecting managers, minimizing turnover, optimizing conditions for development, designing training and educational programs, and evaluating promotability would be markedly improved by more sophistication about motivational factors.

DEFINING AND MEASURING MANAGEMENT CAREER MOTIVATION

Management motivation may be thought of at two levels. One subsumes interest in and taking steps toward having a career in management. For some, the decision to seek a management career is based on real, although perhaps indirect, familiarity with what managers do on a day-to-day basis. One or both parents may be managers, and mealtime conversations over the years may have revealed some of the positives and negatives of that occupational role. Others, however, may be attracted by the vague image of a well-paid white-collar job and have little appreciation of its nitty-gritty aspects. The senior author has pointed out elsewhere (Bray, 1984) how poorly grounded motivation to manage may crumble when a manager is faced with tedious tasks, difficult supervisors, and recalcitrant subordinates.

At a deeper level, motivation to manage is the degree to which persons possess motives which lead them to strive for success in a managerial role. For example, one who is impelled to coordinate and direct the activities of others would find satisfaction in at least that aspect of managing. The more of such relevant motives people possess, the more overall motivation to manage they have.

Some decide to enter management careers because they have a valid sense of their own motives and the relevance of these motives to management. Others do not, however, and find themselves in an inappropriate career. This is not uncommon since, as will be discussed later, some end up in management because they did not elect to prepare for a profession such as medicine or law.

Types of Managerial Motivation

An in-depth analysis of management motivation is provided by the longitudinal studies of managerial careers conducted at AT&T over the past thirty years. In the Management Progress Study (MPS), a cohort of managers has been followed from their start in management in the 1950s until today. Young managers of the late 1970s and early 1980s have been tracked in the parallel Management Continuity Study (MCS). The methodology of this research will be described only briefly here because a complete description is available elsewhere (Howard and Bray 1988).

The participants in MPS underwent three comprehensive assessment centers: one at the start of their careers in management, another eight years later, and a third twenty years later. The assessment centers included multiple measures of abilities and motives. These measures were examined as predictors of career outcomes and analyzed to learn the structure of management potential. The repeated assessment centers also permitted the study of changes in abilities and motives over the years. The MCS participants have been assessed only once so far, but the patterns of assessment results parallel those from MPS.

Analyses of the assessment center measures revealed several factors of importance in management career motivation. One of these was labeled advancement motivation, although insistent ambition might be an even more apt term. Those scoring high on this factor were rated high on the assessment dimension of need for advancement and low on the dimensions indicating willingness to wait for promotion, need for job security, and realism of career expectations.

A second important factor was work involvement, made up of the dimensions of primacy of work and inner work standards. Primacy of work refers to the importance of work compared with other sources of life satisfaction. Inner work standards indicates the motivation to do quality work even in the absence of external demands. Inner work standards and advancement motivation are positively related, which is fortunate. There are, nevertheless, significant personality differences between those who score high on one factor but low on the other (Bray and Howard 1983).

A third factor is leadership motivation. Those high in this factor like to take charge of things in group situations and propel the group toward its goals. They tend to be dissatisfied with a subordinate role. They are more independent and less affiliative than others.

Measuring Managerial Motivation

The assessment centers provided insight into motivation from several different types of assessment exercises. In evaluating advancement motivation, the in-depth interviews and the projective tests were most important, supplemented by personality questionnaires. These exercises were also important in rating inner work standards, but here the quality of work in the simulations was additionally revealing. It is clear that getting at motivation is more difficult than, say, testing general mental ability and requires more elaborate evaluative methods.

Elaborating on such methods, London (1985) described a two-day career motivation assessment center developed in the Basic Human Resources Research section at AT&T. Although few organizations would apply such an ambitious procedure at the point of employment (it was used to study newly employed managers), some of the paper-and-pencil assessment instruments would be useful on their own. One short simulation—fact-finding about a hypothetical job choice—could easily supplement a selection interview, and additional simulations could be devised. There is a recent trend, in fact, toward adding mini-simulations to interviews, which inspires the comment, "Better one interview and one simulation than two interviews!"

Yet management employment interviews have been much improved in recent years by a focus on past behavior rather than on the interviewee's projected behavior in future or hypothetical situations. This focus has, however, been directed primarily to the evaluation of managerial skills. It could and should be expanded to encompass motivation.

Recruiters can find leads in the types of college activities and accomplishments of those they interview. Howard's (1986) research investigated several aspects of college experiences and their relationship to managerial performance. Grades, for example, were predictive of inner work standards but not of advancement motivation. To optimize advancement motivation, graduates with MBA degrees were better bets than those with only bachelor's degrees. Involvement in many extracurricular activities often signaled high primacy of work, while humanities and social science majors were more motivated to take leadership roles than those with technical backgrounds.

Few human resource administrators would reject the statement that managerial motivation is an important organizational asset. Yet they are often at a loss as to how to evaluate whether the organization is well off in this regard or not. This is in contrast to management skills, where training needs analyses provide information about abilities. Attitude surveys are not infrequent, but they do not address motivation completely or effectively. Attitudes may result from the balance, or imbalance, between motivation and the perceived organizational environment. What is needed are organizational motivation analyses.

An appraisal of management motivation in an organization does not mean that every manager would have to be evaluated. A representative sample could be drawn sufficient to compare management levels or departments or locations, as desired. Furthermore, confidentiality with respect to individual results could, and probably should, be maintained. Not only would some of the information obtained be quite personal, but more complete cooperation would be obtained under such conditions. Individuals might, however, be given private feedback if they so desired.

There is also the possibility of comparing the results in one organization with those in another. This was one facet of the Inter-Organizational Testing Study we carried out in ten different organizations as a supplement to the AT&T research. It would be valuable to know, for example, the motivational qualities of new college recruits in one's organization as compared with those just hired by others. If deficiencies were found, changes could be made in the recruiting and selection process.

FACTORS AFFECTING MANAGEMENT CAREER MOTIVATION

General mental ability, an important managerial quality, may increase throughout adult life, but individuals line up almost exactly the same on this characteristic in middle age as they did earlier. In the MPS, for example, the correlation between general mental ability test scores earned in the 1950s and those twenty years later was .89. This very high relationship is just about what would result had the participants been tested on two successive days.

Managerial motivation is quite different. It is much less fixed either in sum or in its components. This means that it is dangerous to make any

Figure 1.1
Key Motivation Scores over Time for MPS College Graduates

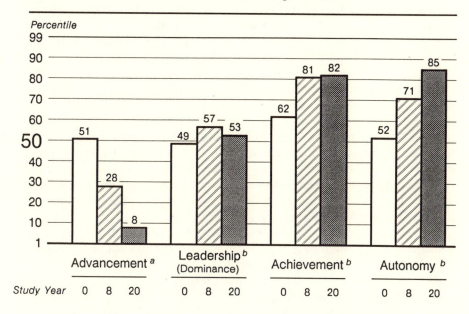

^a *Sarnoff Survey of Attitudes Toward Life, MPS College Norms, 1956–60*
^b *Edwards Personal Preference Schedule, Bell System College Hire Norms, 1958*

assumptions about the level of motivation of any particular group of managers. Evaluating the current state of motivation is always advisable.

Life Changes

The motivation of young managers entering an organization is of key importance as the foundation for future levels of motivation in the organization. It will not, however, remain constant for many individuals or for the group as a whole. As the MPS participants were followed through the years, many changes were observed. Some of these were general changes, apparently the result of age and common experiences. Others varied markedly by the degree of success in management, as reflected in management level attained.

One of the most striking changes, among those illustrated in Figure 1.1, was a sharp drop in motivation for advancement as the years went by among those who remained with the company. After eight years, the study participants were only at the 28th percentile on an inventory measuring advancement motivation as compared to the 51st percentile at the time they started in management. The decline continued, so that after twenty years they scored at only the 8th percentile.

This decline was due in part to some having reached a level which satisfied them, even though that level might still be far from the top. More important, however, was an adjustment to reality as many realized that their chances for a high-level position were essentially nonexistent. In any case, by mid-career the drive for advancement was a salient characteristic for only the small minority who were moving into higher-management and officer positions.

There was little average change in leadership motivation over the years (also shown in Figure 1.1), but there was a sizable increase in motivation for achievement—to do a difficult job well. At year twenty, the study group stood at the 82nd percentile as compared to the 62nd percentile at the start. Another impressive change was in the desire for independence. On a scale of need for autonomy, the group was at the 85th percentile in middle age compared to the 52nd twenty years earlier.

Changes over time varied widely, however, among different levels of management. Although all groups declined at least somewhat in motivation for advancement, this decline was small for those who had arrived at the department head and officer levels and greatest for those who stayed at lower levels of the organization. There were level differences also in job involvement and leadership motivation, with those who wound up at or near the top of the heap showing strong increases in these characteristics while those whose career led to average or below levels showed little gain or even a decline. To illustrate such differences by level, Figure 1.2 shows involvement in the occupational life theme as coded from interviews over the years for those who reached different levels of management after twenty years.

A very important observation is that these differences in motivational growth or decline start to develop surprisingly early in management careers. The trends are clearly apparent five years into the career, and the differences keep widening from then on. It appears that some combination of preexisting motivation and the experiences of the early years results in a highly positive response on the part of some, little response in others, and a negative reaction in the remainder. The early years of the career are critical.

Social Vicissitudes

Motivation is changed by influences other than growing older and experiencing different degrees of career success. The tides of societal change are a powerful factor, having their greatest effect on those growing up under different conditions than their predecessors. The effects of cultural changes were apparent in the participants in the MCS, college graduates who joined

Figure 1.2
Occupational Life Theme (Average Score over Time by MPS: 20 Level)

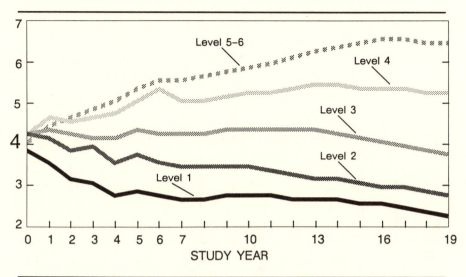

the Bell System in the years 1977 to 1982. They were thus one generation removed from those in the MPS.

One great cultural change immediately apparent was the appearance in the group of many women and minorities. In the less enlightened years of the 1950s, all the MPS participants, who were selected as representative of young managers with a reasonable chance of attaining middle management, were white males. By contrast, the MCS participants, selected in the late 1970s and early 1980s using the same criteria as used for MPS, consisted of one-third minority group members and nearly one half women. The findings to be presented here, however, are not influenced by the different composition of the two groups. They held true when only white males were compared.

The new group was substantially lower in most aspects of management motivation than those employed twenty years previously, as Figure 1.3 shows. They scored at only the 25th percentile on a scale measuring motivation for advancement as compared to the 50th percentile for the MPS group at the start. Neither were they as motivated to lead. Here the typical new recruit was at the 29th percentile as against the 49th percentile in MPS.

The MCS participants were no different than the original MPS participants in involvement in work. Their expectations about life in the company they had chosen were, however, far less favorable than those of their predecessors. On an Expectations Inventory, on which they rated their expectations that a number of work-related outcomes would characterize their

Figure 1.3
Key Motivation Scores for MPS versus MCS College Recruits

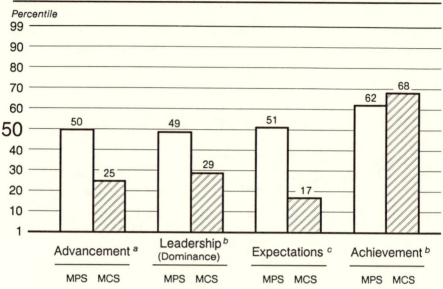

	Advancement [a]	Leadership [b] (Dominance)	Expectations [c]	Achievement [b]
MPS	50	49	51	62
MCS	25	29	17	68

[a] *Sarnoff Survey of Attitudes Toward Life, MPS College Norms, 1956–60*
[b] *Edwards Personal Preference Schedule, Bell System College Hire Norms, 1958*
[c] *Expectations Inventory, MPS College Norms, 1956–60*

lives as managers five years hence, the MCS group stood at only the 17th percentile as compared with the 51st percentile for their counterparts twenty years previously. Some frankly stated that they weren't at all confident that a career in management would be right for them.

On the positive side, the MCS men and women were just as motivated for job challenge as the MPS group had been, and their desire to do a quality job was just as high (motivation for achievement in Figure 1.3). Since they were also interested in a good salary, it seemed that *work* motivation was not lacking. What was lacking was *managerial* motivation.

Although no single cause can be isolated for the motivational changes between this and the previous generation, observers have suggested a number of possibilities. Howard and Wilson (1982) mentioned the post–World War II baby boom, abundance of material goods, and permissive child-rearing practices as possible factors undermining the previously influential Protestant Work Ethic. Also cited as important was the disillusionment produced by such events as the Vietnam War and Watergate.

Since the MCS group has not been reassessed, no data are at hand to say what will happen to their motivation as their careers progress. We saw that in MPS the work involvement of the average manager tended to rise, leadership motivation was constant, and advancement motivation declined. The MCS managers are starting with significantly less drive for leadership and advancement. If they decline in these respects, managerial career motivation will be at a low ebb indeed.

These findings about motivation are among the most important to emerge from the AT&T longitudinal studies. They demonstrate that taking account of motivation in managerial selection and development is a complex matter. One cannot make easy assumptions about what people really want from work either at the time they are employed or in the years that follow.

IMPLICATIONS FOR HUMAN RESOURCE PROFESSIONALS

Human resource professionals, whether concerned primarily with initial selection, advancement, development, or training of managers, would do well to attend to managerial motivation as well as management abilities.

Implications for Selection

It is perhaps ludicrous to urge college recruiters to add more sophisticated evaluations of motivation to their procedures when the whole recruiting process is generally so loose. In their recent study of college recruiting in Fortune 1000 corporations, Rynes and Boudreau (1986, p. 750) concluded:

College recruitment is not typically regarded as a major strategic function. . . . as indicated by the low emphasis on program evaluation, the low perceived status of the recruiting function, only moderate status of recruiters, low top executive involvement, low importance of recruiting performance to individual rewards, and low attention to recruiting procedures.

Nevertheless, for those recruiters who make a serious effort not only to attract future managers but to select them, explicit attention should be paid to evaluating managerial motivation. This is particularly true since becoming a management trainee is often a residual choice. Those who become physicians, lawyers, or accountants, for example, do so not only because of the extrinsic rewards expected but because of the content of the work. They expect function pleasure from the work itself. They have, therefore, planned their college and post-graduate programs toward training in the knowledge and skills such occupations require.

Some of those choosing management have tried to prepare for it, such as by majoring in business administration at either an undergraduate or graduate level. Others have planned on management careers without attending business schools. It was not unusual for engineering graduates in the Management Progress Study to say they had majored in engineering as a route into management although others wanted to stay in technical work.

In addition to such candidates, the recruiter will be confronted by those who did not aim for a profession. Many may have majored in the liberal arts or humanities. Opportunities in management offer such graduates the possibility of rewarding careers but leave the question of motivation to manage quite open.

The point is not that liberal arts graduates are poor bets for management. On the contrary, Howard (1986), using MPS and MCS data, has shown that they are superior to those with business or technical majors in management potential and in the key motives which serve management careers. The point is, rather, that the recruiter should make no easy assumptions about motivation and should attempt to evaluate it directly.

Implications for Advancement

As previously reported, important changes in motivation take place in the first few years after employment. Those whose motivation has changed in a highly positive direction are often those whose careers will be most successful. For this and other reasons, an assessment center including motivational exercises for managers with about five years of service would be extremely valuable. Such a center would, of course, evaluate abilities as well as motivation.

These suggestions have had in mind the organization which hires recent college graduates as beginning or potential future managers. Other organizations hire graduates for entry-level work and do not attempt to evaluate management potential. They assume that enough will manifest such potential to fill the management openings of the future.

Human resource administrators in such organizations have even more reason to establish an assessment procedure to evaluate those seen by supervisors as likely future managers. It has been well established that supervisors, particularly lower-level supervisors, are quite fallible in evaluating the potential of subordinates, especially when those subordinates are not doing managerial work.

Implications for Training and Development

Since several other chapters in this book will be devoted to career development, no detailed recommendations in this regard will be presented here. We have noted the overriding importance of the early years in management. Once young people have started in management, the task for the organization is one of providing assignments and an environment which will enhance motivation rather than diminish it.

The conditions for achieving such goals have been set forth so often by human resource specialists that they run the risk of becoming trite. They include creating challenging jobs, giving feedback and positive reinforcement, encouraging goal setting, and supervising in a participative manner, among other prescriptions. London (1985) presented a comprehensive overview of such conditions. The problem for human resource administrators is translating such goals into effective action against the realities and inertia of organizational life.

A motivational survey would provide invaluable data for those responsible for development programs and management training. A training director, for example, could tailor the incentives in a program to the level of management to be trained. For example, lower-level supervisors in MPS were much more interested in nurturing and supporting others than were those in higher level management. Thus, helping others might be cited as a training outcome to inspire those at lower levels but would not necessarily motivate those at higher levels.

MANAGEMENT CAREER MOTIVATION AND ORGANIZATIONS IN THE FUTURE

The discussion so far has intimated that managers are subject to changes due to age and experience or cultural trends but that organizations remain constant. There were times, not long ago, when organizations were remarkably stable. Businesses such as General Motors, Sears, U.S. Steel, and At&T rolled along, generally profitably. Managers in these corporations could count on staying until retirement if they didn't do anything dishonest. For many people, career motivation was motivation for a career in one organization.

This placid scene has suddenly been disrupted. Foreign competition, governmental antitrust action and deregulation, mergers, takeovers, and other forces have shaken many seemingly invincible firms. One result has been downsizing, to use the current euphemism for layoffs and dismissals. In more than one organization, 20 to 30 percent of management has gone or is going.

Companies often take steps to soften the blow on those who are told to leave by giving them termination allowances and outplacement counseling. Such ameliorations cannot, however, mute the clear message that no one can count any longer on a lifetime career with an organization that has taken such drastic steps or, probably, with any organization.

One can only guess at what effect such a change will have on those entering management today. We have seen that the recent MCS group was already deficient in several important components of management motivation and did not have favorable expectations about life in large organizations. This outcome was not unique to the Bell System, for the Inter-Organizational Testing Study results clearly indicated that the findings were generalizable across other types of organizations. This generation did not look like a group that would easily have developed loyalty to their employers even under the older, more stable conditions. Under current conditions, it seems nearly impossible.

Since the new generation resembled the preceding one in interest in challenging work and was even more motivated for financial rewards, a good guess might be that many more young managers today will view their employers as strictly temporary. They will pay close attention to opportunities elsewhere that offer the kind of work they want to do and that will pay them a higher salary, either with or without promotion. Assuming business conditions remain relatively good, voluntary terminations may well rise. Management search firms may be a good investment!

Even "lean and mean" companies, however, will need good managers who will stay around long enough to reach middle and upper levels. They will need enough of those with not only sound abilities but with strong motivation to lead and to advance. Yet these motives are not as widespread as they used to be. Moreover, the current promotion of vocationalism may deprive employers of some of the best potential leaders—humanities and social science majors. When such shortages are embedded in turbulent corporate environments that may make some fear to aspire, management staffing executives will have to pay even more attention to the development and maintenance of appropriate motivation. Thus, in organizations of the future, for both the selection and development of managers, much greater attention to evaluating motivation is essential.

REFERENCES

Bray, D. W. 1984. *Assessment centers for research and application.* Psi Chi Distinguished Lecture, meeting of the American Psychological Association, Toronto, Canada.

Bray, D. W., and A. Howard. 1983. Personality and the assessment center method. In C. D. Spielberger and J. N. Butcher (eds.), *Advances in personality assessment, Vol. 3.* Hillsdale, NJ: Erlbaum Associates.

Howard, A. 1986. College experiences and managerial performance. (Monograph). *Journal of Applied Psychology, 71*(3), 530–52.

Howard, A., and D. W. Bray. 1988. *Managerial lives in transition: Advancing age and changing times.* New York: Guilford Press.

Howard, A., and J. A. Wilson. 1982. Leadership in a declining work ethic. *California Management Review, 24*(4), 33–46.

London, M. 1985. *Developing managers.* San Francisco: Jossey-Bass.

Rynes, S. L., and J. W. Boudreau. 1986. College recruiting in large organizations: Practice, evaluation, and research implications. *Personnel Psychology, 39*(4), 729–57.

CAREER EXPLORATION

_____ JEFFREY H. GREENHAUS

A chemical engineer with nearly ten years' of work experience, Bob is
confused. For some reason he doesn't quite understand, Bob's interest
in engineering is waning, and his job performance is beginning to slip
just a bit. Maybe he isn't challenged by his job any more. Or perhaps
his income and status in his company are not what he had expected
them to be at this stage of his career. Unfortunately, Bob has no idea
how to resolve his uncertainties. Should he remain in engineering, seek
a management position, change employers, or even switch to an entirely
new line of work? If Bob is to reverse his recent decline in job performance and career fulfillment, he must begin to take a more active role
in managing his career.

All employees, Bob included, are confronted with a series of decisions—
some small and others rather dramatic—as they pursue their careers. There
are occupations to choose, job offers to accept, career paths to determine,
promotions to seek, career changes to consider, and retirements to plan.
Despite the obvious differences among these decisions, they share one fundamental similarity: They should be based on accurate information derived
from career exploration of information about oneself, one's environment,
and one's options.

This chapter will consider how career exploration can contribute to effective career decision making. It will first examine the career management
process and identify the role of career exploration in effective career management. It will identify the types of information that can be acquired
through career exploration as well as the variations in information needs
that accompany different stages of the career life cycle. Finally, a number

of potential obstacles to effective career exploration will be reviewed, and organizational actions to promote career exploration will be specified.

THE ROLE OF EXPLORATION IN CAREER MANAGEMENT

Elsewhere, I have proposed a model of career management that is shown in Figure 2.1. Career management is a problem-solving process by which individuals can make informed decisions about their worklife. Effective career management requires individuals to gather relevant information through career exploration, develop a greater awareness of themselves and their environment, set realistic career goals (which, by the way, need not involve vertical mobility), develop and implement career strategies or action plans to achieve their goals, and appraise the effectiveness and appropriateness of their efforts.

An active, problem-solving approach to career management is essential for employees and employers alike. From an individual perspective, career management can help employees make career decisions that are compatible with their needs, values, talents, and aspirations. Contemporary employees who are assertive about satisfying their needs and deriving meaning from work should be more productive and fulfilled in careers over which they have some control. Moreover, organizations will profit from effective career management as employees pursue career tracks that satisfy significant needs and more fully utilize their talents. The presence of economic uncertainties, corporate mergers and downsizing, and rapid technological changes puts a premium on active, vigilant career management.

Career exploration refers to the collection and analysis of career-related information. Career exploration is crucial to the effectiveness of the entire career management process. Career goals and strategies—no matter how elaborate they may be—are worthless unless they are based on an employee's awareness of his or her own qualities and the characteristics of the surrounding environment. How can Bob, the chemical engineer, choose between a technical and a managerial career path if he doesn't understand his needs, talents, and interests and doesn't appreciate the differences in duties, responsibilities, and rewards between technical and managerial tracks? How can he choose a particular strategy to attain his goal without a thorough understanding of the requirements of different jobs and the culture of his particular company?

Such awareness does not come automatically. For most employees, career exploration is required to develop a more heightened awareness of themselves and their environment. Many employees simply do not know themselves very well. They may not have a clear picture of what they want from a job, a career, or from life. They may overlook their talents in some areas and overestimate their talents in other areas. They may not have given much

Figure 2.1
A Model of Career Management

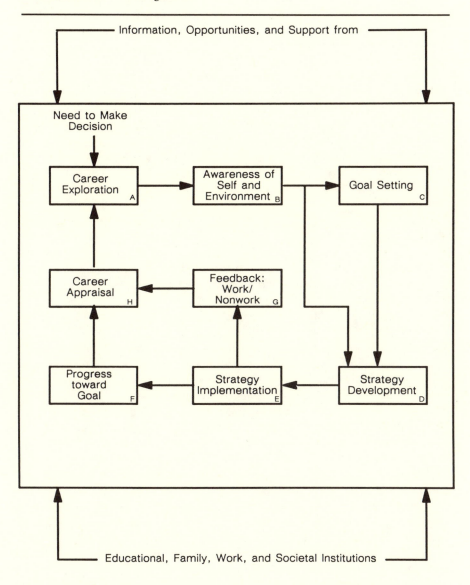

Source: Exhibit 2.1 (A Model of Career Management) In Greenhaus, J. H., *Career Management*. Hinsdale, Ill.: The Dryden Press, p. 18.

thought to the work activities that hold their interest and those that bore them. Many employees sail along in their career without giving these matters much serious attention, basing their career decisions more on what others expect of them than on the satisfaction of their personal needs. For these reasons, a systematic effort at career exploration is required to enhance self-awareness.

Career exploration may also be necessary to enlighten an employee about his or her environment. It is difficult to develop a realistic picture of different occupations, organizations, career paths, and industries without accurate data. Moreover, career opportunities can change rapidly with advances in technology and changes in organizational strategy and structure. Awareness of ourselves and our environment is not always easy to develop. Although some employees may intuitively understand themselves and their environment, most of us need to work at it. And it is career exploration that serves this function.

THE FOCUS OF CAREER EXPLORATION

It is convenient to distinguish two forms of career exploration: self-exploration and environmental exploration. Self-exploration is designed to acquire relevant information regarding one's values, interests, talents, and lifestyle preferences. Values refer to outcomes a person desires to attain or avoid. A particular employee's work values may include a desire for pleasant working conditions, a feeling of accomplishment, and rapid advancement opportunities. Each of us possesses a somewhat unique set of work values that are personally meaningful and are important to satisfy in the workplace. Interests are likes and dislikes attached to specific tasks or activities. For example, whereas some employees may enjoy quantitative and analytical tasks, others may prefer extensive interpersonal contact. Job satisfaction often depends on the availability of tasks in which an employee has a genuine interest. Talents refer to one's aptitudes and skills, one's capabilities and proficiencies—what a person can do or could do with proper training. High levels of job performance are contingent upon a match between an employee's talents and the demands and requirements of the job. A lifestyle preference refers to the desired balance between one's involvement in work and other significant life activities, such as family, leisure, community, and religion. A satisfying balance among life's various activities is a critical determinant of one's overall quality of life.

To summarize, effective self-exploration should help employees become more aware of their values, interests, talents, and preferred lifestyle. It is difficult for employees to make appropriate career decisions unless they understand the values they wish to attain at work, the tasks they find interesting and boring, and the talents they possess or can develop. Moreover, since many jobs can drain employees of their time and emotion, it is essential that individuals understand what balance of work and nonwork involvements is optimal for them.

As critical as self-awareness is, employees also must understand the nature of the environment if they are to make effective career decisions. Environmental exploration is designed to acquire information about occupations, jobs, organizations, and families. How can a person choose a suitable occupation without understanding the duties, responsibilities, rewards, and pressures associated with different occupations or job families? How can an employee pursue a job in a particular organization without understanding the specific requirements of the job and the outlook, culture, reward systems, and opportunities in the organization? And how can one make a career decision that may have far-reaching effects on one's family without understanding a spouse's needs, aspirations, and career stage; children's emotional needs; and the stage of the family life cycle?

TYPES OF CAREER EXPLORATION

Effective career management requires a blend of self-exploration and environmental exploration that sheds light on personal values, interests, talents, and lifestyle preferences and that identifies salient characteristics of occupational, job, organizational, and family environments. What types of career exploration activities can provide useful information? Exhibit 2.1 identifies a number of vehicles for career exploration grouped by the type of information that is sought. Although the list is not exhaustive, it includes many of the most significant career exploration activities.

Note that career exploration may consist of formal and informal activities. Although some of the activities may be formalized into programs (e.g., a career planning workshop), many of the activities do not require the development of a formalized structure. For example, discussions with other people (supervisor, peers, friends and acquaintances, and family members) and extensive readings about different occupations, jobs, or organizations do not necessarily require a formally organized career planning program, although it may be a useful vehicle for initiating such actions. In fact, one of the most significant keys to successful career exploration is the ability to learn about oneself and the environment from everyday experiences—from observing, talking, listening, and reading on matters of interest.

Because many of the career exploration activities are informal and voluntary, employees who assertively take the initiative in collecting information, rather than waiting for the company to set up a program, are likely to acquire more extensive and useful information. Ultimately, the responsibility for career exploration and for career management rests on the shoulders of the employees.

Although Exhibit 2.1 distinguishes activities designed to provide information about oneself and the environment, reality is not so neatly packaged.

Exhibit 2.1
Vehicles for Career Exploration

Information Regarding Oneself

Complete career planning workbooks and learning exercises

Participate in career planning seminars and workshops

Undertake career counseling

Take ability, interest, value, and lifestyle inventories

Participate in assessment centers

Seek performance feedback and appraisal

Hold discussions with peers, friends, and family members

Observe one's own and others' ongoing work experiences

Seek a mentor-protégé relationship

Reflect on one's job performance, values, interest, talents, and lifestyle preferences

Information Regarding the Environment

Read books, pamphlets, articles about occupations, companies, and industries

Read company brochures and annual reports

Conduct information interviews with human resource professionals, supervisors, or others in the organization

Conduct information interviews with a variety of people outside the organization who are knowledgeable about different occupations, companies, or industries

Participate in career planning seminars and workshops

Read job descriptions

Hold discussions with family members about their needs

Seek a mentor-protégé relationship

Observe one's own and others' ongoing work experiences

Attend seminars on opportunities in specific career fields

Read biographies of prominent people

Most of the exploratory activities can provide information about self *and* environment. For example, a discussion with a supervisor can be used to obtain feedback on one's job performance, strengths, and limitations (self-information), as well as to obtain information about the availability of different career options that might be appropriate for the employee (environmental information).

Moreover, each type of exploration—self and environmental—can and should influence the direction of the other. For example, employees should generally engage in a certain amount of self-exploration before extensively exploring the environment. Self-awareness of one's values, interests, talents, and lifestyle preferences can guide one's search for information about an occupation, job, or organization. It is easier (and more productive) to collect and interpret information about the duties and rewards of a particular job if one has a reasonable understanding of his or her own needs and talents. If employees do not understand their own desires, then all the information in the world about a particular job or career path will be wasted.

This does not mean that employees must have a total understanding of their needs or motives before undertaking an exploration of the environment. Since human beings never have a perfect understanding of themselves, waiting for such total awareness is simply impractical. Moreover, environmental exploration can often stimulate self-awareness. For example, an employee conducting a search for information on the differences between a staff track and a general management track may be confronted with specific data (for example, that a management track in a company requires frequent relocations) that can clarify his or her own values—for example, that frequent relocations at this stage of life would not be appropriate.

Therefore, self-exploration and environmental exploration are inescapably intertwined. The better one understands oneself, the more likely one can obtain meaningful information about the environment. And the more thoroughly one understands the environment, the more likely one can relate this information to one's own motives, talents, and aspirations. Thus, employees should use self-exploration to guide or direct an exploration of the environment and should use environmental exploration as a vehicle for stimulating an appraisal of themselves.

CAREER EXPLORATION AND THE CAREER LIFE CYCLE

Career exploration is critical at all stages of career development. The college graduate looking for an entry-level position, the young executive on the rise, the mid-career employee concerned about a lack of fulfillment, and the older employee pondering retirement all have decisions to make. The decisions may be different, but the process of managing a career—gathering information, setting goals, developing and implementing a strategy, and acquiring feedback on one's efforts—are remarkably similar across different career stages.

Nevertheless, employees may have somewhat different information needs as their careers unfold over time. Many researchers agree that careers develop in somewhat predictable ways: Individuals pass through a series of career stages, each of which is characterized by a somewhat different set of themes, issues, and tasks. I propose five stages of career development shown in Exhibit 2.2. Each career stage is associated with an approximate age range, a set of relevant career-oriented tasks, and a somewhat different pattern of information requirements.

Exhibit 2.2
Characteristics of Different Career Stages

---

1. **Preparation for Work**

   Typical Age Range: 0–25

   Major Tasks: Develop occupational self-image; assess alternative occupations; develop initial occupational choice; pursue necessary education.

   Significant Information Needs: personal values, interests, talents, lifestyle preferences; different occupational fields and their education and training requirements.

2. **Organizational Entry**

   Typical Age Range: 18–25

   Major Tasks: Obtain job offer(s) from desired organization(s), select appropriate job based on accurate information.

   Significant Information Needs: personal values, interests, talents, lifestyle preferences; characteristics, duties, rewards, and pressures of job(s) under consideration; outlook, resources, human resource practices, culture of organization(s) under consideration.

3. **Early Career**

   Typical Age Range: 25–40

   Major Tasks: Learn job and organizational rules and norms; fit into chosen occupation and organization; increase competence, pursue Dream.

   Significant Information Needs: personal values, interests, and talents; requirements of new job; organizational policies, practices, expectations, norms, and culture; level of performance on current job; desired balance of work and nonwork involvements; presence/absence of a match with chosen occupation and organization; availability and appropriateness of alternative career paths; opportunities for additional learning experiences; appropriate career strategies; accessibility of mentor.

4. **Mid-career**

   Typical Age Range: 40–55

   Major Tasks: Reappraise early career and early adulthood; reaffirm or modify Dream; make choices appropriate to middle adult years; remain productive at work.

   Significant Information Needs: emergence of new talents; possible changes in values, interests, and desired balance of work and nonwork involvements; organization's future plans and needs; advisability of mid-career change; level of performance on current job; availability and appropriateness of vertical or lateral mobility opportunities; feasibility of improving current job if mobility is unavailable or unwanted.

Exhibit 2.2 (Cont'd)

---

5. **Late Career**
   Typical Age Range: 55–Retirement
   Major Tasks: Remain productive in work; maintain self-esteem; prepare for effective retirement.
   Significant Information Needs: possible changes in values, interests, and desired balance of work and nonwork involvements; level of performance in current job; feasibility of lateral or downward mobility or improving current job; opportunities for part-time employment or other employment opportunities involving reduced level of involvement; options for timing of retirement; personal resources required for retirement; required psychological transition between work and retirement.

Source: Adapted from Table 5.4 (Five Stages of Career Development) in J. H. Greenhaus, *Career Management*. Hinsdale, Ill.: The Dryden Press, p. 87.

Preparation for work is primarily concerned with forming an initial occupational choice and pursuing the necessary education to implement the choice. This stage of career development should witness the formation and refinement of an occupational self-image and at least a tentative decision regarding the way that self-image can be played out in the world of work. Not surprisingly, an individual at this stage of career development requires a considerable amount of information about his or her salient values, interests, talents, and lifestyle preferences, as well as information about the duties, rewards, and training requirements of different occupational fields.

The primary task of **organizational entry** is the selection of a job and an organization that can satisfy one's career values and best use one's talents. Unfortunately, many job selections result in a mismatch because the recruit's information about the job and the organization is incomplete or inaccurate. Therefore, individuals need to be aware of their own qualities as they relate to the job search. Needless to say, recruits must also receive accurate information about the job and the company so they can enter the organization with realistic expectations.

In the **early career**, the employee must first become established in his or her career by mastering the technical aspects of the new job and by learning the ropes (the norms, values, expectations, and practices) of the organization. Once accepted as a valuable contributor to the organization, the new employee can concentrate on achieving greater levels of competence, responsibility, and accomplishments (what Daniel Levinson referred to as the youthful "Dream"). As Exhibit 2.2 shows, employees require a great deal of information—about themselves and the organization—to accomplish the tasks of the early career.

The **mid-career** years typically involve a reappraisal of one's accomplishments and failures, of one's hopes and fears, and a consideration of the most appropriate career direction to pursue in the future. Stimulated largely by the mid-career transition or crisis, employees often must evaluate where they have been and how they wish to spend the remainder of their working lives. Information required to make such decisions may be painful to acquire and accept, but unresolved issues confronted during mid-career are likely to impede personal development during the subsequent years of one's career.

The **late career** is characterized by two significant tasks: to remain productive on the job (often in the face of stereotypes regarding older employees held by the organization) and to plan for retirement. As with earlier stages, the information required during the late career should promote a greater understanding of oneself and the options available in the environment.

In summary, career exploration is critical to effective career management at all stages of career development. Although some types of information needs are common to all stages (e.g., feedback on job performance), each stage also has its own somewhat unique information requirements as well.

OBSTACLES TO EFFECTIVE CAREER EXPLORATION

Although career exploration is an essential ingredient in the career management process, exploratory activities do not always promote a greater insight into oneself or the environment. A number of significant obstacles to effective career exploration are summarized here:

1. Incomplete Exploration. Some employees participate in an insufficient amount of career exploration despite an obvious need for information. Often, the reluctance to engage in sufficient exploration is due to complacency, hopelessness, or fear. Complacency can arise among employees who place so little importance on their work and career that career exploration and career decision making are not thought to make a substantial difference in their lives. Other employees may complacently accept the views of others (supervisors, peers, friends) and see no real need to collect any information on their own.

   A feeling of hopelessness can also discourage active career exploration. People who see no hope of improving their future, who see no real opportunities that excite them, who feel they have no control over the events in their lives are unlikely to engage in extensive exploration. Finally, fear of the unknown can become an impediment to career exploration. Those employees with fragile self-concepts may be reluctant to confront their own weaknesses or limited opportunities. Of course, extensive hopelessness and fear can produce a vicious cycle because the failure to explore options can doom such people to a hopeless and frightening future.

2. Coerced Exploration. Coercion is not a useful strategy to promote career exploration. A supervisor, human resource professional, colleague, or friend can pressure an employee to participate in a career exploration activity. However, people learn best when there is a strong motivation from within and when there is a personal commitment to the learning process. Therefore, employees have to be

psychologically ready to deal with learning opportunities for career exploration to be most productive.

3. Random Exploration. Unfocused, diffuse exploration is not likely to produce maximum learning. Rather, exploration is most profitable when it builds on prior exploration and learning and forms part of an overall information-seeking plan. Therefore, a systematic, organized, planned approach to career exploration needs to be encouraged and reinforced among employees.

4. Ineffective Forms of Career Exploration. Employees committed to career exploration must decide which exploratory activities to pursue. There are career planning seminars to attend, colleagues or friends to speak with, counselors to meet, and literature to read. Undoubtedly, not all of these activities will be equally appropriate in all situations. Some employees take the path of least resistance by choosing those activities that are most accessible and most comfortable, thereby avoiding exploratory activities that are more difficult to pursue and are more threatening psychologically. Such a strategy, although certainly understandable, is likely to give an employee a false sense of security. Often, the most productive activities require substantial effort and a willingness to endure some uncertainty and discomfort.

5. Defensive Self-Exploration. As noted earlier, self-awareness is the foundation for all subsequent career exploration and career management efforts. In self-exploration, employees must process information about themselves accurately and honestly. A failure to do so defeats the very purpose of self-assessment. Research suggests that highly anxious people may not profit maximally from self-exploration. Such people, who are extremely anxious about their lives or their careers, can react defensively to information about themselves and may neglect, distort, or misinterpret information they do not wish to hear. Although a certain amount of tension probably aids the learning process, excessive anxiety may produce more defensiveness than real learning.

6. Exclusion of Nonwork Considerations. Effective career exploration must consider the impact of one's work on personal and family involvements, as well as the effects of family and personal lifestyle on one's career. Excessive time and energy devoted to work and a stressful work environment can impair the quality of one's family and personal life, and family demands (such as a working spouse) can affect one's career involvement as well. All too frequently, employees fail to consider the implications of career decisions for other parts of their lives. Work, family, community involvement, leisure pursuits, and religious practices all need to be examined as they bear on career decision making.

7. Exclusion of One's Current Job. To many employees and employers, career management is synonymous with planning for promotions and climbing the corporate ladder. However, in today's society, with a glut of baby boomers competing for a smaller number of jobs in organizations that are increasingly concerned with downsizing and efficiency, remaining in one's current job may be an appropriate and realistic career goal. Remaining in a current position, however, need not be a stagnating experience. Employees (in concert with their supervisors) need to explore ways in which their current jobs can be redesigned and improved, and their feelings of accomplishment and growth maintained or even enhanced.

ORGANIZATIONAL ACTIONS TO PROMOTE CAREER EXPLORATION

Although it is ultimately the employee's responsibility to manage his or her career, organizations can support the career management process by providing employees with information and with opportunities to develop and refine career decision-making skills. A comprehensive career exploration/career management program should be responsive to employees' needs and should attempt to overcome as many of the obstacles to effective career exploration as possible. Such a program should ideally:

1. Be voluntary. The attractiveness of the program, rather than coercion, should be the incentive for employee participation.

2. Provide extensive opportunities for self-exploration. The use of career planning workbooks, learning exercises, one-on-one counseling, and structured instruments to assess interests, talents, values, and lifestyle preferences can all aid the self-assessment process.

3. Provide opportunities for groups of peers to share their insights, hopes, and concerns. Such group experiences can help participants understand themselves and others more clearly and may help reduce feelings of anxiety and hopelessness regarding career management.

4. Involve the immediate supervisor of the participants early in the career exploration process. The supervisor can provide the participant with constructive performance feedback and emotional support, can suggest useful career strategies, and can discuss ways in which the participant's current job can be improved, if necessary.

5. Incorporate participants' nonwork aspirations into the exploration process. The interaction between work and nonwork lives can be incorporated in the individual self-assessment activities as well as the group discussions. Moreover, families can be encouraged to provide input into the career management process by collaborating with the employee in his or her self-assessment and by participating in some of the group discussions.

6. Expose participants to senior management during the program. Such exposure can help participants learn more about the company's goals, strategies, and resources and can inform top management about the needs, aspirations, and concerns of its human resources.

7. Provide up-to-date, written information regarding the organization's structure, the duties and requirements of specific jobs, and the availability of alternate career paths.

8. Encourage each participant to emerge from the program with a tentative career management plan, including a statement of goals, action plans, and timetables. The participant's supervisor, human resource staff, and senior management should review each plan for realism, and follow-up discussions should be held periodically to review progress toward the goals and the continued viability of the plan.

HUMAN RESOURCE SYSTEM SUPPORT FOR CAREER EXPLORATION

To be most effective, career exploration programs should be supported by a variety of human resource systems. The organization's mechanisms for forecasting its human resource needs and for recruiting, selecting, training, developing, appraising, promoting, and rewarding its people must be consistent with the employees' career exploration efforts, and information regarding these practices should be communicated clearly to all employees.

Organizations' business plans and human resource forecasts should also be communicated to employees so that self-assessment and career planning activities are not conducted in a vacuum. Employees' goals must be consistent with organizational needs if there is to be a match between the employee and the employer. Additionally, organizations must develop valid measures of employee performance and potential that can help organizations make effective assessment decisions and help employees in their self-assessment efforts.

Perhaps most important, organizations should create a climate of trust, openness, and candor. Most employees will be unwilling to reveal their hopes, weaknesses, fears, and concerns in a punitive, secretive organizational climate. Effective career exploration and career management require collaboration between the individual and the organization, and collaboration requires mutual trust and respect.

SELECTED BIBLIOGRAPHY

This chapter is based on material from the author's recent book, *Career management,* published by The Dryden Press in 1987, where more detailed information regarding the career management process is presented. Permission by The Dryden Press to present portions of the book and to reprint Figure 2.1 is appreciated.

A considerable amount of research on career exploration has been conducted by Stephen A. Stumpf and his colleagues at New York University. Interested readers are referred to a technical article by Stephen Stumpf, Stephen Colarelli, and Karen Hartman (*Journal of Vocational Behavior*, 1983, 22, 191–226) that describes the development of their Career Exploration Survey. A number of empirical research studies have investigated the usefulness of career exploration in career management. Illustrative articles include Stumpf and Hartman's "Individual exploration to organizational commitment or withdrawal" (*Academy of Management Journal*, 1984, 27, 308–29) and Thomas Sugalski and Jeffrey Greenhaus's 1986 article, "Career exploration and goal setting among managerial employees," published in the *Journal of Vocational Behavior*, 29, 102–14. Suggestions for effective career exploration and planning can be found in Manuel London and Stephen Stumpf's *Managing careers* (Addison-Wesley, 1982).

The five-stage model of career development presented in this chapter is described in more detail in the author's *Career management.* Alternative models of career development may be found in Hall's 1976 book, *Careers in organizations* (Good-year), and in Edgar Schein's 1978 *Career dynamics* (Addison-Wesley). A fascinating and informative view of adult life development is presented by Daniel J. Levinson and his colleagues in their 1978 *The seasons of a man's life* (Knopf). The interplay among work, family, and personal considerations in career management is demonstrated in Abraham Korman and Rhoda Korman's 1980 *Career success/personal failure* (Prentice-Hall).

James Walker and Thomas Gutteridge's 1979 book, *Career planning practices: An AMA survey report* (AMACOM), reports on the implementation and effectiveness of a variety of career planning programs offered by a large sample of companies. One specific comprehensive career exploration/management program is described by Eckblad, Target, and Westlake ("Career investigation: A comprehensive career management process," *Career Center Bulletin*, Columbia University Graduate School of Business, 1984, 4(2), 2–4).

THE SOCIALIZATION PROCESS: BUILDING NEWCOMER COMMITMENT

⸻⸻⸻⸻⸻⸻⸻⸻⸻⸻⸻ GEORGIA T. CHAO

One of the most frustrating situations for managers can be the awkward, difficult period of breaking in new employees. The first few months of employment are typically learning experiences for both the newcomer and the organization. Daily interactions between a manager and newcomer allow both parties a much closer look at each other and to understand whether early expectations about the other party will be fulfilled or not. In many cases, these expectations do not match reality.

Kennedy (1986) reported that 10 percent of all newcomers are either fired or strongly encouraged to leave the organization within the first six months of employment. Furthermore, over 50 percent of all newcomers will leave their jobs within the first five years of employment (Dalton and Thompson 1986). Why is this early turnover so high? From her interviews with executives, Kennedy (1986) states the number one reason for this turnover is the newcomer's failure to fit into the organization's culture.

Despite all the advances made in employee selection systems, many newcomers who are qualified to perform a job are apparently not qualified to make the necessary adjustments to "fit in" a job situation. The concept of organizational socialization addresses the latter issue, and it is the purpose of this chapter to examine the psychological processes involved in organizational socialization and to describe how human resource professionals may facilitate this process. If valid selection systems can be matched with appropriate socialization strategies, managers may be able to reduce the early turnover rate. This dual system for managing newcomers will ensure that the most qualified people are selected into an organization and that these new hires will be properly taught to perform their jobs within the organization's existing culture.

Organizational socialization can be defined as "the manner in which the experiences of people learning the ropes of a new organizational position, status, or role are structured for them by others within the organization" (Van Maanen 1978, p. 19). This learning occurs in two general content areas: learning about the necessary knowledge, skills, and abilities to successfully perform the job, and learning about the way the organization functions in terms of its culture. For naive newcomers who are just starting their careers, the organizational socialization process is compounded by learning about worklife and organizations in general, in addition to learning about the individual's role with a specific employer.

Current models of organizational socialization are based on general adult socialization theory (Van Maanen 1978), which recognizes that an adult assumes multiple roles throughout a lifetime (e.g., worker, spouse, parent, leisurite, and so forth). Furthermore, the manner in which an individual defines certain behaviors and attitudes that are appropriate to a particular role is directly influenced by his or her interactions with others and their reactions to the role. As an adult ages and experiences major life events (e.g., marriage, children, career changes, geographical moves), the forces that help an adult to define appropriate roles may change. Thus, we undergo a continuous socialization process, learning how to define our roles, maintaining role behaviors and attitudes that help us, and redefining roles that need to serve us better.

As a subset of adult socialization, organizational socialization focuses on how an individual defines his or her role as an employee. However, this work-role definition may be influenced by how the person defines himself or herself as a spouse, citizen, and/or parent. Thus, organizational attempts to socialize a newcomer must recognize that the individual already brings a rich history of socialization experiences that may facilitate or hinder effective socialization on the job. Employers, however, do have several powerful techniques that can facilitate organizational socialization in order to enable newcomers to begin their careers on the right foot. The factors that are most likely to affect organizational socialization for newcomers are shown in Figure 3.1. Several of these factors are brought in by the newcomer; several are controlled by the organization. An understanding of how these issues affect one another, and how they may be managed to facilitate good socialization, can be a critical resource for human resource professionals who are interested in developing commitment and high productivity from their new hires.

ANTICIPATORY SOCIALIZATION

Anticipatory socialization is generally recognized as the first stage of organizational socialization and represents all of the newcomer's learning experiences prior to joining a specific organization (Feldman 1976). These

Figure 3.1
Organizational Socialization Model for Newcomers

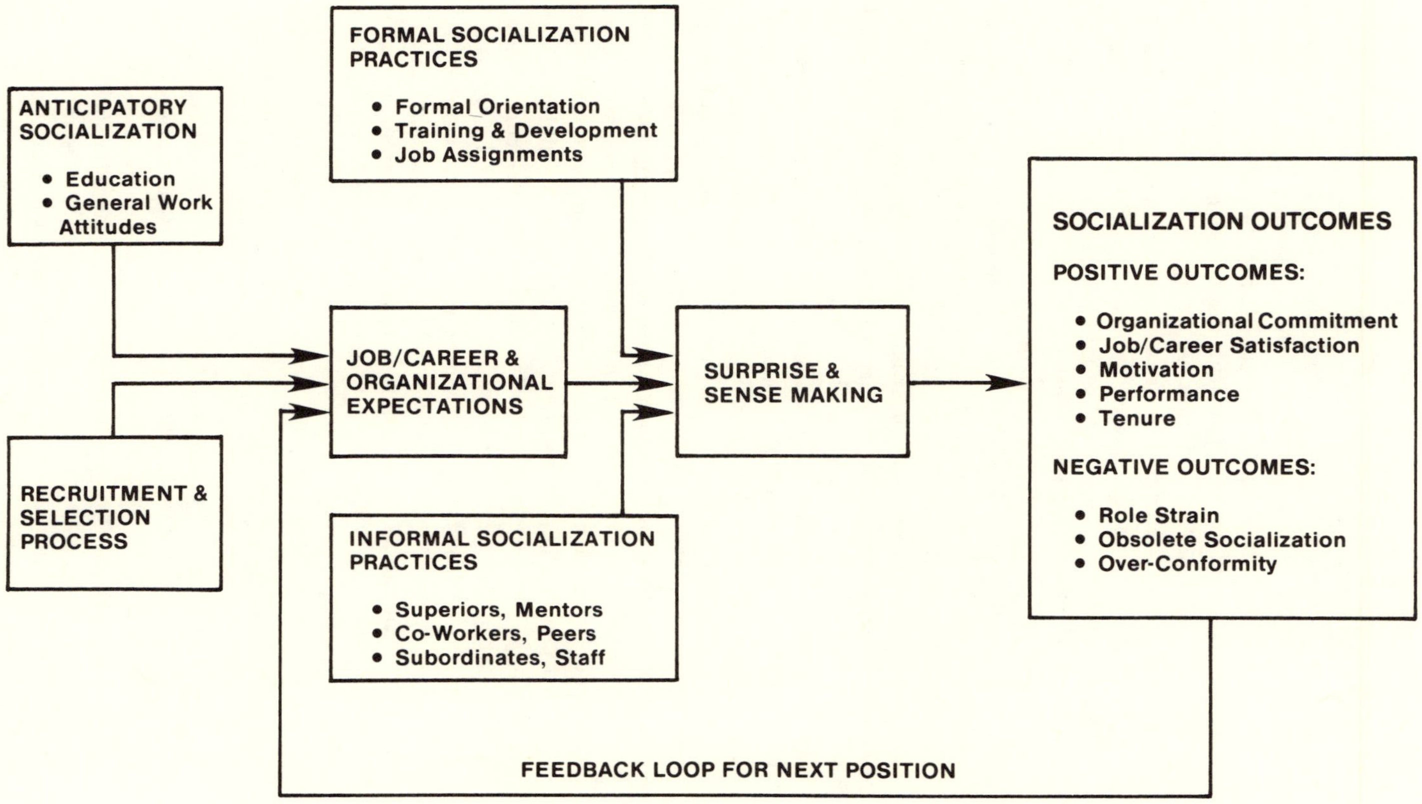

ANTICIPATORY SOCIALIZATION
- Education
- General Work Attitudes

RECRUITMENT & SELECTION PROCESS

FORMAL SOCIALIZATION PRACTICES
- Formal Orientation
- Training & Development
- Job Assignments

JOB/CAREER & ORGANIZATIONAL EXPECTATIONS

INFORMAL SOCIALIZATION PRACTICES
- Superiors, Mentors
- Co-Workers, Peers
- Subordinates, Staff

SURPRISE & SENSE MAKING

SOCIALIZATION OUTCOMES

POSITIVE OUTCOMES:
- Organizational Commitment
- Job/Career Satisfaction
- Motivation
- Performance
- Tenure

NEGATIVE OUTCOMES:
- Role Strain
- Obsolete Socialization
- Over-Conformity

FEEDBACK LOOP FOR NEXT POSITION

learning experiences typically are influenced by the newcomer's education and contacts with people who are knowledgeable about the newcomer's chosen career. For example, college students who major in engineering not only learn about the field of engineering, but they also learn what a career in engineering will be like. This learning occurs in formal class settings as well as in informal interactions with family members, friends, and acquaintances who are engineers. In addition, anticipatory socialization encompasses basic learning experiences that shape an individual's general work values and attitudes (How hard should I work? How important should the job be in relation to my total lifestyle? and so on).

These early socialization experiences may or may not help newcomers adjust to organizational life. Obviously, the technical training provided by a newcomer's education can determine how qualified that person is for a particular job. However, the nature of the educational process can impede effective organizational socialization. Dalton and Thompson (1986) describe how engineering students are trained to work alone. Indeed, collaboration on student projects may be perceived as cheating. Yet when these students begin their careers, a critical predictor of job success may be an engineer's ability to work with others on group projects. Similarly, MBA graduates often encounter difficulty making the transition from a student perspective, where case studies of business problems were solved from a hypothetical executive position, to an employee perspective, where the reality shock of solving minor problems from a low-status level of junior management is experienced. The degree to which the anticipatory socialization experiences of newcomers match the organizational reality of a prospective employer can be a key determinant of an individual's ability to quickly and successfully adjust to the new environment and role demands.

The past learning experiences that a job candidate brings to a potential employer obviously are not under the organization's control. Yet the organization does specify the recruitment and selection criteria that determine which job candidates will be hired; thus, the selection process can be a powerful tool to identify those applicants who can be successfully socialized in the organization.

RECRUITMENT AND SELECTION PROCESS

The current research examining organizational recruitment and selection practices offers human resource professionals a wide variety of valid methods to identify applicants who are most likely to be able to perform the job. In particular, the evaluation of selection procedures such as application blanks, interviews, intelligence tests, and personality and interests tests have identified the extent to which these measures may be useful in selecting good employees (Schneider and Schmitt 1986). When appropriate selection methods are properly used, valid selection decisions can be made based on specific performance criteria. However, the criteria used in most of the selection research are usually confined to supervisory ratings of an employee's performance or objective performance measures that are applicable to a limited number of jobs. These criteria are typically limited in capturing a newcomer's total assets and liabilities to the organization.

One way to increase the utility of a recruitment and selection process is to expand on the selection criteria. Perhaps, if organizations can systematically and validly select those applicants who would be most likely to successfully socialize themselves in the organization, the retention rate and commitment of those newcomers could be maximized. Schneider and Schmitt (1986) suggest that the selection interview be used to measure an applicant's interests, motivation, or attraction to specific jobs. The interview often represents the only direct contact between an applicant and his or her potential organizational colleagues; thus, it can be a valuable test of how well the applicant may fit in with the rest of the work group or department. If other aspects of a selection system are designed to test whether the applicant possesses the necessary knowledge, skills, and abilities that are required for job performance, the interview can extend the selection process to the socialization level. Thus, the selection system not only identifies who can do the job, but, of those qualified applicants, it can also identify who would best fit in with the rest of the organization.

Other selection methods can also be used to identify applicants who could be easily socialized by the organization. For example, realistic job previews (RJPs) can give applicants a clear, true picture of what organizational life will be like for the potential newcomer. RJPs can be used to inoculate newcomers from carrying unrealistically optimistic expectations into their new jobs and later suffering major disappointments and low commitment due to the ensuing reality shock (Wanous 1980).

One note of caution must be mentioned here. It would be a serious error to interpret the selection of applicants who will be successfully socialized in an organization as meaning the selection of applicants who are demographically similar to the current group of job incumbents. Ideally, the human resource professional should maintain a work force that represents a wide variety of knowledge, skills, and abilities by utilizing a recruitment and selection system that is legally sound. Such a policy would maximize the flexibility of human resources as well as minimize charges of unfair employment practices. Thus, selection decisions that consider the socialization potential of an applicant must focus on the newcomer's ability to learn new role demands and not focus on demographic characteristics.

The number and kinds of expectations newcomers bring to their first jobs are largely determined by their anticipatory socialization. To some extent, an organization can minimize the number of person-job misfits it hires, through the recruitment and selection process. However, even if employers seek to identify qualified people who are also judged to be able to fit in with the rest of the organization, newcomers are still likely to require some adjustments when they actually report for work. In this situation, the kinds of socialization practices that a newcomer experiences after organizational entry become critical to later organizational performance, satisfaction, and commitment.

JOB/CAREER AND ORGANIZATION EXPECTATIONS

Initial job expectations are heavily influenced by anticipatory socialization. In contrast, initial expectations about the organization are often based upon the early contacts between the newcomer and organizational recruiters and interviewers. Together, they form the basis for directing the newcomer's initial attitudes and behaviors about the job. To what extent does the newcomer try to adapt to the organization's practices? To what extent does the newcomer try to resist established organizational politics? Most of the literature about organizational newcomers indicates that these people are highly motivated to create a good impression on their new employers. Thus, few managers need to motivate newcomers to learn how to do the job and get along with others. However, some newcomer efforts toward this goal may backfire if they expect organizations to readily abandon long-held traditions in order to experiment with the newcomer's suggestions for improvement.

SURPRISE AND SENSE MAKING

As the newcomer gains more experience as a member of the organization, certain evaluations about the job and organization are formed. These evaluations may occur in isolated events (e.g., the office is too small, the food in the cafeteria is lousy, the people are friendly, the parking is convenient); but together, they serve as valuable information cues that allow the newcomer to make some sense out of the overall experience of working for a particular organization. Very often, the early experiences differ from the initial expectations and can be surprises to the newcomer (Louis 1980). These surprises can be positive ones that please a new employee (e.g., I can travel first class, my office has a great view), or they can be negative ones that are sources for disappointment (e.g., I have to share an office with others, the clerical support is inadequate).

The sense making that results from the surprises of overmet/undermet expectations of the newcomer help shape the new attitudes and behaviors that will guide future job plans and actions. From the socialization perspective, the kinds of experiences that will be important in this shaping process can be managed along formal organizational programs, or along informal communication channels. Either approach can exert a profound effect on subsequent commitment and performance.

FORMAL SOCIALIZATION PRACTICES

Several techniques have been used from various organizational levels to shape a newcomer's attitudes and behaviors about the job. This section will describe only a few that will illustrate the extent to which managed programs can facilitate organizational socialization.

Formal Orientation Programs

Most organizations provide some type of formal program for newcomers. These programs typically present information about the organization's history, products, and philosophy as well as the employee's compensation, benefits, rights, and responsibilities. Formal orientation programs allow the organization to communicate its overall expectations of newcomers and to present an image that is consistent with the organization's objectives. Despite the benefits of formal orientation programs, many often are poorly designed or poorly executed and subsequently do not aid newcomers in their socialization efforts. Common problems that are encountered include programs that are too general and vague, programs that present too much information and overwhelm the newcomer, programs that are outdated and present inappropriate information, programs that assume newcomers will read and understand all written materials, and programs that do not provide necessary resource materials or follow-ups for newcomers.

Good orientation programs will make newcomers feel welcome in the organization and will clearly articulate how the organization expects newcomers to perform their jobs. These programs often combine verbal, audiovisual, and written forms of communication in order to teach newcomers the organization's mission, goals, and culture. One example of an effective orientation program at Texas Instruments Corporation is described by Hollmann (1976). This program emphasized newcomer socialization by describing the personalities and behaviors of the supervisors, common hazing experiences new hires might encounter, and expectations regarding job success. This program was compared with a more traditional orientation program that did not focus on socialization issues. Although the comparison found the socialization program was six hours longer than the traditional program, newcomers in the socialization program showed at least a 50 percent reduction in training time, training costs, waste, and tardiness/absenteeism. It was concluded that the costs involved in the longer socialization program were well invested.

Training and Development Programs

Training programs are generally designed to teach required knowledge, skills, and abilities that are necessary for successful job performance. The emphasis in these training programs is placed on job requirements. Development programs, on the other hand, are generally designed to provide necessary tools and experiences that allow an individual to assess his or her strengths and weaknesses and to take actions that will minimize weaknesses, highlight strengths, and direct career plans to achieve personal goals. In contrast to training programs, the emphasis in development programs is on the individual employee. Development programs also take a long-term perspective in an individual's contribution to the organization over the course of his or her entire career; whereas training programs typically take a short-term perspective in teaching an individual how to perform his or her current job. Although one program may incorporate both training and developmental aspects, the distinctions between the two types of programs are presented here to illustrate how these programs parallel the two content areas of socialization (e.g., specific job performance content and organizational culture content).

One type of training and development program that is often viewed as a powerful socialization technique is a mentoring program. A strong mentoring relationship between a senior-level mentor and a junior-level protégé provides personalized instruction for the protégé to learn how to perform the job as well as how to behave within the organization's culture. Mentoring has been demonstrated as an effective technique for newcomers to learn about the organization (Kozlowski and Ostroff 1987), and some formal mentoring programs have been able to achieve many goals that informal mentorships have attained (Noe and Schmitt 1987).

Job Assignments

As mentioned previously, most newcomers are motivated to create a good impression with their new employers and are willing to learn and adapt to the organization's climate. However, many naive newcomers often believe their selection to the organization means they have been accepted as they currently are, and that changes are unnecessary. For these people, the first step in an organizational program designed to facilitate the socialization process may be to teach newcomers to recognize that the current organizational practices are to be respected and learned. Thus, there may be a need to demonstrate to newcomers that there is a great deal to learn if they want to be successful and remain in the organization. Schein (1964) describes two types of debasement experiences that are designed to unfreeze the newcomer's preconceptions about his or her role in the organization and to maximize the newcomer's willingness to accept the organization's authority in shaping job attitudes and behaviors. The debasement experiences are intended to highlight the newcomer's inadequacies and thereby identify the new hire's reliance on the organization for guidance. One method is a sink-or-swim situation that vaguely defines a difficult task so the newcomer is forced to seek help. Another method is known as an "upending experience" that requires the newcomer to perform a task that is guaranteed to fail, or to perform a menial task that degrades the position of the newcomer. These upending experiences are designed to sufficiently humble the newcomer so he or she will be receptive to organizationally sanctioned attitudes and behaviors. Thus, the organization asserts itself as the newcomer's superior, and it is the role of the newcomer to adapt to the organization and not vice versa.

Use of debasement experiences are typically surprises to the newcomer and must not be too negative and thereby serve as an impetus to leave the organization. Essentially, they should only be used when newcomers attempt to change the organization to fit his or her expectations and when these changes would not be in the best interests of the organization. Only in rare cases—and typically they are at the executive level—are newcomers brought into an organization with the expressed goal of implementing major changes.

Other examples of job assignments do not involve debasement exercises but attempt to match newcomer expectations by providing challenging, stimulating work for the new employee in order to encourage good job performance and build commitment to the organization. Research on early job experiences indicates that those newcomers who were assigned challenging work were found to perform at higher levels than did new employees who were assigned more mundane tasks (Berlew and Hall 1966). Challenging work for newcomers indicated the company valued these new employees and held high expectations for them. It was speculated that the high expectations helped newcomers to internalize positive work attitudes and behaviors which then were reinforced by subsequent career success. Thus, the quality of early work assignments can serve as a way to communicate how the organization values its newcomers and what types of performance it expects from them.

INFORMAL SOCIALIZATION PRACTICES

Much of the literature on organizational socialization argues that the most powerful sources of influence in shaping a newcomer's adaption to the job are informal sources of communication between the newcomer and his or her superior, co-workers, and subordinates (Klein and Ritti 1984). The extent to which these people uphold the formal organization's position on work values, attitudes, and behaviors can affect the newcomer's ability to quickly adjust to his or her new job. Organizations with a satisfied work force who are committed to the organization's mission and policies present a congruent picture of organizational life to the newcomer. Examples of informal socialization that reinforce formal socialization practices are these:

"The Company really supports hard workers. I won a trip to Hawaii last year when I set a new sales record."

"We consider ourselves one big family here and try to take care of one another."
"It's important to follow these work procedures carefully, otherwise someone could get hurt."

However, organizations with dissatisfied or alienated employees often build an antiorganizational culture that articulates work values, attitudes, and behaviors that are not sanctioned by the formal organization. Examples of antiorganizational socialization are given by the following types of comments:

"Everybody uses sick leave days for personal holidays. You should make sure you take all of those days off too."
"If we did everything by the book, nothing would get done around here. I'll show you how to get by all the red tape."
"We're having an office party next week. Everyone is calling it a business meeting so the company will pick up the tab."

When newcomers are given little or no formal organizational socialization, they rely on the informal sources for direction. These sources may be divided into three general groups of employees: the newcomer's superiors, the newcomer's colleagues, and the newcomer's subordinates.

A newcomer's superiors are most likely to espouse the formal organization's position regarding the socialization of new hires. Managers generally reaffirm the organization's performance expectations of a newcomer and assume the formal organization's role in helping the newcomer to adapt to the company's values, attitudes, and behavior. Newcomers are most likely to respect his or her superior, and the desire to create a good impression further motivates a newcomer's socialization attempts. When a superior singles out a particular newcomer for individualized attention and development, an informal mentorship begins that may benefit both parties. This type of relationship helps newcomers to sort out important information that should be quickly learned from relatively unimportant information that will not affect the newcomer's career. Mentoring often serves as a stabilizing force in organizations, allowing a smooth passing of the baton from one generation of organizational leaders to the next. However, problems may develop from a mentorship that could include (1) creating newcomer's overdependence on the mentor, (2) cloning newcomers to be just like the established group that may not be able to adjust to current business demands and changes, and (3) creating dissatisfaction among nonmentored newcomers who may regard a mentorship as an unfair advantage for the chosen protégé. In these situations, the negative consequences of mentoring may offset the potential benefits.

Interactions between a newcomer and his or her colleagues may far exceed the number of contacts a newcomer has with superiors and/or subordinates.

Thus, this group may have the greatest potential in socializing the new hire. Research on role modeling shows people are most likely to adopt attitudes, values, and behaviors of other people who are most like them (Decker and Nathan 1985). Explanations on "how *we* do it here" can be powerful socialization strategies. However, if current employees are low in their commitment to the organization, they may socialize newcomers to accommodate an antiorganizational culture and thus perpetuate the organization's problems with its human resources. Organizations that use a buddy system to help newcomers learn the ropes must be careful that the selected buddy teaches the new person the kinds of attitudes, values, and behaviors that are desired by the organization.

A third group of employees who can help socialize newcomers are subordinates and/or staff support people. Examples of how these employees can influence a newcomer's attitudes or behavior can be found in all organizations. One manufacturing organization recently hired a former military officer to supervise a work group. The ex-officer met his new subordinates and told them each day would begin with the group lined up at attention. His announcement was met with riotous laughter and a quick introduction to labor relations. A service organization hired a young consultant who wanted to impress everyone with his professionalism. He made it clear that he was "better" than the secretaries and that they were only there to serve him. When he noticed that his travel reimbursements were the only ones lost and that his reports were given last priority, he learned how other consultants treated the secretaries as a valued and vital part of the department. Gradually, he discovered that a different approach toward the staff allowed him to be a more efficient consultant.

Subordinates or support staff personnel can be valuable sources of information, and many newcomers may seek help from these people in order to avoid asking potentially embarrassing questions to their colleagues or superiors. For example, nurses who work with new interns are often asked basic questions about patient care that should have been part of the doctor's training. Rather than expose their ignorance to other doctors, the interns turn to the nursing staff for help. These people have the necessary expertise, yet they have a lower organizational rank and thus represent a less threatening reference for the newcomer's performance evaluation.

SOCIALIZATION OUTCOMES

As a newcomer tries to integrate all the information he or she learns about an organization, this sense making can resolve a number of discrepancies that may be perceived by the individual. Discrepancies between early expectations and actual experiences, between formal organizational policies and informal practices, and among different people and groups of employees need to be understood for the newcomer to form his or her own evaluations about the job and the organization. How the newcomer evaluates specific aspects about the job, fellow employees, and the organization as a whole will shape his or her commitment to the organization as well as his or her commitment to the chosen career.

Organizational commitment can be described by three components: (1) identification with the organization by adopting its values and goals, (2) involvement with the job and willingness to devote a large portion of one's life to work activities, and (3) loyalty to the organization (Buchanan 1974). A newcomer who is beginning his or her career may be compared with a child who is learning about life in general. The early job experiences are critical factors that will shape the newcomer's attitudes and values about work. To the extent that they represent major discrepancies from original expectations, these early experiences will be traumatic and require a great deal of sense making. To the extent that formal and informal socialization processes will affect the newcomer, these early experiences will influence how well the new hire will fit in and be a satisfied and productive employee who is building commitment to the organization.

Most of the literature on organizational socialization focuses on the advantages and types of socialization strategies. These advantages may have a direct impact on bottom-line criteria of productivity measures. However, there are some potential disadvantages to socialization strategies as well. A sample of disadvantages and advantages is presented here as possible outcomes from socialization practices.

Potential Disadvantages of Organizational Socialization

Perhaps the most common disadvantage is the role strain that results when newcomers try to absorb all the technical, political, and social information they encounter during their first weeks on the job. Information overload and surprises on the job can be major sources of stress for the newcomer. Furthermore, these new role demands often occur with other lifestyle changes such as marriage, children, or geographical move. Organizations can minimize this role strain by providing several resources for newcomers to learn more about the job and company (e.g., employee handbook, feedback from the supervisor and colleagues, training programs) as well as providing resources to help new hires make general lifestyle adjustments (e.g., relocation services, credit union, orientation programs).

A second possible disadvantage to organizational socialization concerns the use of inappropriate socialization strategies. Attempts to teach a newcomer the attitudes, values, and behaviors that are espoused by the organization may be inappropriate for a number of reasons. The background and anticipatory socialization of newcomers may have changed, thus making traditional socialization strategies unsuitable for the latest generation of newcomers. To illustrate, today's young managers are less willing to accept work assignments that involve relocations. The development technique of job rotation often involves periodic moves for junior managers to learn about different facilities and functions of the organization. As more managers refuse to move their families to accommodate job rotations, other strategies (e.g., junior boards, business games) have been suggested to avoid this problem. Thus this method of teaching different aspects of the organization is less likely to be accepted by today's newcomers. In addition to a changing work force, top management may be changing the organization so that current policies and practices in supervision and work expectations would become obsolete. In this situation, continuing socialization practices may reinforce a status quo that would no longer be valued.

Finally, a potential problem of overconformity exists when a newcomer totally accepts the organization's culture and is unable to contribute creative new ideas to change and improve the organization. If total conformity stifles creativity and innovation, the organization may lose some flexibility in anticipating and accommodating change. Thus, socialization strategies ideally would balance strategies that teach a newcomer to accept organizational values with strategies that would give the newcomer enough slack to allow him or her to express individuality and creativity that could benefit the organization. If this balance were achieved, several advantages to this type of socialization would be enjoyed by the organization and the newcomer.

Advantages of Organizational Socialization

Perhaps the most obvious advantage of organizational socialization would be the efficiency of bringing a newcomer up to speed on work productivity. A good socialization program would quickly teach a new hire how to do the job well and how to work effectively with other employees. Without such a program, a newcomer would learn about the job and organizational culture from the informal socialization process. If the informal processes match the formal organization's expectations of newcomer performance, the learning will still occur; however, it may take longer to complete because it is dependent on the quality and quantity of interactions between the newcomer and the more established employees. Formal and informal methods of socialization communicate to the newcomer that the organization cares about new hires and has specific expectations about their role as employees.

The structure of the early socialization experiences can help newcomers focus on the most important features of the job, and the attention can help newcomers build their self-confidence and commitment to the organization. As newcomers learn how to perform the job and how to work well with others, the satisfactions derived from successful job performance and the friendships that are built among employees help develop outcomes such as internal motivation and organizational commitment—outcomes that cannot be taught directly to new hires. Although bottom-line benefits of organizational commitment are difficult to measure, highly committed employees are most likely to make an extra effort, put in extra hours, and be more involved in their work than less committed employees. Successful employees who are highly committed to their work and employer would be the organization's best representatives for the informal socialization of newcomers. The selection of these people to develop newcomers can be managed to be a form of recognition for their loyalty and expertise, and many often derive personal satisfaction in mentoring new hires. Finally, if the socialization process reaffirms the newcomer's decision to join the organization, their subsequent decisions to continue their employment and to work toward certain goals that satisfy both personal and organizational needs would be positive. Thus, possible outcomes from the socialization process would also include job satisfaction and a long organizational tenure.

The outcomes of formal and informal socialization practices may range from overconformity to a productive employee who is committed to the job and organization. These outcomes shape the future expectations employees have about their career. The extent to which these future expectations match organizational reality will determine the long-range organizational commitment and career plans for the individual. Thus, the socialization outcomes serve as feedback for the new expectations that guide future career plans and decisions.

CONCLUSIONS

Organizational socialization concerns the learning process as an individual develops from a naive newcomer to a fully adjusted employee who knows the ropes of the job and understands how to work within the organization's culture. How quickly and how well the newcomer learns how to successfully perform the job in a particular organization is influenced by factors that affect the individual before accepting a position and after entering the organization as a new hire.

For the human resource (HR) professional, the socialization process for newcomers should be managed through formal and informal socialization practices. Formal socialization practices involve direct contact between HR professionals and newcomers and begin with the organization's recruitment and selection systems. Before accepting a job, a potential newcomer has formed certain expectations about it from the anticipatory socialization that educates and trains the individual for the chosen career. Given this anticipatory socialization, hiring managers should base their staffing decisions on two major criteria: (1) Selection criteria would focus on the necessary knowledge, skills, and abilities that are required for successful job performance; and (2) Socialization criteria would focus on the necessary role adjustments required for effective job performance within the organization's existing culture.

After hiring a newcomer, the formal socialization continues via orientation programs, training programs, and specific job assignments. The design, implementation, and evaluation of these early organizational experiences must be carefully managed by the HR professional in order to ensure that a newcomer learns the job efficiently and can take satisfaction with his or her role in the organization. If these activities are not personally conducted by HR professionals, it remains their responsibility to ensure that the line managers are properly trained to provide a good orientation, appropriate training, and challenging job assignments for their new employees.

Working with established employees, and with line managers in particular, HR professionals can have a major impact on the informal socialization practices of newcomers. The extent to which line managers are able to effectively coach new employees, provide good answers to newcomers' questions, and can promote a healthy organizational climate within their units can be influenced by the line managers' own training and career development. Thus, the HR professional's influence on the career management of line managers can indirectly affect the career management of newcomers. In addition to training line managers on the importance of organizational socialization for newcomers, several general programs designed by HR professionals can have a dramatic impact on newcomer experiences. Programs designed to increase the quality of worklife or to provide incentives for superior work can enhance the organizational commitment of all employees. The success of these programs could be perpetuated when highly committed employees are informally socializing newcomers to accept and appreciate the organization's values and goals.

Together, the formal and informal socialization experiences help the newcomer make sense out of his or her role in the organization. How the individual evaluates this sense-making process will affect outcomes that will shape future expectations about the employee's career within the organization. If the socialization practices were effective in teaching the newcomer how to successfully perform the job in a satisfying manner, the individual is likely to be motivated to continue good performance and thus build the person's commitment and loyalty to the organization. However, if the socialization practices were teaching inappropriate or conflicting ideas to the newcomer, the information overload may result in role strain, or the newcomer may learn obsolete practices that would not benefit the organization. Furthermore, socialization practices that are taken too seriously may result in overconformity in newcomers. This total conformity may discourage newcomers from offering creative and innovative ideas to improve current work practices. Thus, a balance must be achieved by socialization practices that teach newcomers to work within the system but still protect the individuality that is needed for creative improvement. Finally, the outcomes from socialization practices serve as a primary reference source for the formation of new job expectations. Based on this feedback, a new phase of socialization begins when past job experiences shape expectations about new jobs.

Thus, the initial problem posed at the beginning of this chapter—early turnover of organizational newcomers—can be minimized through planned socialization programs that aid the new hire in learning and adjusting to organizational life. An employee who is successfully socialized not only understands what his or her role is in the organization, but also shares the attitudes and values of the company. These adjustments offer stability to the work force and help organizations develop employees who are committed to successful work performance and take satisfaction in their work.

REFERENCES

Berlew, D. E., and D. T. Hall. 1966. The socialization of managers: Effects of expectations on performance. *Administrative Science Quarterly, 11*, 207–23.

Buchanan, B., II. 1974. Building organizational commitment: The socialization of managers in work organizations. *Administrative Science Quarterly, 19*, 533–46.

Dalton, G. W., and P. H. Thompson. 1986. *Novations: Strategies for career management.* Glenview, IL: Scott, Foresman & Co.

Decker, P. J., and B. R. Nathan. 1985. *Behavior modeling training.* New York: Praeger.

Feldman, D. C. 1976. A contingency theory of socialization. *Administrative Science Quarterly, 21*, 433–52.

Hollmann, R. W. 1976. Let's not forget about new employee orientation. *Personnel Journal,* May, 244–47, 250.

Kennedy, M. M. 1986. 10 reasons people get fired. *Business Week Careers, 4*, 39–41.

Klein, S. M., and R. R. Ritti, 1984. *Understanding organizational behavior* (2nd ed.). Boston: Kent Publishing Company.

Kozlowski, S. W. J., and C. L. Ostroff. 1987, April. The role of mentoring in the early socialization experiences of organizational newcomers. In G. Chao (chair), *The role of mentoring in organizational settings.* Symposium conducted at the meeting of the Society of Industrial/Organizational Psychology, Atlanta.

Louis, M. R. 1980. Surprise and sense making: What newcomers experience in entering unfamiliar organizational settings. *Administrative Science Quarterly, 25*, 226–51.

Noe, R. A., and N. Schmitt. 1987, April. The role of the mentor in career planning and exploration and career and job involvement. In G. Chao (chair), *The role of mentoring in organizational settings.* Symposium conducted at the meeting of the Society of Industrial/Organizational Psychology, Atlanta.

Schein, E. H. 1964. How to break in the college graduate. *Harvard Business Review, 42*, 68–76.

Schneider, B., and N. Schmitt. 1986. *Staffing organizations* (2nd ed.). Glenview, IL: Scott, Foresman & Company.

Van Maanen, J. 1978. People processing: Strategies of organizational socialization. *Organizational Dynamics*, Summer, 19–36.

Wanous, J. P. 1980. *Organizational entry: Recruitment, selection and socialization of newcomers*. Reading, MA: Addison-Wesley.

CHAPTER 4

PROMOTING CAREER-ENHANCING RELATIONSHIPS IN ORGANIZATIONS: THE ROLE OF THE HUMAN RESOURCE PROFESSIONAL

DAVID A. THOMAS AND KATHY E. KRAM

What factors have been most important in my career development? Well, of course, technical competence and determination, but there have also been a few very important people who have influenced my personal and professional development. Perhaps the most important was the second supervisor I ever had. I had been in the company two years, fresh out of the training program. John was his name. He took me under his wing and showed me the ropes. There's a lot about this business you only learn by apprenticing. John was almost like a surrogate father to me. He struck the right balance between encouraging and affirming me and letting me make the mistakes you need to in order to become your own person. Interestingly enough, John was highly respected, but he wasn't on the fast track.

The second person is Janet, my current boss and vice president of the company. She had heard about and seen some of the work I did for John and asked me to come work for her. She has been an important sponsor for me at the corporate level. Over the last three years, we've developed a good working relationship. When it comes to my social and emotional needs now, I think I look more to Helen and Sid who are peers of mine. We started in the company together and have always shared information and problems arising from the work.

Only recently, I've begun to play somewhat of a developmental or mentor role for some of my subordinates. I find that I gain a lot from these relationships. The young people I'm involved with keep me technically up to date, and I get a sense of accomplishment by seeing them do well.... There's no question that their performance enhances my position in the company.

I could also name a few people above me in the organization who I think at, ᵣtant times, put in a good word for me, but we really

didn't have what I'd call a relationship. They sponsored me because
they saw it to be in their own, and the company's, interest.

                          Bradley, 35 years old, middle-level manager

Where in organizations do people find support for their career development?
Surveys and interviews with managers and professionals echo the experience
of this manager. The ability to form supportive relations in the workplace
has been positively linked to job satisfaction (Kirmeyer and Thung-Rung
1987) and career mobility (Kanter 1977; Roche 1979). There are also positive organizational outcomes associated with the development of career-
enhancing relationships. When young employees have supportive relationships early in their careers, the socialization process is often facilitated, and
their task competence develops more rapidly (Zey 1984). Therefore, to
further both organizational and employee effectiveness, human resource
professionals must understand and promote the formation of career-enhancing relationships in organizations.

In recent years the concept of mentor-protégé relationships has received
a good deal of attention in the popular press. Articles with titles such as
"Everyone Needs a Mentor" have been frequent occurrences. While we
agree that mentor relationships are important sources of support for individuals, it appears that the concept has lost much of its original meaning
(Levinson and others 1978). The term "mentor-protégé relationship" has
been uniformly applied to all superior-subordinate career-enhancing relationships; in fact, there are a range of career-enhancing relationships, each
providing different types of support and possessing different relationship
qualities. In addition, there has been undue focus on the instrumental purposes of the mentor-protégé relationship, deemphasizing the psychosocial
support this type of relationship can give. Also, overlooked in the literature
and by practitioners in the area of human resources has been the role that
peer relationships play in enhancing individuals' career development (Kram
1988; Kram and Isabella 1985).

This chapter is inspired by the belief that in order for human resource
professionals to be effective in their efforts to facilitate the formation of
career-enhancing relationships, they must understand the range of relationships possible and the benefits to be derived from each. This chapter begins
with a discussion of the types of superior-subordinate career-enhancing
relationships that are possible and the special nature of boss-subordinate
relationships. Then the importance of peer relationships as sources of career
development support will be addressed. The work force is becoming more
multiracial at all levels, and more women are moving into nontraditional
jobs. Issues associated with the development of cross-race and cross-gender
career-enhancing relationships will be examined. The final section examines

a number of strategies available to organizations for facilitating the formation and positive development of career-enhancing relationships.

SUPERIOR-SUBORDINATE CAREER-ENHANCING RELATIONSHIPS

Broadly defined, a superior-subordinate relationship occurs between two persons who are differentiated by hierarchical levels and/or professional status within the organization. This includes boss-subordinate relations, relations involving persons who are not in a boss-subordinate relationship but are nevertheless hierarchically differentiated, and relations between persons who technically have the same job title but are differentiated in terms of organizational status. An example of this latter category is found in law firms in which two professional hierarchical statuses are officially recognized—partner and associate—yet the organization does differentiate between senior associates and junior associates. The latter often work for the former, as apprentices, and are given relatively less responsibility.

Are all superior-subordinate relations career enhancing? Frequently, superior-subordinate relations, especially boss-subordinate relations, imply that the superior has some responsibility for the assessment and development of his or her subordinate(s). A structural reporting relationship is not enough, however; there must be some interest and action taken by the senior party to enhance the junior party's career development. Thus, not all superior-subordinate relationships would meet this criterion. In addition, parties in such a relationship might differ in their perceptions of whether a career-enhancing relationship actually exists, and what kind of relationship is desirable.

Much of the popular literature on mentor-protégé relationships promotes the view that superior-subordinate career-enhancing relations are primarily concerned with sponsoring the junior person into higher levels of management by providing exposure and endorsements. While these activities can be an important part of these relationships, they are not the only or necessarily the most important ones. Kram (1988) found that career-enhancing relationships perform two types of functions for the parties involved: (1) career functions, and (2) psychosocial functions. Career functions are those activities which enhance career advancement and increase one's share of organizational rewards and resources, such as providing sponsorship, exposure, visibility, protection, and challenging assignments. Psychosocial functions enhance one's sense of competence, identity, and effectiveness in the professional role, such as role modeling, acceptance and confirmation, counseling, and friendship. While most of the activities listed for both types of functions imply effort by the senior party on the junior party's behalf, both individuals benefit from both types (Kram 1988).

Figure 4.1
Typology of Career-Enhancing Relations*

| | | Developmental Relationships | |
Criteria	Temporary Instrumental	Sustained Career–Support	Mentor/ Protege
(1) Level & duration of contact	Impersonal/ Short–term	Personal/ Short–long	Personal/ Long–term
(2) Mutuality	Low	Medium	High
(3) Interdependence	Low	Low to High	High
(4) Relationship Functions Career vs. Psychosocial	Career	Career	Career & Psychosocial

* Adapted from Thomas (1986).

A Typology of Career-Enhancing Relationships

Little work has been done to define the various types of superior-sub-ordinate career-enhancing relationships and the dimensions along which they are differentiated. From Bradley's experience, it is clear that his relationships with John and Janet were different in terms of both the functions served and the level of personal attachment. Yet, both met Bradley's needs and enhanced his career. Also, there are the relationships Bradley describes at the end of his comments which offered him needed sponsorship, but lacked the personal element found in the other relationships he describes.

Drawing upon current research in both psychology and sociology, Thomas (1986) proposes the typology of career-enhancing relationships illustrated in Figure 4.1.

Career-enhancing relationships involving superiors and subordinates are conceptualized as falling on a continuum ranging from temporary instrumental relationships to mentor-protégé relationships. These relationships are differentiated along four criteria: (1) level and duration of the relationship which refers to the nature of the personal contact between the parties—personal versus impersonal—and the length of time the relationship existed; (2) mutuality is the extent to which the relationship is characterized by trust and openness on issues of both personal and professional importance to the parties; (3) interdependence is the extent to which the parties feel the actions of one have consequences for the other; and (4) relationship functions refers to the type of support function(s), career and/or psychosocial, that the relationship provides to the parties.

Temporary instrumental relations. This type of relationship serves solely career functions, most notably sponsorship. It requires little or no mutuality and is not dependent on the parties having personal knowledge or contact with one another over a significant period of time. Likewise, the parties need not see themselves as being interdependent. Bradley's reference to superiors who sponsored him on occasion, but with whom he had no personal contact, is an example of this type of relationship. The implication is that both he and they derived only career benefits from the relationship.

Sustained career support relationships. This type of relationship is perhaps the most common. It is structured to provide primarily career functions. Mutuality is required only to the extent that the parties are able to exchange positive and negative information relevant to their task performance. The sense of interdependence in these relationships is likely to vary depending on the design of the task. If the individuals are in a loosely coupled structural relationship, such as that between persons who are not in a direct line of reporting, perceived interdependence may be low compared to that between a boss and his or her immediate report.

Bradley's relationship with Janet can be classified as sustained career support. The relationship is personal and seems to have lasted a significant amount of time. He sees the relationship as having provided him with significant career support, especially exposure to upper management and sponsorship. However, he does not rely on it for a great deal of psychosocial support, as he did with John.

Mentor-protégé relationships. This type of relationship is characterized by a high degree of mutuality and interdependence. Mentor-protégé relationships provide significant amounts of both career and psychosocial support. Levinson et al. (1978) note that these relationships often possess dynamics and emotions similar to those found in the parent-child relationship. Individuals in these relationships are usually differentiated by hierarchical level and age. The parties also view themselves as interdependent both personally and professionally. The average duration of a mentor-protégé relationship is five years (Kram 1988; Levinson et al. 1978). Bradley's relationship with John can be classified as such. Both career and psychosocial functions were served, and the relationship seemed to possess a significant degree of mutuality. Bradley even goes so far as to describe their relationship as similar to that between father and son.

Sustained career support and mentor-protégé relationships can also constitute a subcategory of relationships known as developmental relationships (Kram 1980; Clawson 1979). Developmental relationships occur between individuals who have a personal knowledge of one another and rely on the relationship, over a significant period of time, to provide important services to the junior party's career development. Developmental relationships—sustained career support and mentor-protégé relationships—are important because they offer more benefits to the parties involved than do temporary instrumental relationships. Also, most human resource professionals' efforts to facilitate the formation of career-enhancing relationships are intended to foster developmental rather than temporary instrumental relationships.

A Note on the Importance of Boss-Subordinate Relationships

Recent research (Thomas 1986) illustrates the importance of the boss-subordinate relationship as a potential career-enhancing relationship. In a study of 199 managers from a Fortune 500 company, it was found that 65 percent of all career-enhancing relationships involved these individuals with their bosses, while only 27 percent of the relationships were with persons two levels or more removed from the respondent. Furthermore, 60 percent of all boss-subordinate relationships were found to possess the characteristics of mentor-protégé relationships, while only 40 percent of all other superior-subordinate relationships were found to have these characteristics.

Immediate supervisors are especially important in the socialization, training, and development of young employees and new organizational members. Some of the fallacies that have grown out of the misrepresentation of the mentoring concept in the popular press have, perhaps, led some to lose sight of the importance of this relationship. The idea that mentors are powerful people, levels removed from their protégés, has left out the critical importance of the boss-subordinate relationship as a potential mentor-protégé relationship. Just imagine the young professional who enters an organization and feels she must develop a mentor. Without a clear understanding of the range of career-enhancing relationships, and instilled with the myth of the powerful mentor, this individual might overlook the most valuable source of mentoring available to her. Likewise, bosses who are not well placed or high up in the organization may diminish their importance as a mentor and not pursue development of such a relationship. It is also interesting to note that most training courses for middle- and lower-level management personnel do not include modules which explicitly address the issue of career-enhancing relationships, especially mentor-protégé relationships. The inclusion of such modules would help to legitimize managers' and supervisors' involvement in developmental relationships.

This discussion of superior-subordinate career-enhancing relationships points toward the need for human resource professionals to develop an understanding of the range of career-enhancing relationships that may develop and the conditions which foster them. It is also important to acknowledge that individuals usually rely on multiple relationships, over the course of their career, to provide the type of support they need. Given the importance of the boss-subordinate relationship as a source of career development support, it seems appropriate that efforts should be made to enhance the probability that such relationships will become developmental.

THE NATURE OF CAREER-ENHANCING PEER RELATIONSHIPS

There is a tendency among practitioners and scholars alike to assume that career-enhancing relationships are limited to superior-subordinate alliances. Considerable evidence suggests, however, that relationships with peers also have the potential to support individual development at every career stage (Kram 1988; Kram and Isabella 1985; Shapiro, Hazeltine, and Rowe 1978; Thomas 1986). In the same way that superior-subordinate relationships vary in the range of career and psychosocial functions they provide, and in the degrees of mutuality and interdependence, so do relationships with peers.

While peers are not generally in a position to sponsor or create opportunities for exposure and visibility, they can offer career support in the form of information sharing, career strategizing, and job-related feedback (Kram 1988). Indeed, in the absence of a mentor or sponsor who can provide necessary career functions, individuals do find it helpful to look to their peers for knowledge and insight that can further their preparation for advancement. Similarly, peers can provide emotional support, personal feedback, role modeling, and friendship—a range of psychosocial functions that enhance self-confidence, well-being, and clarity of professional identity. Studies of cross-race and cross-gender developmental relationships have indicated that relationships with same-race or same-gender peers often provide psychosocial support more difficult to achieve in relationships with mentors of a different race or gender (Thomas 1986; Kram 1988).

Relationships with peers offer several unique advantages over hierarchical developmental relationships. First, they offer the opportunity for both individuals in the alliance to receive and provide support—this mutuality furthers a sense of competence, responsibility, and the mentor's identity as an expert which is particularly important for those in the early stage of a career. Second, peer relationships are more available at every career stage than mentor or sponsor relationships. Everyone has, in his or her immediate work context, more potential peers than mentors because of the narrowing organizational pyramid and the ease in contacting those at the same age or hierarchical level. Third, it appears that peer relationships can endure far longer than mentor relationships; whereas the latter generally last between three and eight years, some peer relationships begin in early career and last through late career. Such long-term relationships provide continuity over the course of a career, along with a variety of developmental functions through periods of change and transition.

Both age peers and level peers are frequently overlooked as sources of career and psychosocial support, even though it is precisely the similarity in age and/or level that makes empathy, communication, and trust easier to achieve than in relationships that cross hierarchical and/or age boundaries. Individuals will maximize the range of supportive alliances that they have at work if they consider the untapped possibilities in relationships with their peers. It appears that the value of peers is most likely to be discounted in the novice stage of a career when individuals are focused upward on establishing relationships with bosses and other superiors who can pave the way for advancement. With experience, individuals begin to learn that peers are an essential resource both for getting the job done and for developing one's career (Kram 1988). The human resource professional can facilitate this career-enhancing perspective through education, training, counseling, and consulting efforts.

FACTORS THAT SHAPE CAREER-ENHANCING RELATIONSHIPS

What factors influence the type of career-enhancing relationship that will develop? One might wonder whether this typology of superior-subordinate career-enhancing relationships outlines a developmental model (i.e., relationships may be seen as starting as temporary instrumental and evolving to mentor-protégé). While this may happen, research does not support this view as an axiom (Thomas 1986). The characteristics which career-enhancing relationships take on are determined by the interaction of organizational and individual-level factors.

Organizations influence the formation of career-enhancing relationships in various ways. Kanter (1977) and Alvarez (1979) have stressed that the senior parties to career-enhancing relationships offer sponsorship to junior managers only when the instrumental benefits of doing so outweigh the perceived cost. This suggests that organizations can develop incentive structures that encourage the formation of such relationships. For example, affirmative action requirements may influence white and male managers to sponsor minorities and women into positions from which they were previously absent. Kram (1986) also found that reward structures that have short-term, bottom-line orientations mediate against the formation of positive developmental relationships. While the reward structure is important for facilitating the formation of career-enhancing relationships, excessive reliance on extrinsic motivation factors is most likely to produce temporary instrumental rather than developmental relationships. On the other hand, if extrinsic rewards become the primary motivating factor for individuals to engage in career-enhancing relationships, it is most likely that temporary instrumental rather than developmental relationships will form.

Kram (1988) has noted that an organization's culture, task design, and performance management system can influence the formation of developmental relationships. Organizations whose norms and values legitimize the developmental roles that superiors assume tend to create an atmosphere conducive to the formation of developmental relationships. Task design influences the formation of developmental relationships by defining the technical interdependence and interactions between members of an organization. To the extent that the task system maximizes the opportunities for interaction among people with complementary career needs, developmental rather than temporary instrumental career-enhancing relationships are likely to form. The performance management system can influence the formation of developmental relationships by providing a forum for various relationship functions such as coaching, counseling, providing feedback, and career planning. It is essential, however, that the parties have appropriate interpersonal skill and knowledge of the developmental purpose of the superior-subordinate relationship.

One of the most critical factors in determining the type of developmental relationship that two individuals are likely to have is the degree of complementarity between their career stages.

For example, Bradley notes that his relationship with Janet is different from his relationship with John, partly because his need for nurturing has declined. Researchers have found that in the early stages of an employee's career, he or she is most in need of, and open to, developing a mentor-protégé relationship (Baird and Kram 1983; Dalton, Thompson, and Price 1977). Concomitantly, persons in the middle to late stages of their career and in the midlife stage of adult development are often open to developing mentor-protégé relationships in order to meet their own needs for generativity—to influence the course of an organization's direction and to leave a legacy. However, when the developmental needs of the parties are not complementary, developmental relationships are likely to take the form of sustained career support relations. It is also likely that a lack of complementarity that emerges after a relationship has formed can lead to its dissolution (Levinson et al. 1978).

The potential of relationships with peers to support development at successive career stages is rarely realized. Individuals' attitudes toward self and assumptions about others, as well as characteristics of the organizational context, can fuel competitive dynamics that prohibit the formation of supportive alliances. For example, an individual who feels uncertain about his or her competence is unlikely to form a trusting relationship with a peer with whom performance may be compared in the future. If the organization rewards individual effort and discourages collaboration, it is difficult for peers in the same setting to support one another. It is not surprising the closest relationships frequently occur outside the immediate work group where competition is minimized.

CROSS-RACE AND CROSS-GENDER RELATIONSHIPS

The number of minorities and women in organizations and positions that were once almost exclusively white and male has grown significantly over the last twenty-five years. Much of this change was brought about by affirmative action pressures placed on organizations by government and by the moral and social responsibility felt by the leaders of these institutions. We would be remiss and naive, however, if we assumed that racism and sexism no longer exist or that most minorities and whites and males and females no longer experience anxiety and difficulty when interacting with persons different from them in these salient dimensions.

While legislated efforts to promote minority and female representation may result in important instrumental sponsorship for minorities and women, especially at the entry level, it is doubtful that these efforts will, by themselves, foster the type of developmental and peer relationships necessary for positive career development (Thomas 1986).

A thorough treatment of all the issues associated with race and gender relations in organizations will not be presented (for such a treatment, see Chapter 16 by Fernandez in this volume), but some of the complexities associated with the formation and development of cross-race and cross-gender career-enhancing relationships can be described.

The ability to form a positive identification with an individual is an important aspect of the development of the mentor-protégé relationship (Levinson and others 1978; Kram 1988; Thomas 1986). When individuals are similar on salient demographic dimensions, the identification process is facilitated in a positive direction. Parties are able to develop empathic and mutual responses to one another. When race and/or gender differences are salient features of a relationship, the parties may find difficulty making positive identifications and developing a significant level of trust and openness. The ability to use other individuals as role models can also be impaired by racial and gender differences (Kram 1988; Thomas 1986).

It has been found, however, that when individuals are cognizant of the fact they may have difficulty making positive identification across racial lines, they can compensate by becoming more conscientious about engaging their own resistance and looking for biases in their reactions (Thomas 1986). It should be noted that the necessity of having to make more conscious the identification process may also mean that the amount of time required to initiate cross-race and cross-gender developmental relationships may be longer than when persons are of the same race or gender. This suggests that efforts to educate individuals about career-enhancing relationships would do well to include modules on cross-race and cross-gender relationships, highlighting the issue of identification.

Parties to cross-race and cross-gender relationships have been found to employ several distinct strategies for managing their demographic differences. The strategy employed is dependent on the level of consciousness the parties have about issues of race or gender, and their beliefs about how racial or gender differences should be managed in the contexts of interpersonal relationships and the organization. When the parties are complementary in their views, the relationship is likely to become developmental. When they are not complementary, at best, the relationships will sustain career support but lack mutuality and be prone to premature termination.

Three relationship strategies for managing differences have been identified (Thomas 1986): (1) denial and suppression, (2) direct engagement, and (3) dual support. The first two represent strategies for managing the cross-racial and cross-gender relationship, while the third speaks to a recognition of the protégé's need for identification with persons like himself or herself, as well as to the limitations of cross-race and cross-gender relationships. The first two strategies may be coupled with the third.

The denial and suppression strategy is used when both parties feel race or gender is an issue inappropriate for discussion and does not influence the relationship, or when one party (usually the minority or female) feels the other is unwilling or unable to engage around the issue of race. The common dynamic in both circumstances is that the parties are unable to address issues related to their racial or gender differences; even when such issues seem relevant or important, they are suppressed or their relevance denied. In the first circumstance, the parties' views are complementary, and they will find it easier to form a developmental relationship; while in the second, the minority or female protégé engages in the relationship because of instrumental necessity and finds it hard to be open and trusting.

The direct engagement strategy is possible only when both parties have a high level of racial or gender consciousness and view differences as important and relationship-enhancing when acknowledged and managed. Under this strategy, the parties' views are complementary, and positive developmental relationships are most likely the result. Minorities and women report that it is easier to "be themselves" in these relationships, because they feel less pressure to act in prescribed ways and to ignore issues important to them because of their racial and gender identification.

The dual support strategy is one in which the protégé (usually the minority or female) develops a support system that includes both same- and cross-race or gender relationships. This strategy usually emerges for one of two reasons. One is that the individual realizes, or comes to realize, the importance of having support persons with whom he or she shares a salient demographic characteristic that influences his or her organizational experience (Dickens and Dickens 1982; Thomas 1986). The second reason is that the limitations and stress associated with being involved in cross-race or cross-gender relationships that employ the suppression and denial strategy propel one to seek other outlets for expression and support.

Organizations have a great deal of influence in determining available strategies for managing racial and gender differences. If the organization is characterized by norms and values that treat racial and gender differences as taboo topics, only mentioned when racism manifests itself in overt ways, all employees are likely to get the message that denial and suppression insures survival, whether or not it enhances the relationships. Furthermore, if minorities and women find themselves in organizations which prove to have limited job mobility and growth opportunities, they become disillusioned and angry and withdraw from potentially developmental relationships. Finally, if organizations have few or no minorities and women employed, especially in positions of authority, it will prove difficult for these individuals to utilize the dual support strategy.

PRACTICAL ALTERNATIVES

There are several options available to the human resource professional who wants to actively influence the quality of relationships that support employee development. Each strategy has its strengths and limitations, and the appropriate route to follow will depend on the resources available, the level of support and involvement from senior management, the specific objectives to be met, and the character of the work context in terms of its culture, reward system, and formal organization.

Three basic approaches to improving the quality of developmental relationships can be identified: (1) a formal mentoring program can be created to match those with complementary needs and skills for the purpose of providing mentoring functions to the less experienced employee; (2) training and education can be offered to individuals at early, middle, and/or late career stages that enhance self-awareness, understanding of the developmental relationship process, and the interpersonal skills to build and maintain career-enhancing relationships; and (3) an organizational change approach can be used to diagnose factors in the work environment that impede an effective mentoring process, so that structural and educational interventions can be designed to create a more supportive context for career-enhancing relationships.

Formal Mentoring Programs

While a formal mentoring program frequently appears to be the most direct approach to improving the quality of career-enhancing relationships, it has a number of subtle and unintended consequences which can be costly to individuals and to the organization as a whole. Sometimes those who are matched may feel anxious about their capacity to carry out the expectations of the formal role, and this discomfort can undermine both the performance and morale of both parties to the relationship. Second, those who are not chosen to participate in a formal program may feel increasingly pessimistic about their own prospects for growth and advancement, which can lead to lowered performance and morale as well as increasing resentment toward peers who have been chosen to participate. Finally, a formal program emphasizes the role of a single relationship designated to provide a range of career and psychosocial functions. This contradicts strong evidence that a constellation of several developmental relationships with peers and seniors is more enriching than a single relationship, which is shaped by a number of psychological and organizational forces that can disrupt the alliance at any time.

These unintended consequences can be minimized so that the benefits of a formal program—easy access to mentors, legitimization of developmental activities, ongoing monitoring of the quality of career-enhancing relationships, and increasing competence and motivation among those who participate—outweigh the costs. When participation is truly voluntary, individuals are less likely to feel coerced or resentful of the new responsibilities that the program entails. Second, if training and education are offered to participants at the outset of the program to sharpen conceptual understanding, self-awareness, and the interpersonal skills required to fulfill counseling and coaching roles effectively, then anxiety and incompetence in the new role will be minimized, and such formalized relationships are more likely to succeed. Finally, if the program is introduced carefully by the human resource professional so that nonparticipants understand its purpose and scope, then supervisors and peers of those who join the program may be less inclined to be negatively affected by its implementation.

While there has been little systematic evaluation of formal mentoring programs to date, it does appear that those designed to minimize the unintended consequences have achieved some positive results in terms of developing human resources for the organization (Kram 1986). Frequently, such programs have been introduced to facilitate mentoring alliances for high potential employees, for women and/or people of color, or for organizational newcomers. When a particular population is targeted as being in need of better access to coaching and counseling, and when educational support is offered to insure effective participation, a formal program is viable. However, it is clear that the formalization and engineering of relationships contradicts the spontaneous and mutual attraction that characterizes the early stages of a strong mentoring alliance (Thomas 1986; Kram 1988; Levinson et al. 1978). Also, the effort to match juniors and seniors conveys the inaccurate assumption that establishing one mentoring relationship—rather than several relationships that provide various mentoring functions—is optimal.

Education and Training

Education and training can increase understanding of the role of relationships in career development and create a context in which individuals learn about the range of developmental relationships that are possible, increase their self-awareness, and enhance their interpersonal skills in building and maintaining supportive alliances. This approach, in conjunction with a formal mentoring program, increases the likelihood that participants will benefit from the matched relationship. By itself, this approach can empower individuals to build more supportive developmental alliances on the job, as it offers a new foundation of knowledge and interpersonal skills that facilitate relationship-building efforts. In addition to enhancing knowledge and skills, effective education can change the culture of an organization by reinforcing new values that give priority to relationship-building activities.

Many educational offerings are possible, and the appropriate design depends on the setting and objectives that create the need for intervention (London and Stumpf 1982). For example, when performance appraisal, career planning, and employee development activities are firmly established and functioning reasonably well, education related to career-enhancing relationships can be incorporated into ongoing training that supports these personnel systems. Alternatively, when the human resource department of an organization is expected to offer state-of-the-art programs to employees at every career stage, a specific program on the role of mentoring and other developmental relationships in careers, for example, can be tailored to training populations in early, middle, and/or late career stages. Finally, when higher quality and greater availability of mentoring for women and minority group members are desired, specialized training events for these groups and their potential mentors can be designed (Lean 1983; Phillips 1982; Kram 1986, 1988).

The design of education and training can take various forms, ranging from short (e.g., half-day session) information-sharing events, to longer skill-building experiences (e.g., two to four days). While the latter certainly offer greater benefits, they will only be worthwhile if participation is voluntary, if experiential methods are employed effectively to facilitate personal learning and risk taking, if there is a clear rationale about how the educational objectives fit with participants' job situations and with broader organizational goals, and, finally, if organizational practices support the attitudes, knowledge, and skills that are discussed and practiced. Without meeting these basic conditions, it is very likely that new learning will fade rapidly back on the job.

Having the support of senior management is essential to ensuring that such education and training is viewed as legitimate and important (Leibowitz, Farren, and Kaye 1986). Ideally, these managers should actively articulate how career-enhancing relationships contribute to organizational objectives; they should model effective mentoring behavior in their relationships with subordinates and reward participants who take the time to build and maintain supportive developmental alliances. However, these ideal conditions usually do not exist, and the impact of education and training is limited. If organizational norms and practices contradict new attitudes and skills, then those who have participated are likely to become more frustrated or angry and ultimately fail to use their newly acquired skills.

The limitations of formal mentoring programs, as well as education and training efforts, indicate the need to attend to characteristics of the organizational context that either encourage or obstruct career-enhancing relationships. For even if individuals develop the interpersonal and conceptual skills to build supportive alliances, and the culture of the organization discourages attention to relationships or is characterized by low trust, poor communication, or dysfunctional stereotyping of particular groups, efforts to build career-enhancing relationships will be undermined. Similarly, if the reward system acknowledges only short-term, bottom-line results in the appraisal process, then attention to relationship-building activities will be viewed as a distraction from what is essential to good performance, and efforts to build developmental alliances are likely to be abandoned. And if the structure of jobs and work groups does not allow for frequent interaction among colleagues who might have complementary relationship needs, then it will be quite difficult for individuals to find appropriate others with whom they can establish developmental relationships (Thomas 1986; Kram 1986, 1988).

Organizational Change Approach

An organizational change approach to improving the quality and availability of career-enhancing relationships systematically identifies environmental factors that are impeding effective developmental alliances. The human resource professional who recognizes significant limitations of a formal mentoring program and education and/or training activities can employ this systemwide process of data collection, diagnosis, action planning, intervention, and evaluation (Beer 1980) to determine what actions should be taken to create more favorable conditions in the work context. This diagnostic process usually involves a collaboration among the target population of individuals for whom mentoring is desirable, the management group that must commit resources and support, and the internal and/or external change agents who have the behavioral science knowledge and skill to orchestrate the effort. As part of the data collection and diagnostic phases, organizational members are asked about their experiences in relationships, career concerns, and perceptions of the organization, so that the human resource staff can identify for whom career-enhancing relationships are lacking, the obstacles to forming effective alliances, and features of the organization that may be contributing to these obstacles (Kram 1986).

The result of a systematic diagnosis may be a decision to implement educational offerings or possibly a decision to set up some kind of formal mentoring program. What makes this approach unique, however, is that it ensures that the requisite organizational conditions are simultaneously developed so that programs are not undermined by inconsistencies in the reward system, the culture, the task design, or ongoing human resource management practices. It may be, for example, that before education can have its intended impact, the reward system must be examined and modified to insure that individuals are encouraged to implement new relationship skills back on the job. Or it may be that task forces and project teams that facilitate interaction among individuals at complementary career stages—rather than a formal program or education—are all that are needed to enable individuals to build career-enhancing relationships. Thus, strategies that are effective in one setting may be inappropriate in another; the human resource professional must consider which educational and structural interventions are most practical and most promising given the specific objectives that underlie the interest in promoting career-enhancing relationships as well as the resources available for such developmental efforts.

Frequently, in order to conserve resources, organizations choose the intervention that appears to be most efficient; yet this same alternative may be inadequate in altering the practices that create the most significant obstacles. For example, in one typical situation, a formal mentoring system that was set up for women and minority professionals in an attempt to support affirmative action objectives failed because of these factors: white male seniors resented the new responsibility and lacked the interpersonal skills required to build mentoring alliances or address racial and gender issues that surface in work relationships; the reward system did not recognize efforts to actively develop subordinates; and the culture was such that trust and communication across hierarchical, racial, and gender boundaries were poor. Clearly, other actions had to be taken to create more favorable conditions before such a formal system could possibly succeed.

An organization change approach ensures that the necessary sequence of education and change in culture, systems, and practices is identified. While promoting career-enhancing relationships is demanding in terms of time and resources, the benefits promise to be longer lasting than those of the more efficient approaches discussed earlier. In fact, a systemwide diagnostic approach incorporates the other approaches when appropriate, thereby insuring that benefits of each are maximized. An organizational change approach points to the need to involve individuals at all levels and career stages in the diagnosis, action-planning, implementation, and evaluation phases. Each phase in the process is enhanced by having representatives of major interest groups involved to insure that all relevant factors that are shaping the nature of career-enhancing relationships are considered.

The human resource professional has choices to make regarding the optimal way to promote career-enhancing relationships in his or her organization. While the organizational change approach is most comprehensive and most likely to have enduring impact, available resources may limit the alternatives to education and training or to a formal matching program of some kind. It appears that the costs and unintended consequences of a formal program generally make this the least preferred option, although some companies have reported positive outcomes for some participants.

If few resources are available to warrant consideration of any of the three major approaches outlined here, the human resource professional who wants to promote career-enhancing relationships can, at a minimum, incorporate exploration and discussion of enhancing and problematic relationships into ongoing career counseling and consulting efforts. Such dialog can begin to educate clients about the nature of developmental alliances and how to maximize their role in individuals' careers.

CONCLUSION

There now exists a body of knowledge about the nature and complexity of career-enhancing relationships that can be of value to human resource professionals and organizations. It is important, however, that efforts to facilitate the formation of career-enhancing relationships not be undertaken without full regard for these complexities.

Mentor-protégé relationships are not the only type of career-enhancing relationship available to individuals, nor should they be the only type that human resource professionals attempt to promote. Individuals should be encouraged to develop and nurture a constellation of relationships that reflects their career and psychosocial needs at successive career stages. Included in relationship constellations are likely to be relations with superiors and subordinates and peers.

The formation and development of career-enhancing relationships can be influenced by both individual and organizational factors. Career stage, race, and gender are the individual factors discussed here—each of these represent complex issues which interventions to facilitate the formation of career-enhancing relationships should take into account. Attempts at changing the organizational context, or implementing programs, to promote the development of career-enhancing relationships should be preceded by a diagnosis of the organization's current state, needs, and obstacles with regard to the formation of these relationships. To do otherwise, heightens the probability that such efforts will meet unanticipated resistance and produce unintended, negative consequences.

REFERENCES

Alvarez, R. 1979. *Discrimination in organizations.* San Francisco: Jossey-Bass.

Baird, L., and K. E. Kram. 1983. Career dynamics: Managing the superior-subordinate relationship. *Organizational Dynamics,* Spring, 46–64.

Beer, M. 1980. *Organization change and development.* Santa Monica, CA: Goodyear Publishing Co.

Clawson, J. 1979. Superior-subordinate relationship for managerial development. Unpublished Dissertation, Harvard University Business School.

Dickens, F., and L. Dickens. 1982. *The black manager.* Chicago: Amacow Publishing.

Kanter, R. 1977. *Men and women of the corporation.* New York: Random House.

Kirmeyer, S. L., and L. Thung-Rung. 1987. Social support: Its relationship to observed communication with peers and superiors. *Academy of Management Journal, 30*(1), 138–51.

Kram, K. 1980. Mentoring processes at work. Unpublished Dissertation, Yale University.

Kram, K. E. 1988. *Mentoring at work.* Lanham, MD: University Press of America. 2nd. printing originally published in 1985 by Scott, Foresman & Co.

Kram, K. E. 1986. Mentoring in the work place. In D. T. Hall (ed.), *Career development in organizations.* San Francisco: Jossey-Bass.

Kram, K., and M. Isabella. 1985. Mentoring alternatives: The role of peer relationships in career development. *Academy of Management Journal*, March, 110–32.

Lean, E. 1983. Cross-gender mentoring—Downright upright and good for productivity. *Training and Development Journal*, May.

Leibowitz, Z., C. Farren, and B. Kaye. 1986. *Designing career development systems.* San Francisco: Jossey-Bass.

Levinson, D. and others. 1978. *Seasons of a man's life.* New York: Knopf.

London, M., and S. Stumpf. 1982. *Managing careers.* Reading, MA: Addison-Wesley.

Phillips, L. L. 1982. *Mentors and protégés.* New York: Arden House.

Roche, G. R. 1979. Much ado about mentors. *Harvard Business Review*, January/February, 565–84.

Shapiro, E., F. Hazeltine, and M. Rowe. 1978. Moving up: role models, mentors and the patron system. *Sloan Management Review*, Spring, 51–58.

Thomas, D. 1986. An intraorganizational analysis of black and white patterns of sponsorship and the dynamics of cross-racial mentoring. Unpublished Dissertation, Yale University.

Zey, M. 1984. *The mentor connection.* New York: Dow Jones-Irwin.

MAINTAINING EMPLOYEE INVOLVEMENT IN A PLATEAUED CAREER

———— DOUGLAS T. HALL AND SAMUEL RABINOWITZ

GREAT EXPECTATIONS

The future isn't what it used to be. When a person joined an organization, he or she expected to put in years of hard work, long hours, relocation, and many other forms of sacrifice to build a career there. Over time, the employee would develop a reasonable level of loyalty to the organization. In return, the company was expected to provide a measure of job security, a long career with the organization, perhaps some promotions, and a level of concern for the employee's career development. Such was the psychological contract when the employee entered the organization ten, twenty, and thirty years ago.

The psychological contract has changed. In contrast to these earlier expectations, today's employee often experiences a dead-end job in a turbulent, financially constrained organization, which has just been restructured (or acquired or divested) and which cannot even promise that the present job will be there next year. In addition to fear of job loss, the most common form of career stress in today's organizations is the feeling of constricted career opportunity. Promotions will be slower and fewer, and plateauing will be more common. And the plateauers will be the fortunate ones: The less fortunate will lose their jobs.

As Carol Hymowitz (1986) describes it:

The corporate ladder—the symbol of an [employee's] path to the top—has assumed a new shape. Once predictable rungs have been replaced by a much narrower staircase, difficult to maneuver, with several steps missing and prone to collapse. (p. 33)

A career plateau is defined as "the point in an organizational career where the individual is unlikely to experience additional hierarchical mobility" (Stoner, Ference, Warren, and Christensen 1980, p. 1). In contrast, promotion involves a real increase in duties and responsibilities (not necessarily bonuses, cost-of-living increases, merit increases, or changes in title which do not bring increased authority).

Plateauing generally occurs in mid-career, following the earlier career stages of exploration, trial, and advancement (Hall 1976). It usually is experienced as a shock or jolt, because the earlier parts of the career were full of activity, movement, and change. And each new assignment was better than the last one. There was a sense that there was a path to the career, and that it was headed generally upward, sprinkled perhaps with a few lateral, developmental moves along the way. It felt like a plane taking off, full of power.

Then, all of a sudden, it was as if the plane had leveled off, and the power was cut way back. Everything became quiet; nothing seemed to be happening. The person might try to deny it for a while. But finally he or she had to admit it: "My career is going nowhere."

Early Signs of a Plateau

It is possible for the person to see a plateau approaching without waiting for this dramatic jolt of career inactivity to hit. Here are some of the early warning signs that we have observed:

1. Being in the same assignment for a much longer time than any previous assignment.
2. Feeling the "disappearing firsts": not having done anything of note for the first time in the last year.
3. Not having any more surprises in the job; feeling that the job is under control (too much so).
4. Feelings of boredom; no "zing" in work.
5. Feeling anxious or competitive or angry about younger colleagues.
6. Feeling that the costs of making a career or job change are getting too high.
7. Seeing pay raises level off.
8. Feeling you're defending your position more often.
9. Not learning and growing in the job.

Some of these indicators occur earlier than others. Feeling the loss of learning and surprise happens much sooner than being in the same assignment for many years. The feelings of boredom may hit before the pay increases level off. The sooner the person—or the manager—recognizes a plateau, the sooner remedial action can be taken. We will discuss possible actions later.

First, let us consider the consequences of the plateau for the person and for the organization.

Effects of Plateauing

Strictly speaking, the most important effect of a career plateau is that the person remains at a particular level in the organizational hierarchy for a long period of time. It is important to keep this simple fact in mind, as most people, if given a free association test, would attribute a host of disastrous outcomes with the words "career plateau": stagnation, early death, frustration, dead wood, being "on the shelf," or failure, for examples. These perceptions are difficult to change; it is true that some of these experiences may result from plateauing, *but they don't necessarily have to*! Let us look at the research.

From the individual's point of view, a career plateau is usually associated with feelings of low marketability, dissatisfaction with advancement prospects, and career impatience (Veiga 1981). Plateaued employees also tend to report, compared with their nonplateaued counterparts, lower job involvement, psychological success, and recognition (Hall 1985). So, in general, a lot of the negative free association terms linked to plateauing appear to be true in dealing with the personal perspective.

From the organization's perspective, plateauing is sometimes associated with performance problems, but, on the other hand, some plateauers are strong performers. The work of Stoner et al. (1980) has found that plateauing (or, more precisely, potential for further advancement) and performance were two separate dimensions. A person can be either a strong or a weak performer, and this is a separate matter from whether the person is plateaued or not. Figure 5.1 shows the four possible combinations of these two dimensions.

People who are high in both performance and potential for advancement (i.e., nonplateauers) are, obviously, stars. These are the people at whom our traditional management and executive development programs are directed, and they are known by a variety of names: hi-po's, achievers, water walkers, crown princes and princesses, five-percenters, jet jobs, high flyers, comers, and so on. People who are low on both dimensions (dead wood) are obviously problem cases and those who are probably most traditionally associated with plateauing.

However, there is a very important group of people in any organization who are excellent performers but who, for a variety of reasons (organizational bottlenecks, delayering, strong competition, lack of fit for a higher level job) are seen as plateaued. These are the solid citizens. Solid citizens are the backbone of any organization. They may represent 80 percent of the company's work force, and they are the reliable, everyday performers who enable the organization to get its goods and services out to the customer.

Figure 5.1
Grid for Analyzing Plateauing and Performance

		Performance:	
		HIGH	LOW
Potential For			
Advancement:	HIGH	STARS	LEARNERS
	LOW	SOLID CITIZENS	DEAD WOOD

Source: From Stoner et al. 1980.

There is a risk, however, that today's solid citizen could become tomorrow's dead wood if he or she is not challenged, stimulated, and rewarded so that job involvement stays high. With effort on the part of the organization and the employee, it can be done. Professionals (such as lawyers, doctors, engineers, and ministers) spend their entire careers in one role, and the notion of advancement is often simply not relevant to them. When a professional works in an organization, however, the traditional cultural norms of success equaling upward mobility usually take over, so that it is harder for plateaued professionals in organizations to experience psychological success.

What can be done, then, to maintain the involvement and performance of the solid citizen (and to increase these for the dead wood employee)? To answer this question, let us turn to what we know about job involvement.

What Is Job Involvement?

Job involvement is the extent to which the person identifies psychologically with the job. It is a measure of how important the job is in the context of the person's total life and self-identity, an indicator of how much meaning the job provides in the person's life.

What causes high involvement in one's job? It appears that a combination of factors in the person and in the work situation are responsible. In the person, traditional work ethic values, as well as needs for achievement and personal growth, tend to be related to high involvement. Also, life experience makes a difference, as older employees tend to be more involved than their junior counterparts.

In the work situation, challenging, satisfying jobs which offer employees a variety of activities, autonomy, and the chance to do entire nontrivial tasks and to get frequent feedback contribute to higher levels of employee involvement. Participation in decision making is also a major input to job involvement. Furthermore, the job-involved employee tends to have better attendance and is a more stable organizational citizen (i.e., is more committed to the organization's goals and is less likely to quit) (Rabinowitz and Hall 1977; Hollenbeck, Connolly, and Rabinowitz, 1984). Please notice that none of these factors implies the prospect of future promotions.

High-Involvement Organizations

Recent developments in the area of participative management and quality of work life (QWL) have shown that it is possible to manage an organization in such a way as to increase the mean level of involvement of the work force. Edward Lawler (1986), in his book, *High Involvement Management*, discussed some of the design features which lead to employee motivation and involvement. Participative gain sharing plans, such as the Scanlon Plan, produce a congruence of individual and organizational goals. Open, public information on operating results gives employees knowledge of results and helps them see the need for improvement. Economic education on the business, its industry, the global competitive scene, and other business realities aids the employee's ability to contribute intelligently. A lean structure eliminates top-heavy staff work which could interfere with line operators' identifying and solving their own problems. Structures for participative employee input, such as quality circles and department meetings, give employees voice. Self-managing teams, with cross-training and job rotation, provide responsibility and authority to employees. Goal setting, clear tasks, and contact with customers and other facets of the environment create a clear sense of what needs to be done. All of these conditions, or subsets of them, can lead to a strong sense of psychological involvement in the work force.

Involvement for Plateauers: Two Forks in the Road

The individual also has various ways to approach the job sanely. Let us consider two possible forks in the road through the workday.

The high-involvement fork. One option for a plateaued employee is to try to heighten his or her job involvement. We would argue that the conditions that Lawler has identified for a high-involvement organization can also be the basis of increasing or maintaining the involvement of plateaued employees. Putting experienced, plateaued employees into self-managed work teams (or task forces or project teams) can be an excellent way of tapping their experience and expertise, as well as exposing them to employees from different areas of the company from whom they can learn. Pay incentive plans or employee bonus plans or special achievement awards can be a way to provide recognition for outstanding performance and to heighten involvement. Lean structures, which are becoming daily more common, will have a silver lining of increasing employee participation in decision making, tapping expertise, and raising involvement. (A risk here is that such restructuring may produce excessive involvement and work pressure, leading to stress and burnout. This should be monitored periodically.)

The low-involvement fork. Much of what we have written so far is based on the assumption that an employee wants to be involved on the job. This may be a questionable assumption for many plateaued employees. One way of adapting to a career plateau is to seek growth, stimulation, and meaning in other parts of one's life, as long as one can maintain good performance on the job. This response is also consistent with the direction in which most people's concerns tend to move in the mid-life transition, as well: There is a shift from investments in worklife to home and family life, in an attempt to obtain better balance between the two (Levinson 1986).

Therefore, another option is to find ways to help plateaued people manage work so that their jobs are less involving psychologically. Work schedules might be revised so that a low-involvement employee might work a four-day week, giving more time off. Part-time positions might be more attractive to this employee, as might job sharing. Rather than job enrichment to provide stimulation, perhaps job rotation might provide sufficient variety and novelty. More focus on extrinsic rewards, such as pay, benefits, and working conditions, rather than on intrinsic rewards, may be more appropriate here. Time off or leaving work early can be a powerful reward for a less involved strong performer. As an alternative to a lateral cross-functional move, if such would be required during a reorganization, the person might prefer a move down to permit remaining in the present department, where less change and learning would be required. Rather than a high-involvement performance management process, such as MBO, this employee may simply want a more directive performance appraisal, informing him or her of how the performance was evaluated, with suggestions for how to improve.

These alternative work designs all provide a means of spending less time on the job. They are often used where the work itself cannot be made more rewarding or where the employees have a preference for low job involvement. Once we develop better ways of identifying jobs which cannot be enriched and employees who prefer low involvement, we may see dramatic increases as well as dramatic decreases in employee involvement within the same organizations.

One example of these two alternatives was in a Motorola assembly plant in Fort Lauderdale several years ago. When the plant started making miniaturized "Pageboy" radios, the industrial engineers and the plant manager gave employees a choice of two different jobs. They could work either on an assembly line making the new radios or individually producing entire radios by themselves (this was called unit assembly). The people doing unit assembly received special training in reading electronic circuit diagrams, soldering techniques, trouble-shooting, and so forth, while the assembly line operators required little training. People developed marked preferences for one type of job or the other. The unit assemblers became far more involved in their work, but some didn't like the pressure from the individual responsibility they had and opted to move to the assembly line. Others moved in the opposite direction after they had a chance to see unit assembly in action. We're not saying either method was better or worse from the employees' point of view. The important thing is that the employees had a choice about which job was the best fit for them. Realistic job previews, as well as activities such as self-selection and career planning, represent other ways to help people fit better into work which matches the level of involvement they desire.

The Two-Path Career Model

To carry this idea one step further, it might be possible to present a new employee with a choice of career development tracks, representing high or low levels of involvement, to enhance self-selection into the best-fit job. These paths are shown in Figure 5.2. At entry, the person would be given a realistic job preview, after the job had been offered, but before the person had decided whether to accept the job. Next, the person would complete a questionnaire assessing his or her involvement preferences, and feedback would be given about how this preference fits the job to be filled. If a choice of job is available, the person is given the choice of high- or low-involvement career paths. If the high-involvement path is chosen, the person would be

Figure 5.2
Two-Path Career Model

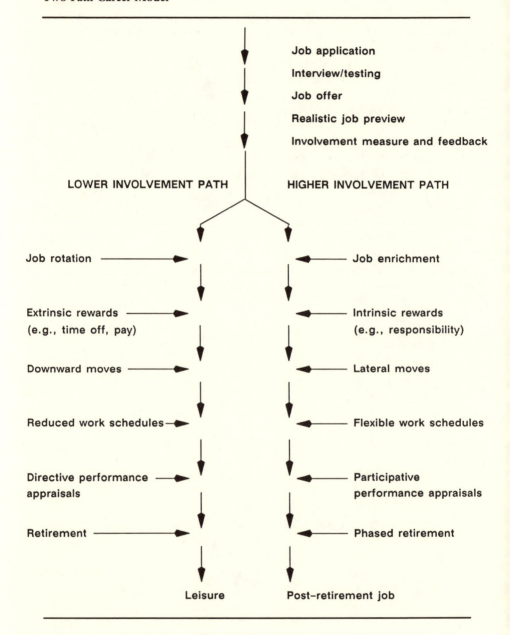

Job application

Interview/testing

Job offer

Realistic job preview

Involvement measure and feedback

LOWER INVOLVEMENT PATH   HIGHER INVOLVEMENT PATH

Job rotation ──────────▶   ◀────── Job enrichment

Extrinsic rewards ────────▶   ◀────── Intrinsic rewards
(e.g., time off, pay)   (e.g., responsibility)

Downward moves ────────▶   ◀────── Lateral moves

Reduced work schedules─▶   ◀────── Flexible work schedules

Directive performance ────▶   ◀────── Participative
appraisals   performance appraisals

Retirement ──────────▶   ◀────── Phased retirement

Leisure   Post–retirement job

placed in an involving job. If a job enrichment program were under way, this person might be given the opportunity to participate in it. Career planning would be made available as well. Performance appraisal with this person would be conducted in a problem-solving way, with a stress on work planning and objective setting. At retirement, this person might be offered a consulting position with the organization, or perhaps a part-time job.

The person who prefers low involvement would be given different work experiences, ones stressing extrinsic rewards and opportunities to leave the job more often. This person might be a candidate for the four-day week, permitting more concentrated leisure time. Job rotation may be another way of not spending too much time in any one unrewarding job. Positive reinforcement programs would also be effective for the noninvolved employee, using rewards such as pay, bonuses, time off, and recognition from management (e.g., awards, special status, write-ups in the company newspaper). Performance appraisals for this person would be more directive, with a stress more on feedback and evaluation than on goal setting and future planning. Regarding retirement, this person might be a candidate for early retirement, since most of his or her rewards in life come from nonwork activities.

Of course, in keeping with the idea of increased choice, it should be possible for a person to switch from a high-involvement track to a low-involvement one, or vice versa, as in the Motorola plant. By not having everyone in the organization in the same track, it should be possible to provide more of the activities in each track to just those people who choose it. With resources becoming scarcer, it is becoming increasingly important to get maximum mileage from the rewards we do have to offer. Involving jobs will be able to attract people at relatively low pay because of the high intrinsic rewards, while noninvolving jobs will have to offer better extrinsic rewards to attract people. In each case, the available rewards can be focused more efficiently to meet the important needs of the employee, with few rewards wasted on unimportant needs. For example, several years ago, New York City ended its shortage of sanitation workers not by enriching jobs (which were hard to enrich), but by drastically raising annual pay! Jobs and career paths will complete for people, and the free market will provide adjustments so that a good match is obtained.

PROJECTS AS PLATEAU ANTIDOTES

We will conclude with a general area of recommended action for all plateaued employees, regardless of their desired level of involvement. This section is based on a study of professionals and managers in a declining engineering organization (Hall 1985). The organization had an unusual triple ladder for career advancement. In addition to the usual technical and administrative ladders, there was also a project engineer ladder. On this third path, an individual could move to higher and higher levels of project management responsibility. The work entailed a large technical component but also a lot of coordination and matrix interfacing. It was a hybrid technical/administrative role.

A funny thing happened when plateaued and nonplateaued employees in the three different ladders were compared. On the technical and administrative ladders, the negative effects of plateauing described earlier were found: dissatisfaction, frustration, low career optimism, low psychological success, and low involvement. However, in the project ladder, the opposite effects of plateauing were found: Plateaued project engineers reported more recognition, more challenge, more psychological success, and more job involvement than their nonplateaued counterparts! Obviously, something in the nature of project work was enhancing the career experiences of the plateaued professionals.

Examination of interview data indicated that project work was broader and more applied than a technical specialist's work or an administrator's work. Every project was new and different and demanded learning and the development of new skills.

Thus, project work puts a premium on experience; the skills and value of the project person grow as he or she matures in the career. The technical specialist, on the other hand, becomes increasingly narrow and eventually obsolete, while the administrator becomes more and more organization-bound over time. Project skills are more transferable to other organizations and make the project specialist quite mobile on the job market.

Thus, project work appears to have potential not just for avoiding the negative aspects of plateauing but for creating positive career experiences for the plateaued employee. Therefore, one implication is that organizations should attempt wherever possible to design work activities as projects, with specific objectives, time frames, and responsibilities. Many organizations, such as Ford Motor Company and General Motors, are already doing this.

As organizations experience increasingly turbulent environments, they have correspondingly greater needs for rapid adaptation and change, through quicker response times, shorter product planning cycles, and so forth. As a result, we are seeing more and more temporary organizational structures and job designs. The project management job design is an ideal way to meet both this organizational need and the career growth needs of the employee. A project can get around the limitations of a shrinking hierarchy; it can exist anywhere in the formal organization, it can (and should) draw people from different levels and functions, and pay can be based on the needs and resources of the project, rather than on formal position level. A good example of projects for organizational and career development is IBM's use of autonomous design teams for new computers, such as the one that designed the personal computer.

However, it is not feasible for all work to be structured as projects. Another idea, then, is to take some of the elements of project work and to incorporate them into more traditional jobs. Hall and Louis (1988) have identified three critical elements of project work: a whole task, a complete activity life cycle, and end result accountability. Rather than giving a person four objectives to achieve in the next year or six months, redefine what you are ultimately trying to accomplish and make it a single major project to be accomplished as part of the present job.

For example, rather than giving a sales manager ten separate indexes of sales volume, sales growth, costs, and customer service to achieve, assign him or her a project of setting up the sales district as a profit center in which all of those dimensions may represent input to a final profit figure. From then on, the manager's "project" would be to increase district profits by a certain percentage. Or, more simply, each manager could be required to develop a major project each year to improve the business. At the end of the year, he or she would be evaluated on both the nature of the project and its completion, in addition to the other traditional performance measures.

In addition to incorporating more project-type features into the job, Hall (1985) has proposed other methods of helping plateaued employees broaden their skill base. We will present them briefly:

1. *Periodic rotation of specialists.* Even if a person is going to remain in a specialist role, variety can be added by moving the person into a new area after a certain number of years (say, five). This could be as simple as a move within a function to a different type of product or process (e.g., a pharmaceutical sales representative being moved from a district full of private practice physicians to one where the customers are mainly in hospital settings). The military uses a dual specialist model in which the person spends the first five or seven years of the career in one field and then moves into a second area of specialization.

2. *Facilitating lateral, cross-functional moves.* As organizations become flatter, employees' expectations regarding promotions will decrease. Lateral movement will become more acceptable to employees, if that is the only alternative to stagnation. Such movement will also become more necessary to the organization as a way of growing a broader, more adaptive skill base in its employees. Lateral broadening is already becoming a critical method for developing high-potential candidates for senior management positions.

3. *Temporary moves.* Another way to provide the benefits of a new assignment without all the costs of a permanent move is a temporary move to a new position. Here the person would be told in advance that he or she would only be there for a limited time (e.g., six months, two years), after which there would be a return to the original location. Thus, the employee could keep the original house, and the company could help rent it, as well as provide rental housing in the temporary location. Or if the assignment

were just for a few months, the family could stay home, and the company would pay for weekend transportation home.

A variant of the temporary assignment is to have a person fill in for another employee who is out on vacation, sick, or at a conference, for example. This gets the job done and provides great learning for the fill-in person.

4. *Downward moves*. With restructuring, organizations are being forced to make greater use of downward moves. Often this is the only alternative to termination. Or it may be the only way for the employee to get "unstuck" from a dead-end career path. For the company, it may be a way to salvage an unsuccessful promotion and put the employee back into a position where he or she can perform well; this can be a better alternative than firing a person you know can do well at the lower level.

The critical factor in a developmental downward move is that the new job should demand some skills which the employee does not have. Or the assignment should be new in some other way—new location, new customer base, new business area, new types of subordinates. With pay becoming more and more decoupled from position (a benefit of flatter structures), it is often possible not to cut pay when a person is moved down. The worst possible kind of downward move is to put the person back into the same position and the same location where he or she has worked before. More detail on how downward moves can provide career development is found in Hall and Isabella (1985).

5. *Job switches*. Another way to provide temporary new work experiences is to facilitate the trading of jobs by employees. Usually the trade would be for a specified period of time—long enough so that real learning takes place. It can be a way of testing whether the person might want a permanent move into that area. The person's original salary grade would be maintained during the switch. This process requires a strong third-party "broker" role by the human resource department. Ford Motor Company is experimenting with this procedure.

6. *In-place career development*. Generally, people assume a person has to move to a new position for career development to occur. However, it is possible to develop new skills and abilities, as well as new ways of viewing oneself, in the context of the same position. To accomplish this requires setting objectives for development (i.e., specific skill areas to be improved) and then working on a plan for achieving them. This is done more effectively through mentoring, coaching, and other forms of developmental relationships (Kram 1985). Many organizations now provide training to managers in these career-facilitating skills.

7. *Eliminate tournament mobility; promote older employees*. Most career systems operate under the tournament model of success: As long as the person keeps winning promotions at each level, he or she stays in the game and is considered at the next level. However, if the person makes one big

mistake or does not win the next promotion by a certain age, he or she is out of the game. What this leaves is a lot of competent people who are being declared "out" at ever-earlier ages—in their thirties now in many organizations. However, people learn and change, and the company and situations change. These older people represent mature, competent, committed resources to the organization. There should be mechanisms for identifying potential for advancement in older employees. Among other benefits, this would increase the pool of potential candidates in the succession-planning process. As our population ages, this will become an increasingly critical issue.

8. Promote and recognize slower advancement. Even though promotion rates have slowed in many organizations, the culture still stresses success. Promotions are glorified in the company newsletter; lateral moves are rarely mentioned. High potentials are given "plum" assignments and training experiences; plateaued people are not. It is time to publicize information about the frequency of various types of moves—promotions, lateral moves, downward moves, exit. Promotion rates for younger employees should be slowed to promote better mastery in initial assignments and to moderate expectations for future moves. More stress and rewards should be attached to performance rather than promotability. The solid citizen should be made a prized corporate resource.

CONCLUSION

The facts are simple. Increasing numbers of a given organization's work force are or shortly will be in a plateaued position. It is quite easy to ignore this and try to carry on with a business-as-usual attitude, which only contributes to an increasingly unhappy and potentially ineffective human resource.

Within this chapter, we have examined early signs and consequences of plateauing. Research has clearly demonstrated that most plateaued employees still have much to offer to the organization and are well worth developing. By considering the option of low as well as high involvement, it is possible to take into account personal needs and desires related to time and psychological effort spent on the job. Either fork in the involvement path model allows the organization to match worker needs with organizational realities in order to get the maximum benefit out of the work force.

Finally, alternative ways of dealing with plateaued employees, regardless of their desired level of involvement, were examined. The notion of adding project-work-type features to a job is well worth exploring, as well as periodic rotation to different areas. The stigma of upward mobility being the only way for a person to go is unrealistic. As organizations take on a new shape, the facilitation of lateral, cross-functional moves, temporary moves, and/or downward moves should be legitimized as slower advancement paths become part of the corporate culture. Job switching or new skill development within the context of one's current position are also ways which allow the plateaued worker to remain vital. A final thought here is that the up-or-out mentality surrounding a tournament model of success should be eliminated. The next few decades will give us an increasingly older work force. It might very well benefit the organization to try to continue to develop this resource rather than eliminate it at a relatively early stage.

REFERENCES

Hall, D. T. 1976. *Careers in organizations.* Glenview, IL: Scott, Foresman & Co.

Hall, D. T. 1985. Project work as an antidote to career plateauing in a declining engineering organization. *Human Resource Management, 24,* 271–92.

Hall, D. T., and L. Isabella. 1985. Downward movement and career development. *Organizational Dynamics,* Summer, *14,* 5–23.

Hall, D. T., and M. R. Louis. 1988. When careers plateau. *Research technology management,* March–April, *31,* 41–45.

Hollenbeck, J., T. F. Connolly, and S. Rabinowitz. 1984. Job involvement, 1977–1982: Beyond the exploratory stage. Working Paper, New York University.

Hymowitz, C. 1986. More executives finding changes in traditional corporate ladder. *The Wall Street Journal,* November 14, p. 33.

Kram, K. 1985. *Mentoring at work.* Glenview, IL: Scott, Foresman & Co.

Lawler, E. E., III. 1986. *High involvement management.* San Francisco: Jossey-Bass.

Levinson, D. J. 1986. A conception of adult development. *American Psychologist, 41*(1), 3–13.

Rabinowitz, S., and D. T. Hall. 1977. Organizational research on job involvement. *Psychological Bulletin, 84,* 265–88.

Stoner, J. A. F., T. P. Ference, E. K. Warren, and H. K. Christensen. 1980. *Managerial career plateaus.* New York: Center for Research in Career Development, Graduate School of Business, Columbia University.

Veiga, J. 1981. Plateaued versus nonplateaued managers: Career patterns, attitudes, and path potential. *Academy of Management Journal, 24,* 566–78.

CHAPTER 6

CAREER SUCCESS AND PERSONAL FAILURE: MID- TO LATE-CAREER FEELINGS AND EVENTS

ABRAHAM K. KORMAN

Something has happened in the world of work and organizations for which we have been unprepared as scholars, as management practitioners, and as citizens of a society which has traditionally greatly valued career achievement and success and the rewards that go with such achievement. This unexpected event has been the continuing reports of negative emotions and feelings of personal failure among successful career people in mid- to late-career stages. Increasingly, we have anecdotal accounts, journalistic reports, and academic studies reporting, sometimes in painful and even tragic detail, negative feelings and emotional problems among those who have met our societal norms for work and career achievement. Yet, despite their achievement, their rewards have not been what they, or we, might have expected; and we now find, among highly career successful people, clear evidence of alienation, life dissatisfaction, burnout, and depression (La Bier 1986).

The following discussion is structured around three major goals. The first is to document the extent and character of this phenomenon, which we will define as career success and personal failure or CS/PF, and its potential significance for individual and organizational functioning. Following, I will then develop a tentative explanatory framework for understanding why such negative emotional feelings may be characteristic of those who are successful in their careers. I will then conclude the analysis by examining the implications of CS/PF for human resource professionals.

EVIDENCE FOR CAREER SUCCESS/PERSONAL FAILURE AT MID-LIFE

CS/PF has been reported anecdotally in the popular press and has also been studied from a research perspective. Among the more recent anecdotal accounts have been the following:

1. Reports of eating disorders, smoking, drug abuse, and other forms of self-de-structive behavior among successful executive women (Deutsch 1986);

2. Analyses and discussions of the agonies associated with career success among older executives, of the depression that sometimes comes at the pinnacle of a career, and of the dashed hopes that have resulted from the false fantasies as to what success would bring (Goleman 1986);

3. Continuing reports of feelings of personal failure and life dissatisfaction among such illustrations of career success as physicians, judges, venture capitalists, in-vestment bankers, models, professional athletes, and executives from the Bank of Boston, Digital Computer, and IBM (Berglass 1986).

A problem with anecdotal accounts is that they are open to questions of generality. In order to fully substantiate the existence of this phenomenon, we need to have systematic research studies which are consistent with these journalistic analyses and which reach similar conclusions. Such studies have become increasingly common. One investigation reported that of 554 founders of firms on *Inc.*'s three most recent annual lists of the fastest-growing private companies in the United States, approximately 36 percent said the pressure of running the business had damaged their relationship with their spouse; 22 percent said their marital relationships were a major source of stress; 15 percent said their relationships with their children were stressful; and 44 percent said they had underestimated the burden on self and family that would result from their work careers and success (*USA Today*, 1986). Also supporting this conclusion have been such studies as the following:

1. A major longitudinal study of executives in a large American corporation which found no relationship between hierarchical level and life satisfaction (Howard and Bray 1980);

2. A questionnaire study of several thousand managers which reported great degrees of alienation from one's career role and from one's organization (Tarnowieski 1972);

3. An intensive interview study of highly successful executives who reported great feelings of personal stress, loss of personal alertness, and an increasing sense of meaninglessness in one's everyday life (Bartoleme 1972);

4. An interview study of executives which reported significant loss in personal affect and a general decrease in emotional ties with others (Maccoby 1976);

5. A study of 450 successful entrepreneurs which found common among them a loss of psychological well-being and a sense of social isolation (Gumpert and Boyd 1984).

Taken together, these research studies and the anecdotal reports point strongly to the conclusion that these are not isolated events but instead reflect a major problem in our society—a lack of relationship between career success and personal life satisfaction among mid- to late-career individuals.

Stated explicitly, the research literature supports the conclusion that there is little or no relationship between career success (when defined by traditional, financial, or organizational-level criteria) and personal reports of well-being (Korman et al. 1986). Such lack of relationship indicates that among those who have been successful according to financial and/or organizational-level criteria, there are as likely to be included among them those who describe their lives in negative terms as there are those who describe their lives in positive terms.

These findings have posed two sets of problems. One group of questions revolves around the definition of career success and its meaning. What, then, does career success mean and under what conditions does its meaning change? More specifically, we need to raise the question as to the conditions under which career success may be expected to lead to feelings of personal failure in mid-life and, alternatively, the conditions under which career success may be expected to lead to feelings of personal success or personal life satisfaction.

A second set of questions concerns the implications of these varying effects of career success for human resource management (HRM). If career success cannot be assumed to have generally positive effects on individuals, what implications does this have for HRM in terms of motivational incentive programs, reward systems, and the overall structure of HRM practice in general? What changes or innovations in HRM might be desirable as a result of these findings?

AN EXPLANATORY FRAMEWORK FOR CAREER SUCCESS/PERSONAL FAILURE AT MID- TO LATE-CAREER STAGES

In this section I present a tentative explanatory framework for understanding the phenomenon of CS/PF with this caveat: Since the ideas I will propose do not as yet have major research validation, readers are cautioned to view these proposals as essentially tentative in nature. However, it is hoped that by stating the proposed explanatory framework in as clear a manner as possible, I will encourage both research scientists and administrators to begin examining this issue and the questions that are raised by it.

The framework proposed here views feelings of failure at mid- to late-career stages for successful career people as a function of a general factor which appears to be common to all or most cases and to a number of specific factors which may vary in saliency in different situations. The general factor that appears to be common to all or most situations are the emotions resulting from and associated with what has been termed the mid-life crisis. In addition, there may also occur in different situations one or more of a number of specific factors relevant to a particular situation, but perhaps not to others. Such factors may therefore vary across situations in the significance of their contributions to feelings of personal failure among those who are career successful. One such specific factor may be an emotional realization of the illusions that may have been previously attached to money and higher levels of income. Such realization may be a factor of considerable significance in a society which is as highly materialistic as ours.

In other cases, there may be other contributing factors to CS/PF such as, for men, guilt as a result of unresolved Oedipal conflicts and fear of punishment for being a success and a loss of affiliative satisfactions (e.g., family life, loss of roots, and so on). For women, among the specific contributing factors to CS/PF may be the feelings of exhaustion from trying to maintain a lifestyle in which they attempt to satisfy both achievement and affiliative needs concurrently. In addition, other factors which may be of relevance in specific situations (and also to be discussed later) are feelings of meaninglessness concerning the value of high income levels, feelings of normlessness resulting from confusion as to how one may attain both achievement and affiliative satisfactions, and the difficulties of developing positive relationships with others when one has hierarchical power over them.

A General Factor: The Mid-Life Crisis

Perhaps most important over most cases as an explanation for feelings of personal failure in the mid- to late-career successful individual is the emotional trauma that we call the mid-life crisis, a trauma that seems to affect most individuals regardless of financial and/or career success. While specific details may vary from individual to individual, the mid-life crisis is thought to be brought about by a number of factors that become salient as one reaches mid-life. One factor is the anxiety that occurs as a result of the realization of the reality of one's eventual death. Also crucial are the changes that take place at this time in one's cognitive and attitudinal structures. Such changes often include an increasing sense of personal obsolescence and one's emotional reactions to the realization of the growth and maturing of one's children and the necessary acceptance of reality (and loss of illusion) that may take place with such maturation. Also significant in contributing to this sense of crisis are the emotions that one may undergo upon experiencing the aging and death of one's parents and, frequently, one's social peers through illness and disease, along with the often-perceived inability to affect significantly any of these processes.

There are also other problems at this period that have career implications (Trinkaus 1981). Often there is a perceived loss of career mobility and a consequent sense of "narrowing opportunities" rather than a sense of being able to "grow and develop." There is the need for the individual to accept the realization that he or she is now old as well as young, and there are questions about sex roles and what is proper behavior when one is in his or her fifties (as opposed to being in the twenties or thirties). As a result of these emotions and these conflicts, mid- to late-career individuals may show

1. A decline in achievement interest and a decreased value for what achievement can bring and for what is being offered by one's organizational leadership as an incentive for engaging in achievement-oriented behavior (e.g., increased income or status);
2. A decreased interest in looking to the future and the possibilities that are available (assuming one's work activity is deemed successful by others);
3. A lower level of desire to have impact on others through increased work activity;
4. A greater orientation toward the inner self and one's personal needs and desires and a decreased receptivity to the incentives and promises offered by others.

The Complex Effects of High Income Levels

An explanation for career success/personal failure which may vary in salience in different contexts is the proposition that as one's income increases, the effects of such financial success may be negative in some cases instead of or along with being positive. In a society which values so greatly materialistic success and the satisfactions this success may bring, the realization of such complex outcomes and the possibility that one may feel worse rather than better as a result of having been financially successful in one's career may clearly be a significant emotional experience. Such realization may lead the individual to view money and career success in one's life and the supposed benefits to be derived as essentially meaningless since there is no clear relationship between such acquisition and the benefits to be derived. Such a sense of meaninglessness may then be highly significant as a causal factor in the occurrence of CS/PF in mid- to late-career individuals (Seeman 1972).

There are also other possible mechanisms by which higher levels of income may come to have such negative effects. One such mechanism is suggested in the work of psychologists and sociologists such as Milner (1968), Slater (1970), and Deci (1975). While differing from one another in some details, these theorists are similar in suggesting that income level, because of its objectivity, its clarity, and its social acceptance in our society, often becomes the most significant way that we evaluate ourselves, other people, and various activities such as our job demands. Since the likelihood that we will use income and money as a basis for evaluation will be greater the more money we make (since money has been at least part the driving motivation to begin with in acquiring such income levels), one might then expect that high-income individuals may become alienated from other ways of enjoying life in all its different dimensions. In this sense the power that money has to become our dominant way of evaluating ourselves and our experience tends to make us one-dimensional individuals, alienated from other aspects of human experience and unable to enjoy nonfinancially based types of life satisfactions.

Another way in which high income levels may come to have negative effects at the mid- to late-career state is that parents may, through the use of their high income, generate a lack of achievement motivation and a high degree of dependency in one's children—a behavior pattern that would impact negatively on the degree of life satisfaction of such parents. Although counter-indicated behaviors such as these have become increasingly noticed in our media, it may be noted that such patterns were predicted more than two decades ago by McClelland (1961) in his famous study *The Achieving Society.* According to him, a major reason for a lack of achievement motivation among the children of the affluent was that their parents had used their money to buy their children out of all the difficult, less exciting life experiences that they (the parents) had had to go through but which had, nevertheless, built in them the drives toward achievement leading to their career success.

Now, however, the increased income of the parents might be used to buy their children out of the types of challenging, difficult experiences which will tend to generate achievement motivation. Once such actions are taken, it would then be predicted that there would be a decreased capability in handling life situations on the part of their children and a decreased life satisfaction and perhaps a sense of personal failure on the part of the parents who were career successful. Of particular significance for our purposes here is that children of the affluent may normally be expected to exhibit such counter-productive behavior when their parents reach their mid- to late-career stage.

Unfortunately, the arguments and evidence are still mostly analytic and descriptive, rather than being based on systematic research data. For example, although Korman and his co-workers (1986) have summarized a body of empirical research findings showing minimal or no relationships between income levels and feelings of psychological well-being, we still have few empirical research findings actually evaluating whether the possible negative impact of high income occurs for the reasons suggested by such people as Deci, Milner, Slater, and McCelland.

Guilt from Surpassing Parents

A possible explanation for CS/PF in the mid- to late-career stage that may be of some value in explaining such emotions among males in some contexts stems from psychoanalytic theory and its suggestion that, for men at least, a feeling of fraudulence may sometimes become associated with success.

According to this argument, men may, as a result of unresolved conflicts remaining from the Oedipal life stage, tend to suffer from an unresolved feeling of rivalry with their father and a sense of anxiety concerning possible punishment from one or both parents for surpassing the father. One way to overcome such feelings and the possible punishment that may ensue (such as loss of love) is to deny that they have had greater success than their fathers, perhaps by the son coming to embrace the view that he is an imposter in his career success. However, there is a cost here for those individuals who have decided to reduce their anxiety in this manner for they then live in fear that they may be found out by others to be the "frauds" they have convinced themselves they are. Such exposure would then make him subject to all the penalties that being a fraud involves. Stated as clearly as possible, the successful man, in adopting this defense against anxiety, has put himself in a double bind. The more successful he is, the more he needs to convince himself that he is a fraud in order to avert (the possibility of) punishment from his father and, perhaps, his mother. However, the more his feeling of fraudulence grows, the more fearful he is that he will be discovered as a fraud by others with all the punishment that such discovery might lead to.

It may be noted also that this double bind and the associated feelings of CS/PF may be particularly acute among men who are the first generation in their families to become successful. As such individuals rise about their roots, deep feelings of guilt also increase. Career success has, unconsciously, become equated with betrayal of the family. Consciously, the male in such cases fears failure because he wants to and is expected to succeed. Unconsciously, however, he fears success because of the loss of love it may bring. This latter point is well illustrated in a research study of a number of male managers and their wives in the New England area who had risen from working-class origins into middle-class status (Sennett and Cobb 1972). Despite such career success, the research provided considerable evidence as to the self-doubts of the managers concerning the value of their work compared to the work of their fathers. Similarly, the research also pointed to the loneliness of their wives in their affluent surroundings when they compared their current lives to the lives they knew in their more crowded, family-involved, working-class backgrounds.

There is an important limitation to this possible explanation that we need to keep in mind, regardless of its eventual value for enabling us to understand feelings of failure despite career success among males in their mid-career stages. This limitation is that it will not be able to help us in explaining analogous phenomena among women since psychoanalytic theory does not suggest such a similar rivalry between daughter and father. Yet, there may be analogous phenomena among women stemming from other causes.

Thus, CS/PF may also occur for women as a result of anxiety concerning the possible loss of love of parents or of one's husband if the woman has succeeded at too high a level in her career. However, the original source of such anxiety may be different, stemming perhaps from such factors as social role expectations concerning traditional female roles. A somewhat similar argument to this was noted two decades ago by Horner (1972) in her conceptualization of the "fear of success" syndrome among women. While this particular view of female achievement motivation later became quite controversial, it may be that an understanding of CS/PF among successful women executives will require us to reexamine an idea such as this from the viewpoint of its particular fruitfulness for the problem of concern here.

The Affiliative Costs of Success

This explanation for career success/personal failure suggests that the negative emotions that mark such individuals may have their origins, at least in part, in the increasing recognition of the affiliative costs that one may have paid for attaining career success. Such experiences may then lead to specific questioning as to how one is supposed to live *if* achievement has led to affiliative costs rather than affiliative benefits and, eventually, perhaps to increased doubt as to the continued validity of the rules and norms by which one has guided one's life. Should this take place, one would then be in a state of normlessness, a factor proposed by Seeman (1972) as important for understanding the emotional state of alienation.

One group of such costs may come in the area of family life, both in terms of one's nuclear family and perhaps also in the giving up of one's roots as a result of the geographic and other types of mobility sometimes demanded by one's career (and perhaps, also, as a result of the unresolved Oedipal and/or traditional female role conflicts discussed earlier). In some cases of the reexamination that often comes with mid-life, one may come to realize that in the pursuit of career success one has given up much of family life and the retaining of one's roots and one's identity and the satisfactions that may go with such retention. Evans and Bartoleme (1981) have provided extensive evidence for such costs among managers and executives in Great Britain and France, but such costs are certainly not limited to those from these nations. Research conducted in the United States has shown that income has few positive effects for males for whom the attainment of career and financial success has come at a cost of giving up of affiliative (family) satisfactions (Korman et al. 1986).

There is some indication, however, that such affiliative costs may not develop in the same way for successful women. As opposed to men who may have ignored their affiliative needs during the seeking of career success, it may be that women are less likely to seek career success without a continued maintenance of at least some affiliative ties during the course of their careers. However, such retention may cause other problems such as an increasing sense of exhaustion from juggling the jobs of wife, mother, social butterfly, keeper-of-the-flame (i.e., accepting responsibility for maintaining family traditions), and executive (Deutsch 1986).

Thus, women at mid-life may begin to question whether the juggling act has been worth the effort. In this sense, then, the association of feelings of personal failure with career success for women takes place because they have been so concerned with maintaining affiliative ties all along and have undertaken the effort and work necessary to maintain such ties, in addition to the work called for by their careers. Also adding to the complexity of these possible gender differences is that there are also indications that women executives may react to stress differently than men. Deutsch (1986) has suggested that successful women are more likely to have eating disorders (bulemia, anorexia) than men, smoke more, and (perhaps) drink less (although evidence for the latter is somewhat ambiguous).

Another possible affiliative cost of career success, at least in organizational hierarchies, may be the loss of friendships and the social alienation that may come with the attainment of power. High levels of power may generate alienation from the self and others (cf. Kipnis 1976; McClelland 1975).

Thus, while the attainment of power may often bring satisfactions, it may also lead to behavioral actions designed to maintain power and the hierarchical system in which one is higher than others. This generates an alienation from others and also a denial of the impulses and values in oneself that would want to maintain affiliation with others but which cannot be engaged in because of the possible loss of power that this might entail. Furthermore, this realization of how one may have become corrupted by power may generate anger at the self and an increasing anxiety that one cannot and will not be able to change things because one has become trapped by the "golden handcuffs" of power.

WHAT TO DO: SOME SUGGESTIONS FOR THE HUMAN RESOURCE PROFESSIONAL

In developing some possible recommendations for the human resource professional in this area, it is most important to be realistic in terms of level of aspiration. There may be a limit to what management can reasonably be expected to do about the phenomenon of career success and personal failure among those in middle age since there are certain reality factors about which little can be done. The individual *is* getting older, and events are occurring over which he or she has little control and which will impact on his or her sense of well-being and work commitment. Friends and family members are more likely to become ill. Health problems among those people with whom one is more familiar do increase at this life stage, along with all the possible anxieties that follow. These events cannot be denied.

Also important is that the individuals involved and the organizations which employ them not allow themselves to be rushed into major change programs without due consideration. Change programs, no matter how well intended and well designed, are far from guaranteed in their effects, and sometimes no change attempt may be better than rushing into change interventions. One of the most commonly suggested approaches to CS/PF is to encourage the individuals involved to move toward a more internally directed lifestyle where personal needs and aspirations become more significant as driving forces than do social role obligations. While such suggestions are normally acceptable and frequently made, they do not always result in better outcomes for the individuals involved.

In an interview study of mid-life individuals who moved to Santa Fe, New Mexico, as part of career change decisions, Krantz (1978) pointed out that the results were far from uniformly positive even though each of the individuals now had a more internally directed lifestyle. A key factor, he found, in determining whether the change was successful appeared to be the extent to which the person had been able to maintain a social reference system of some sort.

A continuing problem also is that the individual at mid-life has come to the realization at some level of awareness that the basic value system under which he or she has been living has been found somewhat meaningless. However, while they may now be more open to the process of change and to engaging in behaviors reflecting different values, such change will not be easy since the value system they are open to changing from is still considered meaningful and is highly reinforced by our society and by our organizations (i.e., the money-success-power syndrome). Similarly, it is also a system they have accepted up to now.

A second problem is that the direction in which change is most likely to be acceptable to them—that is, for them to become more intrinsically oriented—is a direction opposite to the values of a society which values extrinsic achievement and outward signs of the attainment of such achievement. Also, the extent to which organizations can provide opportunities for more self-directed lifestyles, even if they should be willing to do so, may be quite limited in some instances.

Yet, some people and some organizations in our society have dealt with the problem of CS/PF at mid- to later-life meaningfully and successfully, and there are possibilities to examine. This section offers three suggestions designed to deal with the problems outlined here. Each is reasonable and attainable, but they all pose a problem for contemporary organizational management and to the individuals whom they are designed to aid because the basic values underlying each recommendation are not necessarily consistent with the value system that guides much of contemporary organizational life and that has guided these individuals up to their current life stages. The contradictions are, therefore, real and will need to be faced if change is to be implemented.

First, encourage the individual to develop a more intrinsic lifestyle and to search for and help the organization to find ways in which they can

provide him or her with work challenges that will lead to intrinsic satisfactions.

One of the keys of the mid-life stage is the realization that previous value
systems have broken down and that one must now begin to rewrite one's
contract for living. How shall one spend the rest of one's career? one's life?
There is much evidence that the ability to attain intrinsic satisfactions from
one's life and one's career assumes increased relevance and importance at
this stage. Frequently, this may involve changing one's job either totally or
in part, but this is not always the case. Sometimes the individual may remain
in the same position or in the same organizations. The important point here
is that these questions are asked: "What shall I do now?" "Shall I stay with
the same career or should I make a change?" "If a change, what kind, and
how do I evaluate costs and benefits?"

From the perspective of the human resource manager, key here is the
degree to which the employing organization will be able to provide the
opportunity for such increased self-implementation and the role that he or
she can play in facilitating this process. To the extent to which this can be
done, then this is a desirable aim for the human resource professional.
However, such opportunities may be limited in a particular setting or often
are not capable of being achieved at all, particularly in these days of shrinking organizational size and the increased use of other strategies such as
layoffs (temporary or permanent) and mergers/acquisitions/divestments as
paths to organizational profitability. This changing climate has made even
more crucial other avenues for possible organizational responses to the
individual with a sense of CS/PF at the mid- to late-career stage, assuming
there is a mutual desire on both parts for the individual to remain employed.

Second, encourage and seek ways in which the individual may be able to
exhibit and attain a sense of competence in his or her work.

The significance of a sense of personal failure resulting from an inability
to feel competent on one's job and a feeling of a lack of self-efficacy would
seem to be highly important at this stage of life. Levinson (1981) has suggested that the types of situations which are most likely to be marked by
feelings of personal failure and burnout among executives are those that
place enormous burdens on the individual; that promise great success if
attained but which are nearly impossible to complete successfully; that expose
the manager to risk of attack for doing their jobs without providing a way
for him or her to fight back; and that overwhelm the individual with complex
detail and conflicting forces. The key, then, is to provide the manager suffering from CS/PF with a sense of self-efficacy (i.e., with assignments and
job opportunities that provide him or her with a sense of competency and
a resulting sense of self-esteem). This recommendation can be developed
and used in almost all job settings either in whole or in part through temporary assignments and the like. It is therefore probably generally more
attainable and capable of implementation in most organizational settings

by the human resource manager than increased opportunities for self-implementation and intrinsically satisfying job opportunities.

Third, encourage the individual to pay more attention to his or her family life and/or other social relationships.

The importance of the need to maintain and develop social affiliative relationships in times of career distress and changes has been pointed out by Krantz (1978) in his study of mid-life career changers, but it is also supported by much of the research on the affiliative costs of success cited here earlier. There are, however, two problems which the human resource professional will have to deal with in implementing this suggestion.

One of these problems has to do with the historical reluctance of most organizations to interfere in any way with an individual's private affiliative relationships. There are good historical reasons for such reluctance, and caution is important. Yet, it is clear that recent decades have seen an erosion of the barrier between work and family/affiliative considerations—an erosion which has been seen as justified because of the increasing evidence of the interrelationships between these two dimensions of life at different levels.

A second problem concerns the difficulties which problems stemming from affiliative relationships often pose for male executives in particular. As Bartoleme (1983) has pointed out, such individuals often have very unrealistic attitudes concerning their family lives and the efforts needed to develop a meaningful relationship with one's family members. Sometimes they make an incorrect assumption that family life is easy and problems simple to resolve. Sometimes they are afraid of confronting conflict in their family life because of fear of rejection, fear of facing the unknown (which may develop if one tries to face family problems and change develops), and an unwillingness to confront difficult decisions. Sometimes they have a "manana" complex—in other words, there's plenty of time to deal with family problems. As a result of these attitudes, Bartoleme argues that executives need to be helped considerably in these areas.

SUMMARY

A phenomenon that has become increasingly a matter of concern for human resource professionals is the occurrence of feelings of personal failure among some mid-life individuals who have been successful in a career sense. One major factor that seems to be involved in such emotions is the mid-life crisis, increasingly recognized as one of the major factors in the adult life span. Typically characterized by such emotional states as the anxieties that come with recognition of the inevitability of death, changes in one's relationships with friends and family, and one's personal changing relationships to his or her career, the impact of these changes may be even greater when they are accompanied by an overreliance on money and income as mechanisms for self- and other-evaluation, a loss of belief in the meaning of money as key to greater life satisfaction, and difficulty in attaining affiliative satisfaction along with achievement in one's career.

While there are some strategies human resource professionals may employ in responding to this problem, they should recognize that aspiration levels in this area may need to be modest because some of the difficulties involved may be beyond the competence of any management, regardless of how committed and capable they may be.

REFERENCES

Bartoleme, F. 1972. Executives as human beings. *Harvard Business Review*, 50, 62–69.

Bartoleme, F. 1983. The work alibi: When it's harder to go home. *Harvard Business Review*, 61, 67–74.

Berglass, J. 1986. *The success syndrome*. New York: Plenum Press.

Deci, E. 1975. *Intrinsic motivation*. New York: Plenum Press.

Deutsch, C. H. 1986. Women's success: A darker side. *New York Times*, September 10, pp. C1, C10.

Evans, P., and F. Bartoleme. 1981. *Must success cost so much?* New York: Basic Books.

Goleman, D. 1986. The strange agony of success. *New York Times*, August 24, section 5, pp. 1, 12.

Gumpert, D. E., and D.F. Boyd. 1984. The loneliness of the small-business owner. *Harvard Business Review*, 62, 18–20, 22, 24.

Horner, M. 1972. Toward an understanding of achievement-related conflicts in women. *Journal of Social Issues*, 28, 157–76.

Howard, A. and — Bray. 1980. *Career motivation in mid-life managers*. Presented at the Annual Convention of the American Psychological Association, Montreal, Canada.

Kipnis, D. 1976. *The powerholders*. Chicago: University of Chicago Press.

Korman, A., J. Greenberg, D. Lang, C. Lavy, S. Mahler, K. Omran, and S. Hartog. 1986. *Income and well-being: On the relationship between income and alienation*. Presented at the Convention of the International Association of Applied Psychology, Jerusalem, Israel.

Krantz, D. 1978. *Radical career change*. New York: The Free Press.

La Bier, D. 1986. *Modern madness: The emotional fallout of success*. Reading, MA: Addison-Wesley.

Levinson, H. 1981. When executives burn out. *Harvard Business Review*, 59, 73–81.

Maccoby, M. 1976. *The gamesman*. New York: Simon and Schuster.

McClelland, D. 1961. *The achieving society*. Princeton, NJ: Van Nostrand.

McClelland, D. 1975. *Power: The inner experience*. New York: Irvington.

Milner, E. 1968. *The failure of success* (2nd ed.). St. Louis: W. H. Green and Co.

Seeman, M. 1972. Alienation and engagement. In A. Campbell, and P.S. Converse (eds.), *The human meaning of social change*. New York: Russell Sage Foundation.

Sennett, R., and J. Cobb. 1972. *The hidden injuries of class*. New York: Vintage Press (Random House).

Slater, P. 1970. *The pursuit of loneliness*. Boston: Beacon.

Tarnowieski, D. 1972. *The changing success ethic*. New York: American Management Association.

Trinkaus, R. 1981. The effect of the mid-life crisis on personality. Working Paper, Baruch College.

USA Today: International Edition. 1986. The hard part of business—Staying alive. May 24, p. 15.

Part II

Organizational Strategies for Career Development

This section describes corporate strategies for employee development. The chapters bring out the themes of organizational resources and leadership support affecting career development.

Mirian Graddick examines corporate human resource philosophies that guide employee development. These philosophies emphasize that people can give a firm its leading edge in the marketplace and that human resource departments need to be positioned as a strategic arm of the business, rather than being reactive, administrative, paper-intensive systems. Graddick's chapter is based on visits to six Fortune 100 companies which are well known for clear people philosophies tailored to the needs of their business. She discusses how human resource philosophies articulate corporate values (standards or qualities considered desirable), the concept that people are a critical resource, characteristics of the work environment (for example, the importance of teamwork), guiding principles, roles and responsibilities in the developmental process, and strategies for development.

Graddick then describes how the philosophies are inculcated. She notes that each firm had identified key transition points in employees' careers when communicating and reinforcing the philosophy would have maximum impact. These transition points include when the person enters the firm, is promoted or is transferred, is asked to be part of a major corporate transition or change in business direction, and leaves the firm. These are the times when individuals are primed to learn new information and to understand how their actions or behaviors can make a difference. Corporate learning center courses and special forums may be used to present, discuss, or possibly identify corporate human resource values. Overall, the goal is to have a well-articulated philosophy statement to help the firm differentiate itself from others and create a shared vision among employees.

Lynn Summers writes about an approach to setting management development policies. He recognizes that the responsibility for career development is shared by the boss, the subordinate, the chief executive officer, and the training department. Summers describes sticky problems that put a drag on management development efforts. One is the "no-road-map syndrome" that occurs when the supervisor tells subordinates what they need to do to improve but does not help them figure out how to do it. Summers outlines the responsibilities, roles, knowledge, skills, and abilities required of a manager. Given these components, management development happens by identifying what the manager needs to be developed, by determining the underlying causes of weaknesses, by deciding how to measure whether the subordinate is progressing, and by designing a development plan. The chapter concludes with an example of such a comprehensive development program.

Edward Del Gaizo's chapter describes a project to identify the components of effective management in today's business world. Del Gaizo's research involved 501 managers from 150 companies. The result is a taxonomy of four managerial roles: the visionary, the investor, the information manager, and the influencer. Managers need to be proficient in each role; however, the importance of a particular role at any one time will depend on the situation. Del Gaizo shows how the four roles can be integrated into a practical framework to guide career development. The framework includes focusing on a job (one's current position or another job the individual wants to have, targeting the critical aspects of the position, evaluating one's strengths and weaknesses, and preparing action plans. In following the process, managers use the four roles by envisioning a new job, obtaining information, influencing others to assist in the education and goal attainment process, and investing in themselves and encouraging the organization to invest in them.

The last chapter in this section describes critical links between human resources, career management, and business strategy. Too often, career development programs are developed without thought as to what is needed to make the organization successful. John Slocum and William Cron propose that different business strategies require distinctive competencies required of employees, and this influences human resource programs and policies. Their comprehensive framework depicts relationships among the organization's strategy (for example, skill requirements and competitive position), the external environment (for example, competitors), and the internal environment (for example, top managers' values). Together these components influence staffing, appraisal, and development procedures in the organization. These human resource strategies define career issues in the firm and ultimately influence employees' job attitudes and performance levels.

Slocum and Cron focus on two business strategies: the defender and analyzer firms. Defender firms carve out a niche in relatively stable markets. In order to achieve a low cost position in their industry, they require employees with competencies in production, industrial engineering, finance, accounting, and quality control. Analyzer firms continuously study their markets and achieve growth through product and market development. They need expertise in marketing, applied research and development, engineering, and production. Slocum and Cron argue that the strategy developed by the human resource department must be consistent with the business strategy pursued by the firm. For instance, defender firms are likely to have performance appraisal standards which are clear and quantifiable; whereas analyzer firms are likely to have less formalized and less quantifiable appraisal criteria. Defender firms will have slow rates of upward movement; whereas analyzer firms will have moderate rates of mobility. Defender firms are likely to have employees whose careers have reached a plateau; whereas analyzer firms will be likely to have more high-potential/fast-tracked managers. Defender firms will have employees who are unhappy about their career prospects, and these companies need human resource strategies that deemphasize promotion as the ultimate reward for good performance, and instead provide such rewards as autonomy, money, recognition, and involvement in important decisions independent of promotion.

CHAPTER 7

CORPORATE PHILOSOPHIES OF EMPLOYEE DEVELOPMENT

MIRIAN M. GRADDICK

In recent years many firms have attempted to move from slow-growth bureaucracies to fast-growth, high-performance organizations, whose internal infrastructures can easily adapt to environmental fluctuations. Those known to have accomplished this transition successfully realize that their most important lever for gaining and maintaining a competitive edge rests with their people. Technological breakthroughs often become obsolete overnight, and innovative advancements are easily accessible to others within a relatively short period of time. With the dynamic and often unstable marketplace for products or services, people become a critical element in helping a business succeed, particularly during times of change.

The growing awareness that people can give a firm its leading edge in the marketplace has led many firms to reposition corporate human resource (HR) departments as strategic arms of the business, rather than being reactive, administrative, paper-intensive functions. The new challenge to the HR professional is to identify developmental strategies which inspire commitment to the firm's mission and values, are adaptive to change, and result in employees who are motivated to help the firm gain and maintain a competitive advantage.

Several trends are emerging from this reexamination of human resource strategies and systems. First, firms are recognizing the importance of having a well-articulated people philosophy that transcends all developmental systems and is closely tied to the strategic business plan. This philosophy can help to differentiate one firm from another and serve as an extremely valuable tool in attracting potential applicants. It can also help to solidify the relationship between the employee and the firm by providing employees with a clear set of expectations and direction. Second, many training and educational experiences are being viewed as levers for introducing and reinforcing the philosophy at key transition points in an employee's career cycle. When the direction of the firm shifts, training and education may also provide a useful vehicle for stimulating behavioral change so that employees can successfully adapt to changes in the work environment. Finally, firms are moving away from having a set of isolated and disconnected developmental experiences. Developmental strategies are being positioned within an overall framework with the people philosophy woven throughout.

This chapter examines various people philosophies and shows how firms incorporate these philosophies into the web of their developmental systems. The chapter is based on a visit to six Fortune 100 firms. These firms were selected because they are well known for having clearly identified people philosophies tailored to meet the unique needs of their businesses. Realizing that people make a difference, these firms have identified key levers to help employees understand the philosophy, as well as ensure that the philosophy permeates the entire organization.

In each firm, interviews were conducted with HR managers responsible for management or executive development. The data were analyzed to learn more about the essential elements of a people philosophy and how the philosophy can transcend human resource systems and programs.

PHILOSOPHIES OF EMPLOYEE DEVELOPMENT

Each firm described three essential components to any people philosophy. First, it must be closely tied to what will make the firm competitive in the marketplace. Second, there must be a strong commitment to the philosophy at the top of the firm. Finally, the philosophy must find its way into the heart of every employee.

Probably the best way to envision a people philosophy is to think about how one might describe a firm to a potential employee. Each firm I visited had captured many of the core elements of its people philosophy in a brochure. Media such as brochures are useful for creating a picture of what the firm stands for regarding its people and differentiating the firm from its competitors. Having a clear and tangible people philosophy gives employees something to evaluate their own behavior against and provides a benchmark for evaluating the success of various developmental strategies.

After reviewing and comparing each firm's philosophy statements, six themes were identified which seem to capture the core elements of a people philosophy: (1) values; (2) people as a critical resource; (3) characteristics of the work environment; (4) guiding principles; (5) roles and responsibilities in the development process; and (6) strategies for development. The following discussion of these common themes includes examples which illustrate choices and alternatives in articulating philosophies.

Values

Values are principles, standards, or qualities considered worthwhile or desirable. Each firm interviewed had a set of values designed to influence a person's behavior in the work setting. Values are never chosen arbitrarily. They represent a few short but powerful statements that define the elements most important to helping that firm succeed in the marketplace. For values to be credible, people must know what they are and understand how to incorporate them into their day-to-day work activities.

One firm had *appreciation for diversity* as one of its values. This firm has divisions that are extremely diverse in terms of its product lines, strategy, and to some extent culture. Yet, the firm expects its people to contribute to the success of the total enterprise. The importance of this as a value is the recognition and acceptance of diversity as a key factor in the ability of that firm to succeed. Thus, the environment should be one that allows the different perspectives to emerge and recognizes that various divisions may have different strategic thrusts. Recognition of diversity couples with the overarching goal of helping the entire enterprise succeed. Diversity also means taking into account the diverse backgrounds and experiences of employees and capitalizing on these as a strength. Hence, environments should be structured to allow the constructive blending of the various perspectives and talents in the organization.

Examples of other values include *excellence, integrity, service, teamwork*, and *profit*. Value statements are most effective when there are only a few of them, representing the most important factors contributing to the success of that firm (Schein 1985). Many firms display their value statements by including them in brochures and on cups and other company paraphernalia. The ultimate test of the effectiveness of each value is the way it is reflected in all products or services the firm offers.

People as a Critical Resource

The theme, people as a critical resource, describes the ultimate investment in its people a firm is willing to make. Many people philosophies highlight that investment by making statements such as these: "Best managers are made not born, therefore development of people is key to accomplishing objectives." "Business growth is directly related to people growth," and "People are key to the company's success—development must therefore be well managed."

Many of these kinds of statements offer clues as to whether the firm endorses a promote-from-within philosophy, thereby investing heavily in the development and retraining of its people. An alternative strategy is to recruit the needed talent primarily from the external marketplace.

Consideration of each employee as an individual, respecting his or her dignity, and recognizing individual merit are other ways firms actualize their philosophy that people are a critical resource.

Characteristics of the Work Environment

Characteristics of the work environment define the context within which a person will be working and can be directly translated into the kinds of behaviors that are necessary for success in that environment. For example, some firms described how the organization is structured and highlight important elements such as the scope of the various divisions, responsibilities, the types of products or services produced or sold, and whether the firm's major focus is marketing or manufacturing. Other elements key to understanding the environment include the degree of competitiveness, pace, and the stimulation of collegiality and teamwork versus independent, individual contributions.

Guiding Principles

Guiding principles are statements designed to guide the behavior of individuals in the firm. Some firms articulate values, some guiding principles, and others both. Guiding principles are designed to operationalize value statements and should serve as standards against which behavior can be measured. Reward structures should consistently reinforce the desired behaviors.

One example of a guiding principle is an "ongoing commitment to growth and development." This suggests that management should have systems in place to enable employees to realize their potential. Employees also have the responsibility to seek out opportunities to continually enhance their own skills. Commitment to growth and development means that the firm realizes that every manager, beginning at the top of the organization, invests a significant percentage of his or her time on people issues.

Another example of a guiding principle is "quality comes first." Here, the firm believes that the quality of products and services must be the number one priority for achieving customer satisfaction. The quality ethic in this firm permeates everything employees do or produce.

Roles and Responsibilities in the Development Process

This theme focuses on understanding the set of responsibilities the individual, the supervisor, and the organization must fulfill to enhance and strengthen the relationships between each pair. Many philosophy statements aim to ensure that the nature of these mutual roles and responsibilities are clear to employees. This is sometimes referred to as a psychological contract or shared understanding. More important than what it is called is the extent to which these roles and responsibilities are clearly articulated and understood throughout the organization.

All of the firms interviewed believe that individuals should take ownership for their own development and career management. Employees should not expect someone to "take them under their wings" and guide them along a career path. The onus is on the individual to take the initiative and seek out developmental opportunities.

Supervisors have certain responsibilities as well. According to these firms, subordinates have a right to receive timely and open feedback regarding strengths and areas for improvement. The supervisor can also act as a catalyst in career discussions by offering his or her knowledge of the different types of jobs in the firm.

Finally, these firms agree that even if a strong boss/subordinate relationship exists, the firm has a responsibility to provide the resources necessary to make career planning a reality. This includes providing employees with information about job opportunities. It requires the kind of environment that allows movement which may cross various jobs and organizational units. Some firms have become fairly sophisticated in this area and have computerized data banks where employees can log on and access data related to job openings.

Strategies for Development

Articulated strategies for development provide the underpinning for a firm's effective development of employees. Some firms, for example, have generated a development model describing how development occurs and at what point in a career cycle certain events should take place.

All developmental activities can be grouped into the following three categories: (1) education/training; (2) on-the-job experiences; and (3) relationships with others. While everyone agrees that most development occurs via on-the-job experiences, some firms have chosen to identify key transition points in an employee's career cycle and offer more formal events. One firm, for example, has a long-standing belief in the fundamental value of education. As a result, everyone in the firm is required to attend a certain number of hours of training per year. This ensures that employees are constantly revitalized and have an up-to-date perspective on where the business is going.

An important issue emerges when evaluating the strategies a firm employs to invest in its people. The issue is whether or not the firm believes that everyone should benefit in some way from development. Several firms expressing this belief have built centralized and formalized activities so that everyone has an opportunity to participate in learning events. This kind of philosophy takes into account the fact that people grow and move both horizontally and vertically. Formal events accommodate both types of career paths.

Other firms believe in more formalized investment targeted to those who have been identified as having potential to advance. Firms that primarily invest in the development of high-potential managers have hierarchically driven development strategies. The goal is to ensure that top talent is identified early and developed according to the kinds of experiences needed to successfully move into higher levels of management. Development is encouraged for others, but left primarily in the hands of the boss/subordinate. A corporate HR role in these instances is to ensure that all employees have access to the tools necessary to do effective career planning.

This has been a review of the core elements of a philosophy statement. The next section looks at periods in an employee's career cycle when introducing and reinforcing the philosophy can be most beneficial.

CRITICAL TRANSITION POINTS IN A CAREER CYCLE

Once a people philosophy has been clearly articulated, it is equally important to determine how the philosophy will be communicated to new hires as well as to existing employees. Each of the firms we interviewed had identified key transition points in an employee's career cycle when communicating and reinforcing the philosophy would have maximum impact. While people philosophies can be well entrenched in a culture, they should be dynamic and well integrated with the direction the firm is headed. Continual reinforcement of the philosophy ensures employees know how to behave in ways that will allow them to grow and make a contribution.

Many transition points exist, yet there appear to be four general clusters: (1) entering a firm—new hires; (2) increase in scope of responsibilities or move to different organizational unit; (3) major strategic changes in the business direction; and (4) exiting the firm. In each case, employees are primed for learning new information and eager to understand how their actions and behavior can make a difference.

One of the most important transition points for communicating the corporate philosophy occurs when new hires enter the business. Research on the socialization process of new employees has focused on the importance of clearly articulating information such as the firm's mission and values, as early as possible (Schein 1980). Corporate-wide orientation programs are the most common vehicles for accomplishing these objectives, and the firms I interviewed stated that the most important mission of the orientation program is to communicate the people philosophy. Discussion of administrative issues such as benefits and policies is only a secondary goal. Features of various orientation programs include helping employees understand the firm's mission, strategy, and values, with the belief that when employees first enter the firm, it is important to foster a single enterprise perspective. Even though employees will later be dispersed into various units within the organization, some of which may have their own goals and objectives, it is critical that initially employees hear a common message to rally around. Employees are generally excited and eager to make a contribution at this point, and every effort should be made to capitalize on this enthusiasm by helping them to understand how they can make the enterprise a success and at the same time grow professionally.

A significant increase in responsibilities or a move to another part of the business defines a second key transition point, with an opportunity to again reinforce the people philosophy. Becoming a new manager is one example. This represents an excellent opportunity to communicate to each manager how he or she can, in the new role, help to make the philosophy a reality. New managers, for example, can benefit from a greater understanding of the future, focusing on creating a shared vision and meaning. Other topics might include transition into management and strengthening the manager/subordinate relationship by acquiring key skills such as coaching and giving and receiving feedback. Other key transitions involving an increase in scope of responsibility are promotions to middle management or executive ranks.

An international assignment illustrates a transition point representing a move to another part of the business. This is a critical time to articulate the goals and objectives of that organizational unit and define how the people philosophy is implemented in that unit to help the firm succeed.

A third important transition point for reevaluating the philosophy and subsequently communicating it to employees occurs when an organization undergoes a major change such as a reorganization, downsizing, or acquisition. These events can be traumatic. For example, there has been a fairly dramatic shift in careers at AT&T over the past decade, stimulated in part by the breakup of the Bell System (Campbell and Moses 1986). Employees have a high need to know what has changed and what is now expected of them. As a result, AT&T is reexamining its people philosophy to ensure that it fits with the new strategic direction.

Several firms discussed the impact of a new chief executive who had a contemporary view of the relationship between the firm and their employees. Radical shifts in the people philosophy can often occur during change in leadership. It is incumbent on the new leadership to restate what the firm values and expects of its people. In the absence of this, the instinct for survival will often drive employee behaviors, and a new and sometimes undesirable philosophy may emerge.

Finally, exiting the business can be viewed as an important transition point. Firms should consider people leaving the business as future customers and major constituents. Ensuring that employees leaving the business are treated according to the people philosophy the firm espouses is crucial. It sends signals to the remaining employees and may potentially impact recruitment of future employees.

Establishing a Building-Block Approach

While formal programs have typically occurred as isolated events, recent attention has shifted to building on the knowledge and insights gained from one event to another. While the people philosophy transcends all events, the manner in which the events play out may vary depending on where someone is in his or her career cycle.

One firm, for example, begins its sequence of activities with new hires. The initial focus is on creating an awareness of where the firm is headed and how to maximize individual contributions. As employees progress and take on greater responsibilities, the focus changes to understanding how the people philosophy can be applied to motivating and stimulating teams. As some managers move even further up the corporate ladder, the emphasis shifts to helping create the strategic vision. At this level it is crucial to understand the people implications that emerge from the strategic direction that has been set and how a people focus can become an integral part of the fabric of the firm. It is also important to understand when changes are needed to successfully adapt to a changing environment.

THE ROLE OF CORPORATE HR ORGANIZATIONS

The role of many corporate HR departments has undergone significant change during the past decade. Today's HR professional has responsibilities for establishing a corporate-wide people strategy and direction. New perceptions of people as key to the success of the business make human resource activities become critical. Corporate HR departments that have managed to get ahead of the train have shifted the emphasis from being viewed as an administrative promulgator of rules and procedures to architect of HR strategies and systems. Building collaborative relationships with line organizations is critical in implementing the various systems. HR professionals are therefore channeling their efforts toward helping line organizations understand the people philosophy and incorporate it into their human resource systems.

During my interviews, many firms talked about the unique role corporate HR serves by providing the glue for linking various diverse units together to foster a single-enterprise perspective. Several firms have capitalized on this role in a very strategic way. For example, HR professionals can design and implement events which bring managers together from different parts of the firm at key transition points. In several firms, managers attend a corporate learning center at various career crossroads, such as becoming a new manager. The fact that the various activities or events are sponsored by corporate HR is not nearly as critical as ensuring that employees know there is a place where they can acquire a better understanding of the total business, meet others from different operating units, establish networks, and strengthen the relationship between the individual and the firm.

One firm, after having several years of poor financial results, decided to readdress its people philosophy to ensure that its employees could help regain a competitive edge. Corporate HR led an activity designed to bring vice presidents together representing all organizational units to form a development council. The initial purpose of the council was to articulate a management development philosophy providing a foundation for building developmental strategies. Once consensus was reached on the development philosophy, the council became a permanent group (with rotating membership) responsible for reviewing and approving human resource strategies and policies to ensure consistency with the people philosophy. Not only is this a way to ensure buy-in from the top of the firm, but the representation from the various business units helps to guarantee relevancy of developmental strategies across the firm. The council also identifies some of the unique needs of individual business units and makes certain that developmental strategies address these needs as well. One decision the council made, for example, resulted in the creation of a special annual award for individuals who are recognized by others for excellence in developing people. Over time, these employees have comprised a cadre of role models who are often asked to participate in events such as new manager orientation.

While the development council was one example of how a people philosophy can be articulated, another firm had corporate HR create a team representing diverse perspectives to address training and educational strategies across the corporation. This type of partnership ensures that a consistent people philosophy is woven throughout the educational experiences and helps to eliminate redundancy across business units. This effort resulted in the development of a core curriculum sponsored by corporate HR which is different from the courses that are designed and delivered in the field. Most firms believe that corporate HR should conduct orientation for new managers to nurture a single enterprise perspective.

Another strategic role that corporate HR can play is to help high-potential managers obtain the kinds of developmental experiences necessary to move up the corporate ladder. Movement across major operating units to learn the business is critical for advancement in most firms. Corporate can often be a broker for this activity by facilitating sessions designed to move managers across units. Helping to establish a common set of standards for potential is an essential role that HR professionals can play. In this way, managers can bring candidates who are ready for interdepartmental movement forward and have a common language by which to communicate strengths and nature of experiences.

SUMMARY AND IMPLICATIONS

Key to the success of any firm is the extent to which it understands the important role its people can play in operationalizing the corporate strategy. Well-articulated philosophy statements help a firm to be differentiated from others and to create a shared vision among employees. HR professionals can help leaders crystalize the shared vision and relate it to day-to-day behaviors.

In many instances, the process of reassessing the firm's commitment to its people can be a useful and ongoing dialog. One activity to stimulate this type of discussion among the senior officers is to have them design a recruiting brochure. This would force them to think about the characteristics which make the firm stand out from its competitors. It might also reveal a discrepancy between what they would like to see and what actually exists. Successful firms understand that a people philosophy must come from the leadership of the firm and go beyond empty rhetoric.

Based on examining several different philosophy statements, it is clear that one best philosophy does not exist. It is not possible to successfully lift a philosophy from one firm, because it works well there, and export it to another firm. Philosophy statements often define the culture of a firm and should be tailored to match the unique characteristics of that firm. People philosophies should be future-oriented and linked directly to the strategic business plan. Several firms noted the difficulty in changing a people philosophy. Some said that it takes years to successfully transform a culture. The role of an HR professional is to understand the relationship between developmental strategies and people philosophies and ensure that the philosophy transcends all human resource systems.

The value in having a clearly articulated philosophy statement is that potential employees can evaluate whether their own values and expectations match those of the firm. Having something tangible that employees can periodically read and evaluate their own behavior against can help to solidify the relationship between the individual and the firm in terms of specifying mutual expectations. More broadly, a philosophy statement can also be used as a benchmark against which to evaluate the success of various developmental strategies. Not all firms included every core element as part of their philosophy statement. Enough elements are present, however, to obtain a sense of what the firm stands for with respect to people, to highlight mutual expectations, and to specify how it invests in its people.

The most important time to communicate a philosophy is with new hires. New employees are ripe for knowledge about the firm and how they can make a contribution. Communicating the people philosophy should be the most important component of a new manager orientation program. Since the strategic direction of a firm is never static, the people philosophy should also be an ongoing part of all developmental strategies and programs.

An important challenge for HR professionals is to help a firm identify key transition points when communicating the philosophy can have its greatest impact. The focus should be on reinforcing the commitment and strengthening the bond between the individual and the firm. Most firms are moving away from having a series of isolated events at each transition point. They have recognized the importance of having one experience build on another and are capitalizing on learning that has occurred during prior events. This method takes into account where a manager is in his or her career cycle and focuses on the specific needs of that individual or group of individuals.

The recognition of the strategic role that corporate HR can play to help make the firm competitive is key. As HR professionals work more collaboratively with the field, they begin to be viewed as value-added rather than as overhead. Corporate HR should realize its unique role in contributing to the success of the total enterprise and build interventions to help the line organizations successfully inculcate the people philosophy into their human resource systems.

The proper selection and development of people in support of the corporate philosophy is one of the most important levers a firm has in gaining and maintaining a competitive edge. Ultimately, the success of any philosophy statement is the extent to which it is an integral part of the firm's developmental systems and the extent to which every employee believes it and effectively carries it out.

REFERENCES

Campbell, R. J., and J. L. Moses. 1986. Careers from an organizational perspective. In Douglas T. Hall (ed.), *Career development in organizations*. San Francisco: Jossey-Bass.

Schein, E. H. 1985. Organization culture: A dynamic model. In R. H. Kilmann, M. J. Saxton, and R. Serpa (eds.), *Gaining control of the corporate culture*. San Francisco: Jossey-Bass.

Schein, E. H. 1980. *Organizational psychology*. Englewood Cliffs, NJ: Prentice-Hall.

CHAPTER 8

HOW TO WIN FRIENDS AND DEVELOP MANAGERS: AN APPROACH TO SETTING MANAGEMENT DEVELOPMENT POLICIES

LYNN SUMMERS

If you are responsible for the management development function in your organization, you probably have faith in the changeability of people's behavior—and faith in the belief that planned individual development is more than the diaphanous vision of an idealist. But do the influential executives and managers in your organization share your faith? They spend the organization's dollars on advertising, and they believe that such an investment results in sales. But do they send their "kids" to you for development? Do they believe that doing so gets them any results? (Careful—these are trick questions! Check your responses against the correct answer given at the end of this chapter.)

The purpose of management development is to change the behavior of certain people in ways that make those people more valuable to the organization—to mold managerial talent in ways that help the organization achieve its business objectives, make a profit, and remain a "going concern." In so doing, management development, whether intentionally or unconsciously, takes advantage of every possible instrument of change.

One such instrument is maturation. Maturation is the normal developmental process in which people change as a result of the accumulation of experiences within an ever-aging nervous system. The management development function can't take any credit here, because maturation produces change whether or not there is a management development function. The problem with relying on maturation to produce individual behavior change

I thank Ben Rosen, Dick Levin, Dave Neumann, and the editors for very thoughtful comments on an earlier version of this chapter.

of value to the organization is that it is slow and it doesn't always produce change in the right direction.

A second instrument of change is the battlefield commission in which the individual is given a special, challenging assignment, for which he or she usually is not prepared. Drastic situational changes do indeed cause people's behavior to change, and change quickly. That's the upside of the battlefield commission. The downside is that it is a trial-and-error instrument of change with a low success rate. Not everyone rises to the occasion.

The third instrument of change is planned development—individual behavior change brought about through the sensible application of what we know about human development and about how things happen in organizations. As you know, planned development is the most difficult of the three instruments to use. But, if properly designed and executed, it decreases reliance on chance and increases the likelihood of getting desired results. Planned development is the instrument of choice of organizations who fund legitimate management development functions.

In this chapter I'd like to treat a number of issues that, to me, appear to be important in the execution of planned management development. For anyone involved in establishing management development policy, these issues represent decision points. We at Hardee's are continually struggling with many of these decision points. We can't say for sure that our philosophy and consequent practices are indeed the best, even for us, let alone for any other company. But I do believe these are some of the more important choice points. So, with this caveat of modesty out of the way, let's get bold!

I've organized the chapter around four major sections:

1. Sticky Problems. These are the pitfalls that traditionally have ensnared the well-intentioned efforts of management development functions. I describe these problems based on experiences of someone I know real well.

2. Where to Aim? What does the organization expect a management development function to develop its managers to do? Although we properly answer this question through needs analysis, it also helps to have in hand a model that ties together the critical elements of management behavior. In this section I describe a model we've concocted at Hardee's.

3. Executing. Once you've settled on a model, how do you apply it in individual cases? Here I outline a process we are now attempting to instill.

4. A Scenario. In the final section, I play the whole process out through a case study. Although fictitious, it does show how all the pieces can potentially come together.

STICKY PROBLEMS

There are at least five sticky problems that put a drag on management development efforts. Summarized in Exhibit 8.1, these problems are beliefs

Exhibit 8.1
Five Sticky Problems

The Problem	Evidence It Exists
1. The No-Road-Map Syndrome	*Boss*: "I told him a dozen times to delegate more. Why won't he do it?"
2. The Merit Badge Infatuation	*Subordinate*: "I attended the seminar. Now where's my promotion?"
3. The Round-Peg-in-a-Square-Hole Dilemma	*Head of Management Development Function*: "We did a thorough needs analysis. And we're teaching them hyper-extended decision trees. Why isn't the program working?
4. Who's Got the Monkey?	*Line Manager to Head of Management Development Function*: "I'm sending Jane to your program. I know you can work wonders with her!"
5. Political Shyness	*President*: "Did you say *our* company offers that program? I didn't know!"

and consequent behaviors that reduce the likelihood of management development's being successful.

The No-Road-Map Syndrome

It's like when we tell our friends from Idaho, whom we would prefer to avoid spending another minute with for the rest of our lives, "Drop by when you're in our neck of the woods!" We scrupulously avoid giving them any directions and hope they forget how to spell our last name if they ever do get to the East Coast.

The manager who tells his subordinate, "You need to plan more effectively," period, is partaking of the same, uncharitable no-road-map syndrome. Tell the subordinate that he's now at A (substandard behavior), that he needs to get to B (standard behavior), but share nothing with him to help him figure out how to get from A to B. Hence, no road map.

The no-road-map syndrome leaves the individual alone to figure out (1) what body of knowledge is available to apply to this journey, (2) how best to apply it, and (3) which, of the many possible routes, are acceptable to the boss and the organization, and which are not.

The management development function needs to devise ways to help bosses avoid falling victim to this syndrome. The best approach is a positive one: Devise a variety of tools for bosses to use for guiding planned development of their subordinates.

The Merit Badge Infatuation

When I was a Cub Scout, I enjoyed ticking off the requirements for merit badges. Fix a peanut butter and jelly sandwich, and you get a merit badge in cooking. Take a walk in the woods, and earn the wildlife merit badge. Do this, do that. I had tons of merit badges.

Similarly, development efforts can easily become exercises in activity completion. To develop planning skills, for example, a manager may go off to a seminar on strategic planning. However, attendance at the seminar does not imply that development has occurred, only that an activity has been completed. Will the manager's boss rate him higher on planning ability on his next performance appraisal just because he's attended the seminar?

More important than activity completion is the actual change in the manager's behavior that results from his engaging in development activities. And the behavior change needs to happen on the job, not just at the seminar. An organization can be lulled into a false sense of confidence in its management development function by merely looking at the numbers of people going to seminars and being run through company training programs.

The management development function can help the organization focus on on-job applications, using discrete activities as catalysts. For example, don't give credit for attending a program until the participant has applied some predetermined set of learnings to his or her job.

The Round-Peg-in-a-Square-Hole Dilemma

The inflexible obsessive-compulsive tries to jam the round peg into the square hole because, "This is where it's supposed to go!" Similarly, we human resource professionals often try to fit a round approach to management development into a square organizational context. This is a complicated problem which plays itself out on at least two levels.

First, there's the problem of the contents of our management development programs. All management development programs have contents in the sense that, for every development need, there is a body of knowledge that can be tapped in some way to help an individual change his or her behavior in an appropriate way.

For example, to become a more effective planner, a person can benefit from learning how to assess the adverse consequences of a course of action. Tapping into this body of knowledge is a more efficient way of developing planning skills than having to figure it out by trial and error. It's part of the road map for moving from novice to master planner.

However, not all contents are consistent with the organization's culture.

For example, in creating tools to help develop managers' interaction skills, the management development function may conclude, after searching the research and practitioners' literature, that maintaining subordinates' self-esteem is an essential ingredient of effective supervision. This, in fact, is the pillar of contemporary behavior modeling approaches to supervisory training—one of the most effective training techniques ever to emerge from human resource research. But what if the organization's top and middle management exercise the KATN style of supervision? (That means "kick ass and take names.")

No matter how sound the research, no matter how solid the ethics supporting the maintenance-of-self-esteem approach, it won't fit in a square hole.

Second is the issue of the process by which management development is carried out. At one extreme of the process continuum is the silver spoon approach, and at the other is the Darwinian approach to planned development.

The silver spoon is most often used in large, administratively oriented organizations. Here, planned development is carried to an extreme, with multitudes of programs and procedures to help an individual through the growth process.

The Darwinian approach is used in more entrepreneurial organizations. Here, individuals are exposed to greater risks in the development process, partly because the organization does not devote many resources to the planned development effort and also because it just believes that there should be a strong element of struggle, pain, and survival of the fittest in growing its people.

Both approaches work, within their contexts. The task of the management development function in the administrative organization is to avoid sinking its planned development programs with excessive procedural ballast. And in entrepreneurial organizations, the function must work to inject some planning into the development process to balance the organization's natural predilection to return to the jungle.

Who's Got the Monkey?

Something very basic needs to be settled before you can move into a truly integrated management development system: the delineation of responsibility among manager, boss, and management development department.

Paul Banas and his associates at Ford dramatically flashed this insight in our eyes when my colleagues and I did an article recently on management development. They said:

The biggest mistake ... is that the ... management development ... function believe they are responsible for development. And when they take on that type of

Exhibit 8.2
Management Development Responsibilities

Manager
- Perform the job
- Seize opportunities to learn and to grow

Boss
- Train and develop subordinates
- Coach, supervise, encourage, give feedback, set example, correct, push, cheer, and so forth
- Use all appropriate development tools available
- Identify subordinates' training and development needs

Management Development Function
- Create development tools
- Provide guidance in how to use them
- Assist bosses in identifying training and development needs

---

responsibility, they are assuming the job of the line managers. And usually, what that means is that they don't have [management] support...

Management development, to the surprise of many directors of management development, is the responsibility of the line manager, and to the extent you involve them in a collaborative way in the development of the management development program—you even involve them in doing the... training—the stronger your management development program will be.

We have suggested the delineation of responsibilities shown in Exhibit 8.2. This is one way to cut it. A different fit may be required in other organizations. The management development function should spearhead the effort to clarify these responsibilities and then shrewdly avoid falling into traps. The most damaging trap, of course, is the belief that they are responsible for developing people. Remember, that is a line function!

By the way, we use the word "tools" rather broadly. A tool can range from an on-the-job development guide to a university-based mini-MBA program for executives.

Political Shyness

Few management development programs ever succeed on their own merits. You have to sell 'em! No matter how sound they are. No matter how much research supports their contents or their design. You still have to sell 'em!

In designing experiments, scientists take great pains to identify and control for threats to validity. But, in organizations, the threats to validity are often the variables that can most efficiently produce the desired effects. To make management development work, you not only need to put together a solid, research-based, technically proper, contextually congruent program, you must also work the culture in ways that win support for the program. This requires involving management in the development of programs and going beyond involvement to outright politics!

Conclusion: It helps if your CEO is the first to use your new appraisal system—and talks about it—and the word gets around. And it helps if key executives inaugurate a new training program by being the first participants—and participate fully—and talk about it.

WHERE TO AIM?

Develop what? Some companies spend big bucks on management development. So what is it the management development function needs to do to satisfy expectations? What is it that managers and executives need to be developed to do? What are we aiming at?

A large body of research has developed over the years in defining what it is that managers and executives do. Each line of research takes a slightly different perspective, like the blind men confronting an elephant. To apply all this research, therefore, requires boiling it down to something that is easier to understand and to use. And what executives do must be specified before you can design and implement management development processes to help them do their jobs and grow into future jobs more effectively.

Here's one way to tackle the issue. We took three bodies of existing research, added a fourth of our own invention, and wrapped them together in a model of executive behavior. We wanted the model to promote development action rather than merely intellectual understanding. We involved management in defining some elements of the model. See if it makes sense.

1. Responsibilities. The core responsibilities for executives are planning, organizing, leading, and controlling. This is the classic, prescriptive list of executive functions, the list of things an executive should do.

But these responsibilities are concepts. They are not observable behaviors. So, like the elephant's trunk, responsibilities only tell part of the story. We needed to look at the executive's job from additional perspectives, especially if our ultimate goal is to change behavior in the direction of becoming more effective at doing what executives are supposed to do.

2. Roles. Second, we considered the roles executives play. Interpersonal, informational, and decisional roles capture the broad range of actions an executive performs in a day. We can think of each specific role as a different hat the executive wears. Research, and casual observation, tell us that the executive changes hats rapidly—in fact, he must be able to make quick

transitions in order to be effective. And frequently he must wear several hats simultaneously.

Understanding roles gives us another perspective and a more complete grasp on what executives do. But we have yet to determine what it takes to effectively fulfill the executive's responsibilities and perform in the executive's roles.

3. Dimensions. That is the purpose of the third layer of our model. Dimensions are clusters of knowledge, skills, and abilities that are presumed to underlie effective performance of an executive job. They are individual characteristics that permit a person to perform executive roles effectively.

Let's step back and look at the model as I've described it so far. The model says that we can prescribe what an executive should do by talking about his or her responsibilities. We can describe what he or she actually does by referring to the roles performed. And we can explain why one executive is good at some aspects of the job and perhaps not so good at others by making inferences about where he or she stands on the dimensions.

We have identified and defined, through job analyses and training needs assessments, a pool of slightly more than a dozen dimensions. We have grouped these into interpersonal, cognitive, management, personal, and communications "bags" or categories. We've also added a bag called technical knowledge and skills which embraces the specialized domains of subject matter for experts, specialists, and professionals. Together, these account for most of the variability in individual performance of managers and executives, controlling for situational differences—at least to our subjective satisfaction.

So, dimensions are useful in explaining different levels of effectiveness in executive performance. But knowing an executive's dimensional profile does not automatically open the door to development for the executive. Knowledge that he or she is weak in leadership does not presume knowledge of what to do about it. (Remember the no-road-map syndrome?) An additional step is required.

4. Skills. That additional step, the fourth layer of our model, is skills. In this step, we pinpoint the specific skill the deficiency of which causes a person to be less than effective on a dimension.

For example, Marie may be less than effective in leadership because she is unskilled in persuading others or because she does not seek the involvement of others. Those are two very different potential causes. Knowing which is the true cause would help Marie focus her developmental efforts.

Development is not always a matter of strengthening people where they are deficient. Often it involves putting to better use a strength that is presently underutilized. Joe may be much more than effective in planning and organizing because of his skill in managing his personal time, or because he is very good at setting and using objectives. Again, knowing which is the true cause of Joe's strength in planning would help his boss devise ways

Exhibit 8.3
A Sampling of Skills Underlying the Leadership Dimension

- *Persuading others.* A large part of leadership is simply the act of convincing others to do something the way you want it done.

- *Seeking involvement of others.* Effective executives involve their subordinates in the problems, decisions, and plans that will impact them. Subordinates who are involved in these processes tend to become more committed to the work and to the organization, thus making close supervision unnecessary and your job as boss easier.

- *Maintaining others' self-esteem.* Effective leaders boost and maintain their subordinates' feelings of self-worth. They do so consistently in order to develop a solid base of commitment and self-motivation within their subordinates. Some people are "naturals" at maintaining others' self-esteem; others have to work at it.

- *Being assertive.* Assertiveness is the happy medium between aggressiveness and passivity. Getting your point across in a way that gets others' attention yet doesn't provoke angry reactions toward you enhances your ability to lead.

- *Being concrete.* In other words, being specific. In many situations, leaders can be more effective in their communications with their subordinates if they are specific rather than vague. People understand better when you give them a specific example than when you give them a generality.

- *Setting and using objectives.* Leaders who have a clear target and share this target with their subordinates are much more likely to hit it than the leader who either doesn't share information about the target with his subordinates or who doesn't have a target to begin with.

- *Being enthusiastic.* This is an "amplifier" skill in that your enthusiasm can intensify the results of applying the other leadership-linked skills. If you are weak on all the preceding skills, being enthusiastic will probably worsen the effect of your efforts to lead. But if you're fairly strong on some of the previous skills, enthusiasm can dramatically enhance the results of your leadership efforts.

---

to make better use of his strengths. Before assigning Joe the task of chairing a strategic planning task force, it would be helpful to know that cause.

For your information, Exhibit 8.3 contains an excerpt from a "development directory" that we recently put together. It lists and comments on some of the skills that underlie the leadership dimension. Remember, each of these skills is a potential cause of an individual's strength or weakness on the leadership dimension.

EXECUTING

With this model in hand, how can you make management development happen? There are at least four critical things that need to happen.

1. Identify the Development Need. What does the individual need to be developed on? Information concerning the development need could come in the form of a dimensional profile based on assessment center observations, on-the-job performance summarized in a performance appraisal, or from any other source. It doesn't really matter, so long as the information is accepted as valid by both subordinate and boss and is in synch with what the organization defines as important.

Now some priorities need to be set. If there are several development opportunities, on which should developmental efforts be focused? Subordinate and boss need to agree on what dimension to attack, taking into account several issues. One issue is: Should development efforts be directed at performance on the current job or at some future job? Another issue: Should the subordinate work on correcting a deficiency or on making greater use of a strength?

Note the importance of the boss's involvement in all this. The success of the development effort rests in large measure on the boss's buying into the process and supporting the subordinate in his or her efforts. This is accomplished by involving the boss in measuring strengths and weaknesses and in setting developmental priorities.

2. Determine the Causes Underlying the Development Need. This is an important step. In solving a problem, you can't take corrective action until you uncover the cause of the problem. Without knowing the cause, the best you can do is treat the symptoms or apply a Band-Aid. Likewise in development, it is difficult to accurately aim developmental efforts without first understanding why development is needed.

Here's where the performance model comes into play. Boss and subordinate can explore the tickler list of skills in tracking down the causes. Once the underlying skills are pinned down, they become the targets of the subordinate's development efforts.

3. Decide How to Measure Development. How will boss and subordinate know if the subordinate is making any progress? What are the behaviors on the job that should change? How should these behavioral changes be reflected in results?

Note that the boss's accountability for his unit's results is the strongest bond he has to the development of his subordinate. Therefore, it's not just the subordinate's behavior that they want to track. It's also the organizational results that that behavior affects. Deciding on how to measure progress also makes it easier for follow-up to occur.

4. Design a Development Plan. It is tempting for the boss to say, "Go to the leadership seminar and 'get fixed.' " This, of course, puts the monkey on the wrong back. It won't work.

The development plan will most often result in positive change when it is very closely tied to the job. This includes tying the measurement of progress to on-the-job behaviors and results. It also requires that special development activities be linked to the job. Special activities might include seminars, readings, temporary assignments, and the like. The important thing is that these activities be tied somehow to the specific development need and to on-the-job application of new behaviors.

Darwinian development occurs when the subordinate gets thrown into that special assignment in marketing. He or she either sinks or swims, rises to the occasion, or is overwhelmed by the novel demands of the situation. I suspect that the success rate for Darwinian approaches to development is rather low, although its success stories may be quite glamorous. No wonder!

Planned development occurs when the subordinate and the boss work out a game plan and then design opportunities to play it out. It involves exposing the subordinate to some body of relevant new knowledge or set of new behaviors. Seminars and other special activities become the ways to acquire this new "body." And some structure must be provided back on the job to enable the subordinate to apply this new "body"—to effect change in the old ways based on his or her exposure to the new ways.

A SCENARIO

We've been speaking in generalities. Let's get down to specifics. How can the model and the execution steps be used to overcome the sticky problems and produce planned individual development? Let's consider a hypothetical case.

Brent Goes to Training

Brent is a lower- to middle-level line manager in a large retail organization. In his last performance appraisal, Brent received a good overall rating, but his boss told him he needed to become a more effective leader.

Together, they discussed the leadership issue. Brent's boss, Joe, shared his observations that led him to conclude that Brent needed work in the leadership dimension. Brent could recall the incidents Joe described—in fact, he remembered discussing them with Joe at the time of their occurrence. Their perceptions of the impact of Brent's behaviors in these situations were congruent. Brent agreed that to assume broader supervisory responsibilities and to advance he needed to exert greater leadership. He was open and eager to develop.

They then explored the causes of Brent's ineffective leadership behavior. After looking over the tickler list of skills underlying the leadership dimension, they identified the two most likely causes of Brent's leadership problem.

First, they agreed Brent was very directive and rarely asked his subordinates' input on issues that affected them. Consequently, when Brent asked them to carry out a task, they seldom acted committed and had difficulty bringing the task to completion on time or on standard. So, one skill Brent agreed to work on was *seeking involvement of others*.

Second, Brent was often vague in answering questions. It was hard to pin him down to specifics. Brent agreed that this could cause frustration among his subordinates and was probably adversely affecting his efforts to be an effective leader. He thus agreed to work on *being concrete*, too.

Brent and Joe agreed on ways to measure Brent's progress in developing each of these skills. They identified behavioral measures, many of which Joe would be able to observe periodically. And they also listed several outcome measures—unit results that should be favorably affected by Brent's leadership development.

Since Brent would soon be eligible for promotion, Joe scheduled him to attend a training program designed to help prepare managers at Brent's level for the next level of responsibility. Brent's boss had attended the program two years earlier and thus was familiar with its contents. He knew one of the program's modules dealt with the two skills Brent was working on.

Joe worked with Brent to help him prepare for the program, using workbooks sent out in advance by the management development department. He placed special emphasis on the pre-course material dealing with Brent's development areas. Circumstances prevented Brent from attending as originally scheduled. (Not everything goes as planned, right?)

By the time Brent eventually attended the program, he was primed to make the most out of it as a catalyst and testing ground. It was an opportunity to try out the new behaviors he knew he had to start practicing in order to be more effective at involving others and being more concrete.

His confidence bolstered by the insight he gained into the leadership process and by the opportunity to practice new behaviors in the relative safety of a training environment, Brent practiced the new skills even more intensely back on the job. Joe gave him feedback every time he visited Brent's unit and had a chance to observe Brent interacting with his people. Brent's behavior had changed, and he began to see changes in his people's behavior and in his unit's results as well.

In this hypothetical success story, planned development actually occurred. It was structured around the four development steps. It used a training program as a catalyst for Brent to acquire a new body of knowledge and to begin practicing new behaviors directly related to his development needs. But the bulk of the actual development efforts occurred on the job.

Brent's boss, Joe, was intimately involved in the process, motivated in part because he knew developing Brent would enhance the financial performance of his own unit and in part because he has been rewarded in the past for producing people who go on to further success elsewhere in the company. The company had structured contingencies in such a way that the roles of the boss and the subordinates, as well as the role of the management development department, in planned development were clearly defined and appropriately rewarded.

And note that the parties involved did not get so bogged down in an elaborate management development scheme that the development activities became an end in themselves—a glorified merit badge. The process was simple, job-oriented, and results-focused.

Note also that this scenario might have been very different without a training program that was firmly rooted in on-the-job preparation and application and that did not actively involve the boss. The implication is that, for this approach to planned development to work, traditional training programs will have to be dramatically modified.

CONCLUSION

You may wonder what happened to the "policy" so prominently featured in the title of this chapter. No written policy can serve quite as effectively as a philosophy of people development that is ingrained in the day-to-day speech and behavior of every member of the organization. This philosophy can best serve as your policy. The critical elements that weave through this chapter—responsibility, political involvement, on-the-job application, a usable model, and so on—make the policy work.

To answer the trick question posed at the beginning of this chapter: Your top executives should invest happily in management development. They do this because *they* are the ones responsible for management development. And they do this because they perceive as theirs the programs you, as head of the management development function, have made available to serve as catalysts for planned individual development. They invest in the tools you provide because those tools—whether booklets or seminars or major programs—work and are consistent with the organization's way of doing things. And because the organization rewards them for developing people.

SELECTED BIBLIOGRAPHY

References to executives' responsibilities and roles can be found in most management texts. We used Henry Mintzberg's analysis of roles (*The nature of managerial work*, Harper and Row, 1973). John Kotter offers an equally useful classification of roles ("What effective general managers really do," *Harvard Business Review*, November-December, 1982).

The dimension concept is widely used. Our dimensions are adapted from Development Dimensions International's programs. See any of Bill Byham's writings on the integrated human resources system.

The skills concept described here is strictly home-grown. See David Whetton and Kim Cameron, *Developing management skills* (Scott Foresman & Co., 1984), for an approximation. See also Del Gaizo's chapter, next.

References to responsibilities and roles in the management development process

(Who's Got the Monkey?) are more difficult to find. The quote from Paul Banas and associates is from an article I did with Dave Neumann, "Understanding management development . . . and doing it" (*The Industrial-Organizational Psychologist,* November, 1985). Another source that has been vitally influential in our efforts at Hardee's is Jim Cook and the Practical Management Associates organization. See Cook's article, "ROI: What should training take credit for?" (*Training,* January, 1987). Closely allied to all this are the points Peter Block makes in *Flawless consulting* (Learning Concepts, 1981).

Some real progress is currently being made in understanding how management development works. See the recent work from the Center for Creative Leadership (as reported by Lombardo in Chapter 18). Herbert Simon has reported some interesting insights into the management decision-making process that relate to how we might more rapidly grow managers from novices to masters ("Making management decisions," *The Academy of Management Executive,* February, 1987).

CHAPTER 9

A TAXONOMY FOR MANAGERIAL EFFECTIVENESS

EDWARD R. DEL GAIZO

Planning, organizing, directing, staffing, and controlling were once considered the traditional roles of the manager. For decades, proficiency in these skills equaled success as a manager. But in the contemporary business world, new challenges confront managers. They must contend with rapid change, increased competition, a differentiated work force with diverse values and expectations, as well as external influencers such as unions, the media, or government regulators. They must take more direct responsibility for the corporate bottom line, work within an increasingly interdependent organizational structure, and cope with information overload and sophisticated technology.

For today's managers, the traditional roles, while still important, no longer suffice. The challenges managers find in their current jobs, as well as those they face in jobs to which they aspire, point to new ways of looking at the manager's role. These challenges demand a reexamination of the skills, knowledge, and attitudes required to manage successfully in the present, complex business environment.

Managers need to (1) understand the new roles they must play, (2) assess their own strengths and weaknesses in these roles, and (3) use these understandings to enhance their current positions or prepare themselves for increased responsibilities into higher positions.

RESEARCH SUMMARY

Research, commissioned by Learning International, provides the foundation for conceptualizing the manager's role and a corresponding framework for career development. The objective was to identify the behaviors and actions that distinguish outstanding managers from less effective managers.

The two-year study involved 501 managers from 150 companies representing a cross-section of industries and government agencies. Approximately 2,300 surveys were completed by managers, their subordinates, superiors, and colleagues for the three phases of the research: defining the scope of the manager's job; refining the definition and describing the domain of the manager's role; and validating the findings through statistical techniques.

Phase 1: Defining the Scope

The first task in the research was to develop an empirical definition of the full scope of a manager's job. To accomplish this, two types of critical incidents were collected from senior and middle managers: one that described an effective manager and one that described an ineffective manager. Content analysis of these critical incidents isolated common elements that could be considered potential indicators of managerial effectiveness.

Then a survey based on the critical incident data was developed so managers could be evaluated with respect to the elements. This survey was pilot tested to ensure that the items adequately covered the elements.

Phase 2: Describing the Manager's Role

Senior managers first identified among their direct reports those managers they considered effective and those they considered ineffective. The senior managers were instructed to base their selections solely on their own judgment of effectiveness, not on the managers' positions in the organization's hierarchy. Selection criteria were as follows:

• Effective managers were considered to be in the top 10 percent of direct reports, and in the top third of all managers known to the senior managers in terms of overall effectiveness.

• Ineffective managers were considered to be in the bottom 10 percent of direct reports, and in the bottom third of all managers known to the senior managers.

Analysis of the two groups of selected managers showed no significant differences in demographic characteristics (e.g., years of service with current organization, number of levels below CEO).

The managers selected for both groups (effective and ineffective) completed the survey that resulted from phase 1. The survey contained two sections dealing with the elements, one section dealing with importance, and one asking for a self-assessment. Analysis of the responses showed that the relative order of element importance was similar for both groups; and,

Exhibit 9.1
Decision Points for Phases 2 and 3

Decision Points	Phase 2	Phase 3
1. Who selected managers?	Senior managers selected effective and ineffective managers	Managers selected at random
2. Who determined effectiveness?	Senior managers, based upon their own judgment	Work group members, based upon their ratings on separate overall effectiveness scale
3. Who completed survey?	Managers in sample	Managers in sample plus their work group members
4. What data did survey participants provide?	Importance ratings and self-assessment completed by targeted managers	Assessment ratings completed by targeted managers themselves, as well as their work group members

while the effective managers appeared to rate themselves higher on all the elements than did the ineffective managers, self-ratings showed no significant differences between the groups.

All the survey data were subjected to factor analysis to identify the underlying themes embedded in the responses. As a result, the elements were refined into four dimensions, each with several subdimensions.

Phase 3: Validating the Results

A cross-validation study was then undertaken to see whether the dimensions could be verified through a different approach. Exhibit 9.1 summarizes the key decision points of phase 3 compared to phase 2.

Whereas the managers in phase 2 were selected by their senior managers based upon perceived effectiveness, the managers in phase 3 were selected at random from a variety of organizations with no preselection criteria. The managers themselves, as well as their work group members—subordinates, colleagues, and supervisors—completed the survey. In contrast to phase 2, in which senior managers provided the criteria for effectiveness, phase 3 had the rating sources (i.e., subordinates, colleagues, and superiors) assess the managers on their overall effectiveness using an overall effectiveness scale.

As a result of this data collection, those managers given high overall effectiveness ratings by all three rating sources (i.e., upper half of median split for each source) were defined as effective, and those given low ratings by all three sources were labeled ineffective. The data on the effective managers were also subjected to factor analysis, yielding the same four dimensions.

T-tests on the ratings for the effective and ineffective managers showed interesting results. When only the work group data were used, the effective managers received statistically significant higher dimension ratings. This was not the case when only self-ratings were examined. Here, as in the previous phase, there were no significant differences between the groups. These results suggest that intervening variables, such as ego or not having gotten accurate feedback in the past, confounded their ratings.

Finally, regression analyses were performed to determine whether overall ratings of effectiveness could be predicted by the ratings for the management dimensions. The analysis proved that overall effectiveness could indeed be predicted by ratings for dimensions from each source.

Research results concluded that effective managers can be differentiated from less effective managers on the basis of how successfully they engage in management activities clustered into four roles. These roles provide a taxonomy for examining managerial proficiency.

TAXONOMY OF MANAGERIAL ROLES

According to this classification, four primary roles comprise the job of the successful manager in today's business environment, They are the visionary, the investor, the information manager, and the influencer (see Figure 9.1). These dimensions each contain affective and cognitive components essential to management performance. Movement among the four roles is fluid—managers shift easily among them. While it is necessary for managers to be proficient in each, the importance of a particular role, or aspects within a role, are situation specific and will vary depending on the factors interacting with the manager, the job, the unit, and the organization at a given moment.

The Visionary

As a visionary, the effective manager possesses a solid understanding of the organization, its environment, its direction, and the ways in which the parts should function together as a whole to achieve overarching goals. Visionary managers interpret these understandings and use them to align unit goals with those of the greater organization; to challenge and support subordinates and other team members in fulfilling these goals by taking into account how their talents and aspirations can best add value; and to provide both leadership and motivation which help commit subordinates and other team members to goals. Key here are awareness, intuition, interpretation, vision, and communication of goals within the unit and throughout the

Figure 9.1
Managerial Taxonomy

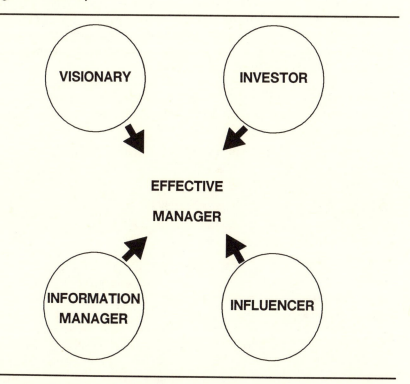

organization. These sample statements describe a manager who is effective in the visionary role:

- Understands the organization's mission and driving strategies
- Understands the general needs of the organization's client base
- Creates a vision of future directions for the unit
- Communicates unit goals to subordinates and colleagues
- Encourages subordinates to show initiative and creativity in carrying out job responsibilities
- Inspires a desire among subordinates and other team members to achieve

The Investor

As an investor, the manager identifies strategies as well as means of implementing strategies to accomplish unit goals. The manager makes conscious and thoughtful decisions about the effective and efficient use of resources, seeking the best return on the investment. In so doing, the manager examines established strategies, evaluates the resources required, considers the potential for flexibility necessitated by a changing environment, and weighs the risks and rewards. The investor monitors outcomes to keep abreast of factors which may affect these choices and searches for new solutions to problems. Managers who are successful investors could be described by these phrases:

- Calculates the amount of time and money necessary to achieve a goal
- Determines short- and long-term effects of implementing a course of action
- Seeks new solutions to problems
- Matches employees' skills and abilities to the requirements of a particular task
- Develops contingency plans for acquiring additional resources in case current resources become unavailable
- Develops plans to address changes affecting the unit

The Information Manager

The information manager seeks information on new ideas, existing conditions, and progress toward goals. The information manager establishes systems to compile and organize data from the multiple sources available through today's communication technology. Proficient information managers seek out sources which are not obvious, disseminate information appropriately, and interpret unit information for others. Essentially, the information manager makes decisions about what information to gather and from where; whether the information is accurate; how to organize and use the information; and with whom to share the information. These are examples of actions taken by the successful information manager:

- Identifies materials and individuals who can provide valuable information on new ideas
- Obtains the information needed to make decisions
- Confirms the facts and information obtained
- Organizes collected information so it is easily retrievable
- Establishes systems to monitor the unit's progress
- Informs immediate superior of issues he or she should be aware of

The Influencer

Given the increased dependency among functions in an organization, as well as the shift in norms governing the traditional manager-subordinate relationship, the influencer role is becoming more and more critical to management effectiveness. As influencers, managers foster a support network and mutually cooperative alliances within the unit and across the organization to expedite the achievement of goals. They exert influence by keeping commitments, sharing recognition, preventing or resolving conflict, championing inter-unit support, and demonstrating their ability to increase productivity. The fundamental stance for these managers is one of coach and empowerer: They know how to involve others in problem solving, build effective teams, create a climate of trust, and relinquish authority when appropriate. Typical descriptors of the successful influencer include:

• Builds alliances and mutual goals with other managers
• Involves all concerned parties when seeking solutions to problems
• Develops a climate of open communication and trust within the unit
• Gives subordinates appropriate authority to carry out their work
• Seizes opportunities to enhance the unit's performance
• Publicizes the unit's accomplishments throughout the organization

IMPLICATIONS FOR CAREER DEVELOPMENT

The critical issue surrounding these four primary roles is that their relative importance to managers in their current or future jobs is not often apparent. As previously stated, effective managers are strong in all four dimensions, however, current conditions surrounding a managerial job (such as reorganization or budget constraints) may necessitate temporary emphasis in particular areas. Managers may be successful in certain positions or on certain tasks because their strengths are aligned with the emphasis. But they may only maintain the status quo or even fail as conditions shift. A more typical situation is where a manager who excels at one job moves on to another and does not perform as well. The managers who are really effective (i.e., having strength in all four roles), or managers who are at least aware of their strengths, can move more strategically. Focus on these four roles of the effective manager can help managers improve themselves in their current positions as well as prepare them for desired career movement. For example, an understanding of the four roles can be integrated into a practical framework to guide career development. This concept can best be described by the acronym STEP: Select, Target, Evaluate, Prepare.

Select (the Position)

Managers should determine whether to concentrate on a current job or another position within or outside of the organization. If interest lies in another position, the current position should be examined as well. It is important to consider positions that are a logical extension of one's current job or level. For example, a district sales manager may select the job of regional sales director or district product manager.

The choice should be limited to one position and be as specific as possible in defining what the position is. If there are several jobs of interest, it would be necessary to repeat the next two steps for each position and to focus on the commonalities in preparing plans for further action.

Target (the Position's Critical Aspects)

Target the critical aspects of the position being explored with respect to each role. Behaviors or actions required for the job should be identified as well as the degree of importance each contributes to the overall effectiveness of the job. In deciding the level of importance, think about the job's place in the organizational hierarchy, its scope, and the current business and organizational environment surrounding it.

Evaluate (One's Strengths/Weaknesses)

Managers should evaluate their abilities in relation to the job and the required critical behaviors. This evaluation involves obtaining and examining data pertaining to one's strengths and areas for improvement.

These data may be obtained in a number of ways. The most accurate method would be to obtain feedback from a variety of sources on all the critical elements underlining the four roles. If a validated instrument or process is not available, information from performance appraisals, informal talks with colleagues or subordinates, and a subjective self-assesment of managerial strengths and weaknesses might be used. As implied in the research, managers should not base an evaluation solely on self-assessment.

Prepare (Action Plans)

Managers can now develop action plans to enhance their effectiveness in the key areas. Exhibit 9.2 provides examples of actions and techniques associated with each role that may be used in this preparation.

As managers follow the STEP process, they will use some of the key behaviors linked to the four roles. For example, they would have envisioned a new job based on their knowledge of the organization and developed a strategy to work toward attaining that position; they would have obtained information helpful to their goal and created alliances to assist in that effort. These managers now need to focus more specifically on particular techniques and behaviors and make a commitment to follow through on implementing their plans.

Knowledge and utilization of the managerial effectiveness taxonomy will also facilitate human resource professionals in carrying out some of their own roles. As coach, HR professionals can support managers in the STEP process. As trainer, they can seek or develop programs focused on increasing

Exhibit 9.2
Examples of Actions Required to Improve Proficiency in Each Role

---

Visionary

• Ask successful colleagues about their understanding of organizational goals.

• Find out how competitors, the media, and customers perceive your organization's goals.

• Review your organization's strategic plan.

Investor

• Encourage creative problem solving within your unit.

• Consider the consequences of not addressing perceived change.

• Explore mutual advantages of combining resources from diverse groups within the organization.

Information Manager

• Initiate market or client surveys where appropriate.

• Attend trade shows and conventions.

• Be aware of projects in which others in the organization are involved.

Influencer

• Participate in projects that cross departmental boundaries.

• Explain the rationale for decisions.

• Encourage brief, frequent meetings to keep everyone informed and prevent misunderstandings.

---

proficiency within each role of the effective manager. As interpreter, they can use the four primary roles when translating job requirements to analyze the relationships among jobs and individuals. As counselor, HR professionals can guide managers into appropriate career paths or advise them on what they need to do to prepare themselves in their careers.

SELECTED BIBLIOGRAPHY

The following books were chosen because they provide additional information and ideas related to the four roles of the manager. Relationships to particular roles are noted in parentheses.

Block, P. 1986. *The empowered manager*. Washington, DC: Jossey-Bass. (influencer)
Bradford, D. L., and A. R. Cohen. 1984. *Managing for excellence*. New York: John Wiley & Sons. (visionary, investor, influencer)
Fisher, R., and W. Ury, 1981. *Getting to yes*. New York: Penguin Books. (investor, information manager, influencer)
Hickman, C. R., and M. A. Silva, 1984. *Creating excellence*. New York: New American Library. (visionary, investor, influencer)

Kanter, R. 1983. *The change masters*. New York: Simon and Schuster. (visionary, investor, influencer)

Kelly, R. E. 1985. *The gold collar worker*. Reading, MA: Addison-Wesley. (visionary, investor, influencer)

Kotter, J. P. 1985. *Power and influence*. New York: Macmillan. (influencer)

Naisbitt, J., and P. Aburdene. 1985. *Reinventing the corporation*. New York: Warner Books. (visionary, information manager, influencer)

Peters, T. J., and N. Austin. 1985. *A passion for excellence*. New York: Random House. (visionary, investor, influencer)

Tichy, N. M. 1983. *Managing strategic change*. New York: John Wiley & Sons. (investor, information manager)

CHAPTER 10

BUSINESS STRATEGY, STAFFING, AND CAREER MANAGEMENT ISSUES

—— JOHN W. SLOCUM, JR., AND WILLIAM L. CRON

How well a company performs depends to a large extent on how well its strategy has been thought out and implemented. When clearly outlined, a corporation's strategy gives a unitary focus to its range of businesses and specifies a general priority and competitive posture. A poorly conceived or carelessly developed strategy often precludes a company from maintaining its competitiveness in the marketplace. Great strides have been made in recent years by focusing attention on strategic issues and in developing effective strategies. Yet even a carefully developed strategy's success is not guaranteed unless properly implemented. Many people believe that the critical need of top management in the 1990s lies not in new answers to strategic questions, but in increased attention to the implementation process.

The human resource professional plays a central role in the implementation process, thereby influencing a strategy's bottom-line results. To the extent that the human resource manager employs astute judgment, the quality of a strategy's implementation is affected by the fit between the requirements of the strategic implementation processes and the specific human resource practices adopted by the company. The purpose of this chapter is to further our understanding of the link between a firm's business strategy and its human resource practices.

To accomplish our mission, we present a general framework of how a business strategy affects the development of its human resource strategy.

The authors would like to acknowledge the comments made by Ellen Jackofsky and Randy Schuler on earlier drafts of this paper. Support for the original study was granted from the Bureau of Business Research, Edwin L. Cox School of Business, Southern Methodist University, Dallas.

We propose that different business strategies pose different adaptation problems, require different distinctive competencies, and are aligned with different competitive environments. Strategy, along with both internal and external environmental factors, influences the stream of decisions that are the domain of the human resource manager. The development of a human resource strategy is critical to the deployment of people to achieve the major goals outlined in the business strategy of the firm. To aid in the successful implementation of a company's business strategy, human resource managers must engage in practices that ensure an availability of human resources that fit the skills and requirements of the business strategy. The nature of important human resource decisions and the major personnel consequences of these decisions are inextricably interwoven into the fabric of the firm's strategy.

A FRAMEWORK FOR ANALYSIS

A major purpose of a business strategy is to align the firm with its environment. As shown in Figure 10.1, each strategy has intended consequences for how it solves its problems of adaptation, the firm's distinctive competencies, the managerial orientations of the firm's elites, and the competitive portfolio of the environment in which it operates. Along with external and internal factors, a business strategy should affect the development of the human resource strategy and various human resource practices pursued by the firm. The dotted lines indicate that there are possible linkages between these variables, but for our purposes, we shall simply consider the solid paths to career issues, and then job attitudes and performances. We believe that such a system allows us to develop insights into what impact a particular business strategy has on the career paths of its employees.

Business Strategies

There are various strategies describing how managers create and sustain a competitive advantage in their business. Each of these strategies identifies how a business may compete in its own environment with its own financial, technological, and marketing constraints. For our research, we identified two strategies that our sample of seven mature industrial-product manufacturing companies used to gain a competitive advantage in their industry. These two types—defenders and analyzers—are generic business strategies that enabled us to identify key factors in the development of the firm's human resources.[1] In Exhibit 10.1 we identify those managerial attributes and actions associated with these two strategic orientations.

Defenders carve out a niche in relatively stable markets. These firms rely heavily on an efficient technology and production system to achieve a low-cost position in their industry. They tend to be organized by functional

Figure 10.1
Organization Strategy and Its Consequences on Human Resources in Organizations

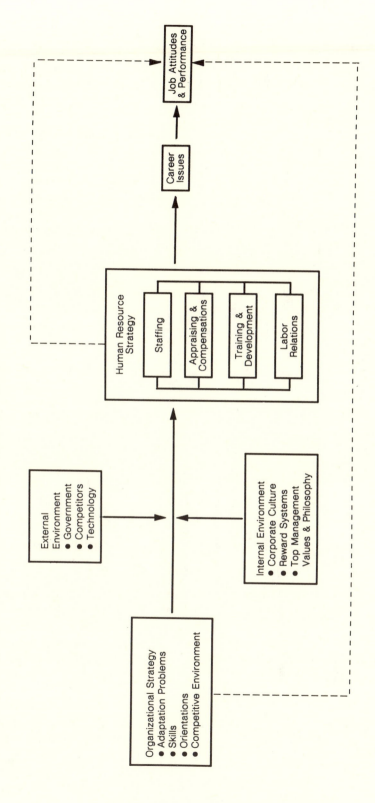

Exhibit 10.1
Summary of Important Managerial Requirements for Defenders and Analyzers

STRATEGY	ADAPTATION PROBLEMS	DISTINCTIVE COMPETENCES	ORIENTATIONS	COMPETITIVE ENVIRONMENT
DEFENDER	**Entrepreneurial** o narrow and stable product domain o competitive pricing and service o tendency to ignore outside developments o growth through market penetration of existing products o product development around existing goods or services **Engineering** o cost efficient technology o single manufacturing process o vertical integration o improvements in industrial engineering **Administrative** o centralized control o organized by function; high degree of formalization o intensive planning with cost emphasis before action is taken o conflict resolved through chain of command	Production Industrial Engineering Finance & Accounting Quality Control	Conservative Stable Single Product Product Reliability	Stars 14% Cows 36% Dogs 4% Question marks 54%

138

Exhibit 10.1 (Cont'd)

STRATEGY	ADAPTATION PROBLEMS	DISTINCTIVE COMPETENCIES	ORIENTATIONS	COMPETITIVE ENVIRONMENT	
ANALYZER					
	Entrepreneurial				
	o operates in stable and changing markets	Marketing	Competitive	Stars	20%
	o surveillance mechanisms mostly limited to marketing				
	o steady growth through market penetration and product-market development	Applied R&D	Balance between risk & stability	Cows	14%
	o imitation of successful products	Engineering		Dogs	6%
				Question marks	60%
	Engineering				
	o applied engineering	Production	Aggressive in new markets; conservative in established markets		
	o maintain efficiency in stable environment, flexibility in changing environment				
	o focus on quality control systems		Flexible		
	o complex coordination mechanisms				

Source: Adapted from R. Miles, C. Snow, A. Meyer, and H. Coleman (1978). Organizational strategy, structure, and process. _Academy of Management Review, 3,_ 3, 546–562. Also see T. Herbert, and H. Deresky (1987). Should general managers match their business strategies? _Organizational Dynamics, 15,_ 3, 40–51.

departments. Defenders dedicate few resources to basic research and development, instead choosing to focus on improving efficiency. Managers tend to have narrow specialized skills and are promoted within their specialized domain. Individuals typically enter defender organizations at low levels, receive considerable on-the-job training, have slow but steady promotions if they demonstrate performance in their functional areas, and plateau in their career at a relatively young age. Because of the emphasis on low cost and efficient production, the powerful individuals in defender firms tend to be those managers with financial, accounting, and production experiences. The effective human resource specialists in these firms are likely to allocate more of their resources to identifying and nurturing production and finance specialists than to other types.

We have borrowed from the Boston Consulting Group the portfolio planning matrix that they have found useful in establishing performance objectives for different business units. Portfolio theory suggests that there are four different kinds of businesses in the growth-share matrix and that each should be evaluated quite differently with respect to growth and profitability. The data from managers in the defender companies are presented in Exhibit 10.1. These data indicate that 40 percent of their products are in low-growth markets (dogs and cows) and only 14 percent of their products are stars. According to the Boston Consulting Group, managers of cows and dogs must be kept from undertaking expensive growth-generating activities and should encourage employees to set priorities on businesses that generate cash.

Analyzers are organizations that operate in two different types of markets. Like defenders, some areas of this organization operate in narrow, relatively unchanging product markets. Other divisions closely watch their competitors for new ideas and then move quickly to develop efficient production methods for those products that appear most financially promising. To achieve synergy, analyzers are frequently organized into matrix structures that combine both the stability of a functional organization and the innovativeness of the product organization. Employees in the new product division(s) are likely to face frequent changes in job duties and assignments as the organization's product lines are modified. Since these divisions frequently explore novel markets, it increases their need to identify individuals with a high tolerance for ambiguity and a willingness to incur risk.

Very different growth-share profiles were found in the analyzer firms. In these firms, only 20 percent of their products were in low-growth markets (cows and dogs); 80 percent of their products were in markets that they considered highly attractive for potential growth. Sixty percent of their products were operating in markets for which expensive advertising, promotional campaigns, and new production facilities might be needed to enhance growth, as opposed to profitability. These markets require entrepreneurial managers capable of creating new products and developing new markets.

Business Strategy and Human Resource Practices

According to our framework in Figure 10.1, the strategy developed by the human resource manager should be consistent with the business strategy being pursued by the firm. While it is beyond the scope of this chapter to comprehensively consider all aspects of human resource management, we believe that key selection, appraisal, promotion, and recruitment practices are likely to be implemented for different business strategies. According to human resource experts, these practices can be related to the generic business strategies of defenders and analyzers.

As shown in Exhibit 10.2, in those companies that have achieved a competitive advantage, key executives in defender companies tend to have functional backgrounds in finance and production. Therefore, they are more likely to identify and develop production and financial specialists than managers from other functional specialities. Because these firms compete on the basis of being low-cost producers and operate in markets with low-growth potential, employees are not likely to face major changes in their jobs. This enables these firms to engage in extensive on-the-job training. The stability of the production process in the defender firms affords them the time to invest in skill building and succession planning programs to internally generate a list of available candidates. Promotions are from within a department, as opposed to across departmental lines, and are slow. Explicit selection criteria and routine methods for assessing performance are employed, such as the Hay system. Since these firms typically hire into lower-level positions and then heavily promote from within, defenders typically use future-oriented screening devices, such as assessment centers and aptitude tests.

Analyzers are likely to engage in different human resource practices. Key executives are likely to have backgrounds in marketing, engineering, and production. Because of the need to introduce new products into growth markets (question marks and stars), and maintain their share in ones in which they have a major commitment (cows), analyzer organizations tend to exhibit two types of staffing patterns: some individuals are hired at entry levels and move into positions of higher responsibility within a function, while others are brought in from the outside to provide immediately needed expertise. Since analyzers are constantly seeking opportunities to develop new products or lines of services, recruiting from different sources is functional. Candidates from within, as well as candidates from other divisions or product lines, are recruited. Because parts of the organization are changing, analyzer firms are more likely to have line managers (as opposed to

Exhibit 10.2
Summary of Staffing Practices for Defenders and Analyzers*

STAFFING PRACTICE	DEFENDER	ANALYZER
Backgrounds of key executives	Finance, production	Marketing, production, engineering
Training & development	o entry level positions o slow rates of upward mobility o past achievements o narrow range of specialized skills	o middle & upper levels o moderate rates of mobility across products o focus on knowledge, skills & abilities that demonstrate achievement across departments o general abilities to adjust to changes
Appraisal standards	o clearly stated levels of quantifiable performance with clear accountability	o less formalized and quantifiable appraisal criteria
Recruitment tactics	o internal generation of candidates	o both internal and external generation of candidates
Job descriptions	o convey information about job descriptions that are well-defined, stressing the need to meet cost standards	o convey information about both job dynamism & stability o stress applied risk-taking

* Adapted from Olian, J. and Rynes, S. (1984). Organizational Staffing: Integrating practice with strategy. Industrial Relations, 23 (2), 170-183.

human resource staff people) conduct job interviews because they are better able to stay abreast of the changing requirements and nature of the jobs to be filled.

Business Strategy and Career Paths

As we have pointed out, the strategy of the firm has an enormous power over the practices of human resource managers. In this section, we will examine empirical evidence of how strategy impacts the career paths and attitudes of employees.

To understand this link, we interviewed managers and employees in seven companies and asked these people to complete an extensive questionnaire. This questionnaire measured employees' attitudes on a variety of issues, such as job satisfaction, job attitudes, career aspirations, and their relationship to their immediate supervisor. Data were also collected concerning job histories and job performance.

The data in Exhibit 10.3 focus on differences between employees in defender and analyzer firms with respect to salient career issues. Note that the job histories of employees in both types of companies were quite similar. While employees in the analyzer firms had slightly less job tenure than did those in the defender firms and had made fewer job moves, the differences are not striking.

Plateauing is an issue that is close to the emotional fabric of all employees. People can be very upset when they're plateaued, because it brings into question how good they really are and how they will spend the rest of their lives in a corporation. While there are many definitions of plateauing, we use the term to denote that the person's probability of further upward movement in the organization's hierarchy is quite low. This type of plateauing is frequently caused by an organization's hierarchy. All of us know that as we climb up the organization's hierarchy, the number of positions decreases rather dramatically, and the opportunities to move upward decrease proportionally. The fact is that everyone plateaus. The only difference among employees is when and how they handle it. Thus, plateauing is a generic phenomenon, but it becomes complicated when organizations and individuals find their values challenged by its occurrence.

Researchers have developed a model to understand the plateauing phenomenon using two basic concepts: perceived likelihood of future promotions and current performance. Using these two concepts, they suggest four categories of plateauing. The stars are employees who are doing outstanding work, have been promoted in the past, and are seen by management as having high potential for future advancement in the company. The comers are individuals who have been identified by management as having high potential for advancement, but who are currently performing below their potential. Solid citizens are individuals who are performing satisfactorily,

Exhibit 10.3
Career Issues for Employees Working in Defender and Analyzer Companies

CAREER ISSUES	DEFENDERS	ANALYZERS
JOB HISTORY		
o Average job tenure (months)	50.3	44.3
o Number of job moves	4.7	3.9
o Number of company moves	3.5	3.9
Plateauing Stage		
o Stars	15%	23%
o Comers	19%	50%
o Solid Citizens	31%	18%
o Deadwood	35%	9%
Career Attitudes		
o Marketability to other companies	Average	Average
o Propensity to leave current firm	Low	Moderate
o Willing to relocate for another job in the company	Most willing	Not high priority
o Desire to get promoted	Want to get promoted	Not really
o Timing of promotion	Immediate future	Long time away

Source: These data were compiled from the following: J. Slocum, Wm. Cron, R. Hansen, and S. Rawlings (1985). Business strategy and the management of plateaued employees. *Academy of Management Journal*, *28*, 1, 133–54; Wm. Cron, and J. Slocum (1986). The influences of career stages on salespeople's job attitudes, work perceptions and performance. *Journal of Marketing Research*, *23* (May), 119–26; Wm. Cron, and J. Slocum, (1986). Career-stages approach to managing the sales force. *Journal of Consumer Marketing*, *4*, 11–20; and J. Slocum, Wm. Cron, and L. Yows (1987). Whose Career Is Likely to Plateau? *Business Horizons* (March-April), 31–38.

but who are plateaued. Finally, deadwood are individuals who have limited possibilities for promotion and who are performing below expected levels.

The data in Exhibit 10.3 indicate significant differences between defenders and analyzers in terms of the mixture of employees at various stages of the career plateauing process. Sixty-six percent of the employees in the defender companies were plateaued in comparison to only 27 percent in the analyzer firms. In our conversations with plateaued employees, many of them indicated that they know their jobs too well. There's not enough to learn. They have become experts in their work and are likely to feel profoundly bored. Since there are limited opportunities for upward mobility in defender companies because they are not adding new products or expanding into new businesses, there is an absence of challenge. The lack of numerous plateaued employees in the analyzer companies is because the company is expanding into new markets with new products. There is intense competition among companies to establish their products in the marketplace and gain market share from their competition. There's always something new to learn, new markets to expand into, and other skills to master.

Employees of both companies believed that they could rather easily move to other firms, but the impetus to leave was more pronounced in the analyzer companies than in the defender companies. Employees in the defender firms are less likely to leave their current employer and more willing to geographically relocate for another job in the company than are employees in the analyzer firms. One might conjecture that because of the relatively stable work environment, opportunities for upward mobility are severely limited in defender companies. Thus, relocation can supply the momentum that is needed for employees to be opportunistic about their future with the company. Relocation can create more possibilities for good things to happen and for employees to learn new skills. The lack of movement leaves people with the task of creating their own sense of what they want to do with their lives.

In an analyzer firm, the dynamic nature of the competitive environment may provide greater opportunity to learn new skills and to be promoted without requiring a relocation. Not surprising, employees in defender companies have a stronger desire to be promoted and want to be promoted faster than employees in the analyzer companies. Plateaued employees are usually conscious that they are probably losing the respect of their peers. This adds to the stress of plateauing and increases the probability of despair. As the possibilities for promotion narrow, the opportunity to move to a new location is seen by many as a vehicle to fill the gap between their aspirations and their past attainments in the company. It's their opportunity to break the plateauing trap. For employees in our analyzer firms, it's not competition between employees for promotions that is a key, but it is the pressure to create new products and expand into new markets that counts.

Job Attitudes and Business Strategy

We have found that a firm's business strategy has consequences not only for staffing practices, but for career paths for employees. In the final section of this paper, we explore the attitudes and job performances of employees working in firms with different strategies.

The data in Exhibit 10.4 indicate that employees who are working for defender firms describe their jobs as providing them with less challenge and are less involved with their work than employees working for analyzer firms. Most of us need to feel the challenge of having something unfamiliar in the task and the satisfaction that we are learning something new. Mastering something that you don't know is engrossing. People usually find the process of learning and achieving more fulfilling than the knowledge that they achieve. Motivated to become an expert in what we do, the paradox is that we are psychologically most at risk when we are expert because that is when we are most likely to become bored and discontented. When we become experts, the challenge is gone. When the job itself does not provide enough challenge and/or involvement, employees become less satisfied with their work. Without deriving much intrinsic satisfaction from their work, and with their upward mobility generally limited by the organization's attempt to run a cost-effective system, employees' ability to influence the system wanes. This is communicated by the fact that senior managers no longer seek their opinion, no longer assign them to special projects, no longer try to have lunch with them, and the like (see data in Exhibit 10.4).

Although it is easy to understand why employees in defender companies tend to have poor job attitudes and express concern over their lack of influence and visibility to senior managers, understanding the role of their immediate manager is more complex. Managers in defender organizations typically rated their employees as more effective performers than did managers in analyzer firms.

There are three possible reasons for this. First, since employees in defender firms have longer job tenure and are more likely to be solid citizens and deadwood, they have mastered their job. Some might argue that these people are content to be plateaued. These people can do their job extremely well without dedicating enormous amounts of psychological energy. Because the organization's metaphor is efficiency, these employees have learned to do their job efficiently and, therefore, are highly valued by their managers. Second, the manager knows that the person's mobility is limited and thus attempts to create a situation whereby a harmonious relationship can be maintained. One way to sustain their relationship is to avoid giving the person a low performance appraisal rating. We have found that employees who were categorized as either solid citizens or deadwood were given performance appraisals that were skewed to the positive. They receive consistent checkmarks in the second-best category—the category that says a

Exhibit 10.4
Job Attitudes and Job Performance of Employees in Defender and Analyzer Companies

JOB ATTITUDES	DEFENDER	ANALYZER
Job Involvement	Low	High
Psychological Success	Average	Average
Job Challenge	Low	High
Satisfaction with work itself	Low	High
Satisfaction with Immediate Supervisor	Average	Average
Satisfaction with pay	Average	Average
Satisfaction with co-workers	Low	High
Opportuniites to participate in decisions that affect my work	Low	High
Pressure to achieve goals and objectives set by company	Low	High
Visibility and influence to senior managers	Low	High
Job Performance, as Evaluated by Immediate Supervisor	Positive	Negative

person is an above-average performer but not quite exceptional. When appraisals are inflated, the manager can then assign the blame for the person's lack of mobility to senior managers. Finally, we have found that managers who recently experienced a medium career transition themselves—a change in job or functional area, and received a promotion—were more likely to give subordinates higher performance appraisal ratings than were those managers who had experienced no career transitions themselves. The career transition state of one's boss, therefore, is a salient factor affecting how bosses rate subordinates reporting to them.

Employees in analyzer companies reported a different attitudinal profile. These people are highly involved with their work, describe their jobs as challenging, and get along well with their fellow workers. It is appropriate for them to be involved in decisions facing the firm because the firm is constantly looking for new avenues to gain a competitive edge in the marketplace. Making presentations to top management is not unusual nor is their assignment to strategic task forces. Morale is high because employees are challenged by the job. Their immediate supervisor may feel free to give more honest appraisals because employees know that promotions and advancements are still possibilities. As shown in Exhibit 10.3, 73 percent of employees in our analyzer sample were rated as people likely to get promoted.

The reasons for these employees' lower performance appraisals, in comparison with those employees in the defender firms, may be explained by the competitiveness of the environment and the large number of employees in the comer plateauing stage. As depicted in Exhibit 10.1, 60 percent of the analyzer firm's products have a low market share, but high-growth potential (question marks). The performance objectives for employees facing this competitive environment are to undertake expensive projects in advertising and promotional campaigns that have the immediate effect of consuming cash and thus resulting in lower profitability. If profitability goals are set, usually they are quite low in order to encourage growth-promoting activities. Therefore, the current performance of employees is likely to be low, with the expectation of high performance sometime in the near future. The employees are cognizant of this situation. The data in Exhibit 10.3 show that 50 percent of the employees have been rated as comers by their boss.

Human Resource Management Strategies

Our results suggest that more effective human resource strategies are needed for organizations who choose to gain a competitive advantage by adopting defender business strategies. The more negative and/or passive attitudes of people in these organizations appear to be closely linked to the early occurrence of plateauing in their career and job. Forecasts of slower economic growth among developed countries suggest that more and more companies will employ defender-type strategies in the future.

One particularly intriguing strategy suggested by human resource experts is to deemphasize the importance of promotion within an organization's corporate culture. This requires that an organization admit to its employees that the big rewards of promotion and compensation are available to only a select few and for a limited period of time. Organizations and managers have been reluctant to admit this because they are afraid that people will lose their motivation to work hard if they know the truth. Avoidance of these issues in defender firms results in the majority of its employees feeling punished and disappointed because the firm cannot provide rewards that are implicitly promised.

How can promotion be deemphasized as the ultimate reward for good performance? Experts have suggested several strategies that an organization can adopt to change this fundamental element of their corporation's culture. One tactic is to widen the criteria of success so that plateaued employees can feel that they are winners. This may be accomplished in concert with another current trend in business which is to reduce the number of hierarchical levels in the organization. This may help to reduce the content plateauing that is likely to occur with lengthy tenure at the same level in the organization. Second, significant rewards should be given for meeting a challenge and mastering it. This requires that people have the opportunity to do increasingly independent and challenging work. It also means that rewards such as increased autonomy, money, publicity, and recognition have to be given independent of promotion. A third strategy is to expand the number of people involved in decision-making groups, especially those responsible for doing in-depth studies.

One study found that the return on financial investment of firms using this practice was nearly twice that of those firms using traditional authoritative structures. Obviously these changes must be initiated with support at the executive level. The top executive must assume a leadership role in this effort to uproot the ingrained element of most corporate cultures: promotion being the ultimate and most important symbol of success.

CONCLUSIONS

The strategy adopted by a firm to gain a competitive advantage in the marketplace has important implications for the human resource professional. We developed a framework for describing two, among the many, strategies that companies have used to gain this competitive advantage: analyzer and defender. The analyzer strategy poses adaptation problems that are different from those of the defender. How these adaptation problems are resolved depends on the distinctive competencies of the firm, the managerial competencies of top management, and the nature of the firm's competitive environment.

The business strategy of the firm has an important impact on the strategy developed by the human resource professional. Since each strategy is implemented differently, the human resource manager must fit his or her human resource strategy with the overall strategy adopted by the firm. When one considers the human resource practices typically found in a firm, the human resource professional should align these with those of top management. For example, human resource professionals in a defender company typically face staffing decisions different from those found in an analyzer firm. Because these practices vary, they have important consequences for employees' career paths, job attitudes, and job performances. We found that employees in defender firms are more likely to be plateaued by the firms than are those employees in an analyzer firm. Similarly, because of these differences, managers face employees who have different career goals and aspirations.

NOTE

1. A third strategy in the Miles and Snow typology is prospectors. Among other characteristics, these firms focus entirely on high-growth market opportunities sacrificing short-term profits for superior growth performance. Because of the natural evolution of markets and organizations, few firms embrace a pure prospector strategy, and none was found in our study.

SELECTED BIBLIOGRAPHY

Several articles have been cited in the text that aided us in drawing useful conclusions about the relationships between business strategy and the role of the human resource manager. To this list, we add Jeff Kerr and John Slocum, "Managing corporate cultures through reward systems," *Academy of Management Executive*, May 1987; Charles Fombrun, Noel Tichy, and Mary Anne DeVanna, *Strategic human resources management* (New York: The Free Press, 1985); Randy Schuler and Ian MacMillan, "Gaining the competitive advantage through human resource practices," *Human Resource Management*, 1984, 23, 241–55; and Randy Schuler, "Personnel and human resource management choices and corporate strategy," in Randy Schuler and Stewart Youngblood (eds.), *Readings in personnel and human resource management* (3rd ed.), St. Paul, MN: West, 1987.

A number of books have been written lately that focus on career issues and their management. Judith Bardwick, *The plateauing trap* (New York: AMACOM, 1987); Jeffrey Greenhaus, *Career management* (Chicago: Dryden Press, 1987); Duane Brown, Linda Brooks, and associates, *Career choice and development* (San Francisco: Jossey-Bass, 1984); Douglas T. Hall and associates, *Career development in organizations* (San Francisco: Jossey-Bass, 1986); and Kathy Kram, *Mentoring at work: Developmental relationships in organizational life* (Glenview, IL: Scott, Foresman & Co., 1985). A book written by two medical doctors that focuses on the management of one's career is Barrier Greiff and Preston Munter, *Tradeoffs: executive, family, and organizational life* (New York: Mentor Books, 1980).

Part III

Career Development Tools, Techniques, and Programs

This section shows how training methods and other resources contribute to self-understanding and long-term career development. The section highlights these themes by describing self-assessment programs, assessment centers for development, a career workshop for high-potential managers, simulations for assessment and development, and a way to train managers to be better developers of their subordinates.

Cynthia Smith states that self-assessment is the first step in effective career planning. Her chapter describes methods for self-assessment such as values, interests, skills, feelings, personal resources (physical and emotional health and support from friends and family), and styles of decision making and initiating change. An example of a self-assessment method shows how self-assessment can be integrated with other information to form a career direction and plan.

Virginia Boehm outlines a process for designing assessment centers that provides information about individual needs development, as opposed to the traditional purpose for assessment centers for selection and evaluation of potential for advancement. An assessment center collects data about a person using several methods such as behavioral exercises (for example, group discussions and in-baskets), interviews, personality tests, and ability tests. Observers integrate the information by making judgments of the individual's managerial skills. Traditional assessment centers are designed to determine a person's suitability for a specific target job or level. Developmental assessment centers must be broader because they need to direct people toward jobs that are right for them and suggests areas for development to obtain job and career goals.

The results from a traditional assessment center are provided to higher management to make decisions about individuals. The results from a developmental assessment center must be in more detail and usable by the assessees. They receive information about their skills and abilities and also developmental recommendations, with feedback and the assessment results serving as a bridge between assessment and career development plans and actions. Steps for designing a developmental/career planning program are determining the goals of the program, analyzing the kinds of tasks and activities employees perform in a cluster of jobs and in job levels, determining the skills and abilities required to perform these tasks, selecting or developing exercises that allow opportunity to evaluate the relevant skills and abilities, and developing training and administrative procedures for assessors.

Peter Cairo and Karen Lyness describe a follow-up program to an assessment center. They show how the assessment center components relate to career planning and how the post-assessment development program they designed draws on the assessment center results to facilitate exploration of career goals and plans. The assessment center was intended to be an opportunity for high-potential managers to learn about themselves in ways that might influence their careers. The post-assessment program helps them work with the results of the assessment center. The cornerstone of the post-assessment development program is an organizational simulation. Other elements of the program are lectures, exercises, and discussions aimed at providing a voluntary, nonevaluative learning experience.

The program is organized around small discussion groups co-lead by staff psychologists with whom the participants work during the assessment process. Topics for discussion include the extent to which current work situations are satisfying and the implications of the assessment center results for development. Information about career development opportunities is presented by executives who are in a position to understand the direction of the business and the implications of that direction for career opportunities. Another part of the program focuses on how the participants can help their subordinates manage their careers, for instance, by role playing career development discussions with their subordinates. Finally, the small groups are given time to develop a strategy for monitoring career plans that makes sense for all members of the group. This usually includes continued networking among the participants and ongoing feedback to each other.

Stephen Stumpf's chapter describes the advantages of business simulations for skill diagnosis and development. Business simulations concentrate on realistic experiences that ordinarily take years to diagnose and learn on the job and compress them into a few days. Business simulations re-create a corporate entity. Participants assume roles as managers of the organization faced with varying business problems. Stumpf covers large-scale behavioral simulations and computer-based organizational simulations. A large-scale behavioral simulation is an intensive, interactive experience involving many different roles in the organization. Such simulations highlight the interpersonal dynamics which occur among participants and offer a controlled setting for analyzing patterns of behavior. After several groups from one organization go through the same simulation, it is possible to analyze the organization's culture, managerial strengths, and training needs. When people from different corporations go through a simulation together, individuals receive feedback about their own behavior in the different situations arising during the simulation.

Computer-based simulations focus on the individual's formulating a strategy through analyzing financial and accounting information, then making specific decisions that are put into the computer model of the business. Such simulations can be done individually or in teams. In general, business simulations are valuable tools when they are compatible with the organization's learning goals. Similar to assessment centers, they can be a diagnostic tool and part of a development program as a source of learning. They may also generate a sense of corporate identity as managers from the same organization who participated in the simulation share ideas in a nonthreatening environment.

In the final chapter of this section, Edward Mone outlines a workshop to help managers understand their role as developers of subordinates. This role is often ignored or not given enough emphasis because managers have other demands placed on their time. They are often measured and rewarded for achieving various financial and production goals, not for how well they develop their subordinates. Yet developing people is essential if they are to continue their contribution to the business today and in the future. Some organizations are recognizing this by encouraging excellence in people management and rewarding subordinates financially for developing subordinates.

The workshop focuses on why the role of developer is so important to good management. Participants discuss who is developed and in what ways—that is, the meaning of development for different types of subordinates (mid-career plateaued managers, young fast-trackers, supervisors newly promoted from occupational ranks, and so on). The workshop then explores the when, where, and how of career development. Participants also consider their own situations—the barriers to motivation for their spending time developing their subordinates and their confidence to be developers. The participants identify resources that support career development (for example, assessment centers to evaluate subordinates' strengths and weaknesses and staffing mechanisms to help move people into different positions). Finally, the participants set goals and plans for developing members of their work groups.

CHAPTER 11 _____

DESIGNING AND FACILITATING A SELF-ASSESSMENT EXPERIENCE

_____ CYNTHIA B. SMITH

"If you don't know what direction to take, you haven't acknowledged where you are" (Anthony 1983). A cliché? Perhaps it is, but one that suggests the key goal of any self-assessment effort—to facilitate an individual's self-knowledge and maximize the chances of making a satisfying career decision. Self-assessment is the first of several steps in effective career planning; occupational and organizational information, goal setting, and implementation complete the process. The self-assessment portion of career planning addresses the question, "Who am I?" in work and not only focuses on self-perceptions but also includes perceptions of others.

The tools and techniques used in self-assessment run the gamut from the simple to the probing. At a minimum they include exercises designed to help individuals identify and articulate values, interests, and skills. More comprehensive self-assessment builds on those three basic components by integrating such factors as feelings, developmental changes, personal resources, timing, situational impact, decision making and change styles, and investment in education, training, and work experience. At AT&T, our corporate and departmental self-assessment experiences have taught us that it pays to take a comprehensive route to facilitating self-knowledge because self-assessment shortcuts contribute to the high costs of unrealized human potential. The company's investment in self-assessment is more than realized when the right people are doing the right job in a way that is right for them.

It is generally acknowledged that a career choice reflects "the implementation of a person's self-concept" (Super 1951). That is, people have some ideas or images of their work personalities and aptitudes in their minds. These ideas are based on perceptions of particular instances or environments from the past. Typically, individuals go a step further and also form an impression of whom they are as seen by others and how they compare. There are big differences to be found in people's awareness of and ability to articulate their self-concepts. Consequently, it becomes the role of a self-assessment facilitator to help clients develop and accept an integrated, adequate picture of themselves in work, to test those images against reality, and to generate ideas or resources for identifying satisfying and beneficial work functions.

Developing a career direction is a deliberate, methodical process during which individuals frequently report feeling as if they are solving a complex personal puzzle. All the necessary puzzle pieces of self-knowledge are present within them, but in the beginning those pieces may seem scattered or unfocused. Self-assessment materials provide the process by combining essential pieces that lead to an integrated whole that is actually greater than the sum of its parts. Although it is rare to find a participant who does not enjoy the self-assessment process, it is important to note that self-assessment may not be for everyone. For example, some may have an abundance of self-awareness and need only skill acquisition or job enrichment resources. Others, for various reasons, simply may not be ready for an in-depth look at self.

On the surface it may appear to be a simple matter to design quality self-assessment questions, checklists, and such that will allow individuals to "see themselves" on a sheet of paper or in a fancy summary booklet and then to follow through with appropriate actions. As a word of warning, however, the age-old concept of that being "only the tip of the iceberg" applies here. The fundamental determinants of the ultimate success of a person's career exploration are found in the following issues (Pedersen and Smith 1986): Self-esteem—"Do I care deeply enough about myself to be successful and take positive steps?" and Developmental Maturity—"Have I sufficiently resolved what life has dealt me to take on new growth producing challenges and opportunities?" Assuming the best, the self-assessment components described here are for those who are able to take constructive steps toward career development.

With a step-by-step approach in mind, the remainder of this chapter will be a presentation of specific self-assessment pieces. These pieces reflect those typically used in AT&T's self-assessment workshops and self-paced materials. Also included are methods used in integrating those pieces into a career direction or plan. The importance of self-assessment to an effective human resource system will conclude the chapter. It was not intended that this discussion contain an exhaustive list of all possible self-knowledge components. Instead, it was meant to provide a framework to which pieces can be added or subtracted, depending upon the specific needs of the person or the organization. Also, for the most part, the following self-knowledge steps can be facilitated either in workshops, in individual counseling sessions, or in self-paced materials.

SELF-ASSESSMENT COMPONENTS

Setting the Stage

In this introductory portion, the purpose is to get the person on board with the process. To achieve this purpose, steps in career planning can first be presented, followed by a definition of self-assessment and how its components fit with the agenda. The facilitator's credentials and career planning experience may be mentioned in this beginning phase. If appropriate, the career development philosophies and career management practices of the organization can also be stated.

Following the sharing of information and agenda, the individual can be asked to share reasons for seeking a structured self-assessment experience. This "Why are you here?" question, plus many other possible getting-on-board questions or sentence completions, can be managed in a variety of ways depending upon the setting and group size. These responses provide helpful information to the facilitator and can be the first personal step into the process for the person.

It is important to establish that career planning and self-assessment are processes and that knowledge of the steps enhances a person's chances of career success. However, there are other processes that individuals need to be aware of as the stage is being set for further self-knowledge. A process that greatly impacts people is that of human development, especially adult development. The following overview of the ages and stages of adulthood can prove quite helpful as a preliminary learning. Theoretically, the career needs of a twenty-year-old adult who looks for mentoring and support are different from those of a person thirty to thirty-five who is striving for upward mobility and feeling the conflicting needs for both stability and freedom. Later, mid-life issues that come into play from thirty-five to forty-five reflect a new-found awareness that time will someday run out and that one has one last chance to "make it." At this same time there emerges a desire to help, nurture, and teach others. After age forty-five there follows a settling down, mellowing career phase when work goals are secondary to enjoyment of life.

Throughout any review of self, but particularly at this point, it will be apparent that change is one of life's few certainties. All individuals and all organizations are constantly changing or evolving. It follows, then, that an overview of societal and/or organizational change can follow the adult development piece and be linked to the changing needs and roles of the person.

In the AT&T Operator Services' "Career Planning with Managers" workshop, these stage pieces are all included and are then pulled together by having the individual construct a career history, a lifeline, complete with job history and career-impacting events and decisions. The facilitator then reflects how societal and organizational events have affected individual careers. Other highly effective techniques are found in the recommended reading at the conclusion of the chapter.

Values

"Work without value is mere labor, and work with value justifies any burden you may have to shoulder or effort you may have to put forth" (Figler 1979). The single most important source of career expression and satisfaction is found in values. Values are usually seen in behavior and reveal what is important to the individual and central to the self-concept. They are the rewards derived from the largest, or even the smallest, life experience in which great effort and energy were expended.

As a values clarification example, an individual who examines past successes and finds the reward of self-expression—or worth—in "influencing the behavior of others" has that example as a value that needs to be achieved. If it is achieved, the person reports satisfaction; if it is not, the person reports dissatisfaction, frustration, or even depression. Prior to a self-assessment experience, that same individual may not yet have clearly identified that influencing others was the reward so strenuously sought in a particular past endeavor. In addition to examining past efforts, much can also be learned from the future. That is, daydreams and career fantasies also hold important clues to work satisfaction.

Checklists and satisfying job or leisure discussions can shed light on what is important if followed by a deliberate, long-term awareness of past and future satisfying activities and dreams. A few sample items that may appear on the numerous values clarification checklists include the following (Comprehensive lists appear in the recommended books.):

• Money/Financial Security/Material Gain
• Helping People/Social Contribution
• Power Over Self/Self-Improvement
• Security/Stability/Predictability
• Mental Challenge/Mental Stimulation

These checklists usually can be grouped according to the nature of rewards realized. For instance, sometimes the reward received is not the direct result of the effort like the influencing people example demonstrated. The value may be in a condition gained such as a large paycheck or time off. No matter how the listings are presented, enlightenment on basic personal motives for working hard and expressing self can result in a richly satisfying worklife for the person.

Interests

Interests are identified through the things people enjoy doing. Interest assessment plays a large role in self-understanding and can increase the chances of individuals' enjoying and being successful with career and lifestyle decisions. The ideal, of course, is to directly transfer a strong interest into a career, such as the landscape architect whose career beginnings are found in the love for gardening. For most people this transference won't be so obvious, and they will need help analyzing what they are actually doing— what needs are being met—when they are pursuing interests. Those needs and activities can yield significant career/work clues.

Interest assessment can be done simply by asking individuals to list those things they enjoy doing in work or play. Lists also need to be made of what enjoyable things would be done if more spare time were available. However, interest assessment is much more than making lists. As was mentioned, each item on a list needs to be treated as a clue to broader patterns. For example, a person who spends his or her spare time reading detective novels and building intricate model ships is not likely to earn a living doing those same things. In analyzing those two leisure activities, though, it may be that the actual enjoyment comes from having to imagine how all the factors or pieces affect each other and come together in a logical way—much the same skill pattern, for instance, that a financial counselor or adviser uses!

Possibly the best-known career theorist who has worked in the area of interest measurement is John Holland, author of *Making Vocational Choices: A Theory of Vocational Personalities and Work Environments* (1985). The basic idea of this theory is that when people are young they try and like certain activities, and some of those activities become interests. Later those interests lead them to have certain groups of competencies which, in turn, produce a particular personal disposition that makes them think, feel, and behave in distinct ways. Thus Holland is saying that from interests comes personality.

"A particular disposition develops because different people have different biological capacities and life histories. The developmental outcomes of these interactions are characterized as personality types and tend to become well defined between 18 and 30" (Holland 1985, p. 11). In fact, Holland says there are six different personality types—realistic, investigative, artistic, social, enterprising, and conventional—which he describes in great detail in his research. Holland also says there are six distinct types of work environments called by the same names. The idea is to match the personality to the work environment so that a realistic person is working in a realistic work environment. Many of the recommended books at the end of the chapter include explanations and exercises based on Holland's interest typology. These tools help individuals to know their choice is right for them and to know that they have not overlooked other careers or jobs that might also be desirable.

Skills

Everyone has hundreds of skills, but few people can articulate many of them. There is a certain vagueness inherent in skill identification—that is, great things get accomplished without an awareness of how. Skill assessment is examining *how* things get done. The key to skills assessment is defining and labeling, one-by-one, each behavior/quality/knowledge that it took to achieve a particular result.

Sidney Fine (1967) proposed the following customarily used, practical method of assessing skills. Understandably, there hardly exists a career planning book or facilitator that does not apply Fine's concepts in skills identification. Especially creative applications were done by Richard Bolles in *What Color Is Your Parachute?* (1987).

According to Fine's theory and Bolles's explanations, people have three types of skills:

1. Functional/Transferable
   - tells the functions performed
   - are transferable from one job to another
   - are usually action verbs followed by direct objects
   - are rooted in aptitudes
   - are acquired as a natural-born talent and refined by experience or are acquired by deliberate, specific training
   - might be used to answer such job interview questions as:

     "Why should I hire you?"

     "Why are you the right person for this job?"

     "What do you bring to this job?"

     Examples: assisting customers, reporting results, compiling information, entering data

2. Adaptive/Self-Management
   - tells how people accept and adjust to the conditions of work (i.e., how they manage themselves at work)
   - describes work qualities or work styles
   - are usually adjectives
   - are rooted in temperament
   - are acquired in early years—from family, friends, schoolmates, teachers, and others—or later in life from hard, personal work or re-education

- might be used to answer such job interview questions as:

"What are you like as a worker?"

"What is your personal work style?"

Examples: friendly, punctual, dedicated, efficient, loyal, accurate, precise

3. Specific Content
   - indicates specific information/knowledge acquired and "stored" in the brain
   - are usually nouns
   - are rooted in experience and personal preference
   - are acquired through work, school, training, reading, or apprenticeships
   - might be used to answer such job interview questions as:

   "What are you knowledgeable in?"

   "What systems/equipment/programs do you know how to work with?"

   Examples: knowledge of a computer language, bookkeeping, car repair, psychology, cooking, football

The way to enhanced skills awareness can be found in the following truth: "Man, unlike any other organic or inorganic in the universe, grows beyond his work, walks up the stairs of his concepts, emerges ahead of his accomplishments" (John Ernst Steinbeck, *The Grapes of Wrath*, 1939). In skills assessment the aim is to get "man" to look back at those accomplishments, at least long enough to identify the skills used to complete them. Methods for examining accomplishments include having individuals write down things that they look back on and feel pleased about, along with writing detailed step-by-step descriptions of what they actually did from beginning to end. Skills checklists (many of which appear in the recommended books list) assist in this process and are reported by most people to be much valued tools in career planning.

The discussion of values, interests, and skills completes the basic components of self-assessment. Even though self-knowledge is greatly enhanced by a thorough awareness of just these three components, numerous additional factors are also present. Some of the typical ones are briefly described next.

Feelings

There exists a common belief in this culture that good decisions are made by logic alone, that emotions impair good judgment. Yet, over and over such statements are made as, "I thought about it for a long time and finally decided to do what I *felt* like doing rather than what I really knew was right." These statements are in line with what the experts teach regarding balance in decision making. That is, logic is very important but mirrors only half of the self; feelings must be considered equally.

Discovering feelings about work activity is an essential part of self-assessment. Not surprising, feelings are usually a manifestation of values. It follows that one way of beginning strong feeling awareness can be with the values clarification checklists previously discussed. Ask people to narrow their values to five or six of the most important to them. Then, ask them to try trading off particular ones. This can be done in small groups, or perhaps even in large groups using an auction format. Feelings about giving up or fighting for particular values can be quite revealing as the individual discovers what constitutes the bottom line of happiness in work.

Personal Resources

The road to self-awareness will be a smoother one if individuals use their resources wisely. Personal resources are said to include such things as physical and emotional health, support available from family and friends, the renewal gained from the thoughtful use of leisure time, and assistance obtainable through various community and professional sources. The task in self-assessment is to facilitate people's awareness of personal resources and to maximize the use of what they have available.

Creative exercises and experiences can be designed with the goal of first enumerating and then evaluating the nature and extent of the resource, plus what must be done to obtain it. Taking just one of the resources mentioned before, "support available from family and friends," individuals can begin by listing (or talking through) the names of five or six people who are important to them, along with how each person best demonstrates support. Next, the individual must report what is actually needed from each and, then, how to go about asking for what is needed. Much the same process can be applied to the other personal resources.

Timing

Another important piece of self-knowledge is how time affects the person. There is a saying in the career planning field that "luck is the crossroads where preparation and opportunity meet." So often those who seek self-assessment feel that others have had all the luck and that great opportunities have passed them by. It can be emphasized that those situations can occur when there is a lack of self-knowledge leading to an inability to act upon opportunities. Timing and luck obviously do play a role in career success, but usually do not have as major a role as some would like to believe. Preparation through deliberate self-assessment and knowledge of the ways people enter specific careers or jobs will greatly reduce the portion left up to luck.

Also on the subject of timing is the significant work done by Bernice Neugarten (1976) as she researched adults in the life cycle. Her work is usually of great personal interest to those involved in a self-assessment experience. Neugarten found that adults are influenced by three kinds of time: historical (or calendar) time, social time (expectations), and life time (chronological age). However, they are especially controlled by social time or the conscious or unconscious expectations that certain things are to happen in their lives at certain ages or stages. An unexpected event (e.g., the loss of a job at forty-five rather than at age sixty-five) can produce a tremendous amount of trauma because it is not "on time." The expectations that all adults have as to when events are supposed to occur for them need to be carefully examined and either kept or discarded. The reason for this is that those timing expectations can actually control and limit the person's constructive career action. Many of these "on time" or "off time" expectations will be revealed in the lifeline exercise suggested earlier. The facilitator may want to reflect on the significance of social time during that exercise.

Decision-Making and Change Styles

Just as there are large individual differences found in the various other components of self-assessment, there are big differences in how people go about making decisions and actually changing. Changes, both voluntary and involuntary, are a part of every person's experience, and it is important to assess how those changes are managed—and managed they must be if growth and enrichment are to occur! However, when working with people on self-assessment, it is not unusual to get to the end of the process and hear them say in one way or the other, "yes, but." All that self-knowledge does indeed clarify the need for and direction of a change, but it will not erase entirely the anxiety and uncertainty about what the change will bring.

You can expect that anxiety surrounding a career change manifests itself in numerous "I can't" types of statements. Loughary and Ripley, in their book *Career and Life Planning Guide* (1976), write of the dilemmas of change and provide a very helpful exercise which analyzes the constraints people identify that prevent them from changing. In the exercise, the "I can't do A because of B" statement is changed to an "If I do A, then I will have to deal with B" statement (Loughary and Ripley 1976, p. 91). This is achieved by carefully examining the validity of underlying assumptions.

As was mentioned, even when people do decide to change certain things, they make changes in very different ways, depending upon their decision-making and change styles. The process of deciding usually involves sensing a need to change, exploring self, evaluating which alternatives match with self, deciding, and implementing. How this gets done varies greatly. Some people prefer less information and quicker decisions; others like to know everything and to keep the decision open as long as possible. Some base their decisions on their personal needs and the needs of other people; others base theirs on "right and wrong." However individuals go about deciding things, it is important that they know it is the right way for them but may not be the right way for the other person. There are numerous inventories available that assist persons in synthesizing their ideas of their style of deciding and changing. Identification of appropriate inventories can be done by consulting with professional counselors and obtaining their recommendations.

Investment in Education, Training, and Work Experience

This is the final self-assessment factor that will be discussed and one that can greatly affect what action an individual takes. Before entering the self-assessment session, people have either wisely or unwisely spent much of their time, money, and personal energy gaining particular credentials or experiences that they—or others—determined appropriate at the time. Whether or not those experiences were actually things they feel good about pursuing, people are very hesitant to "throw all that away and start over." In many cases, self-assessment results not in people "throwing away" their jobs or careers but in identifying and accepting *why* they made particular choices. That knowledge can result in a feeling of more complete personal integration. When that is not the case, individuals may actually decide to make some very big changes in their careers, but rarely without a lot of feelings and concerns.

To facilitate a final assessment of the most critical factors in an individual's career change decision, one exercise that is frequently used is the "Decision-Making Table." Seated around an imaginary table are all the important people/things/events/experiences that will greatly affect that person's decision. There are a limited number of seats, so each factor must be carefully selected and either explained or explained away. For example, in this exercise, "money" may be seated at a person's decision-making table. If so, a realistic discussion of its place in priorities and the amount desired may lend further personal clarification. As each factor is carefully considered, more and more clarity is achieved. In the end, the individual may choose to "unseat" some of the factors around the table or substitute others. As may be evident, this and other similar exercises are a way of synthesizing even further the person's values—the single most important career clue.

IMPORTANT NEXT STEPS

By now it should be apparent that there are many pieces in the self-assessment puzzle and that the way the individual pulls those pieces together is critical. Having answers to a lot of self-knowledge questions on a summary page is a good beginning, but equally important is the next step of questioning those who have actually pursued the career or job of interest. Information obtained from those workers then needs to be compared with the self-assessment conclusions of the individual. For example, if after completing a self-assessment experience a person concludes that a career in public relations may best fit his or her needs, the next step is to research that conclusion by talking with or "shadowing" a person who does public relations work all day. Much can be learned through conversations with those occupying certain positions and through reading everything available on the nature of a particular kind of job or industry.

As was mentioned in the introduction, the ability of an individual to integrate self-assessment information comes from within. Personal integration is a reflection of developmental/emotional maturity; consequently, not all self-assessment participants will end up able to successfully act on their increased self-knowledge. Certainly, those who enter the self-assessment process with a highly formed self-concept can be expected to progress far beyond those who entered fragmented. Because of that, the measure of success for a career planning facilitator is more likely to be found in individual progress toward the self-discovery goal rather than in the unanimous achievement of career goals by all.

As with any process involving self-knowledge and change, the self-assessment experience is a stressful one. A change of career or job may require significant changes in the lifestyle of the individual. It is wise, then, that the career development facilitator be keenly aware of larger lifestyle concerns. Of course, wisdom comes largely through direct experience conducting self-assessment. However, expertise can also be enhanced by joining professional career development networks and associations, attending conferences and seminars, and staying current with the latest career research and information. Since there are many who believe that facilitating a self-assessment experience is less like helping to work a puzzle and more like artistically overseeing the painting of a beautiful picture, it behooves all master artists/facilitators to constantly strive to become better at what they do!

SELF-ASSESSMENT AND THE HUMAN RESOURCE SYSTEM

Communicating and marketing the need for enhanced self-knowledge cannot be done effectively unless one understands the human resource (HR) system and the role self-assessment plays in that system. To gain a clearer understanding of the fit of HR with self-assessment, it is helpful to begin with individual workers and this very basic assumption—people work primarily because of their own career needs. It can be convincingly argued that gone are the days when an employee's identity was so enmeshed with that of the organization that their goals are always one and the same. Across the world of work, the competition of the 1970s and 1980s among organizations and among qualified workers has so challenged job certainty that loyalty typically is first to one's self, rather than first to one's employer. This condition exists at the same time that employers need to minimize costs and maximize human energy and potential.

Based then on the assumption that individuals work in a particular environment because of their own career needs, employers are wise to know and respond to those individual needs in a thorough, systematic way—a way that fits, of course, with the employer's mission and strategic direction. The first steps to a comprehensive HR system begin with assessing individuals regarding their work needs and expectations. Generally, those worker responses include:

- meaningful, challenging jobs
- fair pay and fair treatment through appraisals
- recognition for efforts
- real opportunities and supervisory support in job advancement and in personal/career growth

Moreover, employers generally respond to an HR needs assessment with the following strategic organizational requirements:

- optimum utilization of personnel
- competitive salaries and skills
- flexible work force, able to be trained for future skill requirements
- directed people working hard to achieve organizational goals

It is when all these individual and organizational needs become clear that self-assessment can be shown to play a major role in the comprehensive HR system. The individual needs meaningful, challenging work, but that individual is a constantly changing human being. The self-knowledge he or she had at age twenty will not suffice for the greater challenges yearned for at age forty. Much of the career planning research reflects varying levels of vagueness among most adult workers regarding the skills they have to offer and the motivators that make them work their hardest. That vagueness has a cost to the organization by limiting the amount of talent and desire that can be tapped. A worker who is completely aware of and excited by what he or she has to offer is likely to offer it. That person is particularly likely to offer it to the employer that assisted in the self-discovery process.

Certainly, to the HR professional these last paragraphs are not new information. The problem remains: How do I get particular policy/program executives to support quality self-assessment efforts? At AT&T we have been fortunate in having receptive, far-sighted leaders who have responded positively to the following approach. First, those of us with the responsibility of preparing and marketing self-assessment as an essential part of career management identified the basic indices/measurements of corporate success. Next, we determined the impact that self-assessment can have on improving those indices. For example, absenteeism is an index that affects corporate profit, so we ascertained how enhanced self/career knowledge can actually lower absenteeism. This was accomplished through tracking and analysis of case studies from actual pilot self-assessment workshops and self-paced materials. These case studies were then used as a basis for some financial projections, illustrating lower absenteeism, less job stress, better match of talent to job, and more initiative in seeking new skills and knowledge in order to prepare for jobs of higher interest. The second step in obtaining upper management buy-in was to have the decision makers themselves experience the self-assessment materials. That was easy and fun since executives are people too—people with their own career needs! This combination of addressing key indices, providing pilot and case study data, and conducting self-assessment with the central decision makers has led to success with our self-assessment marketing efforts.

One key programmatic question that needs to be answered by HR professionals prior to marketing self-assessment is that of "who should facilitate the self-assessment process?" The ultimate answer to that lies within each individual organization or department. Quality training and support for in-house facilitators is essential and quite manageable if the organization's HR knowledge and supervisory expertise is available or if there is a willingness to hire a professional to develop materials and train facilitators. This in-house approach is ideal because it can support individual follow-up and the maintenance of relevant organizational information that matches people to jobs. On the other hand, responsible self-assessment efforts require high levels of facilitation skills and an organizational commitment to training and personnel development. Some organizations opt to contract with professional counselors or consultants for self-assessment itself and then to link individual assessment results to existing HR staffing and development functions. Again, that program delivery decision is based on the values, priorities, and resources of the organization.

Another important question to answer when establishing a self-assessment program is "how is the process to be delivered—in workshops, through self-paced written or mechanized materials, through career resource centers, or in one-on-one career counseling sessions?" That answer, too, depends on the preferences of the organization. Workshops are typically two or three days in length and begin with self-assessment (who I am); second is usually job matching (where I fit); and third comes implementing the decision (how I get to my career or job enrichment goal).

Whether it is a workshop, self-paced materials, or individual counseling, that process remains. It is truly up to the HR professional and upper management to determine the costs and benefits of the various approaches. All can serve to effectively facilitate self-assessment. Many organizations offer all of the delivery mechanisms mentioned; the individual worker decides his or her participatory method. If this variety of approaches is available, it is then necessary to have consistency in language and format and in the exercises themselves. For instance, it is confusing to employees to find skills assessed in a certain way in a workshop and then find self-paced materials where skills are defined and identified in an entirely different way.

In concluding this chapter, it seems important to state again that quality self-assessment goes a long way in satisfying one of our important HR areas of responsibility—having the right human resources in the right place at the right time. Self-assessment is the beginning step in seeing that goal realized. True, we have other HR career management responsibilities:

- organization/job design and evaluation
- present and future skills and job vacancies analysis
- supervision/career coaching training
- assessment of potential
- performance appraisal
- staffing and career pathing practices
- analysis of job enrichment and alternative work arrangements

But before reading further, stop and look again at that list. Realize that none of that work can possibly bear the fruit of getting people in the right jobs unless those people themselves have the empowerment gained through self-knowledge. Facilitating that self-knowledge is not an easy task, but if we do it well, we will have people who confidently know they are founded on rock—not on sand—and who will want to contribute enthusiastically to the organization.

REFERENCES AND RECOMMENDED READING

Anthony, R. 1983. *Think*. New York: Berkley Books.

Bolles, R. N. 1982. Specific knowledge skills revisited, and Behind the making of a skill identification instrument. Newsletters published by The National Career Development Project of United Ministries in Education, Walnut Creek, California.

Bolles, R. N. 1987. *What color is your parachute?* Berkeley, CA: Ten Speed Press.

Borchard, D., J. Kelly, and N. P. Weaver. 1984. *Choices, chances, changes* (3rd ed.). Dubuque, IA: Kendall/Hunt Publishing Co.

Crystal, J. C., and R. N. Bolles. 1974. *Where do I go from here with my life?* New York: Seabury Press.

Figler, H. 1979. *Path: A career workbook for liberal arts students* (rev.). Cranston, RI: Carroll Press.

Figler, H. 1979. *The complete job-search handbook*. New York: Holt, Rinehart and Winston.

Fine, S. A. 1967. *Nature of skill: Implications for education and training*. Reprinted from the Proceedings, 75th Annual Convention, American Psychological Association, pp. 365–66.

Hecklinger, F. J., and B. M. Curtin. 1984. *Training for life*. Dubuque, IA: Kendall/Hunt Publishing Co.

Holland, J. L. 1985. *Making vocational choices: A theory of vocational personalities and work environments*. Englewood Cliffs, NJ: Prentice-Hall.

Krannich, R. L. 1983. *Re-careering in turbulent times*. Manassas, VA: Impact Publications.

Leibowitz, Z. B., C. Farren, and B. L. Kaye. 1986. *Designing career development systems*. San Francisco: Jossey-Bass.

Loughary, J. W., and T. M. Ripley. 1976. *Career and life planning guide*. New York: Cambridge, The Adult Education Company.

Miller, A., and R. Mattson. 1977. *The truth about you*. Old Tappan, NJ: Roselle Park Press.

Miller, S., E. W. Nunnally, and D. B. Wackman. 1975. *Alive and aware*. Minneapolis: Interpersonal Communication Programs.

Neugarten, B. L. 1976. Adaptation and the life cycle. *Counseling Psychologist* 6(1), 16–20.

Pedersen, J. S., and C. B. Smith. 1986. A diagnostic model for assessing the effect of developmental issues on career action. *Journal of Employment Counseling* 23(2), 66–77.

Schlossberg, N. K., L. E. Troll, and Z. Leibowitz. 1978. *Perspectives on counseling adults: Issues and skills*. Monterey, CA: Brooks/Cole Publishing Co.

Sher, B. 1979. *Wishcraft*. New York: Ballantine Books.

Simon, S. B., H. Kirschenbaum, and L. Howe. 1972. *Values clarification*. New York: Hart.

Super, D. E. 1951. Vocational adjustment: Implementing a self-concept. *Occupations 30*, 88–92.

Super, D. E. 1953. A theory of vocational development. *American Psychologist 8*, 185–90.

Super, D. E. 1957. *The psychology of careers*. New York: Harper & Row.

CHAPTER 12

DESIGNING DEVELOPMENTAL ASSESSMENT CENTERS: STEP BY STEP

VIRGINIA R. BOEHM

The value of using assessment centers for the selection of managers and supervisors and the identification of long-range managerial potential has been well demonstrated during the last twenty-five years.[1] By furnishing a wealth of behaviorally based information about individual's managerial skills, assessment centers have become an integral part of the succession process in many organizations.

For more than a decade, it has been widely recognized that assessment centers could be used for more than just selection and potential identification. The great promise that assessment centers have as career planning and development tools is well recognized, and there have been a number of successful uses of assessment centers for this purpose.[2] However, there have been many more attempts than successes, and organizations attempting to use assessment centers for developmental purposes have frequently become disillusioned and given up the attempt.

There are several reasons why this has happened. Sometimes, an organization has simply expected too much or expected that developmental needs, once identified, would be dealt with without further organizational intervention. But one major reason for failure, or less-than-true success, is that it has been a common practice to take assessment exercises and procedures developed for use in a selection context and use them, with little or no modification, for developmental purposes. This simply will not work well. Designing assessment centers for selection and for development are two different processes. While the fact that the processes are different has been pointed out, there has been little in the way of detailed presentation of just what the differences are and their impact on the design process.[3]

The process of developing an assessment center for selection or identification purposes basically consists of the following stages:

1. Identifying the target job or job level and the candidate population.

2. Analyzing the job or job level to determine the kinds of tasks and activities
   incumbents perform.

3. Determining what the skills and abilities are that are required to perform these
   tasks, and what the appropriate level of difficulty is.

4. Selecting or developing assessment exercises that allow opportunity to observe
   and evaluate candidates' skills at the appropriate level of difficulty.

5. Developing training and administrative procedures.

6. Developing procedures for the use of the results and the feedback of results to
   candidates.

Each of these stages has a parallel when developing assessment centers
for career planning and development. Using these stages as a model, this
chapter presents a step-by-step outline of what is involved in designing an
assessment center for career planning and development purposes.

DETERMINE THE GOAL AND DEFINE THE POPULATION

Failure to define goals is a very common reason why developmental programs fail. The goal may be quite specific, for example, developing the
managerial skills of technical people who are interested in eventually becoming technical managers. Or it may be broader—that is, identifying the
strengths and weaknesses of entry-level employees to determine what sort
of career path might be feasible for the individual and what training and
development would be needed to move along that path.

A statement of goals should include what the program is intended to
accomplish and identify the target group. In general, the more concrete the
goal and the more tightly defined the target group, the easier the design
work will be and the more likely the program will be to succeed.

Before proceeding further, it is critically important to obtain the concur-
rence of potential users and developers of the program concerning exactly
what the program is intended to accomplish. Development is a word that
means many things to many people, and failure to clarify the program's
purpose up front may lead to unmet expectations at a later time. While a
simpler, less ambitious program may be easier to develop, a broad, ambitious, developmental program can be highly desirable to an organization
and worthy of undertaking, so long as the organization knows going in that
substantial time and resource commitment will be essential if the program
is to succeed.

Analyze the Job

The second step is to analyze the relevant jobs, job levels, and clusters of jobs in the organization to determine the kinds of tasks and activities incumbents perform, their level of difficulty, and how the various relevant jobs are similar and different.

In assessment for development and career pathing, there is no specific target job, and there may or may not be a targeted job level. In a broad-based program, particularly one with long-term career planning aspects, there may be clusters of jobs that require similar skills and abilities within the cluster but where there are differences between clusters. There may also be differences in the difficulty level of the tasks, and these differences in difficulty level do not necessarily correspond to organizational differences in compensation and authority levels. Being an engineering manager may not, and usually does not, require the incumbent to perform engineering tasks greater in difficulty to those performed by the engineers who report to the manager, for example.

Also, the fact that two jobs are on the same organizational level and involve some common tasks does not mean that the task difficulty is the same. For example, the supervisor of a small work group and the supervisor of a larger work group may be at the same organizational level, and both may have to train new employees on the job. It is quite likely that the supervisor in the large group will find this task more difficult since there are more people who have to be trained, and the larger span of control allows less time to be spent with any one individual.

DETERMINE SKILLS

Third, determine the skills and abilities required to perform the identified tasks and activities and the levels of difficulty of these skills and abilities for the various jobs or job clusters. Tasks and activities are clustered into groups that require the same skill or ability. This clustering can be done using a number of different statistical models, or it can be done judgmentally.

However it is done, it is crucial to remember the difference between an activity or task and a skill or ability. An activity states what is done, and a skill states what is required to do it competently. For example, giving a speech is an activity. Oral communications is the skill necessary if the speech is to be an effective one. Scheduling work for others is an activity: Organizing is the skill needed to develop an effective work schedule.

Obviously, an activity can require more than one skill. Developing the annual budget is an activity. It requires skill in planning (to determine what is going to be done during the next year), decision making (to determine the best way of getting the job done), financial analysis (to determine how much the work is going to cost), and just plan arithmetic (to make sure the numbers on the budget add up right).

The end product of these first three steps should be a matrix, outlining the skills and abilities, and the difficulty levels, of the various jobs, job levels, or job clusters and indicating the similarities and differences between them. A very simple example of such a matrix is illustrated here:

Skill/Ability	Job Cluster		
	A	B	C
Oral Communications	H	M	H
Written Communications	L	M	H
Planning	L	M	M
Problem Analysis	L	H	M
Leadership	H	L	H
Decision Making	M	H	H
Delegation	M	L	H
Organizing	M	M	M

In this matrix, an "H" indicates that a high level of the skill or ability is required, an "M" indicates a moderate level, and an "L" a relatively low level.

Such a matrix provides a "portrait" of the jobs in the cluster. In this example, these may be viewed as job clusters in a manufacturing plant.

Cluster A represents first-level supervisory jobs. A supervisor in this environment must be able to communicate effectively orally, but does not have much in the way of written communication to generate. The supervisor must also exercise effective leadership, has some latitude in decision making, and must be able to organize the day's work. But there is little responsibility for long- or medium-range planning, and the problems dealt with tend to be recurring ones.

Cluster B represents various engineering and other technical jobs. While the incumbents in these jobs do not have people reporting to them (and consequently not much in the way of leadership or delegation is required), they do have to be able to analyze complex technical problems and make decisions concerning how to solve them.

Cluster C represents various middle-management positions. Incumbents in these positions must have the high leadership and oral communications skills required by the first-level supervisory positions but must also be able to handle planning and problem analysis at a moderate level of difficulty.

Obviously, this matrix is oversimplified and intended only to be illustrative of the steps outlined previously. But the creation of such a matrix is of critical importance in designing an assessment center for developmental purposes. Without it, the next steps simply cannot proceed in an orderly fashion.

SELECT EXERCISES

The fourth step is to select or develop assessment exercises that allow opportunity to observe and evaluate the relevant skills and abilities at appropriate levels of difficulty. One difference between selection-oriented assessment centers and those designed for use in development is that the assessment center designed for development will have more exercises. It has to, since different levels of difficulty, as well as the appropriate skills and abilities, have to be tapped. For example, a developmental assessment center may use two in-baskets that measure the same skills and abilities but vary sharply in their level of difficulty.

While the exact number of exercises will depend on the number of skills and abilities, and the relative profile of the jobs or job families involved, it seems extremely unlikely that a good assessment center for development purposes could have fewer than seven or eight exercises and may well have ten or more.

Another difference is that the developmentally oriented assessment center should include self-assessment exercises in addition to more traditional ones where evaluation is done solely by assessors. This is the first step in obtaining candidate buy-in to the results. While it is more comfortable for everyone involved if a candidate in a selection center winds up agreeing with the assessors' evaluation, it is not critical. But, in a developmentally oriented center it is critical: Unless the candidate accepts the results and uses them as the basis for further development, the assessment center is essentially a waste of time and money.

A third area where assessment centers designed for developmental purposes are likely to vary from those designed for assessment is that developmental centers should usually include paper-and-pencil tests as well as simulation exercises. There are two reasons for this. In the first place, in a developmental center it is advisable to get at some of the "whys" as well as the "whats" of observed behavior. For example, someone may not have dealt with some of the high-priority items in the in-basket. The kind of development required would be different for someone who was a very slow reader as compared with someone who simply had never learned to establish priorities. Without a reading test, it would be difficult to make appropriate recommendations.

To give another example, a candidate is observed to have poor oral communication skills. The candidate mumbles, uses poor grammar, uses sentences that seem to go nowhere, and in general is difficult to follow. Maybe the candidate is simply nervous, or maybe the candidate has problems with basic language skills. Here again, the developmental recommendations would vary, and, without a paper-and-pencil test, it is difficult to determine which is the case.

The other reason is that the use of paper-and-pencil tests provides an opportunity to get at factors other than abilities that may have relevance for the candidate's future career planning and development. An interest inventory, for example, can provide information concerning what the candidate likes to do which supplements information provided by the simulations concerning what the candidate does well.

Organizations have hesitated to use paper-and-pencil tests in assessment centers because of EEO concerns. In an assessment center used strictly for developmental purposes, these concerns do not apply because the results are not to be used to select (or reject) anyone and are intended to be used to benefit the future career development of all candidates. Professionally developed, valid and reliable tests can play a valuable role in a developmental assessment center.

DEVELOP TRAINING AND ADMINISTRATIVE PROCEDURES

Administrative procedures are a critical part of any assessment center, and one that is too often relegated to secondary status. Granted, it is not very glamorous to sit down and figure out how many note pads are going to be required each assessment session, or to schedule things so that nobody is supposed to be two places at the same time, or to leave time to rearrange the room between the group exercise and the interview simulation, but without consideration of these tasks, and literally hundreds of other details, the assessment center would be simply chaotic.

The administrative area is the one where there is the least difference between the selection and development-oriented assessment center. Logistics are likely to be somewhat more complicated because there are more exercises, but the issues that have to be dealt with are generally the same.

One area, however, where there is a difference in the two types of centers is in the focus of security efforts. In a selection center, exercise security is of great importance since candidates can presumably have an unfair advantage (or at least think they do) by obtaining prior knowledge of the content of the exercises. In a development center where the candidates are not competing with one another, exercise security is of less concern.

But results security is more of a concern in a developmental center. While keeping results out of the hands of those with no need to know is very important in selection centers as well, a breach in results security in a developmental center can destroy the center. No matter how strongly the fact that assessment results are to be used only for developmental purposes is stressed, there will be those in the organization who feel that the information obtained should also be used for selection purposes, either directly or indirectly. This is particularly the case if the organization's assessment centers are also selection oriented. Any such improper use of the results from a developmental assessment center destroys the center's credibility with the candidates and consequently its usefulness to the organization.

Another difference is in the atmosphere the administrator and the assessors create in the center. In a selection center, administrator and assessors should be cordial, professional, but somewhat distant from the candidates as befits people who are making decisions about the candidates that will strongly affect their careers. In a developmental center, on the other hand, the atmosphere should be more of partnership, and informal interactions (excepting, of course, premature evaluations of performance) need not be discouraged. Also, the concept of partnership should change the way the exercises are introduced to the candidates. In a developmental center, there may be an extensive overview of the exercise outlining what skills and abilities it is intended to tap, and a debriefing after it. This, again, is part of the way candidate buy-in is obtained. Candidates should be encouraged to think about, and do self-evaluations, of their own performance.

To promote this atmosphere and assure results confidentiality, selection of assessors requires careful attention. While a selection center can usually function even if the administrator has to train and make the best of whoever the organization designates as assessors, a development center simply cannot operate that way. A developmental center requires far more skill on the part of the assessors, and it is crucial that the administrator be given the authority to both screen assessors in advance and to screen out those who do not measure up during training.

In addition, it may be desirable to use psychologists as part of the assessment team. This is particularly a factor if the center is to make extensive use of self-assessment techniques or paper-and-pencil tests. As well as aiding the other assessors in making effective use of test information, psychologists can provide feedback and work with candidates in devising appropriate developmental plans.

Assessor training is more difficult in a development center than in a selection one, not just because there are more exercises that the assessors must learn but also because the evaluation procedure is different. While in a selection center what really matters is the bottom line (the overall rating), what matters most in a development center are the ratings on individual skills and abilities. Usually, there is no overall rating given. Consequently, each of these ratings must have the reliability required only of the overall rating in a selection center.

Another difference in the developmental center is that the evaluation process will usually involve two stages. First, ratings will be done on the skills and abilities in the usual fashion, then other information (such as paper-and-pencil test results) will be introduced so that developmental recommendations can be made. Assessors must be trained to use and interpret this additional information and must be made familiar with the type of developmental strategies the organization views as being part of the program.

GIVING FEEDBACK AND USING RESULTS

While feedback is viewed as the last stage in the assessment process in a selection center, in a developmental center it is more of a bridge between the assessment and the development phases of an assessment and development program. In a selection center, the candidate doesn't have to do anything with the results, while in a developmentally oriented center, the use made of the results by the candidate is the reason for the assessment.

Consequently, feedback in a developmentally oriented program is much more intensive, covering not only what the candidate did and how the performance was rated but also interactive discussion with the candidate concerning why the results were as they were and what should be done to build on strengths and develop weaknesses. It may be desirable, if psychologists are part of the assessment team, to have them handle feedback (particularly for candidates who exhibited a number of weak areas), but this is not essential providing that whoever does the feedback is extensively trained in giving feedback and is credible to the candidate.

The person giving feedback should have extensive knowledge of the developmental resources available in the organization and elsewhere in the community in order to be able to work with the candidate in the feedback session in developing a draft of a developmental plan. But a finished product cannot be expected to emerge at this point. The candidate has been given a great deal of information at once and requires time to digest it and plan next steps. If a good development plan is to be generated, it is critically important that the candidate be given the opportunity for one or more future meetings, either with the person who conducted the initial feedback or with another resource person.

Development starts with feedback. It does not stop there. An organization that simply presents the candidate with the results and expects the candidate to take it from there with no further organizational input is likely to be very disappointed with the results of its program.

Assessment centers designed specifically for developmental purposes require a substantial commitment of organizational resources. But if they are properly designed and conducted, and the results are used effectively, they can play an important role in preserving and enhancing the quality of the organization's most important resource, its people.

NOTES

1. Readers are assumed to be familiar with the basics of the assessment center method and its use in management selection. Readers who do not have this background might wish to refer to the following sources:

Bray, D. W., R. J. Campbell, and D. L. Grant. 1974. Formative years in business: A long term AT&T study of managerial lives. New York: Wiley Interscience.
Mosse, J. L., and W. C. Byham. (eds). 1977. Applying the assessment center method. New York: Pergamon.

2. A number of developmental uses of assessment centers are reviewed in Boehm, V. R. 1985. Using assessment centers for management development: Five applications. *Journal of Management Development*, 4(4), 40–52.
3. Other discussions of the topic can be found in the following sources:

Keil, E. C. 1981. Assessment centers: A guide for human resource management. Reading, MA: Addison-Wesley.
Thornton, G. C. III, and W. C. Byham. 1982. Assessment centers and managerial performance. New York: Academic Press.

CHAPTER 13

STIMULATING HIGH-POTENTIAL CAREER DEVELOPMENT THROUGH AN ASSESSMENT CENTER PROCESS

PETER CAIRO AND KAREN S. LYNESS

Because assessment centers focus on observed behaviors, job-related performance dimensions, and detailed feedback, they provide invaluable input for participants to use in charting their careers. This chapter describes an approach to career planning that was developed as part of AT&T's Advanced Management Potential Assessment (AMPA) Program (Moses 1985).

AMPA is a three-and-a-half-day assessment program for high-potential middle managers. The program's strengths reside in the use of multiple measures, such as individual and group simulations, psychological tests, interviews, and aptitude tests, as well as multiple observers, including experienced managers and psychologists. An important program goal is to provide participants and company management with an objective evaluation of the participant's advancement potential, based on specific dimensions that are related to managerial success. Another goal is to help participants get a better understanding of their strengths and weaknesses as managers, the work environments where they are most likely to succeed, and the implications for their own career planning.

After a brief overview of how the various AMPA components relate to career planning, the remainder of the chapter will describe the high-potential career development program designed for AMPA participants. This program, which draws heavily on the assessment results, allows exploration of career goals and plans. Created in 1986, the program has been offered to two separate groups of high-potential managers. Regrettably no formal

The authors would like to acknowledge the important contributions of their professional colleagues in the AMPA program: Joseph L. Moses, Kerry Bunker, Ted Ballard, Karen Calhoun, and Jodi Kassover-Campbell.

evaluation has been undertaken yet; however, participants have reacted very enthusiastically to the program. Therefore, the chapter will conclude with a discussion of why the program was successful in an effort to be helpful to others who are facing the challenge of designing a similar program.

BACKGROUND

From the beginning, AMPA was regarded as an opportunity for managers to learn about themselves in ways that might strongly influence their careers. Consequently, even before the career development program was added to the AMPA sequence, there were program features which encouraged managers to engage in serious introspection of their careers.

One of these features was the heavy involvement of psychologists in the AMPA program. In addition to the industrial/organizational psychologists who directed AMPA, counseling and clinical psychologists from outside AT&T served on the assessment center staff. These staff psychologists conducted personal interviews, interpreted projectives and other psychological tests, served on evaluation teams, and provided individual feedback to participants. Participants' interest in career development was stimulated in several ways. First, part of the personal interview focused on career history issues, such as reactions to assignments, career satisfaction, developmental goals, and the relative importance of promotion and other career rewards. This information provided a backdrop against which to view the participant's assessment performance.

Psychologists also provided feedback to participants after the results of all phases of the assessment process had been integrated. During the feedback session, the psychologists further integrated the assessment results with the psychological test data and career information provided by the participants. Also included in the feedback were any career development recommendations made by the AMPA staff and assessors. One of the primary objectives of the feedback session was to help participants begin to use what has been learned to formulate realistic career plans.

Another unique feature of AMPA was the post-assessment development seminar. This seminar focused on managing in changing and ambiguous environments and sensitized participants to their own affective and behavioral responses. Alternative approaches were reviewed, and participants were given an opportunity to experiment with different behaviors. The seminar was a nonevaluative learning experience, and participation was voluntary. The cornerstone of the seminar was the unique organizational simulation known as Looking Glass, Inc., developed by the Center for Creative Leadership and enhanced to address AT&T issues. In addition to this realistic simulation, seminar activities included lectures, exercises, and discussions. Although individual career planning was not a specific focus, participants were encouraged, through self-ratings and extensive peer feedback, to explore their own performance and its implications for development.

Despite these efforts to promote the developmental potential of the AMPA experience, many participants expressed strong interest in a more intensive program focused entirely on career development. This interest was triggered by several factors. First, many participants reported having had little or no opportunity to raise career concerns, other than in sporadic and informal discussions with bosses.

Second, the assessment results provided them with new information that had important implications for their future in the company. By providing more than just their overall rating of advancement potential, assessment feedback gave them a richly textured picture of clearly differentiated abilities and preferences that had implications for both the type of job and organizational level where they might be most successful.

Finally, the degree of uncertainty in the organization triggered strong interest in career development. The post-divestiture environment at AT&T had created shifting business strategies, manpower reductions in many areas, and some confusion over corporate goals. Along with changes in the business, profound changes in the nature of the career opportunity structure had also occurred. For many managers the result was a keen recognition of the need to reconsider their personal career plans.

A survey of former AMPA participants was undertaken to determine more precisely the extent of interest in a career program as well as specific activities that would be helpful. The survey results revealed three areas of interest. Predictably, participants expressed a strong desire for information. They wanted to know about existing and projected opportunities throughout the company and what organizational changes were being anticipated that might affect their careers. A second strong interest was having the opportunity to get feedback on their career plans. This included learning more about how to use the results of assessment for modifying existing goals. Finally, nearly all of the participants wanted to learn new methods for helping their subordinates manage their careers. The level of interest in this activity was somewhat unexpected. Managers appeared just as eager to acquire ways to become effective career coaches as they were to discuss their own personal career concerns.

In some respects the needs expressed by these high-potential managers were similar to those associated with any other group of individuals seeking help with career planning (i.e., the need for information, a better understanding of strengths and weaknesses, and feedback on goals and plans). The needs expressed by AMPA participants were consistent with the features common to almost any well-conceived career planning program (Brooks 1984).

Yet, there were characteristics of this population that set them apart from many others: Most were in their mid- to late-thirties with many different career experiences; they had been on a "fast track," achieving a level of success that many others managers had not; and they had been through an intensive and selective assessment program. Typically these managers had worked hard to excel at each assignment they were given, trusting their career management to the company rather than channeling energy into a more proactive approach.

Furthermore, for most of their careers these managers had considered career development to be virtually synonymous with advancement and promotion. This predisposition was now being challenged by organizational realities. Not only did these managers have to confront the traditional reduction of opportunities beyond middle management that is common in most organizations, but they were also faced with company-wide reorganization and manpower reductions at all levels within their own particular organization. In the absence of advancement opportunities, these high-potential managers would have to expand their understanding of career development to include consideration of other possible goals and achievements.

THE HIGH-POTENTIAL CAREER DEVELOPMENT PROGRAM

Preprogram Assignments

The program is designed as a two-day experience, with participation limited to twelve to fifteen managers. In order to make the most efficient use of time, managers are given a comprehensive preprogram assignment. The first part of the assignment is a "High Potential Development Guide." This guide includes many traditional career planning concepts and strategies but is specifically tailored to take into account participants' assessment center experiences. Sequentially structured activities require participants to incorporate their assessment ratings on key managerial dimensions in order to identify developmental needs and appropriate next assignments. Furthermore, they explore work preferences by using dimensions that were part of a company-wide job analysis. Participants rate their preferences for various types of work activities (e.g., coordinating, supervising, planning and organizing); work environments (e.g., fluid vs. stable, high risk vs. low risk); and developmental opportunities (e.g., the challenges of start-up or turn-around assignments).

Also, as part of the preprogram assignment, participants are asked to conduct at least one interview with someone in the organization who has information relevant to one of their current career concerns. Assuming that career needs will differ among participants, this task is left open-ended. Participants are given some general selection criteria for consideration, such as the person's experience, objectivity, and willingness to share information, but are essentially told that they can interview anyone whom they consider to be a source of potentially valuable career information. General guidelines for conducting the interview are provided, but participants are given a free hand in what questions to ask.

Participants are also asked to administer a career development survey to all of their subordinates. The results provide important input for the module on helping subordinates manage their careers. The subordinates are polled about their job and career satisfaction, clarity of their career plans, factors that were instrumental in achieving career goals, perceived organizational support for career planning activities, and the help they received with career issues from their boss. The responses from all surveys are combined into a group profile that is shared with participants. Also, when there are enough subordinates to protect confidentiality, each manager is given a separate profile of the combined responses from their own subordinates.

Finally, two psychological tests, the Myers-Briggs Type Indicator and the 16PF Career Development Profile, are administered prior to the program. These instruments were selected because their results could be integrated effectively with the other information participants were using for career planning, and each instrument was judged to make a unique contribution to self-understanding. Furthermore, the results were reported in a comprehensive and readable narrative geared to career planning. After a thorough discussion of how the results should be used, participants can take the results with them for further reflection.

Discussion Groups

Much of the program is organized around small discussion groups that are co-led by the staff psychologists with whom the participants have worked during assessment. During the sequence of assessment activities and feedback, each psychologist has developed a good understanding of the assets and liabilities of the managers with whom he or she has worked. The established relationship between the psychologist and AMPA participant helps to insure that the groups will run smoothly and productively.

The psychologist's role in the small group is largely to facilitate discussion—keeping the group on task, encouraging mutual feedback among group members, and insuring that each manager has the opportunity to participate to the extent desired. In order to insure consistency among the small groups, the psychologists adhere to a set of general topics for the discussions. Each of these topics is, in turn, related to specific sections of the development guide. These topics include

• The extent to which participants' current work situations are satisfying their most important values and what to do if they are not,

- The implications of assessment results, including the degree of consistency between assessment results and self-assessments based on work experiences, and
- Current and projected developmental needs and how they will be met.

Need for Information about Career Opportunities

The need for career information among AMPA participants was clear from the beginning. Not only was this evident from the survey results, but whenever career development topics arose during assessment, participants noted the difficulty of planning in the face of organizational uncertainty. Some managers believed that important information was being withheld by top management. Others expressed frustration at not knowing what sources to tap for the information they needed. Still others were convinced that until decisions were made about long-term business strategies, there was little chance of getting useful information about career opportunities in the company.

While information about opportunities is widely acknowledged as being essential in any effective career planning intervention, it is particularly important for adults with work experience. For many adults the challenge of career planning is not so much achieving greater self-awareness, but rather discovering the types of positions and assignments that match up with what they know to be true about themselves (Herr and Cramer 1984). Even the most effective methods for helping to enhance self-understanding will founder in the absence of valuable career information. For high-potential managers who treat career development as synonymous with advancement, the challenge of acquiring useful information to make important career decisions is made doubly difficult by the reduced numbers of opportunities for promotion.

The program is designed to address these concerns in several different ways. First, participants are given an opportunity to share the results of their preprogram interviews. Most participants conduct more than one interview and seem to value the assignment because it gives them a socially acceptable reason to raise career issues with knowledgeable people in their own organization. This activity is carried out not only to help participants acquire information that might be useful in their own decision making, but also to begin fostering a more proactive approach to career planning.

Another major activity is intended to help participants get a broader perspective on the different parts of the corporation. This is accomplished by inviting top company executives, who are involved in major staffing decisions, to attend the program and interact with participants. An open forum is held with key human resource officers from each of the company's major lines of business. The forum begins with each executive commenting on existing and projected opportunities in his or her part of the business, including changes that are occurring, staffing implications, and advice on career planning in the current environment. After their comments, each executive responds to questions. Multiple objectives are accomplished through this activity. First, participants achieve a somewhat better understanding of the issues facing company leadership. At the same time, executives report that it is important for them to hear firsthand the career concerns of talented middle managers. Finally, this discussion offers an overview of the existing organizational opportunity structure, which serves to help participants be more realistic in developing their own career goals and plans.

Despite these activities, at least some of the participants remained frustrated that they could not obtain answers to all their questions. This problem was addressed by acknowledging the likelihood that answers to many career-related questions probably did not exist, at least not with any degree of certainty. This led to a discussion of career planning under uncertainty, which is one of the major program themes. Despite rapid organizational changes and the absence of desired information, career choices are still necessary. Thus, participants are encouraged to become more proactive in managing their own careers.

Career planning is described as a problem-solving process, requiring the same flexibility and contingency planning that is common to other forms of managerial problem solving. Also, although participants are encouraged to think about long-term career goals, emphasis is placed on realistic short-term goals and the specific next steps required to achieve them.

Career Goals

A final approach to these issues is to encourage broad exploration of career goals. This takes the form of acknowledging the diminishing numbers of advancement opportunities and encouraging participants to articulate alternative and often more personal definitions of career success. Some participants admit that they are learning to feel good about significant accomplishments rather than always longing for the increasingly elusive promotion.

Ference, Stoner, and Warren (1977), in discussing the plight of the plateaued manager, described the need to encourage those whose advancement is blocked to examine alternatives to promotion, such as lateral moves or developmental assignments. This is particularly important for managers whose advancement is blocked largely by organizational factors, such as diminished opportunities, rather than by individual performance factors.

This theme was prominent in all of the small groups, where participants often expressed interest in lateral transfers to positions in different parts of the business. Among the options they considered were positions that would help them develop new talents or achieve higher levels of satisfaction, whether or not they involved a promotion.

Helping Subordinates Manage Their Careers

There are three phases to this part of the program. The first phase involves discussing the results of the subordinate survey and the implications for the boss's role in helping subordinates to manage their careers. The next phase involves specific strategies for participants to use in conducting career development discussions with their subordinates, including how to prepare, what topics to include, how to review specific goals and plans, and so on. Participants receive a set of guidelines for conducting these discussions as well as a developmental planning worksheet that can be used by the subordinate and manager in connection with the discussion. The worksheet focuses the subordinate on key aspects of the career planning process, including developmental needs, short- and long-term goals, actions required to meet their goals, and ways that the manager can help. The final phase of this module includes role play among participants. With one of their colleagues playing the role of a key subordinate, each participant conducts a simulated career discussion based on the guidelines discussed earlier in the module. Each practice session is followed by structured feedback from other managers and a psychologist.

Following Through on Career Plans

One of the most difficult challenges in any type of career planning is the follow-up on plans that are made. Too often career plans are forgotten soon after the end of a workshop or discussion. The hectic pace of the regular workday distracts attention from goals to be accomplished three months, or three years, hence. Also, contingencies and discontinuities arise in each person's life that may radically change earlier plans. These include work-related factors, such as major organizational changes, and nonwork factors, such as the transfer of a spouse or serious illness of a family member.

Recognizing this problem, and acknowledging that no one solution exists, the managers participating in this program are given the task of arriving at their own solutions. Each small discussion group is given time to develop a strategy for monitoring career plans that will work for all members of the group. Each "solution" is then shared in the plenary session. Most of these solutions involve some form of networking among participants and ongoing feedback to one another. In addition, participants are encouraged to write themselves letters describing what actions they plan to take during the next six months. These letters are held by program staff for six months and then sent to participants as a way of helping them monitor their progress.

OBSERVATIONS AND CONCLUSIONS

The response from those who took part in the program was overwhelmingly positive. Although no formal evaluation of the program was undertaken, participants were asked to rate the usefulness of each major activity. By and large they reported finding almost all activities extremely helpful.

Clearly, however, no firm conclusions about the effectiveness of the program can be drawn on the basis of such limited experience without a more thorough examination of effects. Nevertheless, five observations about what may have accounted for the program's perceived success will be summarized in an attempt to help others.

First, this program differed from many other career development efforts because it was specifically tailored to both the needs of the participants and to the organizational realities they faced. Participants' needs were determined through examination of the aggregate assessment results, review of company data from longitudinal follow-up of previous participants, officer interviews, the survey which asked potential program participants about their career development needs, and an advisory task force of managers who had gone through the assessment process.

While all of these inputs were extremely useful in determining the program content, the program would not have been perceived as credible or relevant without explicit recognition of the existing opportunity structure. Thus, the program was also designed to realistically address the need for career planning in an organizational environment characterized by ambiguity and change. As described earlier, participants' feelings of frustration at diminishing advancement opportunities were acknowledged, and an explicit attempt was made to redirect their energy toward more constructive and proactive approaches. Also, when participants articulated career goals or plans, they received constructive but direct feedback about their feasibility. All of these strategies were intended to keep both the program and the career plans that were generated firmly grounded in reality.

Second, the linkage between this program and the formal assessment center experience was also important. First, participants had the opportunity to incorporate extensive and directly relevant information about their managerial characteristics into a broader career development framework. Furthermore, examination of skills, style, motivation, and talents was not limited to self-report as is so often the case in other career planning interventions, but rather based on behaviors observed during actual work simulations. The value of the program was further enhanced by the continuity provided by staff, in particular, having the same psychologists with whom participants had worked during assessment also play a central role in the high-potential career development program.

Third, participation of key executives from across the company was another important element of the program's success. This became apparent in contrasting the reactions of participants in the two separate trials. For the first trial, several of the company executives, who were invited to attend, delegated the job to a subordinate. In some cases, the subordinate who attended had no more information than several participants. Predictably, participants were disappointed with the results of the forum.

The second time around, however, invited executives attended themselves and contributed information and insight that otherwise would not have been available. This time the reaction of the participants was much more positive. Another clear effect of top management involvement was to signal implicitly the importance of the program itself. Top management support for career development programs has long been recognized as essential for their success (Gutteridge 1986).

Fourth, although the program was tailored to take into account participants' assessment experience and their designation as high-potential managers, the fundamental design was based on standard career planning concepts and principles. Holland, Magoon, and Spokane's (1981) review of career interventions led them to conclude that the effective ones generally included

- Relevant occupational information,
- Assessment methods for helping participants learn about themselves,
- Individual or group activities requiring discussion of specific goals and plans,
- Counselors, groups, and peers to provide support, and
- A cognitive structure for organizing the information about self and occupational alternatives.

Although some of these elements are often thought to be most relevant for people facing an *occupational* choice, they were effective in this program where high-potential managers focused on alternatives within their chosen occupation and organization. Despite the fact that the target group was composed of high-potential managers with successful track records and extensive experience, many were clearly in need of fundamental career planning competencies. This is consistent with Holland et al.'s (1981) observation that most career planning interventions are effective because the individuals receiving them have minimal career planning skills to begin with! This appeared to be no less true of these high-potential managers than it was of the individuals in the studies Holland et al. reviewed.

Finally, probably equally important for these participants was their admitted need for stimulation in career exploration. Most focused their talents and energies on succeeding in their jobs without taking the time on a regular basis to think about where their career was heading. They were encouraged throughout the assessment sequence to capitalize on the opportunity it provided for serious introspection without the daily pressures of job and family responsibilities. The career program further stimulated thinking about career issues as well as challenged participants to develop workable plans and goals. By the end of the program, virtually all of the participants recognized the need to become more proactive in their careers in spite of the organizational uncertainties and challenges they faced.

Despite the program's success in the eyes of participants and staff, well-conceived investigations of specific effects are necessary. This will not only enhance our understanding of critical program components, but also strengthen the rationale for developing programs for other high-potential middle managers.

REFERENCES

Brooks, L. 1984. Career counseling methods and practice. In D. Brown and L. Brooks (eds.), *Career choice and development*. San Francisco: Jossey-Bass.

Ference, T. P., J. A. F. Stoner, and E. K. Warren. 1977. Managing the career plateau. *Academy of Management Review*, 2, 602–12.

Gutteridge, T. G. 1986. Organizational career development systems: The state of the practice. In D. T. Hall (ed.), *Career development in organizations*. San Francisco: Jossey-Bass.

Herr, E. L., and S. H. Cramer. 1984. *Career guidance and counseling through the life span*. Boston: Little, Brown.

Holland, J. L., T. M. Magoon, and A. R. Spokane. 1981. Counseling psychology: Career interventions, research and theory. *Annual Review of Psychology, 32*, 279–305.

Moses, J. L. 1985. Using clinical methods in a high level management assessment center. In H. J. Bernardin and D. A. Bownas (eds.), *Personality assessment in organizations*. New York: Praeger.

CHAPTER 14

BUSINESS SIMULATIONS FOR SKILL DIAGNOSIS AND DEVELOPMENT

STEPHEN A. STUMPF

Research on adult education verifies what many managers have said for years: The best learning occurs when employees perceive the learning to be of value to their life or work situations. Educational opportunities must respond to diagnosed training needs and individual career development plans because adult learning is primarily self-motivated. Adults learn what and when they want to, with a strong emphasis on application. Instructors or trainers do not have the power to implant ideas or transfer skills directly to the adult learner. In the best training situation, they can serve as guides to help adults learn for themselves. Experience continues to be the richest source of learning.

This suggests that the optimal learning situation involves some elements of diagnosis and career development, while drawing on life experiences and integrating theoretical concepts with hands-on practice. Business simulations can be used in training programs to provide this combination; they are able to concentrate into a few days what might ordinarily take years to diagnose and learn on the job.

Business simulations are valuable training tools which satisfy many of the needs of adult learners. Two general types of business simulations are discussed here—large-scale behavioral simulations and computer-based organizational simulations. Both attempt to re-create a company with all of its realities in a training setting; both provide participants an opportunity to see an organization from a senior management perspective; both seek to involve participants so fully that they emotionally become the managers of the simulated company.

According to *Training* magazine, the complexity and availability of business simulations has grown tenfold in the last decade. Now that many such simulations have become available and affordable, human resource (HR) professionals are actively examining them for use in training and other career development programs. And who are the users? Over two-thirds of the Fortune 500 companies, including those often cited as being the best-run corporations in America.

Before examining program design considerations for and the benefits of using business simulations, it is necessary to describe the primary characteristics of business simulations, how business simulation training relates to other HR activities, and how large-scale behavioral simulations differ from computer-based organizational simulations. Business simulations re-create a corporate entity. The various functions of marketing, R&D, finance, personnel, operations, and accounting are present. The simulated company is part of an industry; it experiences competitive, economic, legal, social, political, and regulatory forces just as real companies do. Individuals assume roles as the managers of the simulated organization and seek corporate and individual goals of their choosing. The participants control the simulation outcomes. Depending on the goals, styles, and actions of the people involved, different problems may become important, or different solutions may be found for the same problem.

There are no absolute right answers—but some actions are rewarded more by the training staff than others depending on the concepts and theories presented as part of the total educational experience. Feedback is quick and rich; participants learn more about their analytic and/or management skills in three or four days than they would in several years on the job. Why? Because a large amount of relevant feedback is provided which is linked to specific behaviors, actions, or inactions. Contrary to some people's beliefs, neither large-scale behavioral simulations nor computer-based simulations require past experience in the specific industry or business being simulated. Neither require fluency with computers. Neither involve the ill-structured personal and interpersonal feedback associated with T-groups and sensitivity training.

THE RELATIONSHIP OF BUSINESS SIMULATION TRAINING TO OTHER HR ACTIVITIES

Business simulation training is one of the many types of education that HR professionals examine to fill the developmental needs of the work force. It is also much more. The extensive diagnostic and feedback components of business simulations provide opportunities to link participant self-awareness and learnings with individual and organizational career plans for additional training programs, targeted development efforts, job rotations, special assignments, developmental transfers, and the like. The fact that participants assume a higher-level position in the business simulation than they otherwise have provides an opportunity to diagnose their potential to perform at higher levels. It is a way to have them learn what the demands are like in more senior positions—as sort of a realistic job preview of managerial work.

Business simulations provide participants the opportunity to learn together by giving each other performance feedback—feedback that can be structured to parallel the organization's performance appraisal process. The interactive, experiential nature of business simulations can be used to facilitate the learning of new behaviors that the organization wants to reinforce by having senior managers participate with lower-level managers and/or nonmanagers. The senior managers become role models for the others during the simulation; friendships develop that can become mentor-protégé relationships over time.

Is a business simulation a type of assessment center to be used as a selection or promotion tool? Probably not. The strengths of most business simulations are in diagnosis, feedback, and development, not in assessment per se. Business simulations differ from assessment centers in that in business simulations each participant has a unique position typically in a hierarchical context. The differences in positions make it difficult to directly compare participants as is done in assessment centers. Extensive feedback is provided by the simulation itself, by peers in the simulation, as well as by the program staff. The ratio of participants to trainers is about one half to one-fourth of assessment centers—there may be as many as twelve participants per trainer depending on the program's design. Their cost is substantially lower than that of an assessment center given the smaller number of staff involved.

LARGE-SCALE BEHAVIORAL SIMULATIONS: WHAT ARE THEY?

A large-scale behavioral simulation is an intensive, interactive experience which differs dramatically from most other educational methods. The emphasis is on experiential learning through doing, rather than on vicarious learning through the case study approach. Case studies generate consultant-like behaviors rather than actual managerial behaviors because there is no management group involved in running the company. Large-scale behavioral simulations let the participants run the company.

Large-scale behavioral simulations involve many different roles—from a president to senior vice presidents, to plant managers, to senior staff roles in operations, marketing, personnel, and data processing. Each role contains extensive information on past business decisions and correspondence on current issues, problem symptoms, and decision situations. Only by identifying important issues, collecting and sharing information, and interacting with others can people manage effectively.

Large-scale behavioral simulations create realistic managerial experiences: the ongoing press for information; the need for strong interpersonal and communications skills; the establishment of priorities and specification of goals; and the management of the conflict between strategic and operating views. As a result, managers behave as they do on the job: exposing individual strengths and weaknesses while responding to some situations and leaving others unaddressed. This provides participants the opportunity to identify and examine typical behavior patterns.

Behavioral simulations are tools to highlight the interpersonal dynamics which occur among participants as they address strategic and operating issues—issues which often involve departmental interdependencies, power relationships, and judgment. Organizations that compete in uncertain and turbulent environments face continually changing opportunities and risks. As such, there is a critical need to balance daily operational problems with long-term strategic issues. Behavioral simulations allow participants to experience this challenge and to receive feedback on how they handle it.

Large-scale behavioral simulations are generally part of three- to five-day training programs in which participants manage a simulated company and then receive feedback on their effectiveness. They are also used in advanced business courses which focus on the application of management theory to actual business situations.

In preparation for a large-scale behavioral simulation, participants receive company annual reports, background information, and an extensive overview assignment. After an introduction to the simulation, participants typically meet individually with experienced staff members to share their personal learning objectives. Together, they identify particular skills for feedback and development. Staff members observe the participants at work during the simulation. The staff meets with them later in small groups, then individually, to discuss behaviors and actions. After receiving personal feedback on the areas previously identified, participants suggest action plans to develop the skills necessary for improved performance and greater management effectiveness.

From an organizational perspective, large-scale behavioral simulations provide a controlled setting for the analysis of company-specific patterns of behavior. Through multiple runs of a simulated company, an organization creates a data base from which it can develop an in-depth understanding of its corporate culture, managerial strengths, and training needs. One company that I am familiar with chose to use a large-scale business simulation over other training tools to obtain such information. The following behaviors were consistently observed over six applications of a large-scale behavioral simulation in a medium-sized publishing and information services company: (1) teamwork beyond information sharing was scarce; (2) the formal hierarchy created boundaries which were rarely crossed; (3) members of one division tended to see members of other divisions as competitors rather than co-workers; and (4) decisions were made alone or with consultation; seldom was a decision a group product.

These observations were made and presented by HR staff to the company's president. After his approval, they were shared with the management committee. Senior management agreed that these attributes (and eleven more patterns of behavior observed in the simulation) were representative of the company's culture and the relative strengths and weaknesses of its 350 managers. Several HR efforts were developed, approved, and implemented within six months to address the areas of concern (and to reinforce the areas of strength). In two years' time, the shift in corporate culture was noticeable by both senior management and the HR staff. But did it make a difference in corporate performance? Management says yes. The firm has maintained its number-one position in the industry while confronting several direct assaults by competitors and coordinating several new internal ventures.

COMPUTER-BASED ORGANIZATIONAL SIMULATIONS

Computer-based organizational simulations are as intensive as large-scale behavioral simulations, but the intensity focuses on formulating a strategy through analyzing financial and accounting information, then making specific decisions that are input into the computer model of the business. How much raw material should we buy? What is our inventory level? Should we run two production shifts? What price should we charge? Are we going to do market research? Should we invest this year or next year in plant and equipment? What will the other firms be doing?

Computer-based simulations tend to generate functional analyses and competitive behaviors. Individuals or groups directly compete within the constraints of the programmed model; decision effectiveness is generally measured against the model's design rather than through the interactions with and the judgments of other participants.

There is growing variation in the type and character of computer-based organizational simulations; some can be done individually, but most involve several four- to six-person teams of participants competing in a computer-simulated industry against other teams of participants. Each round of decisions typically comprises a quarter or a years' worth of financial performance. The analytic model contained in the simulation uses the input data from each team (i.e., company) each period to determine the overall level of industry and firm performance. Running the simulation for four to eight periods is typical in a three- to five-day training program.

Individuals participating in computer-based simulations assume the roles of senior management. Position distinctions among team members frequently reflect an agreed upon division of labor rather than role-specific information or unique knowledge relevant to the particular organizational position one has selected. Some teams do not differentiate roles or formalize any division of labor.

Computer-based organizational simulations have been used in business schools and in many corporations for nearly four decades to examine questions of business policy, corporate strategy, marketing strategy, international trade, and so forth. The number of computer-based simulations has grown rapidly since the widespread availability of personal computers. Today one can find computer-based organizational simulations for over a dozen industries and several functional specialties. Many of these simulations were designed to teach specific analytic models of how a business unit, department, or product line functions within an organizational context and competitive environment. To the extent that the underlying computer model reflects current reality, the simulation has utility. The risk associated with the use of computer-based organizational simulations should be apparent: If the model is in error, one could be etching the minds of participants with logic that either no longer applies to the current business situation or is inappropriately limited by the constraints of the computer program. Large-scale behavioral simulations, which are fewer in number, are not subject to this particular criticism because there is no specified model within them. A potential problem with large-scale behavioral simulations is that the judgmental problems and issues they contain can become dated. An action that required a calculated and precise judgment in 1978 may be trivial and obvious in 1988. Both of these criticisms indicate that the guts of business simulations need to be understood by HR professionals before they are extensively used in an organization.

Another difference between computer-based organizational simulations and large-scale behavioral simulations is the types of behavior exhibited by participants. Computer-based simulations stimulate quantitative analyses, competition, and gamesmanship. The overriding goal felt by participants is to develop a strategy or game plan to win—to grow faster or earn more profits than the other teams of participants. Large-scale behavioral simulations stimulate qualitative analyses, interpersonal interaction, and cooperation. The goal is to run the company as effectively as possible and not to rock the boat. Computer-based simulations place substantial technical and administrative demands on the training staff; large-scale behavioral simulations require the training staff to have good observational, facilitative, and small group process skills. Both use a greater amount of organizational resources in terms of program management time and equipment needs than lecture/discussion or case analysis methods.

PROGRAM DESIGN CONSIDERATIONS

The design of a program using a business simulation is central to the effective delivery of the simulation. In order to be effective, a business simulation must be compatible with the learning goals of the overall program. Business simulations are tools; their potential value is reached when they are well integrated with concept and skill-building sessions within a training or development program.

The design considerations for a program using a business simulation are numerous. However, the overriding consideration is this: What are the training or developmental needs that the program is to satisfy? Without conducting a training needs analysis, it is unlikely that the purpose of a program will be clear, that senior management will support the program, or that individuals will gain maximum benefit from participation. If managerial skills and strategic management skills need diagnosis or development, consider a large-scale behavioral simulation. If functional analysis skills and strategic planning skills need diagnosis or development, consider a computer-based organizational simulation.

Conducting a needs analysis generally involves surveying employees as to their developmental needs. This can be done through a mail questionnaire sent to a sample of potential participants, telephone interviews of select managers, or small discussion groups whose members are invited because of their insight and expertise in the area of training needs. The outcome of such surveys, interviews, and discussions should be a prioritized list of the areas needing to be developed in the organization's work force.

The primary goals of a program should derive directly from the training needs to be satisfied. Primary goals should be stated explicitly to participants. If, for example, there is a need to develop skills of delegation and control, then one goal for a large-scale behavioral simulation program would be to enhance participants' understanding and ability of how to delegate tasks effectively. Alternatively, if there is a need to develop marketing skills in newcomers to the marketing area, then a goal for a computer-based organizational simulation program would be to train marketing concepts such as market segmentation, market share, and channels of distribution.

Several secondary goals can be accomplished with business simulations that may be relevant to program development efforts. These include (1) providing participants with a common experience base or framework from which to manage; (2) evolving a sense of corporate identity through the sharing of ideas and viewpoints in a nonthreatening environment; (3) developing an informal network among participants to augment the formal hierarchical system; and (4) articulating and reinforcing the organization's culture and values.

These secondary goals are generally a part of the HR unit's philosophy and mission—they may or may not be articulated to participants in each program. However, secondary goals should affect design decisions. To the extent that a goal is espoused, the program should be tailored to meet the goal. For example, if a common experience base or framework is desired, business simulation offerings should be well integrated with other training and development efforts. The previously mentioned publishing and information services company espoused this goal. They were careful not to present conflicting concepts or theories in different programs or from those required on the job so as not to undermine the common experience/ framework goal.

Alternatively, if evolving a sense of corporate identity through the sharing of ideas is a goal, group discussions around the behaviors and decisions made during a business simulation would be preferred to lectures or discussions on topics that are not part of this common experience base. Several large, diversified manufacturing companies use business simulations just this way.

Developing an informal network among participants can be facilitated through using business simulations as team-building activities. Some of the feedback focuses on the nature and quality of the interpersonal relationships that emerged and how to improve them. Research by Robert Kaplan and associates at the Center for Creative Leadership has shown this to be a particularly valuable application of a large-scale behavioral simulation in one organization; several other organizations have applied simulations in this way with notable success.

The goal of articulating and reinforcing the organization's culture and values can be facilitated by having participants discuss the culture they created and the values they espoused through their actions in the simulated company. These will typically mirror those of the corporation so well that the participants will make the linkage without prompting by the training staff. The desired values are then reinforced by the training staff in hopes of seeing them perpetuated. Several large financial service companies have found that using business simulations to facilitate accomplishing this goal is particularly valuable as they expand nationally and acquire businesses that have cultures different from the parent company. By involving people from the newly acquired business along with senior people from the parent company in each program, they are able to address issues of culture and values in an open, nonthreatening way after the simulation.

Whatever the secondary goals, they need to be made explicit along with the primary goals in the program design stage. Once the goals are listed— and tagged to specific developmental or organizational needs—design decisions follow. If goal accomplishment is hampered by organizational constraints (e.g., delivery costs, program duration, facility needs), the trade-offs of one design can be assessed against another by examining how likely each design alternative is to accomplish each primary and secondary goal.

DIAGNOSIS AND DEVELOPMENT

There may appear to be an inconsistency in the previous statements in that the decision to use a business simulation should be based on a training needs analysis, yet business simulations can be used to diagnose business skills. This dual role of business simulations is possible because they permit participants to behave in whatever way they view as appropriate; then they allow the participants and staff to examine that behavior. For most people, this is diagnostic data on their specific skills. As long as the general skill area addressed by the staff facilitating the business simulation's use has been identified as being in need of development, then the business simulation can be both diagnosing individuals' skill levels and providing skill development within a program. The participants' skill areas needing further development can subsequently become part of a targeted development effort over a series of years. Manuel London and I have proposed ten guidelines in *Managing careers* for organizations to follow in their use of targeted development efforts. Diagnostic information is essential to the targeted development process. Diagnostic data from a business simulation, coupled with a self-assessment and assessments by peers, superiors, and subordinates yield a well-balanced and powerful baseline from which to design individualized career development programs.

Large-scale behavioral simulations most effectively address managerial skills or strategic management skills depending on how the simulations are positioned within a program and the feedback process used. Core managerial skills that can be diagnosed and developed include setting realistic and challenging objectives, day-to-day planning, clarifying roles and objectives, establishing priorities, informing others, involving others, motivating others, communicating effectively, delegating tasks while maintaining control, and recognizing and rewarding performance, among others. Strategic management skills that can be diagnosed and developed include envisioning, analyzing the business environment, assessing the current business situation, sustaining a competitive advantage, handling ambiguity, behaving flexibly, championing ideas, reconceptualizing issues, and influencing strategy formulation and implementation. These latter skills which focus on strategic management have recently emerged as additional skills needed by middle- and senior-level managers that confront extensive competition in turbulent and uncertain environments.

Computer-based organizational simulations most effectively address functional analysis skills or strategic planning skills depending on the computer simulation used. Functional analysis skills include marketing strategy and tactics, bank asset and liability management, production and inventory control management, portfolio management, and research and development project management, to name a few. Strategic planning skills include economic forecasting, environmental assessments, trend analysis of key business indicators, industry and competitor analyses, and strategy formulation.

The relative emphasis when using a business simulation for diagnosis versus development depends on how precisely the skill deficiencies of the intended participants are known. When development is clearly needed, the use of business simulations can be tailored to those needs. Concepts and skill exercises would precede the simulation to give the participants a chance to understand and explore the new ideas and skills in a simple setting. A business simulation would then be used to test the transfer of learning to an organizational context. The feedback provided would target the skills being developed and suggest ways of further transferring the learnings to the job.

When diagnosis is needed—particularly when different participants are likely to have different but unknown developmental needs within a skill area (e.g., some need delegation skill development, others need skill development in establishing realistic and challenging objectives)—then the business simulation would be used at the beginning of a program and followed by various skill-building modules. Large-scale behavioral simulations are used in just this way by such companies as Dow Jones, Imperial Life, Union Carbide, and Monsanto. Participants conclude the simulation portion of the program with a clear understanding and acceptance of their relative strengths and weaknesses. Because they both own the diagnosis and see the relevance of the skills to effective performance, they are highly motivated to develop abilities in the areas identified as needing improvement.

BENEFITS OF USING BUSINESS SIMULATIONS

The most common benefits sought through the use of business simulations are to help employees see their organizations from a senior management perspective and to stimulate the learning of various cognitive and behavioral skills viewed as necessary to manage effectively. Richard Lepsinger and Stephen Wall of Manus Associates in New York and Tom Mullen and I of New York University have analyzed why business simulations, particularly large-scale behavioral simulations, are able to facilitate adult learning.

First, they are able to replicate much of the fast-paced and fragmented nature of managerial work. There is more information available in a simulation than individuals can digest; there are more possible actions than can be taken individually or by the group; and, the level of uncertainty and ambiguity tends to be high. If the environment changes in ways that require new patterns of managerial behavior, business simulations can be altered or updated to reflect these changes. While the simulated company feels real, the participants are operating in a setting where information and possible decisions are familiar to the training staff. The managers feel as if they are operating in their typical, open-ended environment and act much the way they would on the job. This simulated company setting enables a professional staff to gather data through observation and questionnaires on such things as the goals that were set, the visions shared, the actions taken, the influence processes employed, and the climate created. How well individuals handle ambiguity, reconceptualize issues, and flexibly behave can be observed and discussed.

Second, managers have the luxury of stepping back and looking closely at what they did after the simulation. The data generated provide the basis for discussion and serve as a starting point for an analysis of the organization and their contribution to its success and problems. These discussions allow managers to reflect, analyze, and diagnose alternative scenarios, causes of new problems they may have created, and lessons learned.

Third, the competencies and concepts covered in a program tend to get internalized because they are being used. Discussion alone does not help a manager feel what it's like to effectively influence another person or to create and implement a vision of an organization's future. More important, discussion alone does not help a manager develop an understanding for and skill to overcome failures in these areas. Coming to grips with the reality that one's influence attempts failed and one's vision was ignored can only happen if such attempts are freely exhibited and responded to. To be of value, managerial competencies must be taken beyond cognitive understanding to become part of a manager's day-to-day behavior.

CONCLUSIONS

Business simulations require managers to use a wide range of managerial competencies and skills. Unlike other forms of management development, business simulations allow managers to act on what they think should be done in particular situations. Individuals iterate between thought and action, and they get to see the financial and interpersonal results of their managerial style. Because of the experiential nature of business simulations, managers better understand the cause-and-effect relationships of their actions and gain a keen awareness of their individual strengths and weaknesses.

The replication of a managerial environment within a complex organization facilitates the transfer of learnings back to the job. Managers are better able to integrate key learnings and personal insights from the simulated environment with their job because the two environments have many similarities. The lessons have more meaning and impact because they are presented in a context that is familiar and meaningful to the learner.

A difficult obstacle to overcome in helping people to develop an organizational perspective is the nature of strategy. Strategy formulation and implementation in organizations occurs over long periods of time. This makes it difficult to provide timely feedback on the impact of managerial actions on organizational goal accomplishment. Feedback on how well an individual is performing is a critical factor in personal and professional development. When feedback on actions taken or actions not taken is not available or timely, people continue to act ineffectively, or they act without an understanding of what they are contributing to the desired organizational outcomes. Business simulations overcome these problems to varying degrees depending on how they are used. At the conclusion of a business simulation, participants immediately begin to review the strategies they formulated as well as their implementation efforts. For example: Were actions in support of organizational goals? How were they individually and collectively able to reshape or redefine complex problems? How did they handle critical information? Were their priorities clear and acted upon? Because there is little time lapse between action and feedback, the feedback has a high degree of validity and utility for the participants.

No doubt, the use of business simulations will continue to grow, and their usefulness will continue to be enhanced as HR professionals tailor their use to satisfy specific organizational needs. As suggested by this discussion, care must be taken when selecting different types of business simulations for different applications. Asking the right questions about a particular business simulation's structure and purpose is as important for the HR professional as is the design and delivery of the educational program.

SELECTED BIBLIOGRAPHY

Several articles have appeared on the growing use of business simulations in work organizations. Jack Gordon's "Games managers play" (*Training*, July, 1985) provides a review of several business simulations. Peter Petre's "Games that teach you to manage" (*Fortune*, October 29, 1984) discusses the use of large-scale behavioral simulations. John Soat examines the use of two business simulations—Metrobank and Investcorp—for strategic management in "Mastering the art of strategic management through simulation" (*Office administration and automation*, November, 1984). For more information on business simulations, contact the Association for Business Simulation and Experiential Learning (ABSEL), University of Tulsa, 600 S. College Ave., Tulsa, OK 74104, or the Management Simulation Projects Group, New York University, 40 West 4th Street, New York, NY 10012.

A number of papers are available that more fully describe and detail the use of business simulations. Robert Kaplan's *The looking glass experience: A story of learning through action and reflection* (Center for Creative Leadership, 1984) details the experiences of four people as participants in the large-scale behavioral simulation called Looking Glass, Inc. The program management demands associated with large-scale behavioral simulations are examined by Stephen Stumpf and Monica Shay in *Behavioral simulation program manager and administrator guide* (New York University, 1985). Richard Lepsinger, Thomas Mullen, Stephen Stumpf, and Stephen Wall examine the use of business simulations to assess and develop strategic management skills in "Large-scale management simulations: A training technology for assessing and developing strategic management skills" in S. Mailick, S. Haberman, and S. Wall (eds.), *Advances in management development* (Praeger, 1988). Robert Kaplan, Michael Lombardo, and Mignone Mazique discuss the use of large-scale behavioral simulations for team building in *A mirror for managers: Using simulation to develop management teams* (Center for Creative Leadership, 1983). For people interested in a general resource on career development for managers, see Manuel London and Stumpf's *Managing careers* (Addison-Wesley, 1982).

TRAINING MANAGERS TO BE DEVELOPERS

_____ EDWARD M. MONE

The pace of change is accelerating. But what is required of companies in an environment that can only be characterized as rapidly changing? An environment whose horizon has been transformed by a rainbow of national and world events, including

- The deregulation of major industries (e.g., trucking, airlines, and telecommunications);
- Increased competition from the Far East, including South Korea and Taiwan;
- Rapid technological change resulting in shorter life cycles for new products;
- The restructuring of American corporations through major downsizings, mergers and acquisitions, and strategic alliances with foreign companies; and
- The shrinking of middle-management ranks, particularly in the industrial sector, coupled with a trend toward the growth of a service-oriented economy.

American companies must become competitive. To do so, they must better understand themselves in terms of mission, goals, and the fundamental strategies for achieving those goals. The organization's strengths and weaknesses must be identified, and its competitive advantage must be determined. The leaders of today's organization must establish and then communicate a vision for success, as well as create an environment in which all employees can contribute to company success.

Ultimately, today's corporation depends for its survival—its ability to compete—on the contributions of its employees, both labor and management alike. Innovation, creativity, productivity, and the continued development of people with a focus for gaining the needed skills and knowledge for an uncertain future are key for corporate success into the 1990s and beyond. Once the mission, goals, and fundamental strategies are in place, however, it becomes the manager's job (role) to ensure that the organization's goals can be made meaningful to his or her employees and that these goals are met.

But the questions remain: How can managers help? What should managers do? What role should managers play? And then, what can the human resource professional do that enables the line manager to fulfill this role? This chapter addresses the role of the manager as developer—a role I feel is crucial to achieving long-term success and a national, competitive advantage—and considers what the human resource professional can do to make that role effective, meaningful, and successful.

THE MANAGER AS DEVELOPER

The developer role is an approach to managing people on a day-to-day basis. It is not a once-a-year appraisal and feedback session. It is providing a work environment and behaving in ways that foster the growth, learning, and development of subordinates. When managers truly understand the role, they will never say that they don't have the time to spend on developing their subordinates. They will know that developing subordinates is their job and that is how they will spend their time.

The learning environment that managers create for their subordinates is a direct result of their own attitudes, knowledge, and skills. These factors are manifest through the manager's words and actions, which communicate to subordinates what is and is not important to the manager and, perhaps, the organization. The problem in most organizations today is that managers, although possessing the skills and knowledge required of the developer role, will espouse its importance but not support it by their own actions. Spending time developing subordinates may be viewed as time away from the "real job" because development is not directly measured and rewarded. This inconsistency between the managers' words and behaviors causes subordinates to be suspect about the development focus and may result in performance that benefits neither the individual nor the organization in the long run. Obviously, what is needed is a high degree of consistency between the words and behaviors of managers for the creation of an environment supportive of development—the vehicle for success in today's and tomorrow's marketplace. Helping managers to achieve this consistency is the job of the human resource professional whose goal should be institutionalizing the manager developer role in his or her organization.

THE "WHY, WHO, WHAT, WHEN, WHERE AND HOW" OF THE DEVELOPER ROLE

My experience working with managers in trying to help them implement the developer role has taught me the importance of clarifying its different aspects and the expectations that the role brings. Although most managers agree that the development focus is good for its own sake, managers often need to be reminded and shown that this role is crucial to organization success. Some additional "why's" for this role include

- The positive effect of development on employee motivation and productivity;
- The necessity for having better developed and skilled employees for success in rapidly changing organizations where people, not just technology, provide a competitive advantage; and
- Ensuring that employees will be able to assume and be motivated by different and challenging lateral assignments as upward movement becomes limited.

Some managers my colleagues and I talked with reported that they originally thought of development as something they did with poor performers who were deficient in skills or lacking motivation. Managers must understand and realize that the "who" is really all employees, at all levels in the organization, at any point or stage in their careers. Development is future and growth oriented, not negatively motivated by deficiencies. All employees must be growing and contributing to organization success.

In many instances, both managers and their subordinates felt that the "what" or purpose of the developer role was to prepare subordinates for promotion. However, the focus is broader; it includes gaining more responsibility and greater autonomy in the present job, acquiring the skills and background for the next job (possibly a lateral assignment in a different department), and adding technical and/or managerial skills.

The "when" for most managers was easily answered once they grasped the concept of the role; they realized that development is an ongoing function, not a one-time or once-a-year planning activity.

Finally, development takes place both on and off the job, and so managers, when it came to asking "where," were encouraged to help subordinates determine the best kinds of development opportunities and plan where to get them. Often, this involved one of the "how's" such as formal classroom training sponsored by the organization or outside institutions; it also may have involved self-paced learning. Additional, broad-based techniques or "how's" include career and performance counseling, mentoring, task force assignments, job rotations, and temporary interdepartmental loans.

INSTITUTIONALIZING THE MANAGER DEVELOPER ROLE

In order for the manager developer role to work, the philosophy must become embedded in the organization and have the support of top management. That support must be communicated throughout the organization, preferably by both words and actions, and structures must be in place that will provide the ongoing support for the manager as developer.

The human resource manager can help the leaders of the organization embody this message in the company's mission statement. One company included the following statement: "recognizing that its human resources are the business's most valuable assets, employees will be provided challenging jobs, attractive career opportunities, competitive compensation and a safe working environment."

This same company, further supporting the development focus, stated that one of its key business strategies was organizational effectiveness and employee development. A cornerstone in this strategy was the organization's commitment to provide all employees with meaningful work and the opportunity to grow to their fullest potential, based on the principle that its people constitute the company's competitive edge.

When strategic commitment to the development of people is present, it is often not long before the human resource professional will be asked to help company leaders design and implement plans that drive development as a value and way of life throughout their organizations. The human resource manager can play a crucial role by ensuring that management systems support and reward a development focus and that adequate programs and resources are also in place.

MANAGEMENT SYSTEM SUPPORT

The manager developer role can be supported and promoted through an integrated management system that includes goal setting, management development, performance management, performance appraisal, and compensation. These processes aid in institutionalizing the developer role by providing the necessary motivation and rewards for both managers and subordinates.

Having well-defined, meaningful, and attainable goals is important to motivation and performance. Setting goals for the development of a subordinate holds the manager involved responsible for seeing those goals achieved (fulfilling the developer role); it also motivates the subordinate, since development efforts become real, valued, and rewarded. Therefore, we recommend that managers include as part of the goal-setting process establishing development goals. One organization has its managers formulate specific development goals. Their managers must ensure that these goals are

- Output focused with excellence criteria;
- Connected directly to a particular skill or knowledge area;
- Related to producing outputs required by the subordinate's job; and
- Challenging to achieve but possible to attain.

Exhibit 15.1
Criteria for Evaluating Goal Accomplishments: An Example

Output	Excellence Criteria
Increased knowledge of cost-justification techniques.	• able to direct subordinates to provide appropriate data for cost-justification techniques.
	• demonstrate proficiency by using several different techniques on the job
	• prepare an accurate financial analysis report in ninety days
	• receive positive feedback on accuracy and value of financial analysis reports from higher-level managers.

An example of an output-focused development goal, with its excellence criteria, is shown in Exhibit 15.1.

Closely related to goal setting is the process of management development. In this instance, we define it as acquiring the necessary skills and knowledge to perform in the current or a future job. Both the manager and subordinate need to determine if the subordinate has the skills to achieve and produce his or her goals, including development goals. Here, human resource managers can provide the necessary process or tools to aid in assessing the subordinates' competencies and serve as resources to help them locate the most effective training opportunities, or to structure a developmental assignment. Development can occur in many ways. Exhibit 15.2 is an example of a detailed plan for a subordinate to produce the output "increased knowledge of cost-justification techniques."

Once goals are set and plans to achieve them are created, they are, unfortunately, often neglected. Goals should be monitored on a regular, continuous basis for their meaningfulness and their attainment. It may be that new goals are developed or that previously established goals are renegotiated. But a key part of the developer role is to ensure progress toward goal achievement, including development goals. I recommend that the human resource professionals counsel managers to (1) ask themselves if their subordinates are achieving their goals and developing the required skills for strong performance; (2) find out if there is a performance concern and determine whether it is a function of ability, motivation, or both; (3) share their concerns with the subordinate in question and jointly assess the concern; (4) mutually decide on a strategy that most effectively deals with the concern; and (5) create and later evaluate the action plan based on the performance improvement strategy selected.

Although this five-part performance management process may be more

Exhibit 15.2
A Detailed Developmental Plan for One Goal

DEVELOPMENT GOALS (Output & Criteria)	ACTIVITIES	COMPLETION DATES TARGET/ACTUAL		COMMENTS
Increased knowledge of cost-justification techniques	o Attend A Basic financial awareness seminar	2nd quarter		
- able to direct subordinates to provide appropriate data for cost justification analysis	o Take Financial Analysis I at state college	2nd quarter	not completed	Course cancelled by college
	o Review 3 proposals using different cost-justification techniques	1st quarter/		
- demonstrate proficiency by using several different techniques in on-the-job situations	o Submit monthly budget analysis; schedule half-hour discussion with manager once a month	1st quarter/	1st quarter	
- prepare completed accurate financial analysis report in ninety days	o Work with peer on three cost-justification techniques:	2nd quarter		
- receive positive feedback on accuracy and value of financial analysis reports from higher level managers.	- Cost/Benefit - Internal Rate of Return - Return on Equity			

or less formalized in different organizations, it is an ongoing responsibility of the developer role and an important link to performance appraisal (sometimes it is part of an appraisal system). It helps to foster employee growth through challenging work and may provide input for performance appraisal.

When it comes to performance appraisal, it is important that the human resource professional ensure that subordinates are evaluated on their achievement of development goals, and managers, in their role as developers, are evaluated on their ability to help their subordinates to achieve their goals and grow to meet the future needs of the business. Rewards should be administered accordingly for the varying degrees of success in fulfilling the developer role. This brings us to the final part of the supportive management system, compensation.

It will be important for the human resource manager to ensure that a manager's compensation reflects role efficacy. Experience has shown us too many situations where compensation policy was not philosophically in support of the developer role, and, as a consequence, what finally mattered was production or sales quotas. For the manager developer role to be a vital force in helping organizations to remain competitive over time, managers must be rewarded significantly for these efforts.

PROGRAMS AND RESOURCES FOR THE DEVELOPER ROLE

From numerous interviews and discussions with managers at different levels of the organizations, my colleagues and I learned several key points that help managers grow comfortable with and become competent in the developer role. We needed to

- Enable them to understand the reasons why they needed to develop their subordinates more than ever before;
- Help them to analyze their experience as subordinates and to determine what behaviors from bosses helped their careers and their development;
- Help them to assess and confront their own effective and ineffective behaviors as a manager developer;
- Help them to locate resources and training that would give them the skills and knowledge needed for role performance, and in how to begin—what to do next to effectively engage in the developer role; and
- Help them determine what they need from their boss for their own development.

One approach we found successful for accomplishing these challenges was to give managers the opportunity to explore these issues in a workshop setting. This workshop is outlined in Appendix A. The questions in Appendix B were used in the workshop to encourage participants to reflect on what they need from their own bosses for their personal development.

SELF-REFLECTIVE GUIDE

We wanted to develop a way to help managers quickly and easily grasp the range of the developer role and to see how it impacts several areas of management responsibilities. As a result, we generated a self-reflective tool to help them assess the extent of their ability to create a development-oriented environment. The tool, presented in Appendix C, includes eight different areas of responsibility, goals for the manager to attain in each area, and major performance expectations that lead to achieving these goals. Its intent was not to be exhaustive, but to establish a framework for thinking about and managing a development-oriented environment.

POSSIBLE CONCERNS

Although the suggestions and recommendations made here should contribute to institutionalizing the developer role in most, if not all, organizations, I would like to briefly discuss two concerns that are often heard by the human resource manager when, in effect, acting as a change agent.

The first has to do with costs. Many managers and, worse yet, executives may tell you that the cost of a development focus is too high. We try to remind them that when managers can provide the right environment with a development orientation, and employee behavior is guided and goal directed, the result is that more managers become increasingly involved in solving problems, creating new products, and finding innovative ways of doing the job better, faster, and cheaper. We then ask them to consider the costs of not investing in their human capital.

The second concern has to do with basic resistance to change. We encountered such resistance because of the following reasons:

- Misunderstanding the developer role, thinking it to be a one-time activity;
- Managers believing that they were already developers, but realizing that their efforts were limited—and sometimes frustrated by a lack of skills (e.g., listening, feedback);
- Feelings that managers would be relinquishing control if they became more participative and encouraged more risk taking and autonomy in their subordinates.

But for most managers, the developer role is what they thought was right and would choose, but not currently what they did. We just have to help them take that next step.

APPENDIX A:

This outline is for a one-day workshop for mid-level managers on development. The goal is to increase managers' awareness of their role as a key resource in their subordinates' career development.

The workshop focuses on why the role of developer is so important to good management. Participants identify who is developed and in what way—that is, the meaning of development for different types of subordinates (mid-career, plateaued managers, young fast-trackers, supervisors newly promoted from occupational ranks). The workshop then explores the when, where, and how of development. Participants also consider their own situations—the barriers to and motivations for their spending time developing their subordinates and their competence to be developers. The participants identify resources that support career development (for example, assessment centers to evaluate subordinates' strengths and weaknesses and staffing mechanisms to help move people into different positions). Finally, the participants set goals and plans for developing members of their work groups.

8:30–8:40   ANNOUNCEMENTS

8:40–9:15   *Get acquainted*
             To build group cohesion, promote sharing, and focus the direction for the day. Participants interview each other about their career histories (10 min.) and then take turns introducing the person they interviewed (25 min.). (Times listed are approximate and can be adjusted as needed.)

9:15–9:35   *Agenda clarification*
             To give participants an opportunity to express their expectations and react to the intended purpose of the day. The instructor presents the broad agenda (5 min.) and then asks for additional goals the participants hope to accomplish or issues they wish to address (5 min.). The instructor discusses which of these issues are already incorporated in the agenda, areas where the agenda can be adapted to accommodate participants' needs, and areas that are beyond the scope of the workshop and how they can be addressed in other ways (other courses, discussions with top managers, investigation of corporate policies) (10 min.).

9:35–10:30   *"Why" be a developer*
             To establish the rationale for the manager's role as developer in relation to business needs and changing company cultures. Instructor lecture and large-group discussion.

10:30–10:45 BREAK

10:45–11:30 *The "who" and "what" of career development*
             To understand the needs of different types of employees (for example, early-career managers, newly promoted managers, advancement-oriented managers, those who view themselves as specialists and professionals in a particular discipline, plateaued managers, mid-career managers, and those approaching retirement). Instructor leads a brainstorming session in the large group to identify these different types (10 min.). The focus then turns to what development means for these subordinates (10 min.). Working individually, participants prepare a matrix of subordinate types and development activities (10 min.). The instructor then creates a matrix on easel paper with participant input (15 min.).

11:30–11:45   *The "where," "how," and "when" of development*
To clarify where development activities take place—in the boss's
office, at a career-planning seminar, on one's own. To outline different styles of management—the boss merely provides information
about career opportunities, the boss tells subordinates about their
potential, the boss discusses career possibilities and counsels subordinates. To ascertain the frequency of these activities—once a year,
whenever the boss feels a discussion is relevant, whenever the subordinate feels the need for a discussion. The instructor leads a brain-
storming presentation of these different possibilities.

11:45–12:00   *Applying the development concepts*
To further acquaint participants with these concepts and encourage
them to think about their own development needs as well as those
of their subordinates. Participants complete a self-assessment sheet
on their own work groups and themselves, describing needed career-
development activities and when, where, and how they should occur.
Participants also describe the extent of support for development they
would like from their supervisors.

12:00–1:00   LUNCH BREAK

1:00–1:05   Reviewing and clarifying previous discussions and outlining work
for the afternoon.

1:05–1:20   *Reactions to self-assessment*
To discuss how participants feel about putting themselves in the role
of subordinates. To deal with the boss's motivation in supporting
employee development. Instructor leads large-group discussion of
subordinate, self- and supervisor expectations and roles in career
development.

1:20–1:55   *Motivation for being a developer*
To identify the reinforcements for being a developer and to identify
barriers. The large group breaks into two or three subgroups to
brainstorm about motivators (improved productivity, reputation as
a department for the best people) and barriers (managers are not
evaluated on how well they develop their people, time spent with
employees on career issues takes time away from achieving the basic
goals of the unit) (20 min.). Each group then reports its findings to
the large group for discussion (15 min.).

1:55–2:35   *Competence in and comfort with the development role*
To have participants consider their competence in engaging in a full
range of career development support activities and their degree of
comfort with those activities. Participants complete written descriptions of their support behaviors (15 min.). In the large group, participants report their reactions, feelings, and conclusions (25 min.).

2:35–3:00   *Available resources*
To review and discuss internal and external resources available to
support the developer role. Instructor hands out and reviews a resource guide (10 min.). Resources include ways to learn and improve

skills related to supporting development, such as giving feedback. Participants are encouraged to use each other for practice—for instance, by being helpful to peers in career planning and development and giving each other reinforcement for help (15 min.).

3:00–3:15   BREAK

3:15–4:30   *Action planning*
To move from learning to planning action steps. To emphasize the need to plan if participants are to spend time and energy on development activities for subordinates, peers, and themselves and to engender support from their bosses. Participants individually write their action plans (30 min.) and then discuss and revise them (45 min.).

4:30–5:00   *Wrap-up*
To review the day's work, solicit reactions, and discuss ways to meet needs that were not met by the workshop. Participants discuss each other's career plans, ways to increase support from higher organizational levels for working with subordinates on their career planning and development, and ways to increase higher managers' involvement in the development of their immediate subordinates.

APPENDIX B: THE PERTINENT QUESTIONS REGARDING MANAGER AS DEVELOPER

1. So far, we have been discussing *your* role as a developer. How might you benefit from *your boss's* becoming a career developer for you?

2. What should the focus of development be for you? What would the purpose of the developer role be when taken on by your boss in relationship to you?

3. Where should development take place for you?

4. How, specifically, should your boss go about helping you to develop your own career?

5. How often would you like to be meeting with your own superior to review your development plans?

APPENDIX C: A SELF-REFLECTIVE GUIDE FOR ASSESSING THE EMPLOYEE DEVELOPMENT ENVIRONMENT*

Area of Responsibility	Goal	Performance Expectations
Employee Selection	Selection of the best employee for the position	Reviews past work
		Verifies work and references
		Requires job sample from applicant
		Conducts interview
		Provides information for applicant to self-select
		Conducts realistic job preview
		Provides feedback for applicant regardless of decision
Orientation	Orient an employee to his/her job, department, and company in a way that maximizes that employee's motivation, comfort, and ability to perform excellently	Provides information and exposure to:
		initial job assignment
		company policies and practices
		essential persons and functions
		the manager as a person
Job Structure	Establishing goals toward which an employee's work is directed that are challenging and contribute to that employee's development	Jointly establishes measurable and specific goals
		Includes input of subordinates where possible
		Communicates clearly within work group
		Incorporates innovative ideas
	Establishing performance standards for work which guide an employee's progress toward his or her group's goals	Ensures goals are supported by superiors
		Sets job performance standards which are realistic
		Communicates work group goals to subordinates
		Ensures best person/task match

*This guide was developed in conjunction with James Shillaber of Rutgers University, in New Jersey.

Area of Responsibility	Goal	Performance Expectations
Job Structure	Delegating work where possible	Communicates clearly the end results required
		Allows creativity by subordinates
		Encourages responsibility and problem solving
	Communicating about the organization to enhance an employee's sense of identity and maintain motivation and morale	Communicates relationship of group's work to organization's purpose and policies
		Communicates information about changes and the impact these will have on the employee and work group
		Communicates information about new trends and directions
		Leads to shared vision and purpose among group members
Job Skill Training	To provide job skill training which maximally impacts an employee's present job performance and future development needs	Orients training toward knowledge, skills, and attitudes
		Ensures training is as applied (hands on) as possible
		Coordinates and takes responsibility for all training
		Evaluates and reinforces training outcomes
		Ensures transfer of learning through new opportunities
Performance Feedback	To provide feedback about job performance specifically oriented toward the development of employees	Assess ongoing development needs based on individual's and organization needs

Area of Responsibility	Goal	Performance Expectations
Work Environment	To develop a work environment which maximally contributes to employee development	Creates supportive working relationships
		Facilitates the accomplishment of objectives
		Generates enthusiasm and commitment to development achievement
		Encourages initiative, innovation, and risk taking
		Rewards cooperation and teamwork
		Supports the development and expression of individual competence
		Encourages the honest and timely exchange of feedback
		Reflects integrity and ethics
		Assures best match of talent to task
Career Development	To facilitate the development of subordinate's careers	Holds formal and informal discussions with employees
		Helps employee identify career-related skills, interests, and values
		Helps employee identify career options
		Identifies resources for employee's career development
		Serves as a role model by demonstrating successful career behaviors
		Increases employee's visibility when appropriate
		Provides access to specific career development opportunities
		Provides job experience which prepare employees for their next jobs

Area of Responsibility	Goal	Performance Expectations
Manager as Person	To use the manager's own experience as a source of feedback about, and an opportunity to enhance, the employee development climate	Requests feedback about employee's experience and effects of own supervisory style on employee's development
		Conducts ongoing assessment of key environmental indicators such as productivity, conflict, and morale
		Assesses performance problems broadly, to consider individual group and organizational factors

Part IV

Career Experiences

This section addresses career issues relevant to specific groups of employees: minorities, women, executives, professionals, and those who lose their jobs. It demonstrates the themes that social pressures and other discontinuities create barriers that are dysfunctional for individual career progress and satisfaction and for organizational effectiveness. The chapters suggest ways human resource professionals can help overcome these barriers.

In his chapter on the problems minorities face in the work force, John Fernandez defines racism and analyzes the barriers confronting minorities in becoming full, equal members of corporations. Drawing on the responses of thousands of employee surveys, Fernandez depicts forms of racism and explores the underlying reasons for racism, such as the threat minorities pose to whites' privileged position. He describes how the toughest stereotypes for minorities (and women) to counteract are those related to their abilities and qualifications. Minorities have to be better performers than whites to get ahead, but even outstanding performance is not necessarily enough to break through the informal networks that form the corporate power structure. One way to be sure that the informal work group will be more useful than harmful for minorities is for minorities to have sponsors high on the organizational hierarchy to introduce them and mentor them.

Fernandez's recommendations for human resource professionals include designing reward and recognition systems to reinforce minority sponsorship and advancement. He emphasizes the importance of comprehensive training for employees at all organizational levels, including top management, on understanding how to develop a pluralistic organizational climate. He also highlights the necessity to integrate affirmative action and equal opportunity awareness and actions throughout the organization's existing functions, in all departments at all levels.

Ronald Downey and Mary Anne Lahey's chapter on women in management describes discrimination women face in starting a career as a manager. Social forces in the family, school, and among peers are some of the initial barriers women face to starting a career. Also, discrimination enters into every stage of the organizational selection process, including the job description, advertising the job, reviewing applications, interviewing candidates, and the final selection decision. For instance, job descriptions that focus on activities, skills, and abilities that are status quo encourage looking for someone who is modeled after the current incumbent, who is usually male. While the percentage of women in management has increased during the last twenty-five years, the increase is generally limited to low and middle levels of management.

Downey and Lahey review the evidence that men are not more effective managers than women. Yet the popular belief that there is a difference persists, and women are treated differently from men in terms of the opportunities and salaries available to them. The authors suggest career management strategies for women for overcoming treatment discrimination such as networking and seeking a mentor. Finally, Downey and Lahey cover the conflicts women face between their work and family roles. They discuss the difficulty of this problem and how it can be dealt with by positive actions.

Michael Lombardo addresses the experience of becoming an effective leader. The research he reports finds that executives develop by learning from challenging job assignments, other people, and hard times, as well as from formal course work. Leadership tasks are developmental when they require dealing with new work demands and new groups of people. Also, tasks are developmental when the leader must formulate a strategy or perspective, start up something new, such as a new product line, turn around a troubled unit, or maintain and expand an existing unit. Good and bad bosses are another source of learning what to do and what not to do to be successful. Tough situations and failure experiences increase executives' awareness of their limitations.

Lombardo outlines skills and perspectives important for executive success, such as being resourceful, building and maintaining relationships, and confronting problem subordinates. The purpose of an effective executive development system is to help future executives have a variety of experiences from which they might learn. Handling a career transition (a new job, a demotion, or loss of a supportive boss) is key to executive success or derailment. Organizations can help managers cope and learn by providing a meaningful sequence of jobs and helping managers take their flaws seriously so they can compensate for them or get into situations where the flaws do not matter.

Joseph Raelin examines career development experiences of salaried professionals, such as engineers, accountants, lawyers, and others who are dedicated to technical performance in their discipline. He suggests ways to bridge the gap between managers who want employees who are committed to the organization and professionals who want to develop and succeed in their field of specialization. Ways to merge the two perspectives include dual career ladders, a career path into general management for professionals who want to move in that direction, support for participation in professional associations, rewards for professional accomplishments, increased autonomy and other ways to enrich jobs, support for entrepreneurship (exploring new ideas), and the promotion of ethical consciousness along with corporate effectiveness. These and other strategies discussed in the chapter should assist human resource managers in facilitating cooperation between the organization's managers and professionals as they work together to accomplish individual and organizational goals.

The last chapter in this section is on the experience of job loss. Organizational downsizing as a result of cost-reduction efforts from a new technology or a merger means that employees at all organization levels have faced unemployment, often at mid- or late career when they are least competitive in the labor market. Janina Latack and Harold Kaufman describe this experience. Human resource managers are often involved in developing and implementing forced management plans, which include identifying employees who are no longer needed by the organization, offering financial incentives to leave voluntarily or involuntarily, and providing outplacement services to help displaced employees find new positions. Latack and Kaufman review the factors human resource managers should consider in handling terminations.

CHAPTER 16

HUMAN RESOURCES AND THE EXTRAORDINARY PROBLEMS MINORITIES FACE

JOHN P. FERNANDEZ

This chapter defines racism and analyzes some of the barriers that minorities face in becoming full, equal members of the corporation. The chapter also suggests what human resource professionals should be doing so that minorities are given fair, equitable opportunities to have fulfilling and rewarding corporate careers and to be recognized as valuable contributors to corporate America. The responses in this chapter were collected from surveys of over 12,000 people during 1984–1986 in thirteen companies. The data on stereotypes and problems minorities face in corporate America are from 1986.

RACISM AND SEXISM DEFINED

I define racism and sexism as cultural ideologies that view whites (and males) as inherently superior to minorities and women, solely because of their race and gender. Whites (and men), and thus most strongly white men, wield the power in societal institutions to develop, evolve, nurture, spread, impose, and enforce the very myths and stereotypes that are the basic foundation of racism and sexism, in the minds of not only white males themselves but many women and minorities. These myths and stereotypes are used to maintain and justify white men's dominant social, economic, and political positions.

As we shall see, racism and sexism are still two of the most powerful and complex social forces affecting corporate America. However, the form of these evil forces has changed drastically, especially since 1964. Our present laws are trying to correct the obvious forms of social and sexual discrimination that are called overt racism and sexism. The subtle forms have to do with policies, practices, and patterns of decision making, and they are called institutional racism and sexism. Finally, the ever-subtler overt forms of racism and sexism, such as the issue of "qualification," are called neoracism and neosexism.

PERCEPTIONS OF RACIAL DISCRIMINATION

Minorities confront problems in reaching their corporate dreams that whites—particularly white males—never confront head-on. Minority women must deal with the "double jeopardy" of racism and sexism combined. For them, fulfilling the corporate dream can be overwhelming. The array of minority groups that make up this society face problems that are sometimes similar and at other times quite different.

Economic issues are probably chief in determining the level of race discrimination within this society. Although political and social competition are important, the competition for a finite portion of desirable land, money, and jobs largely determines the intensity and depth of the threat felt by the dominant white society. Once a minority group begins to take something to which the dominant group feels exclusively entitled, minorities become subject to all the manipulation, exploitation, and harassment—in short, oppression—that the dominant group can muster. The relative population of the minority group, as well as its skin color, also influences white America's attitudes and behaviors. The minority group's response to society, in turn, is thereby influenced.

Survey participants' comments about the current problematic situation of minority employees in corporate America give a qualitative dimension to the statistics presented later. The following quotations from minorities present what they perceive as the basic facts about their treatment and work environment.

I honestly believe I have been discriminated against by my second-level manager. However, the only reason I do not file a discrimination suit is because of my family. He already has destroyed me financially.

—Hispanic, male, lower-level manager

I feel that people of color do have to do an exceptionally good job. If they mess up, that is what is noticed, not any of the good things.

—American Indian, male, craftsworker

I feel there is a disparity in the definition of "successful manager" between minorities and whites. White definition: keep your position, lie, cheat, make a lot of money, squeeze your people for all they are worth. Minority definition: build trust, respect, and skills of your people. Build competent teams.

—Hispanic, male, lower-level manager

As a minority, I am (1) in a "token" position to meet AA/EEO; (2) constantly hear racist comments and jokes; (3) handled with "kid gloves" by both peers and upper-level management.

—black, female, lower-level manager

I am totally dissatisfied with my current job. I am constantly harassed due to my being a minority.

—Hispanic, female, craftsworker

I am the only minority person in this office and am stunned and ashamed by the racism in this office. I am always told "it's nothing against me" by other reps and my boss—I have ten years with this company and I have experienced a supervisor that puts down minorities in section meetings and allows ethnic statements and jokes told in the meetings. She always states our meetings are "closed meetings."

—Hispanic, female, craftsworker

I work in the real estate department and am often referred to as the cleaning lady which is racially and sexually discriminating and definitely a stereotype.

—black, female, craftsworker

It seems every time an employee is angry with another employee of color (or opposite sex) they resort to name calling regarding their race/sex.

—American Indian, male, craftsworker

Many people, I've noticed, are still uncomfortable working with people of color, especially if they also happen to be very good at what they do.

—Asian, female, lower-level manager

I have a college degree and experience in the management of people and resources. I would like to use these skills, as well as other skills I feel could benefit the company, in a more challenging position. I question, however, this company's real commitment to pluralism and wonder if I'll get a chance because of my race.

—black, male, craftsworker

People of color can do a good job only with full support from higher managers. I am a person of color, and I can do a better job for this company. Because of my white middle-level manager, I will not get ahead. It is sure funny, I feel I can give this company a great deal, but because of a vain, petty man, I will never get the chance to prove myself.

—Hispanic, male, lower-level manager

Some readers by now might be thinking that these complaints are aberrant and unjustified. A number of comments, especially by our white respondents, tended to blame minorities' problems in the corporations on minorities themselves, if they did not altogether dismiss them. The following comments are symptomatic of such blindness:

I feel that some comments are taken too literally. I feel that some women and blacks have become too sensitive and that sometimes comments are blown out of proportion. I feel that some use racism and sexism as a crutch.

—white, female, craftsworker

I think there are too many instances where people of color "milk the system" as the "hammer" to their unfair advantages. This results in low morale and an "I don't give a damn" attitude.

—white, male, lower-level manager

I have some close people-of-color acquaintances that believe in a full day's work for a full day's pay. However, I have observed many instances of game playing [hide and seek]. The pendulum was too far to the right, but in our trying to adjust and make it better for women and people of color, the pendulum now swings too far to the left.

—white, female, craftsworker

Despite these comments, considerable numbers of whites do clearly see minorities facing discrimination. Their comments are revealing.

People of color at this company continue to experience the effects of tokenism, stereotyping, and/or racism in their relationships with many white employees.

—white, male, upper-level manager

People of color get shafted every day and in every way.

—white, male, lower-level manager

They all think the world is against them. Since they have laws to protect them, they do just about whatever they feel. If I was a black with my own work record, I'd probably be management.

—white, male, craftsworker

In some cases, race discrimination reversal is the norm. The darker the skin or slant eyes shape, the higher you go.

—white, female, craftsworker

I feel that less emphasis is being placed on racism than in the past. I feel a sense of regression both internal to the company and external in society as a whole.

—white, female, lower-level manager

I believe in human rights. I can't imagine how one company can have so many from the white middle class.

—white, female, craftsworker

Many problems are shared by women and people of color regarding obstacles to success at this company. White men are most often the obstacle.

—white, female, upper-level manager

We have not put a high priority [demonstrated by our behavior/actions, not words] on promoting people of color to director level and above assignments. That's not good enough.

—white, female, upper-level manager

The following are some hard data about race discrimination that supports the notion that discrimination still plays a crucial role in the careers of minorities.

RACE DISCRIMINATION IN CORPORATE AMERICA TODAY

In my 1986 survey more than 60 percent of the employees responded that racism exists, at least to some extent, in their companies. As one might expect, a much higher percentage of blacks (92%) than other minorities (77%) and whites (63%) recognize this. To take a more accurate measure of the extent of employee perceptions of racism in corporate America, I asked the participants in the 1986 survey a series of questions, which were then formed into an index. The questions were these:

• Today to what extent do you believe racism exists in your company?
• How frequently do you hear racist language in your company?
• To what extent do you agree or disagree with the following:

> Other employees accept the authority of a minority who is a manager as much as they accept a white person's in a similar situation.
>
> Many white members of work groups listen less to work-related opinions of minorities who are managers than they do to those of white managers.
>
> Many minorities who are managers have a harder time finding a sponsor or mentor than white managers.
>
> Many minority employees are excluded from informal work groups by whites.
>
> Minorities who are managers have to be better performers than white managers to get ahead.
>
> White managers are generally unable to work comfortably with minorities who are managers; they bypass them and go to their superiors.

The vast majority of the other minorities are Hispanic. Since the responses of Asians and native Americans generally are similar to Hispanics, these three minority responses were combined under the title "other" minorities.

Zero percent blacks compared to 10 percent of other minorities and 19 percent of the whites believe that there is no race discrimination in their company. Likewise, 75 percent of blacks, 36 percent of other minorities, and 16 percent of whites believe that a great deal of race discrimination exists in the company. Ninety-two percent of black managers believe that there is a great deal of racism in the company. White craft women and all white men are least likely to see a great deal of racism in the company.

In general, minorities and white women at higher levels are substantially more likely to see racism than those at lower levels. Of white, female managers, 22 percent at the lower level, 44 percent at the middle level, and 57 percent at the upper level believe that there is a great deal of race discrimination in the company.

Most minorities and women at middle levels and above remain consistently critical of the treatment accorded minorities and women. Contrary to

white men's responses, minorities and women do not develop a more optimistic evaluation of their careers and work situation as they move up the
corporate ladder. One explanation is that managers from the dominant
group feel more a part of the group that helped them get there. For women
and minorities, group identity diminishes as they progress up the management ladder, because fewer same-sex or same-race superiors, peers, and
subordinates are found at the higher levels. As their status becomes more
obviously "token," they feel more isolated and thus become more alienated.
Finally, as minorities and women move up the pyramid, they are usually
placed in "no-line," less-powerful departments. Naturally they develop an
increasing sense of powerlessness, in contrast to their white male peers,
whose situations hint at a string of further advancement possibilities.

On the whole, frequency of contact with minorities on the job does not
significantly alter the responses of the employees about race discrimination
in the company. For white women, but not white men, the more frequently
they have social contact with minorities outside of work, the more likely
they are to believe that a great deal of racism exists in the company: 37
percent who have very frequent contact versus 18 percent who have none
believe that there is a great deal of racism.

What this pattern indicates is that perceptions of racial discrimination on
the job in many cases have nothing to do with the actual experience of
working with minorities but with personal feelings. The fact that social
contact outside the workplace modifies white women's perceptions of race
discrimination and not white men's suggests the tenacity with which white
males cling to their subjective perceptions of racism—likely, in large part,
because they sense that their privileged position is under attack. It is easier
to reconcile the obvious inequities by believing that minorities face many
problems as the result of minorities' own deficiencies. Yet we must keep in
mind that more than 75 percent of white males see discrimination in their
company.

THE PROBLEM OF RACIST STEREOTYPES

The dominant white society has developed many stereotypes about minorities. Equal percentages of black men and women (4%) hold at least
some racist stereotypes and attitudes. Twenty-six percent of white men, 21
percent of other minority men, 7 percent of the other minority women, and
19 percent of the white women do also.

Racist stereotypes are carried of course into the corporate world. Middle
and upper-level managers who are willing to admit to it can recall that
almost every discussion pertaining to the upward mobility of minority-group
members has included statements implying some set of presumptive social
characteristics, coupled with generalized assumptions about lack of skills
or ability. The slightest hint of minority behavior, real or imagined, that

seems to support these biases is invariably used as "proof of the pudding." Whole sets of such attributions render minorities and blacks, in particular, less than well suited for influential positions in the minds of traditionalistic white managers.

The toughest stereotypes for minorities (and women) to counteract are all related—directly or indirectly—to their abilities and qualifications. Similarly, legitimate complaints made by minority managers about discrimination are frequently discounted by whites. Sixty-five percent of the whites in the 1986 study believe that a minority could not be demoted without bringing on undeserved charges of discrimination. This leads to other stereotypes such as, "Minorities have chips on their shoulders."

The persistence of racial stereotypes is more likely to be caused by a lack of understanding, insufficient meaningful interaction, especially outside of work, or simply racial bias than by vital cultural differences. Minorities, especially blacks as the "most different" minority group, are not given a chance to disprove the white imputation of undesirable characteristics. Many minority managers interact effectively with whites every day, but many white managers are unable or unwilling to acknowledge effective interaction.

The white managers are not comfortable in these interactions, but they do not identify their own uncertainties as the cause. A white, middle-level manager admitted: "The white community considers blacks to be different without really knowing them. Their lack of social and business contact with blacks has tended to segregate them [blacks] in their own minds. Therefore, they categorize blacks into one group."

In addition, because of racist stereotypes and attitudes, the same behavior on the part of whites and minorities receives different interpretations depending on which actors or actresses are "on stage." Minorities who are assertive, self-confident, and ambitious are characterized as being too aggressive, arrogant, and wanting too much too fast. A white male with these characteristics is viewed in a very positive light.

Now let's turn to some of the specific problems minorities face in corporate America that whites, especially white males, do not have to face.

SPECIFIC PROBLEMS MINORITIES FACE

One of the frustrations minorities must face is that, despite the stereotypes and propaganda about minority advantage, in general they simply have to be better performers than whites to get ahead.

Throughout my sixteen years of survey research, this question has always produced one of the largest disparities in response patterns. Ninety-six percent of blacks, 66 percent of other minorities, and 33 percent of whites agree that blacks must outperform whites to advance. Broken out by race and gender, more than 40 percent of the white women and 25 percent of the white men concur. Even though minorities must be better performers than whites, another frustration minorities have is that they lack certain institutional power and authority that white males wield because of their positions. This takes on added significance when one recognizes that the essence of corporate life is power and authority.

We asked the study participants to respond to four questions related to power and authority. They were:

To what extent to you agree or disagree that:

In general, other employees accept a minority's authority as much as they accept a white's in a similar situation.

Many white members of work groups listen less to work-related opinions of a minority than they do to those of a white.

In general, customers accept the authority of a minority as much as they accept that of a white in a similar position.

Many white employees are generally unable to work comfortably with minorities: they bypass them and go to their superiors.

When responses were formed into an index, 38 percent of blacks, 9 percent of whites, and 16 percent of other minorities responded that minorities do not have any of the same power and authority as whites. On the opposite end of the scale, 52 percent of whites, 10 percent of blacks, and 29 percent of other minorities responded that minorities have the same power and authority as whites.

Two quotations from the study participants add substance to the statistics.

In my office in the suburbs, there are only two people of color. The rest are white. I am black. I have had problems racially with employees because our office deals with contractors, vendors, etc. These people usually are white. Most of them have very serious problems dealing with blacks.

—black, male, craftsworker

I feel that people of color occasionally do not get the respect they deserve when in supervisory positions.

—white, female, craftsworker

A great deal of power in the corporate structure rests in informal networks. Systematic exclusion from powerful, political, and well-connected informal groups can seriously block access to the power and authority that one needs to perform to one's maximum abilities and enhance one's career. Just as women feel excluded by men, many minorities, especially blacks, believe they are excluded from informal work groups by whites. A significant percentage of whites concurs. In 1986, 82 percent of the blacks, 51 percent of the other minorities, and 41 percent of the whites believed that many minorities are often excluded from informal work networks by whites. The following comments by the participants illustrate the problem:

I have found that I am not part of my boss's informal network like my white peers are.
—black, male, middle-level manager

I feel that the informal work networks of white men intentionally make things harder for people of color. What is more, they still have a stereotypical view of people of color.
—black, male, lower-level manager

My peers only include me when they want to talk about sex.
—Hispanic, female, lower-level manager

The difference is still seen on the job. You are excluded. You can try to fit in, but you soon realize your peers and superiors view you differently because you don't think like they do or don't always agree with them.
—black, female, craftsworker

One way in which minorities can be sure that the informal work group will be more useful than harmful to their careers is if sponsors high in the hierarchy introduce them and mentor them. However, as is the case with women, minorities have a much harder time finding such a sponsor than white males. An extremely higher percentage of blacks (92%) compared to whites (41%) agrees with this proposition. Sixty-four percent of the other minorities also agree. Several comments illustrate this problem:

The sponsor/mentor relationships are almost nonexistent for minorities.
—black, female, lower-level manager

Sponsors for people of color are almost nonexistent even when you have tried to be one of the boys.
—black, male, upper-level manager

Minorities do not have sponsors because there are no minorities at high levels.
—Hispanic, female, lower-level manager

The main problems facing minorities and women are directly related to their race (and gender) problems that white males do not encounter.

Besides constantly countering stereotypes about their abilities, women and minorities find that they must meet even higher performance standards than do white men. They must do this despite lacking the power and authority that white men have and despite their exclusion from informal work groups where a lot of corporate power exists and important information is passed on.

THE ROLE FOR HUMAN RESOURCE PROFESSIONALS

The previous discussion has highlighted the most serious problems minorities face in trying to become full participants in corporate America. Now let's turn to what human resource professionals should be doing to assist minorities in achieving the American dream.

The first action human resource (HR) professionals should take is to have a sound understanding of racism and how it presently works in this society and in corporate America. HR professionals must understand that there are still serious questions in the minds of many whites, especially white males, about minorities' ability to succeed in the corporate sphere. Yet, before HR professionals can understand minorities, they must truly understand themselves. Many of them think they know, but they really do not. Schoonmaker (1971) made some comments which all HR professionals should heed: "You may feel that you are too honest to deceive yourself, that you can accept the truth about yourself, but you probably cannot. You are as human as everyone else, and everyone tries to preserve her/his self-image. That is why psychological counseling takes so long" (p. 31). In other words, unless they know and value themselves, HR professionals will find it very difficult to understand the true nature of racism.

It is crucial for human resource professionals to recognize that many problems related to racism (and sexism) can be minimized if corporations address some basic corporate problems. So let's start with some generic solutions and move on to more specific solutions with respect to racism (sexism).

First, human resource professionals must encourage their corporations to begin concerted efforts to develop a realistic corporate culture that admits the inherent problems of bureaucracies and the frailties of human nature and that makes a serious commitment to develop and implement strategies that will provide as fair, equitable, and as healthy a work atmosphere as possible.

A training program should be developed to give supervisors effective and bias-free tools to better evaluate their subordinates' performance and potential and to prepare managers to deal with their subordinates' career development and planning needs. Parallel sessions for subordinates should aim to enhance their understanding of the programs and to stress their individual responsibilities in these processes. A crucial element of these programs is training for supervisors in the skills of clear, honest, supportive, and knowledgeable communication.

Many excellent training programs and policies are not properly used because there are no incentives, beyond individual interest and initiative, for the employees to use them. An effective reward system, with bonuses, special assignments, and promotions, recognizes those managers who have a good track record of developing and using all of their work force and those employees who take the initiative to improve their skills and marketability.

Recognizing that there are limited promotional opportunities for the large numbers of people who desire and expect promotions, human resource professionals must begin to develop new reward systems that focus more on team efforts than on individual ones.

In any reward system, the potential benefits must be weighed against the possible harm to those who are not recognized. In my view, one of the most destructive reward systems is the so-called merit award that is given each year to a select percentage of people for outstanding performance. Corporations that use this system create, from at least two months before the end of the performance period until the awards are announced, a great deal of tension and politicking as employees vie with each other and try to position themselves to be among the chosen few to receive an award. The announcement of the awards has a very negative impact on the 80 percent of the employees who are left out.

Team awards based on the results of the company as a whole or individual units or departments generate much more harmony and cooperation. Making on-the-spot awards for specific projects, activities, or accomplishments is also a way to help motivate people because the reward is immediate and directly related to specific accomplishments.

In addition to such team awards, I strongly urge human resource professionals to develop various pay incentive schemes for those employees who are top talent but must, for corporate reasons, stay in jobs for long periods of time because of their expertise, thus being taken out of the mainstream of promotable candidates. Human resource professionals must discover other informal, nonmonetary rewards. The ultimate goal of these new rewards is to bring corporate promises more into line with realities.

Even if corporations expand their employee rewards and even if they become more fair and equitable, human resource professionals must recognize that the nature of the bureaucracies and of human beings is such that there will always be conflict and dissatisfaction. They should develop strategies to minimize it. The best way to do this is to involve employees in defining the problem as they perceive it and in coming up with solutions and developing, implementing, monitoring, and revising action plans. This should not be a one-shot deal but an ongoing process, because once the process stops, employees will go back to pointing fingers at everyone else, especially upper managers, for the problems that exist. This problem-solving process, if implemented properly on an ongoing basis and with the support of the leadership, is an excellent way to build teams.

Finally, human resource professionals must recognize that, to survive in this new world economy, they must develop programs to make all employees, regardless of race and gender, full participative members of the corporations. They must recognize that a heterogeneous group will produce better ideas and strategies than the homogeneous groups. Sale (1980) makes this point beautifully. He points out that "diversity is the rule of human life." He maintains that the human organism has evolved so far because of its ability "to diversify, not specialize: to climb and swim, hunt and nurture, work alone and in packs." Likewise, social organizations thrive as healthy organisms when they are widely differentiated, capable of a full repertoire of responses. On the other hand, "they become brittle and unadaptable and prey to any changing conditions when they are uniform and specialized." In short, individuals and groups achieve full richness of potential when "able to take on many jobs, learn many skills, live many roles" (p. 403).

EQUAL OPPORTUNITY EMPHASIS

To ensure the full use of this heterogeneous work force so that companies can be competitive and profitable, several strategies are in order. The following recommendations focus on an overall strategy to try to deal with employees' racist (and sexist) stereotypes and behavior. No one method will solve these problems because, in large part, they are so inbred and reinforced from so many different sources that an all-out, multifaceted approach must be implemented. Such an approach should encompass (1) comprehensive training for employees at all levels, including top management, and (2) integration of affirmative action/equal opportunity awareness and activities throughout the company's existing functions, in all departments and at all levels.

With specific regard to the issues of equal opportunity (EO), human resource professionals should encourage their companies to do the following:

- Establish goals and timetables for all departments and levels of the corporation, with respect to hiring and promotion of minorities and women.

- Take concrete, well-publicized action to demonstrate the company's commitment to equal employment opportunities such as on-the-spot awards for individuals who have contributed in a significant manner to the company's efforts.

- Develop and implement race- and gender-awareness workshops as an ongoing part of the company's training and development programs and expand these programs as the company continues its efforts to eliminate racism and sexism.

- Require employees to attend workshops that deal with both racism and sexism because they are interrelated. Previous studies have shown that attending workshops on both issues has a greater positive impact on the employees than attending sessions that deal with only racism or only sexism.

- Make certain that all training programs and systems related to managerial/supervisory skills development have modules that deal with some aspect of racism, sexism, and pluralism.

- Develop race/gender awareness workshops using trained volunteer facilitators drawn from high-potential middle-level and above managers, whose participation should be mandatory.

- Require higher-level managers to become mentors/sponsors to high-potential women and minorities. Measure and reward their success in this task.

- Develop concrete performance measurement criteria to evaluate all managers' efforts in the equal opportunity area. Establish rewards for those who demonstrate a positive record in these areas and penalties for those who do not.

- Demonstrate the company's commitment to EO by promoting individuals who directly or indirectly work in these areas and do an outstanding job.

- Make EO-related jobs necessary work assignments for high-potential people and for any person being considered for promotion to middle management and above. These tours should be for at least a year.

- Provide those in EO-related jobs extra pay incentives above and beyond normal incentives, when they do an outstanding job.

- Require all high-potential managers and those being considered for promotion to middle management and above to belong to and be active participants in community organizations that are concerned with the elimination of racism and sexism, and support their involvement by channeling corporate community-service contributions, financial and in-kind, to the organizations' activities and programs.

- Make certain that issues concerning EO and pluralism have time slots on all middle- and upper-management meetings.

Implementation of these recommendations will make EO an integral part of corporate culture and create an atmosphere in which all employees are fully used and developed. The end result will be a more efficient and productive corporation that will be able to compete effectively in the new economic environment. Human resource professionals who allow their companies to deny, as the federal government is doing, the continued presence of racist and sexist attitudes in their work force and who fail to heed the suggestions just offered will not be doing their jobs as human resource professionals. Whatever the cost of the preventive measures described in this chapter, it is far less than the cost of ignoring racism.

REFERENCES

Sale, K. 1980. *Heman scale.* New York: Coward, McCann and Gecghegan.
Schoonmaker, A. N. 1971. *Executive career strategy.* New York: American Management Association.

CHAPTER 17

WOMEN IN MANAGEMENT

⸻ RONALD G. DOWNEY AND MARY ANNE LAHEY

Just a brief hundred years ago in the history of the United States, a discussion of women in management positions would not have been possible since the majority of women, when they worked outside the home, were concentrated in a limited number of industries (textiles, clothing and sewing, domestic, cigar making, paper, and printing). Even within these industries, women were concentrated in low-paying and low-status jobs, with no mention of women in management positions (Sumner 1910). While the intervening years have seen many changes for women in the work force, one is struck by the timelessness of Sumner's observations on the conditions surrounding employment of women:

The story of woman's work in gainful employments is a story of constant changes or shifting of work and workshop, accompanied by long hours, low wages, insanitary conditions, overwork, and the want on the part of the woman of training, skill, and vital interest in her work. (p. 11)

While federal and state legislation has reduced the problems associated with long hours and overwork, the remaining problems of low pay, changing jobs, poor working conditions, and concentration in low-status occupations are still present for the woman of today.

It is interesting that the root word for manager is *manus*, Latin for hand, and a manager was originally a handler of horses. It may be no historical accident that the male stereotyped occupation of horse trainer has given its name to the equally male stereotyped position of manager (Schein 1973, 1975). Even occupations which are overwhelmingly held by women are managed by men. For example, two-thirds of elementary and secondary teachers are women, while only one-third of school administrators are women (U.S. Department of Labor, Women's Bureau 1978). Although these conditions exist, women are making progress in the field of management, both in the number of positions obtained and their treatment once they gain management positions.

The purpose of this chapter is to document what we know about women in management positions today and to help human resource (HR) professionals to understand the obstacles facing women who are entering or employed in managerial occupations. The chapter is broken into three sections dealing respectively with the entry of women into management, the treatment of women once they obtain managerial positions, and the conflicts between women's managerial and nonwork roles. This is an exciting time for women in the workplace. Many positive changes are occurring, but many barriers and detours are also possible. This chapter will assist HR professionals in devising ways to better prepare both men and women to meet and overcome the obstacles facing women in management.

ENTRY

Career Choice and Development

For the majority of us, the choices we face in life are narrowed and constrained by a multitude of forces which we rarely control or recognize. Less than a century ago in western European cultures, women were barred from many educational opportunities, both by societal expectations and their own views of appropriate behavior. Only a limited number of women were able to break the societal bonds that constricted their roles to certain accepted occupations, and those who did were often criticized or ostracized by their families and friends. While many of the historical barriers to women as managers have been removed, social and individual obstacles remain.

The most common argument against the entry of women into management is that men and women differ in their abilities, skills, emotions, and behaviors and that these differences make men better suited for management than women. Scientists have conducted thousands of studies examining differences between men and women, and, although small differences seem to occur between men and women, the strongest finding is that *women and men are very similar in their cognitive and behavioral abilities* (see Deaux 1984; Linn and Petersen 1985; Maccoby and Jacklin 1974). Although there is no scientific evidence supporting the idea that women do not have the ability to be effective managers, there is a vast difference between having the ability and translating that ability into achievement.

Three social forces influence the expression of abilities in women: family, school, and peers. In a now-classic study of women managers, *The managerial woman*, Hennig and Jardim (1977) concluded that family support was a significant force in their decision to pursue a managerial role. The majority of the women interviewed were encouraged by their parents to succeed in whatever activities they pursued and were instilled with the expectation of independence, the need to support themselves, and the idea that work is a valuable source of self-fulfillment. Thus, the importance of role models and parental support on the behaviors and attitudes of their daughters cannot be denied.

Primary and secondary school experiences also play an important role in affecting the career choices of women. The mechanisms for this are often varied and nebulous and include occupational stereotyping in educational books and materials (e.g., men are portrayed as doctors and women as nurses); use of sexist language (e.g., workers and managers are usually "he"); stereotyping in classes and play (e.g., sex-segregated sports, only girls taking home economics classes); selective expectations from teachers (e.g., girls are not good at math); and differential career counseling. While efforts are being made to reverse this trend (see Tittle 1986), much remains to be done to equalize the treatment of boys and girls in schools.

The choices made in secondary school can make it difficult for many women to be successful in post-secondary educational programs. For example, failure to choose mathematics and science as elective courses in high school can hinder the progress and success of students in economics, statistics, accounting—courses required in most management programs. Many women will need to work to overcome such educational weaknesses in order to be successful in traditional business areas.

The factor that has received the least research attention, peer interaction, may be the most important factor influencing women's socialization. The expectations and reinforcements of our friends and peers shape and mold every day of our lives. Sex-segregation in play and social groups (e.g., Girl Scouts, Boy Scouts, little league sports) almost insures that the primary social interactions for adolescents will be with same-sex individuals. To the extent that peer group activities reflect male and female stereotypes, they will instill stereotypical values and behaviors. These are habits that last long and die hard. Thus, women who choose activities and careers that defy peer expectations often find themselves fighting with their friends and limiting their acceptance among peers.

While the above social forces are strong, women are increasingly entering post-secondary education with management as their career goal. This increases pressure to modify the social institutions that have excluded women from managerial roles and also places pressure to succeed on those women who are seen as "breaking new ground." Each woman who achieves a managerial position and becomes a successful manager serves as a role model for her family, friends, and society and helps to further erode the social barriers that confront women.

Selection Factors

Once a woman has made the choice to enter management and has received the necessary education and training, she faces the difficult task of obtaining a managerial position. The selection process that most organizations use to hire managers involves several discrete stages: definition/description of the job, advertising/search for applicants, review of applications, interviewing candidates, and the final selection decision. While legal and social changes have altered past practices which blatantly discriminated against women, there are reasons to believe that more subtle forms of discrimination operate to exclude women from consideration during different stages of the selection process. A review of the research surrounding these processes and the differential treatment of men and women at each stage may suggest ways to avoid some of the problems.

Job Descriptions. There are formalized procedures for analyzing jobs that aid in the development of an accurate job description (e.g., U.S. Department of Labor 1972); however, informal and less rigorous procedures are most often used when defining open positions. Formal job analysis procedures depend upon an outside person or process to collect information from job incumbents or supervisors, while the informal process is typically based solely upon job incumbents' or supervisors' own description of the position. Informal procedures often result in a job description that focuses on the activities, skills, and abilities that are status quo and encourages looking for someone who is modeled after the current incumbent. To the extent that the incumbent is a male, it is likely that the job duties and requirements will be described in stereotypically male terms. Vigorous efforts must be made to ensure that job descriptions focus on actual job requirements, rather than on the characteristics of a particular person, and to restate job descriptions in sex-neutral terms.

Advertisement/Search. The first step in obtaining a position in management is to find an open job and to have yourself considered for the position. This seemingly simple act has in the past been, and to a more limited extent remains, an obstacle for females. The "old boy" network has been very effective in identifying and assisting fast-track young managers and has been equally successful in restricting from consideration those individuals who are not part of this system. If you do not have access to this network, you may never hear about certain vacant positions. In addition, for many jobs, failure to be recommended by the proper person or failure to be from the "appropriate" school or social group is tantamount to not getting the position.

While recent efforts in affirmative action and equal employment opportunity have required more widespread advertisement of positions and has moderated some of these effects, the network operates unchecked in many private businesses and some public organizations, especially those that prefer to promote managers from within their own ranks. Given the informal nature of advertisement and job posting, such discrimination is difficult to detect and halt. Most efforts to deal with this problem have been directed at helping women to develop their own network systems that will serve to inform women of openings and promotional opportunities (Stern 1980). As long as organizations continue to depend heavily upon personal recommendations, this may be the only effective method to oppose this process.

Application Review. When organizations hire from outside their staff, they generally undergo a "paper" review of each applicant's credentials. A resume or application form, supplemented with recommendations, are typically the only materials available to screening committees who must determine, from a large applicant pool, those who will be reviewed at the next stage (the employment interview). Research on the gender of applicants has not provided a clear picture of the effect of sex bias on screening decisions (Wallston and O'Leary 1981). To the extent that management is seen as a male-stereotyped occupation, some researchers have found that females were rated lower during the application process (Schein 1973, 1975). Other evidence, however, suggests that the majority of people will judge applicants on the basis of their background and qualifications and will only utilize sex stereotypes when qualifications do not clearly distinguish among applicants (Lahey, Stockdale, Downey, and Astley 1986). If screening committees do attempt to consider only job-related information when choosing candidates, great care must be exercised in preparation of application materials to ensure that all job-relevant information is included. It is equally important to avoid inclusion of nonrelevant information that may be judged negatively for management positions. To the extent that members of the selection committee are genuinely biased against females and favor male applicants, little—short of litigation—can be done to avoid the problem.

Interviewing. The next stage in the selection process typically involves an interview of qualified candidates. The job interview is the most widely used method of selecting employees (Dunnette and Bass 1963; and Arvey 1979), and research results for the interviewing process are similar to those for the application review. While there is some evidence that stereotypes impact on interviewers' decisions, there is no clear evidence of rampant overt bias in interview evaluations (Arvey 1979). The bias that does occur at the interview stage may be related to interviewing styles and nonverbal behaviors. Thus, women who interview for jobs should take advantage of every opportunity to practice and improve their skills and avoid some of the problems (e.g., lack of assertiveness, failure to adequately investigate the organization, limited eye contact) associated with a bad interview.

Final Selection. While the available evidence does not indicate a strong bias in favor of men in the early stages of the selection process, it is still undeniable that women are underrepresented in management positions. This discrepancy gets worse at higher management levels. If there is no overt discrimination against women at the individual stages, how is it that this phenomenon continues? Lahey et al. (1986) have suggested that the most likely place for bias to occur is in the final decision. They argue that this happens because candidates who survive all hurdles in the selection process are so similar in skills and experience that it is difficult to differentiate among them. Under these conditions, decision makers must still make a selection decision and may revert to stereotypes and other biases when making their final selection among candidates.

Any attempt to change this effect would be difficult and requires realignment of job stereotypes. The job candidate is in a difficult position to alter this situation. This is one of the strongest arguments for having mandated systems of affirmative action which require that organizations, under these conditions, select equal (or proportional) numbers of male and female candidates. This avoids the tendency for the committee members to favor, when all else is equal, the majority candidate.

TREATMENT

Power, Politics, and Leadership

The increasing number of women employed in managerial positions is encouraging to those women who are considering a career in management. The percentage of women in managerial positions has risen over the past twenty-five years from 5 percent to roughly 25 percent, and the numbers are expected to continue to grow (Gage 1982). Although this is encouraging, recent statistics show that women are typically limited to low or middle levels of the management hierarchy. In fact, fewer than 1 percent of the chief executive officer positions in major U.S. corporations are now held by women (Fraker 1984). Explanation for this phenomenon centers around the contention that women are less effective leaders than are men, and that women are inherently incapable of meeting the demands of management positions.

Research on the relative effectiveness of male and female managers shows a pattern similar to that on male and female abilities. A recent review of studies exploring sex differences in leadership style and effectiveness fails to support the proposition that leader sex exerts a significant influence on leader behavior or subordinate satisfaction. "Male and female leaders differed only on the criteria of effectiveness and . . . only when the study was conducted in a laboratory setting (Dobbins and Platz 1986, p. 125). Thus, in actual work settings, men are not more effective managers than women.

In spite of these findings, popular opinion continues to assume that the reason that women are underrepresented in the managerial work force is that they are not as well qualified as men. Although these attitudes have changed over the past twenty years—only 20 percent of the men and 40 percent of the women readers of *Harvard Business Review* believed that "the business community will never wholly accept women executives" (Sutton and Moore 1985). Two competing explanations for this lingering sexism have been presented. One explanation focuses on personality characteristics and behavior patterns that seemingly differentiate men from women, while the second emphasizes the nature of the work environment. The competing explanations have been termed person-centered and situation-centered, respectively (Riger and Galligan 1980).

Person-centered explanations suggest that women's past experiences and socialization fail to prepare them for the demands of the managerial role, leaving them ill equipped to effectively operate as managers. Those traits that women are believed to possess include fear of success, unwillingness to take risks, shunning of power, noncompetitive spirit, orientation toward relationships, emotionalism, dependency, and lack of ambition and commitment to their careers (Brown 1981). Based on these characteristics, a feminine style of leadership has been proposed and contrasted with the more traditional masculine style. The feminine style is described as relying on qualities that include "the expression of feelings, the use of greater intuition in problem-solving, and an increased emphasis on personal relationships" (Loden 1985). Although many managers feel that two very different styles do exist, they are increasingly seen as complementary, rather than incompatible, and there is growing support in organizations for the expression of feminine leadership qualities by all (Loden 1985; Kasten 1986).

The situation-based explanation for women's limited role in management asserts that characteristics of the organizational situation, rather than the traits and skills of individuals, influence and define women's behavior on the job. Examples of situational factors that may influence women's behavior and resultant treatment on the job include sex-role stereotypes (behavior that matches sex-role expectations is evaluated more positively than behavior that is incongruent with expectations); tokenism (token group members are scrutinized more closely, evaluated more harshly, and seen as more prominent than when more fully integrated into a group); distributions of power (women bosses are seen as upsetting the traditional balance of power which favors male dominance); and social expectations (women are expected to be more nurturing and involved in personal relationships). Thus, focusing on situational characteristics, rather than on individuals, will often result in radically different explanations for identical events and behaviors (Riger and Galligan 1980).

Riger and Galligan (1980) illustrate this point in two examples. The reason for the finding that women tend to consider their relationships with co-workers as a primary source of job satisfaction can be viewed as a lack of training in conflict management or a personal preference for social interactions (person-centered), or it can be alternately viewed as a reaction to limited alternative sources of satisfaction in dead-end or nonchallenging jobs (situation-centered). Similarly, the finding that women focus strongly on short-term tasks and goals could be construed as an inability to set goals and plan ahead (person-centered) or as a way to maximize their satisfaction and self-esteem in a position with limited opportunity for promotion and advancement (situation-centered). The type of explanation one favors will directly affect the types of actions that women in management experience.

Situation-centered explanations appear to be the ones most strongly supported by empirical research. In fact, Terborg, Peters, Ilgen, and Smith (1977) have asserted the following:

It appears untenable to conclude that differential treatment of women vis a vis management positions is justified using behavioral criteria. A more plausible explanation for the differential treatment of women may be found in the existence and pervasive and persistent sex-role stereotypes. (p. 90)

Thus, such stereotypes must be overcome before women are fully accepted and integrated into the executive work force.

Compensation and Benefits

While there is no strong evidence for differences in the performance or effectiveness of male and female managers, there continue to be differences in the organizational rewards allocated to males and females. Regardless of the reason for disparate treatment, the pay, promotions, and benefits offered to male managers still exceed those provided to women.

Salaries are the most frequently compared rewards in organizations. In most cases, women managers were paid less than their male counterparts with salary differentials ranging from 50 percent to 4 percent. Differential compensation was found even when controlling for such factors as length of employment, tenure on present job, education, number of hours worked, and level of responsibility. While most researchers are quick to indicate that females' salaries have gained appreciably in comparison to males' salaries, it has also been shown that salaries tend to become depressed as more women enter traditionally male occupations (Ulbrich 1976). Federal legislation concerning comparable worth and equal pay have focused attention on the issue of salary discrimination and may help to close the gap between male and female managers.

Promotions for male and female managers have also been compared extensively. Again, women appear to be at a disadvantage, with more women being stuck in dead-end career paths. Again, the reasons for this are unclear;

however, a recent survey of males who believed that it was harder for women to advance in their careers cited stereotypes by male upper-level managers, lack of experience in management, lack of mentors and contacts, and lack of commitment to be the reasons for this difficulty (Mason 1985). Although there is limited evidence for some of these explanations, it is important for women to understand the dynamics that may be operating to limit their career growth and to avoid inadvertent support of these beliefs.

Studies investigating fringe benefits, while less prolific, suggest a now-familiar pattern. In general, the benefits packages offered to employees tend to focus on traditionally male needs and have not focused on the particular needs of female employees, especially those with families. For example, few corporate benefits packages provide for maternity leave, nursery and day care facilities, and flexible work hours—issues which are more important to female managers. "Companies that wish to successfully recruit well-qualified women and utilize their talents as managers must focus on programs that permit greater participation of women in the labor force" (Boeker, Blair, Van Loo, and Roberts 1985).

Strategies for Success

If sex-role stereotyping continues to limit women's access to and advancement in managerial positions, the important question becomes, "How do women who aspire to managerial careers overcome these stereotypes and move into positions that will allow them to demonstrate their managerial skills?" A number of studies and self-help books have addressed this issue, offering diverse and often contradictory advice. Career management strategies range from "becoming one of the boys" by acting in a manner consistent with the masculine style of leadership, to improving those skills necessary to be a competent manager (e.g., planning, coordinating, delegating, evaluating, time management).

Some authors suggest that increased training opportunities which focus on the role of the female manager would provide major benefits and advancement for women. Others argue that the skills necessary for successful management are the same for both men and women and that sex-segregated training programs only serve to heighten stereotypes and focus undue attention on the issue of gender. Whether training programs for female managers are limited to women, or incorporate both men and women, it is clear that increased training opportunities are an effective way of helping women to overcome deficiencies in earlier socialization experiences and internalize the norms and values necessary for effective management.

Two related suggestions encourage women in low- or middle-managerial positions to increase their socialization and social support. One technique that is very popular right now is for women to involve themselves in a mentor-protégé relationship. Mentoring relationships are characterized by strong ties to a person at a higher level in the organization: a "coach, teacher, exemplar, counselor, provider of moral support, and facilitator of the protégé's dream" (Brown 1981). Mentors are typically defined as "an older person in an organization who takes a younger colleague under his/her wing and supports that person's career progress until he or she is about 40" (Speizer 1981). Although scientific evidence for the benefits of mentoring is scarce—due primarily to confusions in definition of the terms and the absence of strong research designs—many successful women managers report that they have personally benefited from a mentor's practical and emotional support (e.g., Hennig and Jardim 1977; Collins and Scott 1979; Phillips 1977).

Another popular technique for establishing social contacts and support for female managers is the process of networking. Network relationships differ from mentoring in that they are less formal, less personal, and involve greater numbers of people in the support of female managers. Networks are defined as groups of individuals who share a common interest or goal and whose purpose is to "exchange relevant career information, to provide support for problem solving, and to develop skills and a sense of professionalism" (Kleiman 1980). Again, there is little scientific evidence indicating that networks actually improve females' career opportunities; however, many women testify that such contacts provide emotional and financial support, as well as access to job markets.

WORK VS. NONWORK CONFLICTS

The movement of women from work at home to work outside the home has often created conflicts between societal and personal expectations concerning the proper role of women. For much of history, society's viewpoint was that work outside the home should come *second* for women; their primary roles being wife, mother, and family caretaker. Today that viewpoint is less clear, with the norms of society shifting toward increased acceptance of women as full-time employees. Current norms notwithstanding, many adhere to past beliefs, causing women to be ambivalent about their competing alternatives.

Managers have typically been expected to put the needs of the organization before their personal needs, with the managerial role requiring strong commitments of time and energy. If this commitment must come at the expense of other roles, so be it! Although many organizations have begun to moderate this extreme view by paying more attention to the personal needs of their managers, these are the exception—not the rule. Individuals who are unwilling to provide a high level of time and energy are viewed as not being suitable for management.

Beutell and Greenhaus (1986) have identified three types of work-family conflicts: *time*—limited time to do everything that needs to be done; *strain*—

strains generated in one place spill over into the other; and *behavior*—the roles we take at one place are at odds with the roles we take at the other (e.g., objectivity required on the job versus nurturance required at home). Attempts to balance conflicting demands have led to the "myth" of the superwoman: trying to be all things to all people (behavior conflict), at all times (time conflict), with a smile (strain conflict). The difficulties for women arise from the interactions among three major sources: internal pressures, the expectations of significant others, and the constraints of the workplace.

The majority of women, consistent with female socialization processes, have been found to weigh their personal and family life over their careers (see Fagenson 1986). This value orientation has led to a woman's exclusion from management positions or failure to be promoted to higher managerial levels (Levinson 1982). While this suggests that the importance of women's family role is at odds with the typical expectations for managers, Fagenson found that women in upper-level management positions tended to defy this orientation and were in fact more committed to their careers than were their male colleagues.

Work-versus-family conflicts also arise when the woman manager is faced with significant others (spouses, children, friends) who have traditional work and family orientations. To the extent that others expect that a family's wants and needs should come first, conflicts for the woman manager must occur. Single women are least likely to have the conflicts impact upon their careers; married women with children are most likely to have significant conflicts; and two-career couples (Hall and Hall 1979) experience their own unique problems. Under the best of conditions, managing career and personal requirements is difficult and can become overwhelming when conflicts in priorities arise.

Reactions to this conflict range from mild resentment to overt resistive behaviors. Thus, there is a need for individuals to discuss the potentials for conflicting demands with their significant others and to reach agreements for appropriate solutions. Because the stresses and strains associated with the conflicts often remain high under the best of conditions and may affect the physical health of women managers (Baruch, Biener, and Barnett 1987), actions must be taken to reduce conflicts between work and home.

Beutell and Greenhaus (1986) suggest several ways in which organizational policies and practices can help individuals to manage the conflict between their work and family roles. They propose that the presentation of realistic job and career information may help employees to develop a clear plan of their own career development. In addition, specific information concerning issues such as job-related travel, relocation, and overtime demands will help employees to decide if organizational expectations are in line with their total life expectations. Additional ways in which organizations may help employees avoid conflicts between work and family roles and help employees manage the conflicting responsibilities of job and home are flexible work schedules and job redesign. A third suggestion centered on the establishment of organizational support systems that may help to alleviate work and family stress. Workshops and seminars that strengthen employees' time-management, analytical, and problem-solving skills have been recommended as a means for increasing employees' understanding of their job demands. The establishment of on-site child-care facilities, employee assistance programs, and peer support groups have been influential in diagnosing and treating problems arising from work-versus-family conflicts. In general, Beutell and Greenhaus call for greater integration of career and human resource systems within organizations as an effective means for helping dual-career couples and working mothers to balance their work and family lives.

Even so, there is no clear understanding of the processes that lead women to adopt strong work-role orientations: Do women in management learn to adopt this position, or are women with this orientation drawn to careers in management? Most women are clearly going to find the going difficult. Both society and organizations are changing and have instituted programs that help to reduce work and family conflicts; however, the change is slow. What should be clear is that the problem cannot be avoided, it must be dealt with by positive actions.

SUMMARY

The next few years will continue to be exciting for women who are entering or have been in management. Things are changing rapidly on all fronts, and current signs indicate that women will continue to make strides on entering and becoming fully accepted and functioning members of management. The materials we have reviewed suggest that many of the social and organizational barriers that have hindered the entry of women into management are dropping—some in response to legal pressures, and others in response to greater understanding of the value of women to organizations.

Based on the information presented here, HR professionals must continue to make themselves aware of—and actively work to eliminate—the barriers that limit women's advancement in management. Specifically, we must assess organizational hiring practices to guarantee that sex-role stereotyping does not pervade the job description, advertisement, application review, and interviewing processes used when attempting to fill managerial positions. Once women have been hired into positions in the organization, sex-role stereotyping must still be combated. HR professionals must work hard to ensure that the organizational rewards are not limited to traditionally masculine behaviors and that women are not unfairly scrutinized or evaluated simply on the basis of a more feminine leadership style. In addition, compensation and benefits plans must be continually reviewed for evidence of unfair discrimination.

Finally, the increased participation of women in management has brought the issue of family versus career conflicts to the forefront of many organizations. In order to more fully integrate women into management positions, as well as more fully meet the needs of male managers, HR planners must recognize and actively work to develop programs that advance organizational goals and the personal goals of employees. Increased training opportunities, the development of flex time, child-care programs, employee assistance programs, and the encouragement of on-the-job training through mentoring and networking opportunities have all been advocated as means for advancing women in management.

There is every reason to believe that these processes will serve to place individuals who are more enlightened on women's issues into higher positions of responsibility. With the changing of the old guard, many of the past beliefs concerning the effectiveness of women managers will not be accepted by younger men and women who will have their views altered by working mothers, wives, and daughters. These altered views will, we hope, enable them to accept women managers as full partners in the workplace. Although these gains will be accompanied by risks, potential problems can be reduced or avoided by HR professionals who recognize the issues and take appropriate actions. We all await the day when the need for this discussion no longer exists.

REFERENCES

Arvey, R. D. 1979. Unfair discrimination in the employment interview: Legal and psychological aspects. *Psychological Bulletin, 86,* 736–65.

Baruch, G. K., L. Biener, and R. C. Barnett. 1987. Women and gender in research on work and family stress. *American Psychologist, 42,* 130–36.

Beutell, N., and J. Greenhaus. 1986. Balancing acts: Work-family conflict and the dual-career couple. In L. L. Moore (ed.), *Not as far as you think: The realities of working women.* Lexington, MA: Lexington Books.

Boeker, W., R. Blair, F. S. Van Loo, and K. Roberts. 1985. Are the expectations of women managers being met? *California Management Review, 27,* 148–57.

Brown, L. K. 1981. *The woman manager in the United States: A research analysis and bibliography.* Washington, DC: Business and Professional Women's Foundation.

Collins, G. C., and P. Scott. 1979. Everyone who makes it has a mentor. *Harvard Business Review, 56,* 89–101.

Deaux, K. 1984. From individual differences to social categories: Analysis of a decade's research on gender. *American Psychologist, 39,* 105–16.

Dobbins, G. H., and S. J. Platz. 1986. Sex differences in leadership: How real are they? *The Academy of Management Review, 11,* 118–27.

Dunnette, M. D., and B. M. Bass. 1963. Behavioral scientists and personnel management. *Industrial Relations, 2,* 115–30.

Fagenson, E. A. 1986. Women's work orientations: Something old, something new. *Group & Organizational Studies, 11,* 75–100.

Fraker, S. 1984. Why women aren't getting to the top. *Fortune*, April, 40–45.

Gage, R. 1982. How their lives are changing. *U.S. News and World Report*, November, 55.

Hall, D. T., and F. S. Hall. 1979. *The two-career couple*. Reading, MA: Addison-Wesley.

Hennig, M., and A. Jardim. 1977. *The managerial woman*. Garden City, NY: Anchor Press/Doubleday.

Kasten, B. R. 1986. Separate strengths: How men and women manage conflict and competition. In L. L. Moore (ed.), *Not as far as you think: The realities of working women*. Lexington, MA: Lexington Books.

Kleiman, C. 1980. *Women's networks: The complete guide to getting a better job, advancing your career, and feeling great as a woman through networking*. New York: Lippincott and Crowell.

Lahey, M. A., M. S. Stockdale, R. G. Downey, and S. L. Astley. 1986. *A model for gender-related bias in personnel decisions*. Paper presented at the 94th Annual Convention of the American Psychological Association, Washington, DC.

Levinson, R. M. 1982. Sex discrimination and employment practices: An experiment with unconventional job inquiries. In R. Kahn-Hut, A. K. Daniels, and R. Colvard (eds.), *Women and work*. New York: Oxford University Press.

Linn, M. C., and A. C. Petersen. 1985. Facts and assumptions about the nature of sex differences. In S. S. Klein (ed.), *Handbook for achieving sex equity through education*. Baltimore: Johns Hopkins University Press.

Loden, M. M. 1985. *Feminine leadership or how to succeed in business without being one of the boys*. New York: Times Books.

Maccoby, E. E., and C. N. Jacklin. 1974. *The psychology of sex differences*. Palo Alto, CA: Stanford University Press.

Mason, J. 1985. Opportunities for women. *Management World*, October, 16–17.

Phillips, L. L. 1977. *Mentors and protégés: A study of the career development of women managers and executives in business and industry*. Unpublished Dissertation, University of California–Los Angeles.

Riger, S., and P. Galligan. 1980. Women in management: An exploration of competing paradigms. *American Psychologist, 35,* 902–10.

Schein, V. E. 1973. Relationships between sex role stereotypes and requisite management characteristics. *Journal of Applied Psychology, 57,* 95–100.

Schein, V. E. 1975. Relationships between sex role stereotypes and requisite management characteristics among female managers. *Journal of Applied Psychology, 60,* 340–44.

Speizer, J. J. 1981. Role models, mentors, and sponsors: The elusive concepts. *Signs, 6,* 692–712.

Stern, B. S. 1980. *Is networking for you? A working woman's alternative to the old boy system*. Englewood Cliffs, NJ: Prentice-Hall.

Sumner, H. L. 1910. *Women in America: From colonial times to the 20th century*. Reprinted, 1974, L. Stein and A. K. Baxter (eds.), New York: ARNO Press.

Sutton, C. D., and K. K. Moore. 1985. Executive women—20 years later. *Harvard Business Review*, September-October, 42–66.

Terborg, J. R., L. Peters, D. R. Ilgen, and F. Smith. 1977. Organizational and personal correlates of attitudes toward women as managers. *Academy of Management Journal, 20,* 89–100.

Tittle, C. K. 1986. Gender research and education. *American Psychologist, 41,* 1161–68.

Ulbrich, H. H. 1976. Women and wages. *Atlanta Economic Review, 26,* 44–46.

U.S. Department of Labor. 1972. *Handbook for analyzing jobs* (stock no. 2900–0131). Washington, DC: Superintendent of Documents.

U.S. Department of Labor, Women's Bureau. 1978. *Table: Women are underrepresented as managers.* Washington, DC: Superintendent of Documents.

Wallston, B.S., and V. E. O'Leary. 1981. Sex and gender make a difference: The differential perceptions of women and men. *Review of Personality and Social Psychology, 2,* 9–41.

HOW SUCCESSFUL EXECUTIVES DEVELOP: THE CHALLENGES OF LEADERSHIP, OTHER PEOPLE, HARD TIMES, AND THE CLASSROOM

_____ MICHAEL M. LOMBARDO

In 1982, the Center for Creative Leadership began a series of continuing studies into the question of how successful executives develop once their managerial careers have begun (see references for a listing of the CCL studies). My colleagues and I inquired about the major reasons executives succeeded or derailed (were demoted, plateaued, or fired), key experiences they had had, and major learnings from these experiences. Through analyzing interviews, open-ended surveys, and inventories from over 800 executives in thirteen U.S.-based corporations, we believe we have some reasonable answers to the questions which form the structure of this chapter:

- How do executives say they have developed? What are their pivotal learning experiences?

- Do they really develop this way? What evidence is there that certain experiences or certain learnings can spell the difference between success and a stalled career?

- Then what? To the extent that these findings can guide us, what are the implications for development of more effective executives?

DEVELOPING EXECUTIVES

How do executives say they develop? What do they learn along the way? These are the key questions.

Across corporations, executives believed that three and sometimes four kinds of experiences were critical to their development: certain challenging jobs, hardships they endured, important other people who wended in and out of their lives, and, occasionally, formal courses they attended at pivotal moments.

Why these experiences seem to be critical is that they can teach very different and nonsubstitutable lessons. Certain jobs can contribute a variety of leadership skills and perspectives; other people can trigger us to reflect upon questions of human and management values; hardships can enhance our knowledge of self and remind us of our limitations; and course work can provide a dose of self-confidence and self-knowledge. Put together, these lessons may not produce complete executives, but balanced ones whose skills have been forged in a variety of leadership situations, who have confidence and a sense of their limitations, and who respond well enough to other people to serve as reasonable values models. The major types of experience are explained next.

Leadership Challenges

Across organizations, executives mentioned five types of jobs as having been developmental. Each is important for different reasons, but all pose challenges important to leadership in complex organizations.

Challenge: Learning quickly while dealing with new tasks and groups of people. Project/task force jobs, temporary assignments such as acquisitions, plant closing, and troubleshooting assignments featured tight deadlines, unfamiliar people, and new knowledge to master. A manager might learn that holing up to learn was not a viable option, but that learning to ask questions, rely on the expertise of others, find a tutor, and take the time to thoroughly understand the values and perspectives of others were musts.

Challenge: Developing a strategic perspective. Although "taught" by many challenging jobs, the most focused source was moving from a finite line job to a corporate staff job. Coming to understand the strategic set of the possible meant focusing on the interrelationship among units, considering what could be done from an internal and external perspective, and factoring in the constraints of organizational culture. As a simple example, managers who might think they knew when to fire someone might see the same issue quite differently when they looked across internal units, scanned the outside labor market, legal trends, and what competitors did, then fit this knowledge into the kind of culture their organization espoused.

Challenge: Enhancing take-charge, individual leadership. Starting up product lines, building plants, or creating new units were tests of their capacity for take-charge, individual leadership. Managers started with a blank slate—building teams and plans with few comforting rules to follow. The demand here was to pluck some focus out of ambiguity, act, learn from their mistakes, and move on to shape a unit or product.

Challenge: Turning around units in trouble. Fix-it jobs—turning around ailing units or integrating feuding departments—help answer this question. Managers were likely to discover a good bit about both building and using structure and control systems, and cajoling and persuading others that the new systems were better. Some managers realized for the first time how toughness (tearing down and restructuring) and compassion (motivating and cajoling) can be demanded at once.

Challenge: Maintaining and expanding a large, existing unit. Leaps in responsibility—switching to new businesses and large increases in people, dollars, or functions to manage—left managers with responsibilities they could not manage alone. Such job shifts could trigger a series of realizations—that guiding and prodding and structuring is needed when one can't get intimately involved in every problem or project. Many managers saw such job changes as transitions from doing to seeing that things were done, from controlling to guiding, from setting objectives and delegating to developing subordinates so they could learn to set priorities for themselves.

These five assignments teach the lessons of action: coping with the demands of management jobs, learning the business and requisite technical knowledge, and learning to deal with many different groups of people. These assignments cover a panoply of leadership demands: fix it, start it, maintain and expand it, learn quickly, deal differently with different groups of people, and rise above the day-to-day, to both think strategically and act strategically.

Other People

Learning from challenging jobs was tough but direct; the manager was usually in control and learned by doing. Learning from other people was more subtle; managers learned by watching other people's behavior, seeing its impact on others, and feeling its impact on themselves. What they learned or, more likely, relearned and reconsidered were lessons of human values.

Bosses who served as role models were most likely to be singled out as teaching something enduring. (Ninety percent of those singled out were immediate bosses. Peers, subordinates, outsiders, or those more than one level removed were rarely mentioned.) From the good bosses, managers saw subordinates who were inspired or felt inspired themselves. Unlike in their own roles as bosses, they did not have to guess at impact or rely on feedback. From knowing how good they felt, they realized (for example) the value of motivating others and got some firsthand notions on how to do it well.

Conversely, bad bosses taught them what to do by modeling what not to do. Managers saw people humiliated and fired unjustly and felt demotivated and lousy themselves. The lessons they took away were among their most indelible. As one said, "I never want to feel that way again, and I don't want anyone else to feel that way either." Their learning was preceptive—these are the ways people should be treated as human beings, and the role of a good manager is to do certain things and not others.

A related kind of experience passed on organizational values. Managers told us simplistic, short stories which illustrated "how things work around here." These stories explained both real and ideal states in four settings where values conflict: (1) In tough decision situations, what strategies win out? Are things decided politically or by rational discussion? (2) How are people really treated? When a staff member is distraught, what happens? Do we fire problem performers or do we work with them? (3) How do people get ahead? Is it political or performance based? Are mistakes fatal? and (4) What is the proper role of a manager? What values are sacrificed when times are tough? What is the operational definition of integrity?

Whether reflecting on other people as bosses or as representatives of the organization, executives said they realized that their own values impact was an essential ingredient of leadership. From these experiences executives did not focus on how-tos, instead they focused on moral imperatives. They came to see themselves as representing certain values positions, both personally and as a representative of their organization.

Hard Times

One out of two executives we interviewed volunteered a hardship as having been one of their top three developmental events. Whether they pulled a business boner, had been demoted or "exiled to Siberia," needlessly messed up a relationship, or felt skewered in a reorganization, future executives came face to face with their limits. Their major questions were ones of coping and figuring out what to change in themselves.

Many seemed to adopt a learning attitude in even the toughest of situations. These were their typical responses to a demotion.

1. Executives analyzed the situation objectively. They either got detailed feedback or in some way made sure they got the message (if any). Sometimes they discovered that the demotion was intended as a developmental job, but no one had bothered to tell them.

2. They tried not to react out of shock or anger. They got help if necessary in absorbing their feelings so they could respond appropriately.

3. They developed coping strategies to endure situations beyond their control and made attempts to find out how decisions really got made and what could change them. Some indicated that this was just another tough situation to deal with.

4. Finally, they asked what they could learn about how to cope, what they liked and disliked in a job or an organization, how they could come back, and what their blind spots were.

Executives seem to view hardship situations as a key to understanding their limits and developing more self-awareness, particularly in the area of their relationships with others.

Course Work

Far fewer executives mentioned course work than the three other types of events. In general, executives seem to view it as an ancillary rather than essential source of managerial learning. Courses that made a big difference to executives were not routine: They weren't in the normal, straight-through educational process (undergraduate and graduate work done contiguously) and were rarely limited to specific technical areas. The courses that mattered were usually attended voluntarily, later in one's career, and dealt with general management and business issues or process/self-analysis. Over half occurred in university settings (such as advanced management programs at Harvard, Dartmouth, MIT, and Wharton), and all were conducted away from the job.

Course work that made a big difference did so because it dealt with a relevant issue and occurred at a good time for the manager. Ironically, the major outcome was not the content but the confidence engendered by the experience. This took several forms:

- Self-confidence resulting from being chosen for a plum—an exclusive or high-prestige course (e.g., Harvard or Sloan)
- Confidence from discovering that one knew more about some area than they thought (e.g., a manager who learned finance on the job and discovered that he or she already knew what the course covered)
- Confidence from discovering that the manager was as capable as managers from other well-known firms who also attended the course

The content itself made the biggest difference when the manager needed it at once back on the job. For example, one manager took a course in organizational design while assigned to a task force to redesign the corporation. Another attended a workshop on stress during a particularly rough time.

Course work also exposes managers to different ways of thinking about problems through working with other people with different problem-solving approaches. "It was fascinating to learn how a marketing or finance guy approached issues," one said.

Finally, reexamining their view of the balance between life and work (the who-am-I and what-do-I-really-want questions) often triggered by a traumatic event, sometimes resulted from a course-work experience. When a course included careful self-examination and candid feedback, it sometimes helped managers face such potentially derailing flaws as arrogance or insensitivity or a proclivity to go it alone. The time away, coupled with the stimulation and reflection course work offers, seems to be one of the few safe, reliable ways to help managers with these important questions.

Taken as a whole, the pivotal experiences and the lessons they can teach seem to comprise an executive's model of leadership effectiveness. Executives believe that a mixture of skills and perspectives (see Exhibit 18.1) is critical to success, and that they are developed or enhanced by being tested in specific situations.

Together, these lessons can contribute to personal balance. Confidence which can lead to arrogance can be tempered by a sense of one's own foibles and limits. Toughness, doing what has to be done for the business in spite of the human consequences, combined with a basic sensitivity to human needs can lead to handling difficult situations humanely. One can have the independence needed to take charge and still need others.

Executives were not saying that such a balanced view of leadership was guaranteed, only that it was possible. Their implicit model, which only a few openly described, was that variety in leadership challenge, other people, hardships, and occasionally course work each contributed unique learning to the mixture of qualities that can lead to success. Their formula for success, if there is one, can be boiled down to five components:

- Skills development in different leadership situations
- Refining and questioning personal and managerial values through relationships with others (overwhelming bosses)
- Becoming more self-aware and examining one's blind spots through hardships
- Enhancing self-confidence and problem-solving ability through exposure to peers in course-work settings
- That learning components can fit together in what we might call personal balance

EXECUTIVE SUCCESS

This section explores these questions: Do executives really develop in these ways? What evidence is there that certain experiences or certain learnings can spell the difference between success and a stalled career?

Even though numerous other studies have mentioned pivotal managerial experiences, the CCL studies are the only ones that have looked at managerial experience systematically. One CCL team studied eight U.S. corporations; another CCL team studied executive women in twenty-five corporations; and an independent team from NYU studied Indian executives. While some differences in terminology exist and female executives have a slightly different events pattern, data from roughly 500 executives indicate that these are the kinds of experiences that matter. Nevertheless, further research is needed to identify other developmental events and refine our understanding of existing ones.

The evidence on the learning side is growing clearer. Content-analysis of eighty-six executive interviews led us to hypothesize that each experience had a somewhat predictable learning pattern (e.g., executives in different

Exhibit 18.1
Skills and Perspectives Important for Executive Success

Scale Name	Description
1. Resourcefulness/Situational sensitivity	flexible problem solver; understands and works effectively with higher management; sets up effective structure and control systems; handles pressure and ambiguity; strategic thinker
2. Doing whatever it takes	perseveres through adversity; can stand alone; seizes opportunities; enthusiastic; takes charge of career
3. Quick Study	quickly masters new technical knowledge; learns the business quickly
4. Building and mending relationships	works hard to understand others; gets cooperation of peers; clients; negotiates well; gets along with others
5. Leading subordinates	delegates; uses power wisely; sets clear performance standards; patient and fair
6. Compassion and sensitivity	cares about the hopes and dreams of others; provides wise counsel; sensitive to signs of overwork in others
7. Integrity	doesn't blame or abuse others; relies on substance and straight forwardness; is not cynical or moody; can cope with situations beyond his or her control
8. Setting a developmental climate	encourages growth; leads by example; provides visibility, challenge, and opportunity
9. Confronting problem subordinates	moves quickly in dealing with performance problems; bases decisions on performance
10. Team orientation	focus on others to accomplish tasks; not a loner
11. Balance between personal life and work	believes there is more to life than career; takes family and friends as seriously as work
12. Decisiveness	bias for action and calculated risks
13. Self-awareness	recognizes strengths and weaknesses; seeks feedback
14. Hiring talented staff	recruits the best people; can build a team
15. Putting people at ease	has personal warmth and a sense of humor
16. Acting with flexibility	can be tough and compassionate; can lead and let others lead; is self-confident but has humility

organizations volunteered that fix-it jobs had taught them cajoling skills and how to set up new work systems). We tested this hypothesis by asking an additional 300 executives in three additional corporations what their key learning experiences had been. Although some executives were successful (still promotable) and some were derailed (plateaued or about to be fired), we coded their experiences and lessons without knowing who was in which group.

The results were as follows:

- Particular lessons could be predicted from particular events, essentially confirming the developmental model we had developed.

- Events taught predictable lessons *only* for the still promotable group. Those who had recently derailed said they learned just as many lessons, but their learning had little focus. For example, realizing that "you can't manage it alone," that development of others is not a nicety but a necessity, was cited overwhelmingly by promotable executives (71%) when a significant leap in responsibility occurred. From over a hundred similar jobs, the derailed executives cited this learning not once. While successful executives focused downward, derailed executives looked more often to upper management for help in coping with a job they couldn't quite get their arms around.

Following these studies, we developed an inventory measuring these lessons of experience that executives had recounted. This was administered to 336 executives who rated an immediate subordinate. Again, the results were encouraging:

- The ratings of these lesson scales predicted overall boss ratings of derailment, promotability, and present performance quite well, indicating that the lessons yield data that contribute to bosses' overall view of subordinates.

- With one exception, the items measuring the lessons executives mentioned clustered together. (As an example, behavioral items measuring political behavior grouped together.) This indicates that the lessons reflect a reality that can be measured reliably.

- The ratings of these lessons predicted independent corporate ratings of promotion, providing evidence of external validity.

- A small predictive validity study of thirty-nine promotions and derailments indicated that six of the sixteen lesson scales predicted success or derailment (as did two of the derailment factors and seven specific jobs).

- Finally, skills and perspectives are seen in pairs (tough *and* compassionate) as well as independently. This personal balance measure contributed uniquely to predicting boss ratings and was one of the scales that predicted actual success or derailment.

Although additional work needs to be done, there is reasonable evidence that certain experiences and their predictable learnings can spell the difference between success and a stalled career, even at the highest levels of management. Success or derailment is predicted by different lesson patterns in different organizations, however, and certain attributes appear to fit together as balanced pairs, so the picture is not a simple one. Nevertheless, executives appear to know much of what really matters for their success.

FUTURE EXECUTIVE DEVELOPMENT

What implications can we draw from these findings for the development of more effective executives?

To develop future executives more effectively, we should first examine the rules of development as they see them.

1. Whether they learned something on the job or already knew it, learning became important when it helped them solve a problem (such as building a team) that they were dealing with at that moment. Executives believe specific experiences teach, reinforce, or test one's mettle in using present skills and/or developing new ones. Learning is focused; they do it because they think they have to, so developing executives requires an emphasis on what is important in a particular job.

2. Careers are made or broken in adversity. Executives believe they became accomplished because of, not in spite of, hurdles. To learn, they usually took the hard road. For example, in confronting a new job, it is tempting to try to master the technical core, not doing anything until you are sure of yourself. Successful executives usually took a different route: (a) they focused on learning the management lessons of the job, relying on others for technical expertise; occasionally they tutored themselves in technical topics, often off the job; or (b) they took quick action in areas they did know something about and relied on their management instincts and advice for the rest. While they tried to learn quickly, they did not use lack of technical knowledge as a reason for inaction, and they did not focus on technical knowledge as the route to effectiveness. Knowing that such knowledge takes time (and even so, they might never know as much as their subordinates), they relied on their management skills to set priorities, hone in on problems, and take reasonable actions.

    This taking action in the face of ambiguity and incomplete information was a hallmark of their learning. They usually took the nonobvious and discomforting choice, and learned from it.

3. Their learning appears to spiral back, becoming more specific with each turn. For example, executives discuss both the general nature of interpersonal skills and a series of situation specific ones: There are how-tos for external negotiation, lateral relationships, subordinates, older managers, even older managers to whom they once reported. As skills become higher-order, they become more variegated and individual, implying that upper-level managers should only be assessed against the requirements of a job, and that job skill requirements should be carefully delineated at any level.

4. Executives don't focus on fixing weaknesses. Most learning reported by successful executives involved building new strengths or testing present strengths in new

situations (e.g., developing others is more inspirational in a start-up, more cajoling and negotiative in a fix-up, and more helping others figure out how to set their own priorities after a significant increase in responsibility).

5. Although fixing weaknesses is important to them as well, they sometimes do not confront the weakness directly. They learn to compensate for it (e.g., by staffing wisely) or mentally rehearse how they will act before they go into situations that give them trouble (e.g., confronting a problem subordinate).

6. Mistakes and hardships are most likely to develop in executives some sense of their limits and are critically important to developing personal balance. But many organizations punish mistakes harshly or send high-potential managers to only high-performing units in an attempt to buffer them from failure altogether. Executives reserved their most scathing organizational criticisms for such protectiveness or shortsightedness. They instead tended to focus on learning from mistakes and moving on to do it better next time.

7. Executives implicitly believe there are at least four types of experiences that can teach very different lessons. They are open to learning through job challenge, values situations, hardships, and course work. They have both a more inclusive view of the experiences that matter, and a more specific view of what these experiences teach than the usual systems that attempt to measure their progress.

Inferring from these "rules" of development, the purpose of an effective developmental system would be to help future executives have a variety of experiences from which they might learn varied lessons. To do so, each organization must first answer the question of development for what? What does knowing the business and technical core mean? What are the challenging jobs now and in the foreseeable future? In developing strategic thinking, what should managers be strategic about?

There are many components necessary in an effective developmental system, such as not moving people until they have a chance to complete a job, paying careful attention to what values are really being rewarded or discouraged by the organization, and keeping a cumulative experience record where leadership challenges and lessons learned are documented along with results. (It is common for organizations to move managers after eighteen months or by some arbitrary formula, when research indicates it takes thirty to thirty-six months to take charge of a job, learn from one's mistakes, refine and consolidate changes. In short, both the job and the manager's development are left half-done.) In a brief discussion, only a few components can be detailed, so the three emphasized here are those most directly related to the CCL executive studies.

THE LEARNING ENVIRONMENT

The organization is the manager's classroom, and as in a classroom, the proper learning environment should be developed. Some farsighted organizations may keep low-margin businesses, specific staff jobs, or routinely assign different functional representatives to projects because they offer unique developmental opportunities. Some organizations explain why a person is being given a certain assignment, what the job demands from a leadership skills standpoint are, and try to help the person learn what can be learned from the assignment.

Whether by encouraging time for reflection or bringing someone up short with straight feedback on why they might derail, organizations are acknowledging a fact of life: Bright, talented people who no one thought would derail do so every day. Although it is naive to believe that all or even most derailment can be prevented, it is equally naive to believe that bright people will figure out things for themselves.

Our best guess is that even among the best (those who reach the top 0.5% in their organization), perhaps only half can somehow do this. Structuring one's own learning from jobs, figuring out what one's blind spots are, and internalizing the "right" values which one then puts into action is a tough, never-ending task.

For many people, the ability to learn from their experiences remains largely unfocused. They roll along, intent on results, never realizing that there are different types of lessons to be learned—lessons that will eventually make the difference in their careers. Many derailed executives focus too much on the hard management skills or one type of job challenge or fail to take a learning attitude: They blame others or are blind to the values they model or do not attempt to consolidate their learning.

Providing an environment where learning, not just results, is taken seriously is critical. Whether through feedback, course work, coaching, or placing young managers with exceptional role models, organization intervention is necessary for managerial growth.

CRITICAL TRANSITION POINTS

A career transition (a new job, a demotion, losing a supportive boss) is a pivotal event. Handling that transition is a key to success or derailment. In our research we found six factors that stop careers, all of which are tested when situations change. Managers faced for the first time with complex staffing and team-building requirements, or who must change their management style from hands-on to planning, sometimes derail.

Organizations can help managers cope in several ways. The first involves the principle of progression—for example, having managers go from managing a new group to managing a new-product roll out with a new group to creating a new business or department. Often, organizational assignment patterns are willy-nilly, and a big jump at the wrong time can lead to a big fall.

The second way is to help managers take their flaws seriously. Many models of executive effectiveness are little more than lists of virtues, but all the successful executives we studied had one or more things they did poorly, and many found the notion of "having it all" ridiculous. They had either compensated for their flaws, minimized them, or gotten into situations where their flaws didn't matter (e.g., if they couldn't build a team, they recognized and avoided such situations). So their key was not in trying to have all the skills, but in being aware of what their major strengths and weaknesses were. They relied on confidants who would tell them the truth—spouses, friends, colleagues, human resource professionals, and outside experts.

As mentioned, many otherwise talented managers derail because their blind spots eventually matter—what is seen as hard-driving and results-oriented at age thirty, may be seen as dictatorial and as an inability to persuade at the executive level. For others, an early strength, such as leading subordinates, may become a weakness in the executive suite (always looking down, failing to develop lateral and outside networks, having too tactical an orientation). And for some, success goes to their heads. After an unbroken string of successes, they appear arrogant and make others feel unnecessary. Whatever the flaw or flaws, most appraisal systems stick to results and skills. Flaws are discussed behind closed doors. Bringing them into the open through feedback, "early warning systems," and providing opportunities to overcome, compensate, or minimize them might save countless careers.

The third way is more difficult to spot but perhaps the most important—helping managers make mental transitions. Many executives described their quandary in this way. At some point, after being rewarded for some years for individual achievement and control of what others did, they had to begin the difficult process of learning to manage by remote control—learning to ask the right questions, assisting others in figuring out what to do for themselves, spotting danger signs, learning how to use experts, and learning on the run more efficiently. Making this transition involves relinquishing old habits, staying intimately involved with only a few important projects or problems, concentrating efforts on seeing that things are done by others, and generally finding personal excitement through the accomplishments of a group. This change from an individual to a more altruistic perspective can be a major stumbling block. Some people do not want to make this transition and are well-served by knowing this before the transition occurs; many others want to, but don't know how.

One of the enlightened methods of providing such help is the General Electric course for new general managers. They attend this course at various intervals to discuss their problems and their learning with veteran GE general managers and an expert on the transition to the general management role, Jack Gabarro of the Harvard Business School. Other organizations set up informal dinners composed of present and previous incumbents to talk shop and discuss the tough mental transitions that are necessary.

VARIETY IN LEADERSHIP CHALLENGE

Organizations need to expose managers early to varied leadership challenges before the stakes get too high. By this we mean turning around a small unit in trouble, having to persuade those over whom one has no authority, putting someone in a job where they can't possibly control every activity, starting something (a small unit, a procedure, or process) from scratch. Small challenges are the breeding grounds of leaders because they can teach very different lessons. For example, many of the executives in our studies confronted their first turnaround when the stakes were staggering, and they failed. If a manager has never had to be simultaneously tough and compassionate, manage by remote control, confront problem subordinates, and build morale while tearing down inefficient systems and procedures (all required in a fix-it job), the chance of failure is heightened. Exposure to mini-versions of these challenges at an early age allows time for learning via a strategy of small wins, small losses.

Too often, organizations rely on rotational practices to develop young managers, but in retrospect executives rarely see such assignments as having been pivotal. (This seems to be because functional rotations provide vital business and technical knowledge, but develop leadership skills only incidentally.) In contrast, experiencing variety in leadership challenges and learning from those challenged is strongly related to promotion.

Creating a productive learning environment and taking critical transitions and variety in leadership challenge seriously could benefit both organizations and rising managers. But learning on the job is still a tough and often lonely task—one where the responsibility is largely individual. Most executives have few illusions about this, and they view organizational interventions and systems as valuable but limited. What makes the eventual difference in success or derailment is what they experience and what they can learn.

SELECTED BIBLIOGRAPHY

The Center for Creative Leadership's studies of executive development began in 1982 under the direction of Morgan McCall and are continuing. Many publications have resulted from these investigations and have been referred to throughout this chapter.

The technical aspects of our interviews and surveys of key events and lessons are detailed in *Key events in executives' lives* by Esther Lindsey, Virginia Homes, and Morgan McCall. A nontechnical depiction of our studies, which contains several implications sections, published in 1988, is *The lessons of experience* by Morgan McCall, Michael Lombardo, and Ann Morrison. Other studies include a companion interview study of executive women published in 1987 by Addison-Wesley (*Breaking the glass ceiling* by Ann Morrison, Randall White, and Ellen Van Velsor). Three studies of derailment, *Off the track* (McCall and Lombardo), *Success and derailment in upper-level management positions* (Lombardo, Marian Ruderman, and Cynthia

McCauley), and *The Dynamics of managerial derailment* (Lombardo and McCauley) have been published.

A summary and interpretation of the values-oriented events is *Values in action* (Lombardo); also see a description and interpretation of other research into development experiences for managers, *Developmental experiences in managerial work* (McCauley); a description of the methods used, *Key events and lessons in the careers of executives: Descriptions of methods* (Randall White and Lombardo); and an inventory measuring executive lessons, derailment factors, and challenging jobs, *Benchmarks* (Lombardo and McCauley).

All publications are available from Center for Creative Leadership, Publications, P.O. Box P–1, Greensboro, NC 27402.

CHAPTER 19

THE ROLE OF THE HUMAN RESOURCE PROFESSIONAL IN MANAGING OTHER SALARIED PROFESSIONALS

JOSEPH A. RAELIN

It will not be long before professionals—namely, scientists, lawyers, engineers, accountants, doctors, teachers, and the like—represent one-fifth of our labor force (Raelin 1984). Most of them will be salaried, working in relatively large organizations. Most will also be found in the service industries which already account for more than 70 percent of U.S. jobs. Since we are in a knowledge-based age of civilization, professionals will be increasingly counted on by society for their creative insight and imagination, their technical skills, the ability to handle society's most challenging tasks, and their facility to work with information technology.

As prominent members of their organizations, salaried professionals will be in a unique position to affect the entire course of American enterprise. Whether they will use their position to advance their historic role as the soul of society through their commitment to excellence, service, and social justice, or whether they will become mere pawns in service to the corporate will is to a large extent dependent on how they are managed.

Human resource staff can play a critical role in ensuring that the professional's dedication to technical performance in his or her discipline be merged with a genuine commitment to organizational performance. As professionals themselves, they understand the differences which may arise between the professional and the manager regarding their respective role expectations, cultural predispositions, and career development needs. Some further elaboration of these differences may be helpful.

Role differences have been depicted by some classic sociological studies using the construct of the cosmopolitan-local, wherein the professional is viewed as the cosmopolitan and the manager, as the personification of the organization, the local (Gouldner 1957, 1958). Cosmopolitans are seen as maintaining relatively little integration in either the formal or informal structure of the organization and having little loyalty to the organization as a result of their bearings toward professional referent groups. Locals are just the reverse. They are loyal to their organization, fully integrated, and use an organizational reference bearing. Individual professionals can of course be strong in both orientations or even assume hybrid properties depending on a variety of individual and contextual factors—for example, whether an engineer works in a R&D laboratory or a production department. Managers, on the other hand, except for those with a professional background, tend to be predominantly local.

When we look at the cultural differences between managers and professionals—that is, their values, habits, and beliefs—it is apparent that they come from quite different educational backgrounds and early socialization experiences (Raelin 1985). Professionals are segregated from other students and fields and devote years of study to learn the technical idiosyncracies of their discipline. The early conditions of study are clean and passive, but the professional candidate is gradually given increasing independence to penetrate beyond the confines of the field. Managers, in contrast, although nowadays increasingly subjected to a prolonged term of study, nevertheless learn in very active, interpersonal environments and cultivate a style of engagement entailing the resolution of messy problems depicted in case examples. Students in management schools are not encouraged to develop new managerial theories as much as apply whatever theory or set of practical ideas in order to solve problems whose limits are finite and even knowable.

The educational differences between professionals and managers can become exacerbated in the organizational environment, leading to an almost involuntary conflict over expectations. This can be demonstrated in an example of a bench-level engineer who may have been passed over for promotion to a higher level in the corporate hierarchy, whether as a result of personal preference on the part of the engineer or the individual's failure to attract the attention of superiors regarding his or her managerial potential. The latter result can be particularly threatening to professionals whose organization provides no other outlet (such as a viable dual ladder program) for career advancement. The former result is indicative of a clear choice to remain committed to one's profession regardless of organizational pressures. For these professionals, the sheer amount of time devoted to the study of their field results in a certain amount of emotional attachment and commitment. The investment, in other words, produces an ethos characteristic of professional life, whether through the values of contribution to knowledge, freedom to do independent work, unlimited opportunity to use one's expert skills, service to humanity, or pride in upholding professional standards. When these individuals end up in organizations or departments which reward managerial progression, conflict is bound to ensue. Their cultural predisposition may well be antagonistic to managerial behaviors which entail such practices as working with diverse individuals, coordinating group efforts, configuring the organization system and its subsystems, acting on subjective judgment, using political expediency as a factor in a decision, and dealing with uncertainty (Raelin 1986).

The role and cultural differences between managers and cosmopolitan professionals can become readily apparent in the case of some of the new biotechnology companies. Newly recruited scientists tend to have little experience scaling up from the petri dish to the thousand-liter fermentor. Many potential products, particularly pharmaceuticals, require nearly a decade from discovery in the laboratory to becoming a commercial product. Managers, under constant pressure themselves to produce profits so as to convince outside investors to continue financing their firms, in turn pressure the scientists to speed up their work.

In a final analysis of professional-management differences, career development needs also stand out. Although the work of Driver (1979) and others has convinced us that managers do not conform singly as a unit to the traditional linear career path, which would take one up the hierarchy to the executive suite, most managers are socialized to try to "make it" at least during their early years of service. Professionals, especially cosmopolitan types, on the other hand, may have contrasting career needs, and thus their organizational career paths may look quite different from those of management. Although professionals, too, do not conform to set patterns of career development, my own research has revealed three stages that incorporate a fair number of professional organizational career paths (Raelin 1986).

In the early stage, called *finding a niche*, young professionals tend to be idealistic about their profession. They seek jobs that provide intrinsic satisfaction. They also tend to be highly mobile, preferring to try different organizations if they do not find what they are looking for in the first. Unfortunately, most of their initial work is routine. Yet it is critical that they not get bogged down in this routine work. Indeed, although they must do a satisfactory job, they need to save time to search out and complete more challenging tasks. It is necessary, then, that the young professional show some patience, make the most of the experience shared with older professionals and managers, and gradually take on more independent work as opportunity allows. Dalton and Thompson (1986) believe it is also critical that the young professional seek out a mentor during this early career stage.

The mid-career stage, called *diggin in*, occurring when most professionals are in their thirties to mid-forties, perhaps affords the greatest opportunity for expressing one's professionalism. Professionals during this time are committed to their work, put in long hours, and their skills are at a peak. They tend to seek organizational environments characterized by small work groups, collegiality, and high pay. Having developed a fair degree of trustworthiness, they must adapt to the organizational culture and make their personal imprint without jeopardizing the essential norms of the organization. One way to make a mark is to become a temporary specialist in a critical area without becoming pigeonholed. Professionals during the digging-in stage still need to reconcile personal standards with bureaucratic requirements. They also need to develop trusting relationships with immediate colleagues to whom they might be able to turn for support and advice. In facing technical difficulties in their work assignments, they will need to cope with ambiguity as well as outright resistance to their ideas.

The last stage of organizational career development, which I call *entrenched*, raises the specter of obsolescence as the professional gradually loses touch with recent changes in the field. Yet this is also a time when professionals may decide once and for all to accommodate themselves fully to the organization's value system and expectations. This willingness to compromise may stem from recognition that one is less employable elsewhere than at an earlier stage in one's career, or it may come from a reluctance to uproot oneself and one's family. Nevertheless, by the entrenched stage, the organization and its management have generally conferred certain rights and privileges on the professional employee, such as steady salary increases, promotions, trust in the professional's performance and dependability, the sharing of organizational secrets and other manifestations of membership, the reliable support of a work group, and so forth. The late stage of organizational development typically also entails less supervision of one's own work and more responsibility for the work of others, perhaps through mentorship. Unfortunately, many entrenched professionals do not stay up-to-date in their field. Some display inability to adapt to change. Management may reinforce the potential for obsolescence by assigning senior persons to secondary roles in the organization to make way for the presumed inspiration of youth.

Human resource staff are bound to have great insights into the role, cultural, and career development differences between managers and professionals for at least two reasons. For one, diagnosing and managing interpersonal and inter-role conflicts has been part of their mission historically. Line and staff differences have occurred from the first day large organizations were created, and personnel officers were called upon then not only to recruit staff but also to help them convert their expertise into useful contributions within the organization. Thus, human resource practitioners have long been interested in the development of internal professionals, whether through management development courses which help train managers to understand professionals and help professionals understand and, in some cases, become managers, or through benefits programs which allow professionals to update themselves through such devices as attendance at professional conferences, paper presentations, and patent submissions.

The second reason which explains the sensitivity of human resource staff to professionals is the fact that the human resource field has been striving for many years to establish itself as a profession in its own right. Although there is not wide agreement on what makes an occupation become a profession, there are certainly some commonly accepted attributes which appear to specify increasing professionalism. Among these are prolonged specialized training in a body of knowledge, autonomy in solving problems, primary identification and dedication to one's chosen discipline, commitment to service to clients beyond concern for oneself, and the upholding of standards of practice sustained through the involvement of professional associations (Kerr, Von Glinow, and Schriesheim 1977). The human resource field has clearly progressed along all of these lines. This has occurred especially in recent years given the increasing technical complexity and resulting maturation of the field arising from the needs of the mammoth and diversified organizations of today. Professionalism also arises from deliberate attempts by leaders in the field to increase the occupation's stature and influence in the wider labor market (Johnson 1972; Klegon 1978). Along these lines, a number of prominent human resource professional associations exist to support the field, and a credentialing process has begun through such programs as the Personnel Accreditation Institute (PAI).

Let's consider, then, some of the specific ways in which human resource professionals can assist in managing other salaried professionals.

I have identified six problems, each of which represents a special challenge in the management of salaried professionals. However, each problem can also be addressed through managerial strategies designed to integrate the otherwise opposing needs of professionals and managers (see Exhibit 19.1). The managerial strategies attached to each problem need to be carefully planned and implemented, and it is in this realm where human resource professionals can apply their particular expertise. In many instances, the human resource staff will become the actual agents of change in administering the strategies. Of course, their precise role in this process will be somewhat dependent on their influence in their organization. Regardless of where that influence stands, however, there is opportunity for human resource professionals to assume a leadership position in the difficult assignment of managing professionals. Therefore, in discussing the following six strategies attached to problems in the management of professionals, I shall point out specific ways in which the special expertise of human resource professionals may be called upon to map out and administer these strategies. In this way, it will become apparent how critical the human resource role is in furnishing assistance to management in successfully deploying the entire professional staff throughout the organization.

OVERSPECIALIZATION

Strategies: 1. Linkage devices
             2. Open internal labor market policy

Exhibit 19.1
The Mediation Strategies for Integrating Professional and Management Values

Professionals' Complaints	Mediation Strategies	Management's Complaints
Managers who require over-specialization	Linkage devices Open internal labor market policy Organizational socialization Mentorship	Professionals who wish to remain over-professionalized
Managers who under-specify ends but over-specify the means of practice and who expect adherence to the organizational hierarchy	The "dual ladder" Transition to management Managing ends not means Professional participation	Professionals who demand autonomy over and participation in ends as well as means
Managers who maintain close supervision	Self-management and peer control Professional-administration Management by objectives (MBO) Gatekeeping Professional incentives	Professionals who resist close supervision by insisting on professional standards of evaluation
Managers who show respect for authority and who believe in formalizing control of professional practice	Decentralization Matrix "Soft control"	Professionals who might defy authority or disregard organizational procedures
Managers who in the interest of career and teamwork condone jobs lacking challenge, entrepreneurship, personalness, and stability	Job enrichment Entrepreneurship Personalness Employment stability	Professionals who in the interest of quality of life and individual initiative display little regard for real-world practice
Managers who strive for corporate efficiency	Promoting ethical consciousness Ethical process and structure Institutionalization	Professionals who retain an overriding interest in ethical responsibility

3. Organizational socialization
4. Mentorship

Let's start with the problem of overspecialization, which results when professionals pay exclusive attention to their special competence without sufficient consideration to organizational goals. This problem is especially relevant to the career development function within human resources since proper career management militates against frozen skill development and potential obsolescence. Few professionals ever leave their original discipline, but many wish to try out different facets or subspecialties within it. Not unlike any other employee, they want to try something new. Moreover, given the hierarchical nature of most organizations, the reality that few can afford unlimited vertical opportunities, plus the indifference of some professionals to managerial responsibilities, career development-based strategies offer the best vehicle to promote professional growth and development.

The first managerial strategy to respond to the problem of overspecialization, then, is linkage devices, which, through such methods as meetings, memos, electronic media, cross-disciplinary placements, and user contact, promote professional access to the corporate culture. To the extent the communications function is lodged within the human resource department in the organization, human resource staff can to a great extent control the flow of information between professionals and management. Critical in the linkage strategy is supplying professionals with regular information about the organization's financial and contractual matters as well as its marketing plans for its products and services. Since meetings probably constitute one of the most accessible methods of communication and are relied on a great deal in most organizations, human resource staff should use their expertise in group process to streamline meetings so that they become both efficient and enjoyable. Since the continuing education function also often resides within the human resource department, staff can play a critical role in sponsoring seminars in which professionals can be invited to present a paper or idea or to hear an outside lecturer. These events can serve a dual purpose of recognizing internal professional accomplishment as well as promoting greater interdisciplinary contact among professionals in the organization and also, where appropriate, between professionals and nonprofessionals.

The next strategy, maintaining an open internal labor market policy, relates directly to the career development function. The principal intent of this strategy is to expand skill and career opportunities within the organization so that professionals who wish to grow in their career do not have to feel pigeonholed in their professional specialty. The essential elements of an open internal labor market policy are widely dispersing promotion opportunities throughout the organization, providing abundant information—such as through universal posting—on all corporate job openings, availing professional employees sufficient training to prepare for future job openings, allowing professionals to consider multiple career paths, including lateral and downward transfers into subspecialties or different positions within or even outside their discipline, keeping feedback open regarding the results of job applications, and finally affording individual professionals the means to direct their own career development within the organization (Alfred 1967; Raelin 1984).

Since professionals are not necessarily interested in rapid career progression, as was pointed out in the introduction of this chapter, a managerial strategy of slow promotion through skill broadening may be a preferable internal labor market policy (Hall 1985). What this suggests is that professionals might adopt career paths based on skill rather than on position. Growth is thus interpreted as further development of the skills of one's profession rather than accomplishment in a multitude of vertically linked jobs. Finally, an open internal labor market policy also requires eliminating what has been referred to as the tournament mobility model of career development in which an individual must keep winning promotions at each level or risk being out of the game (Rosenbaum 1979). We have to allow professionals to get back in the game even when they have stayed out for many years as a result of any number of life or career circumstances.

The strategy of assisting in organizational socialization is designed to ease the transition of professionals, often trained under the clean conditions of specialized study in the classroom or laboratory, to the messy, indeterminate problems of organizational life. This process can be initiated under the recruitment function of the human resource department wherein, before hiring actually takes place, professional candidates are given realistic appraisals of the nature of work within the host organization (Wanous 1977). Then, after hiring, the HR staff should, in cooperation with management, provide an orientation which gives professional hires an overview of the organization, familiarizes them with rules and procedures as well as benefits and opportunities, answers their questions, and offers insights into their first job. HR staff should also see that professional hires receive social support in the form of a network of friendly colleagues to turn to as personal problems arise during the breaking-in phase of socialization (Brief 1982).

The strategy of mentorship is really an extension of the socialization strategy except that it is not only a proven policy for professionals but it can also provide benefits to protégés beyond the socialization period. In mentorship, junior professionals are guided toward an eventual broadening of their original field of expertise and are given support to help manage their career and overcome the political obstacles ever-present in their organization. Meanwhile, senior professionals who function as mentors also derive benefits from mentorship, such as access to junior professionals who can help them develop and carry out their ideas. They also tend to derive genuine psychological satisfaction from the process of helping junior people in their field "make it" within their organization (Roche 1979, Kram 1984).

Although the human resource staff does not need to create a formal mentorship program, since grass-root systems have been found to work quite well, they should encourage mentorships and even consider articulating a mentorship policy which might stipulate some of the parameters of successful mentor relationships in the organization, including the risks and rewards.

AUTONOMY

Strategies: 1. The dual ladder
2. Transition to management
3. Managing ends not means
4. Professional participation

The second major problem in managing professionals arises from the dilemma of how to allow them to determine the problems they will examine as well as the means to be used—the principal component of professional autonomy—while at the same time controlling their services to the organization. The dual ladder has the greatest potential of any structural accommodation to date to resolve this problem. It calls for a conventional managerial ladder of hierarchical positions which leads to increased managerial authority and a second nonconventional ladder of professional positions which carries comparable prestige in terms of salary, status, and responsibility.

For many professionals, not interested in advancing by supervising others but by mastering the increasingly challenging tasks required in their professional work, the dual ladder is the perfect solution. However, problems with dual ladders have occurred not so much because of the integrity of the concept itself but to loopholes in their actual operation among participating companies. For example, in some instances, the professional ladder hasn't held its status or has become a dumping ground for failed managers (Roth 1982; Martin 1984).

Human resource staff can play a critical role in monitoring the careful design and evaluation of the dual ladder systems in their organizations. They can ensure that there is a company-wide commitment to professional career growth backed up by a ladder with sufficient rungs, each with distinct job responsibilities and standards, to provide a true incentive to their internal professionals.

In the strategy of transition to management, professionals who are both interested and qualified can make the switch to management where they may acquire greater organizational authority as well as a reception for those who can both manage yet understand the professional culture. This managerial strategy can have enormous benefits to the organization since there is such a great need for good professional-administrators. Yet the human resource department needs not only to specify to available professional candidates what the transition entails in terms of new skills and values, but also to provide adequate training through on-the-job and classroom management development programs to make the transition successful. For example, the assumption of managerial duties may result for some professionals in the gradual obsolescence of their professional skills (Bayton and Chapman 1973). These professionals need to know, therefore, that a transition may not be reversible.

One of the ways of resolving the dilemma of autonomy versus control—the principal value difference between professionals and managers at the heart of this section—is to allow management to control the ends of corporate practice (i.e., the strategic goals which shape the organization's mission) while allowing the professional to control his or her own work when it comes to the means of practice (Bailyn 1985). Since the professional has been expressly trained to deal with rather specialized organizational problems, there is little point in meddling into the means used in attacking these problems.

Management's role in this scenario is to act as a buffer between the operation, of which the professionals are a part, and the upper administration of the enterprise. The manager also coordinates the tasks among the various operating units, provides resources to the professional work groups, and, consistent with managing ends, sets broad corporate policy and articulates the values which guide behavior throughout the enterprise. The human resource staff can support this role distinction between means and ends not only in terms of general policy, but specifically through such personnel practices as performance appraisal whereby professionals are evaluated not on the procedures or means which they use, but rather on the outcomes of their assignments.

Although much has been said previously about the need to release professionals to manage their own means of practice, the last management strategy in this section—professional participation—suggests that the operational autonomy granted to the professional be constrained by the criterion of accountability. Most professionals will impose checks on their work as a part of the natural process of professional practice. Many of the participation vehicles appropriate for professionals have been advanced in the fields of organizational development and industrial relations, both of which may be found within the human resource function.

Organizational development strategies span such diverse techniques as team building, interdepartmental corporate assignments, attitude surveys, and communications workshops, but normally begin with a diagnosis of the appropriate interpersonal strategy based on the needs of the individuals involved (French and Bell 1978.) The industrial relations approaches considered for inducing professional participation include stock ownership plans, co-determination, and, to a limited extent, professional unionism

(Sloane and Witney 1985). This latter set of strategies, however, in my view, have not been particularly successful in the United States in producing long-term professional participation.

SUPERVISION

Strategies: 1. Self-management and peer control
2. Professional-administration
3. Management by objectives (MBO)
4. Gatekeeping
5. Professional incentives

A third major problem for management is knowing how to manage professionals considering their distaste for close supervision. Managers tend to be under pressure to demonstrate performance as quickly as possible; whereas professionals tend to be comfortable with longer-range results since most of their work entails protracted thought and action. Chemists, for example, need to organize innumerable trials on a compound before they may consider it ready for public consumption. There is, thus, a natural inclination among managers to closely supervise professional work. Fortunately, as is disclosed in the first strategy in this section, professionals can be relied upon to control themselves through self-management as well as peer control. However, these two methods of control require human resource input to assure management of their comparable or even superior effectiveness to supervisory evaluation. For example, peer evaluations can be distorted if not administered anonymously, if results are unwittingly used to thwart a group effort, or if professional raters are not competent in the same subspecialty as the colleague under evaluation (Latham and Wexley 1981).

Another strategy to overcome the professional's distaste for close supervision is to recruit professionals to perform administrative and project management roles. Professional-administrators who use their good instincts and are allowed a natural and thoughtful transition to a supervisory from an individual contributor function can make very good supervisors. Especially where the supervisor is competent technically, that individual can be viewed as more of a colleague than merely an administrative functionary, and hence can participate in peer control which was just cited as so critical to professional performance. Nevertheless, project management and professional-administration are not natural roles for most professionals trained in the norms of professional practice; hence, training is again vital. Particularly important is learning the complex interpersonal communications, risk taking, and decision-making skills of management.

Although abused in its implementation, the development strategy of management by objectives (MBO) is considered to be an excellent strategy for promoting a critical review of professional performance while avoiding the necessity for close supervision. MBO consists of having professionals decide mutually with their managers what the objectives of their job should be, how long it will take to accomplish the objectives, and what the criteria should be in evaluating progress toward or accomplishment of the objectives. MBO is particularly adaptive to professional work environments since it recognizes the dignity and maturity of subordinates in taking responsibility for their work goals. Further, since it is person-specific, creative professionals and managers can attempt to measure some of the more intangible or idiosyncratic aspects of professional work, whether it be the generation of new ideas, the development of current ideas, assistance to colleagues, or favorable impact on clients. As was mentioned already, however, MBO has had problems in its implementation, so HR staff have to play a very active role in carefully setting up its mechanics. Particularly critical would be training in proper goal setting, in conducting the feedback session between manager and professional after the term has expired for achieving the objectives, in handling intervening conditions which may have distorted the original objectives, in tying the objectives to corporate plans, or in making the MBO system universal so that it is consistent throughout the organization.

A fourth strategy, known as gatekeeping, wherein an influential professional serves as an information conduit between the professional staff within any one organizational department and other departments or with the outside environment, serves a critical supervisory function. Without the assistance of a gatekeeper, many professionals might lose sight of the latest uses of particular professional technologies, which could have far-reaching performance considerations within the organizations which employ them. Human resource staff can assist in nurturing the gatekeeping role in a similar way as in the case of mentorship. There need not be a formal program to designate gatekeepers, but there can be informal support of the gatekeeping role. Individual professionals with the psychological maturity to communicate beyond disciplinary and organizational boundaries should be encouraged to develop their aptitude along these lines, even though they may actually operate without formal authority. As spokespersons for their department or organization, gatekeepers also need to know that they have a fundamental responsibility to protect the interests of the party they represent.

Last, professional incentives should be deployed selectively as a strategy to stimulate professional productivity on behalf of the organization. However, human resource staff will recognize that some professional incentives are different from nonprofessional incentives. Clearly, professionals are just as interested as managerial employees are in basic financial benefits such as salary increases, bonuses, or profit sharing or in other nonfinancial benefits such as office space, a private secretary, flexible schedules, and access to top-level decision making. However, other benefits, which are academiclike in character, appeal uniquely to professionals. These incentives—for example, society memberships, paper presentations, patent filings, or even sanctioned bootlegging—wherein professionals are allowed to do work outside the scope of their normal assignments, can have a powerful impact on professional motivation and creativity, although their impact on the bottom line may not be explicit. Nevertheless, professionals allowed to develop professionally through the use of these academiclike incentives will tend to do their utmost to also nourish their organization, hence eliminating the need for close supervision.

FORMALIZATION

Strategies: 1. Decentralization
             2. Matrix
             3. "Soft control"

In the fourth problem of formalization, the management strategies are designed to fuse the rules and regulations required for the smooth operation of any bureaucracy with professional norms. It is typical for professionals, as employees who think of themselves as individuals and who don't readily "buy into" the organization's authority system, to resist formal rules and regulations. Formalization, however, does not have to impede professional development (Engel 1969; Organ and Greene 1981). For example, the strategy of decentralization, although formalizing the operation of smaller organizational units, does tend to bring those procedures which are introduced closer to professional employees. In smaller units, there also tend to be fewer managers at middle levels to report to, thus professionals can rely on themselves and their own standards and procedures to control their work. Furthermore, professionals in most modern organizations need to have sufficient discretion to handle diverse, complex, and specialized assignments. Working often in teams, each professional unit functions as a loosely coupled system, interconnected with other professional units by strategy, culture, and telecommunications technology, but relatively independent in its own role (Mills, Hall, Leidecker, and Margulies 1983).

Human resource professionals need to be trained to adapt their services to the flexible and decentralized structures relied upon more and more in today's organizations. Decentralization is operationalized in project management, new ventures units, spin-offs, and a structural variation known as the matrix. The matrix, by combining the disciplinary specialties of professionals with assigned project work, substitutes flexible and interactive controls for bureaucratic controls. Although it may reduce the control procedures imposed on professionals from many levels above them within the hierarchy, it still submits them to quite rigorous controls at the project level. There are other idiosyncrasies of the matrix structure which HR staff need to explain to participating professionals. For example, they need to adapt to dual evaluation and reporting systems. On one hand, they continue to report to their functional or technical managers; on the other, they need to heed the directives of their product manager. These separate middle managers, in spite of human resource staff intervention, may or may not collaborate in the professional evaluation process (Kolodny 1979).

When working with professionals, formal control methods can also be replaced by "soft control" which as a people-centered approach elicits commitment on the part of professionals to the organization's mission by communicating to them a sense of shared purpose. Most formal control processes are impersonal to the extent they are developed to affect everyone in virtually the same way. Professionals as relatively mature employees desire maximum discretion in their work. Control should be exerted on the basis of reason or knowledge as opposed to authority.

REAL-WORLD PRACTICE

Strategies: 1. Job enrichment
                2. Entrepreneurship
                3. Personalness
                4. Employment stability

The next problem of real-world practice stems from the professional's interest in individual initiative combined with a commitment to a high quality of life. "Career" to the professional does not necessarily mean making it to the top as much as doing better and more responsibly the work for which he or she has been trained. Is it possible to manage professionals under this interpretation of the career value in such a way that they heed the realities of corporate life? Can they be induced in some way to merge their interest in professional integrity with corporate purpose?

The essential ingredients of the managerial strategies developed in this section are common to the applications field of human resource management—namely, human resource development (HRD). In the first strategy of job enrichment, the intrinsic need of professionals—their interest in the challenge provided by the content of the work itself—is addressed. Job enrichment entails a design or redesign of jobs which allows professionals to stretch their intellectual abilities to the limit, to be involved in their work, to identify with what they're working on, to try new ways to solve problems in their assignments, and to see the results of their contribution (Hackman and Oldham 1980). Further, human resource staff can ensure a commitment on the part of professionals to organizational goals by making them salient throughout the term of employment. Under job enrichment, these goals are unlikely to be rejected by the professional staff as long as their relevance to the professionals' work is adequately explained.

Entrepreneurship, which encourages willing professionals to choose and work on their own projects without constant oversight, is another strategy for stimulating personal and organizational motivation. Although it is unreasonable to expect the majority of the company's professionals to initiate successful new ventures, the thrust of the entrepreneurial strategy is to create a climate where the professional feels free to try new things or to recommend new ways. Moreover, commitment to the real-world practice of the organization is normally assured when the professionals see that they are also allowed to fail.

A third strategy referred to as personalness, defined as treating employees as people, not as numbers, and emphasizing knowledge over organizational politics as the way to obtain corporate rewards, can also inspire professionals to commit themselves to real-world problems especially because of its inherent egalitarianism and such HRD principles as team building and trust. A true team while accomplishing a unified purpose also recognizes the achievements of the individual. This kind of team does not happen overnight. Through the personalness strategy, it is founded on a climate of trust, wherein professionals feel free to take risks without others' suspecting hidden or illicit motives.

Finally, in the employment stability strategy, management makes the commitment of insuring its professional staff continuous employment as long as they live up to the terms and conditions of their contractual obligations and as long as the organization remains viable. Employment stability, however, need not be introduced all at once; rather, it can be viewed as a goal to work toward. Further, it needs to be preceded by so-called buffer or anticipatory strategies involving the organization's human resources, such as overtime, transfers, and subcontracting, so as not to allow the work force to grow faster than the work load (Zager 1978). Professionals will respond favorably to any sincere attempts by the employer to promote employment stability. They will see such a policy as being a commitment to the individual. They will also be more apt to contribute or to try new things when they know that their management not only will not fire them for actions which are taken in good faith, but also will do everything it can to protect their jobs during both good times and bad.

ETHICAL RESPONSIBILITY

Strategies: 1. Promoting ethical consciousness
2. Ethical process and structure
3. Institutionalization

This last problem emanates from my contention that professionals tend to be more interested in ethical responsibility than their managers. Under the stakeholder concept, however, wherein management displays an interest in all of its constituencies beyond the ownership, modern management has begun to align its orientation with the progressive professional view. Nevertheless, most managers see their first responsibility as maximizing profit or efficiency for their organization. Do professionals have any right to dispute this convention? It is a lot easier for a professional to resist corporate malpractice when supported by a professional association, compared with a manager whose standards are set almost exclusively by the employer. Perhaps the best tack is for management to adopt a social policy wherein it can learn how not only to respond but also to anticipate the social and political consequences of its actions in society. The strategies of this section address how corporate management may embark on such a policy.

Through the initial strategy of promoting ethical consciousness, the top management of the organization raises ethical consciousness by a pronouncement that the organization will be continually responsive to the interests of its various stakeholders. Although this pronouncement can be issued through various forms both within and outside the organization, it should also be embodied in a corporate policy available to all corporate citizens. Meanwhile, the professional staff can be a useful resource in promoting ethical consciousness when their best instincts are tapped. They are characteristically interested in doing things right, rather than doing things expediently. Second, the organization begins to incorporate processes and structures to inquire about and report on their ethical responsibilities, whether through a code of ethics, an internal appeals process, or the appointment of a staff specialist or committee to respond to ethical concerns. These steps assure professionals that the organization is sincerely interested in action and that the firm's social proclamations constitute not merely lip service by the executive staff. Human resource professionals are likely to be actively consulted in this second strategy, especially in the process vehicles, since any internal mechanism of investigation would have to involve standards of due process. Human resource staff should be called upon to establish clear methods of receiving complaints, conducting impartial investigations, defining standards of judgment, providing fair hearings, and reaching objective, fair, and responsible decisions (Hammaker, Horniman, and Rader 1977; White and Montgomery 1980).

Finally, under the strategy of institutionalization, the procedures of the organization are modified, especially those concerned with planning and evaluation, so as to incorporate social and ethical objectives into the plans of operating management (Ackerman and Bauer 1976). Human resource planning considerations become paramount during this last strategy. Ethical responsibilities are incorporated within the managers' and professionals' job descriptions, operating objectives, and performance appraisals. The latter element is perhaps most critical because only when staff realize that they'll be held accountable for their social performance are they truly free to observe ethical principles. Finally, in conjunction with the training and career development functions, human resource staff should see that rewards, whether pecuniary or nonpecuniary, ensue for social performance. By the final strategy of institutionalization, professionals should feel relatively assured that any concern they have for social justice or for the ethical responsibilities of their organization in terms of products, markets, and services will not be overlooked.

The strategies of remediation as outlined in this discussion should assist human resource professionals in two critical responsibilities within their role: (1) to help managers accomplish their assigned objectives corresponding to the organization's mission, while allowing the professional staff to acquire sufficient autonomy to succeed technically; and (2) to help salaried professionals integrate into their organizations without sacrificing affirmative standards of professional purpose. There is no more important role in assuring the smooth integration of salaried professionals into bureaucratic life than that of the human resource professional. But as professionals themselves yet with critical managerial responsibilities tied to the hiring and development of the organization's human resources, they are "naturals" in helping their organization accomplish the valuable and mutual objectives of managerial proficiency and professional achievement.

REFERENCES

Ackerman, R., and R. Bauer. 1976. *Corporate social responsiveness.* Reston, VA: Reston.

Alfred, T. M. 1967. Checkers or choice in manpower management. *Harvard Business Review, 45,* 157–69.

Bailyn, L. 1985. Autonomy in the industrial R&D lab. *Human Resource Management, 24,* 129–46.

Bayton, J. A., and R. L. Chapman. 1973. Making managers of scientists and engineers. *Research Management, 16,* 33–36.

Brief, A. P. 1982. Undoing the educational process of the newly hired professional. *Personnel Administrator, 27,* 55–58.

Dalton, G. W., and P. H. Thompson. 1986. *Novations: Strategies for career management.* Glenview, IL: Scott, Foresman & Company.

Driver, M. J. 1979. Career concepts and career management in organizations. In C. L. Cooper (ed.), *Behavioral problems in organizations.* Englewood Cliffs, NJ: Prentice-Hall.

Engel, G. V. 1969. The effect of bureaucracy on the professional autonomy of the physician. *Journal of Health and Social Behavior, 10,* 30–41.

French, W. L., and C. H. Bell, Jr. 1978. *Organization development.* Englewood Cliffs, NJ: Prentice-Hall.

Gouldner, A. W. 1957, 1958. Cosmopolitans and locals: Toward an analysis of latent social roles. *Administrative Science Quarterly, 2,* 281–306 and 444–80.

Hackman, J. R., and G. Oldham. 1980. *Work redesign.* Reading, MA: Addison-Wesley.

Hall, D. T. 1985. Project work as an antidote to career plateauing in a developing engineering organization. *Human Resource Management, 24*, 271–92.

Hammaker, P. M., A. Horniman, and L. Rader. 1977. *Standards of conduct in business.* Charlottesville, VA: Center for the Study of Applied Ethics.

Johnson, T. 1972. *Professions and power.* London: Macmillan.

Kerr, S., M. A. Von Glinow, and J. Schriesheim. 1977. Issues in the study of professionals in organizations: The case of scientists and engineers. *Organizational Behavior and Human Performance, 18*, 329–45.

Klegon, D. 1978. The sociology of professions: An emerging perspective. *Sociology of Work and Occupations, 5*, 259–83.

Kolodny, H. F. 1979. Evolution to a matrix organization. *Academy of Management Review, 4*, 543–53.

Kram, K. E. 1984. *Mentoring at work.* Glenview, IL: Scott, Foresman & Co.

Latham, G. P., and K. N. Wexley. 1981. *Increasing productivity through performance appraisal.* Reading, MA: Addison-Wesley.

Martin, M. J. C. 1984. *Managing technological innovation and entrepreneurship.* Reston, VA: Reston.

Mills, P. K., J. L. Hall, J. K. Leidecker, and N. Margulies. 1983. Flexiform: A model for professional service organizations. *Academy of Management Review, 18*, 118–31.

Organ, D. W., and C. N. Greene. 1981. The effect of formalization on professional involvement: A compensatory process approach. *Administrative Science Quarterly, 26*, 237–52.

Raelin, J. A. 1984. *The salaried professional: How to make the most of your career.* New York: Praeger.

Raelin, J. A. 1985. The basis for the professional's resistance to managerial control. *Human Resource Management, 24*, 147–76.

Raelin, J. A. 1985. Work patterns in the professional life-cycle. *Journal of Occupational Psychology, 58*, 177–87.

Raelin, J. A. 1986. *The clash of cultures: Managers and professionals.* Boston: Harvard Business School Press.

Roche, G. R. 1979. Much ado about mentors. *Harvard Business Review, 57*, 14–28.

Rosenbaum, J. E. 1979. Tournament mobility: Career patterns in a corporation. *Administrative Science Quarterly, 24*, 220–41.

Roth, L. M. 1982. A critical examination of the dual ladder approach in career development. Center for Research in Career Development, Columbia University, New York.

Sloane, A. A., and F. Witney. 1985. *Labor relations* (5th ed.). Englewood Cliffs, NJ: Prentice-Hall.

Wanous, J. P. 1977. Organizational entry: Newcomers moving from outside to inside. *Psychological Bulletin, 84*, 601–18.

White, B. J., and B. R. Montgomery. 1980. Corporate codes of conduct. *California Management Review, 23*, 80–87.

Zager, R. 1978. Managing guaranteed employment. *Harvard Business Review, 56*, 103–15.

CHAPTER 20

TERMINATION AND OUTPLACEMENT STRATEGIES

Janina C. Latack and Harold G. Kaufman

"The Hazards of Firing at Will"
"People Trauma in Mergers"
"The Agonizing Decision of Cutting Corporate Staff"
"Fire Me and I'll Sue"

Managers are increasingly concerned about handling termination decisions effectively. This concern is reflected not only in newspaper headlines and book titles such as these, but also in the words managers use: *retrenchment, reduction in force (RIF), downsizing, decruiting,* and *dehiring*. These euphemisms cloak a harsh human reality—people are getting fired or terminated. The widespread use of so many euphemisms may well reflect the difficulties managers have in facing squarely the problems created by the need to terminate employees.

The increasing managerial concern about the process and consequences of termination has stimulated one of the major growth industries of the 1980s—outplacement. From a modest start in the late 1960s, outplacement grew to a $220 million per year industry comprised of over 154 firms in 1986, a dramatic increase from 43 firms in 1980 with annual revenues of only $35 million (Mellow 1986). Unlike the euphemisms noted here, however, outplacement is much more than a buzzword for firing. It refers to a systematic program to assist terminated employees in finding other suitable employment.

Managerial attention to outplacement strategies reflects both bottom-line

The research assistance of Judy Tansky was extremely helpful in preparing this chapter.

and social responsibility concerns. Management wants efficient organizations and protection from legal action. Provision of outplacement assistance also reflects a corporate conscience that dictates fair and humane treatment of employees who are involuntarily terminated. In addition, a progressive approach to career development incorporates programs aimed at smoothing the exit process and promoting career success of those employees no longer needed by the organization.

In this chapter, we review the factors human resource managers should consider in handling terminations including practical suggestions and examples of professional, socially responsible solutions to the managerial dilemmas related to firing employees. We begin by discussing the pressures on managers to deal effectively with terminations and outlining how the organization and employees can benefit from effective outplacement. Then we discuss a comprehensive approach to outplacement which includes understanding the trauma for the person fired and the difficulties for the manager implementing the termination decision, reviewing alternatives to termination, conducting dismissal interviews, and providing employees with the appropriate outplacement program components. We conclude with a description of current innovations in strategies for handling excess employees. Our goal is to help managers resolve the inherent conflict in termination decisions by balancing corporate needs with social responsibility.

MANAGERIAL PRESSURES

Several sources of pressure have prompted unprecedented managerial focus on termination decisions: continued publicity about firings, a shift in strategic human resource policy, mergers and acquisitions, and potential legal actions. Public attention to job loss has continued unabated since the recurring recessions of the 1970s and early 1980s when personnel cutbacks affected many sectors of the economy. White-collar and professional employees lost their jobs in unprecedented numbers, and many managers were themselves victims of involuntary job loss, some of them for the first time in their lives (Lynch 1981; Yao 1982).

Despite the economic improvement in many sectors, however, organizations continue to eliminate employees. In fact, managers recently surveyed in *The Wall Street Journal* (Labor Letter, January 6, 1987) listed staff reductions as their number one concern, ahead of complying with the new tax law. As a result, the experience of job loss remains very much in the public eye today.

In many firms, terminations reflect a shift in human resource policy in response to competitive pressures of a global economy. This strategic shift has emphasized downsizing or restructuring to achieve leaner, flatter, more competitive organizations.

In a related vein, Dobrzynski and Berger (1987) report that over the last four years mergers and acquisitions have brought the greatest reshuffling of corporate assets in U.S. history; from 1985 to 1986 alone, the increase in mergers and acquisitions was 12 percent. Since the beginning of 1983, some 12,200 companies and corporate divisions have changed hands. Mergers and acquisitions create numerous redundancies and troublesome decisions about which people and which jobs to retain. There are few signs that this reshuffling will level off in the near future. In fact, if mergers and acquisitions were to continue at the 1986 rate, every public company could be turned over to new owners by the year 2001 (Dobrzynski and Berger 1987).

Recent terminations affecting large numbers of employees have generated widespread publicity, and not all of it presents the organizations in a positive light. In some cases mass terminations have occurred in organizations that were viewed as secure places to work such as AT&T, Kodak, and Wang Laboratories. AT&T stated it would eliminate 27,400 jobs; Kodak's decision to close a lab affected 651 employees. Wang Laboratories announced that it will "adjust the company's operations," and 1,000 employees received pink slips (Zelvin 1986). In some cases, the headlines constitute bad publicity for firms that handle termination decisions in an inhumane manner (Hymomitz and Schellhardt 1986).

Finally, considerable pressure on managers stems from threat of legal action. Employees who have been fired have sued on EEO grounds, age discrimination in particular. Since numerous nonunion employees fired in recent years come from middle or upper management, many of them fall into the category covered by the Age Discrimination in Employment Act (i.e., those over forty years old). Furthermore, the employment-at-will doctrine has become restricted by legal actions and court decisions related to wrongful discharge. *The Wall Street Journal* recently reported that plaintiffs received favorable verdicts in 78 percent of wrongful-discharge cases that went to California juries in 1986. The average award was $424,527 (Labor Letter, March 24, 1987). Employers in some states are also vulnerable to workers' compensation claims that arise out of dismissals. For example, in Oregon, courts ruled that the way a nurse had been fired destroyed her self-confidence, causing her to let her license lapse thus ending her nursing career. She was awarded $50,000.

Managers continue to face termination decisions at a time when it is becoming increasingly difficult to fire employees without repercussions. Developing sound termination and outplacement strategies is an important goal for human resource managers—one that can have major benefits for the organization and for employees.

BENEFITS OF EFFECTIVE OUTPLACEMENT

Outplacement can benefit both the individual terminated and the organization. The psychological trauma and detrimental psychological and social effects of job loss and prolonged unemployment are well documented (Kaufman 1982; Leana and Ivancevich 1987; Nelson 1983). Therefore, efforts to assist employees are laudable because they help individuals through this frequently stressful transition. Organizational payoffs often cited are reduced legal risks; reduced severance pay, unemployment compensation, and other benefit costs; preservation of morale among remaining employees; and maintenance of a positive public image.

Protection from legal actions related to age discrimination and wrongful discharge may come from legal agreements as well as from the positive attitudes generated by an effective outplacement program. In order to participate in some outplacement programs, employees sign a promise not to sue the employer. Because the legal status of these agreements is unclear, however, the more plausible reason for protection from potential legal action may be a psychological one. Job loss often brings an angry reaction from employees, even if the termination came about because of an economic downturn. It stands to reason, however, that employees who perceive the employer as sincerely helpful and supportive are likely to get over their anger and get on with the job search. In short, employees who are not angry and who are busy looking for work are less likely to sue.

Another bottom-line payoff comes from reduced severance pay and benefit costs. Severance agreements sometimes stipulate regular payments and continuation of insurance benefits while the person is unemployed. Since employees may take less time to become reemployed with outplacement assistance, severance pay and benefit costs for the organization may be lower. Unemployment insurance premiums may ultimately drop as well, particularly for firms that have numerous terminations.

Another important benefit from an outplacement program is that it can help to preserve the morale and productivity of remaining employees. It has become increasingly apparent that much of the trauma, especially in the case of major restructuring, merger, or downsizing, accrues to those employees who are left. We are only beginning to understand the complex impact of terminations on surviving employees (Brockner, in press) but researchers report that uncertainty and stress are common (Bennett 1987; Kessler 1985; Schweiger and Ivancevich 1985). Outplacement sends an important message to current employees. The message is that the corporation takes some responsibility for the human effects of strategic changes and other managerial decisions that result in terminations and that help is available for those who are asked to leave.

In light of the extensive media publicity described earlier, maintaining a positive public image is a major goal, particularly in the case of mass terminations. In addition to preserving goodwill among employees and the general public, it may even help to maintain customers. Finally, a positive image is necessary for effective recruiting of new employees when needed.

For the employee fired, the benefits are evident. In addition to the possibility of finding a job sooner, they have support necessary to overcome the psychological impact of job loss. Although hard data are difficult to come by, Henriksen (1982) reported that outplacement consulting firms and in-house programs have achieved a success rate of 90 percent or better in helping employees find new jobs. From 80 to 95 percent of outplacement candidates receive one to three job offers within four months, and 60 percent get better positions at 20 percent more pay. Other limited evidence also tends to support the effectiveness of outplacement (Kaufman 1982).

A survey of 449 large and medium-sized firms revealed that managers see the greatest benefits of outplacement as helping the individual (Drake, Beam, and Morin, no date). The most important help is viewed as psychological in nature, with the rebuilding of confidence and the assessment of oneself as well as one's career ranking highest.

Another highly ranked benefit is maintaining the morale of those employees who remain. Outplacement is also seen as making it easier for the manager to carry out the termination as well as helping maintain a good public image for the company. The latter presumably contributes to avoidance of lawsuits.

The survey respondents ranked financial benefits lowest in importance. This result contradicts one of the key arguments made in favor of outplacement—reduced costs (Hoban 1987). It is possible, however, that less altruistic organizations would not choose to provide outplacement without such a bottom-line argument. It is also possible that the managers responding to the survey wanted to project a socially desirable image as to the reasons they are providing outplacement.

An important departure point for development of an outplacement program is an understanding and empathy for the trauma, not only for the individual fired but for the manager who has to fire.

THE TRAUMA: GETTING AND WIELDING THE AX

What do people lose when they lose their jobs? Although the financial impact may be detrimental, people lose much more than a regular paycheck after they have been fired. They lose social contacts, a regular structure to the day, and a connection with goals and a sense of larger purpose. As Mauer (1979) put it: "Work is not only a livelihood; it is an essential passage into the human community—it makes us less alone" (p. 1). For many people, particularly managers and professionals, a significant portion of their psychological identity comes from their work so "in many respects job loss can be the death of an important part of themselves" (Kaufman 1982, p. 116). Finally, job loss can inflict permanent career damage, particularly for those in the later phases of mid-career (Kaufman 1982; Latack and Dozier 1986), some of whom will never be reemployed in satisfactory positions.

The psychological trauma of job loss is reflected in common colloquial terms for being fired, such as "getting axed," "hatchet job," and "walking the plank." Individuals often use vivid, painful metaphors to describe the experience, such as "a living hell," "like losing a leg," or "like dying professionally" (Latack and Dozier 1986).

Individual reactions to being involuntarily terminated will depend, of course, on many factors, including financial resources, social networks, the amount of psychological identity and satisfaction derived from the job, and whether or not the firing involved performance problems or failure. From studies of people who have been fired, however, we can identify some common reactions that often occur in stages (Kaufman 1982) which have been compared to grief stages experienced by people as they accept death— their own and others (Kubler-Ross 1969).

The first stage of reaction occurs when people hear the bad news. Often they react with shock and disbelief. Even if there were rumors or definite knowledge of cutbacks, many people assume it won't happen to them. Or they may have denied negative feedback and ignored coaching advice. All too often, however, the manager has not provided clear feedback or advance warning about the seriousness of the situation. Individuals frequently become angry and blame the manager or the company. For many, the reaction is a sigh of relief; they've suspected it was coming and have, in effect, been waiting for the other shoe to drop. Some even display euphoria or minimize the event by asserting boldly that "it's the best thing that ever happened." Others display escapism, showing little emotion and wishing to leave the dismissal interview immediately. The newly acquired free time is used by many to relax and even take a vacation. Although a few may break down, the most prevalent reaction during this first stage of job loss is relief and relaxation following the initial shock.

After the short-lived first stage of job loss, a second stage typically begins involving an often lengthy period of concerted effort to become reemployed. When the job search goes on for many months without success, a third stage may begin in which the frustration of not finding work manifests itself in vacillation about one's career, self-doubt about one's abilities, and anger that can involve displaced aggression toward others.

If the job search continues to be unsuccessful, some enter a fourth stage in which the individuals become resigned to being out of work and begin withdrawing from activities, including those aimed at finding work. It is clear that if the psychological deterioration resulting from job loss is to be kept at a minimum, reemployment should occur during the second stage, the period of concerted effort.

Firing someone can also be a stressful situation for the manager who has to communicate the decision. In addition to guilt feelings, there may be fear of the employee's reaction, including concern that the employee might threaten or harm the manager. Managers often compensate for guilt feelings about having to fire someone by avoiding talking about the "real" reason for the firing; instead they find fault with employees in areas that may be unrelated, or they are unnecessarily harsh in communicating the dismissal message. Although the discomfort and guilt are natural human reactions, many managers have never been trained in communicating the firing decision in a manner that balances corporate objectives with human decency. As a result, the firing process may be handled in a manner that is unnecessarily harsh and degrading.

For example, in an architectural firm, a full staff meeting was called at which the head of the firm pointed a finger at three individuals sitting at the table and said, "You, you and you will no longer work here as of Monday." In another instance, a program director for a state agency found out she had lost her job when she looked at a copy of the budget that had been approved to find that the program she headed no longer appeared! A systems group learned that their operation was eliminated when they began work one day and discovered their passwords to log on to the computer were no longer valid.

TYPES OF TERMINATIONS

An employee may be fired for a variety of reasons, and often more than one factor is involved. Although recent media attention has highlighted firings for alleged ethical misconduct (Shad 1987), ethical misconduct or clear-cut violations of company policy account for relatively few firings, particularly of white-collar employees. Other common reasons cited for firing are poor performance or economic conditions. Outplacement consultants point out that especially in the case of managers and professionals, both economic factors and performance issues may be at work. For example, for many organizations, the recession of the early 1980s and the higher mandatory retirement age prompted them to deal with performance problems and, in some cases, fire people whose suboptimal performance had been tolerated for some time.

Finally, there are what we refer to as "positional firings" (Farrant, 1979) which result from organizational restructuring that eliminates a position, a function or department, or even an entire layer of the organization. In some cases, the official reason for termination may be positional (i.e., a response to economic conditions or reorganization), but more often than not, management has considered performance in the decision about who will be retained.

Moreover, performance problems do not necessarily mean incompetence; they often reflect differences of opinion about the way things should be done, chemistry or personality conflicts between boss and subordinate, and organizational politics. It may be that the employee simply does not see eye to eye with the boss on important issues. Firings such as these amount to "wrong place–wrong time" situations (Stybel 1987); as such, they are essentially situations of poor person-job fit that present managers with perhaps the most troublesome firing dilemmas.

In fact, the guilt and discomfort associated with firing reflect the hard reality that, in many cases, the manager and the organization *are* in part responsible for the fact that the employee is not working out. Some management experts put it more strongly, arguing that firing an employee represents managerial failure. It may be a matter of inappropriate selection or placement, inadequate coaching and development, unwillingness to give concrete negative feedback, or simply a shift in strategic direction that renders the employee's knowledge or skills inappropriate for the job. In fact, evidence indicates that the obsolescence of knowledge and skills is caused primarily by the organization (Kaufman 1974, 1975).

In some organizations, inattention to strategic planning, particularly around human resource needs, makes it unfeasible to retrain, reassign, or in some other fashion absorb employees in other areas following organizational changes in direction. Failure to plan strategically in this manner may reflect a relatively low value placed on human resources. The result is that managers do not take the time and the trouble to consider alternatives to termination because this may delay or decrease profits or require compromise or revision in corporate goals.

MAKING THE TERMINATION DECISION

A decision to terminate an employee should be made only after a thorough prior investigation of alternatives to termination. As we noted earlier, job loss can be a major personal and career disruption. Therefore, it is important that human resource managers insure that appropriate efforts have been made to resolve the situation prior to termination.

Exhibit 20.1 lists a series of questions to ask prior to making a decision to terminate an employee. The questions apply primarily to performance-related and wrong place–wrong time terminations. Reviewing these questions with managers will prompt them to consider what steps have been taken to salvage the employee and to document performance problems, along with feedback discussions and developmental efforts that have been made in an attempt to resolve the problem. In short, managers need to carefully review the events that have led to the termination decision. This is not only progressive career development strategy but also bolsters legal protection in case of a lawsuit.

Beyond reviewing these questions with managers, human resource managers should be innovators, proposing creative strategies for absorbing surplus employees elsewhere in the organization if possible. Recent evidence suggests that such creative utilization of surplus employees can have payoffs that outweigh the short-term savings gained from terminating employees (Saporito 1987; Dean and Prior 1986), especially if managers take a longer

Exhibit 20.1
Questions to Consider in Making Termination Decisions

1. Have I made my expectations clear to the employee, both verbally and in writing?
   - Have there been regular performance feedback sessions with clear messages about what is not satisfactory and the nature of improvement desired?
   - Have I set joint goals with the employee for performance improvement and allowed sufficient time for improvement to occur?
   - Has the employee been provided with training and career development opportunities? Have I fulfilled my responsibilities as a coach?
2. Have alternatives to termination been explored relative to reassignment elsewhere in the organization, alterations in job assignments or work flow design, technology, or work schedules?
3. Have I reviewed the decision with my boss and with the human resource staff? (A second and third opinion, with notes or a memo to your file is useful, additional documentation in the event the decision is to terminate the employee.)
4. Have I planned the termination procedure?
   - What is the specific reason for termination?
   - Is this termination consistent with other firings in my organization for similar circumstances? Are all employees aware that circumstances like this one will result in termination?
   - What sort of reaction can I expect from this person, based on my experience, our relationship and my overall assessment of him/her as a human being?
   - What will my reaction be to firing this person? How do I feel about this decision? How will I feel after I communicate this decision to the employee?
   - Do I have the experience and understanding of this person to conduct the dismissal interview by myself? Is there a reason to have a third party present (my lack of experience, possible threats of violence)? If so, who should be present?
   - Have I assembled all of the documentation for this person, including performance appraisal record, notes from coaching discussions and conferences, signed statements from employee indicating awareness of problems and agreed-upon goals?
   - Have I reviewed the severance package and is it fair?
   - What kind of reference will I give for this person?
   - What kind of assistance am I prepared to offer this person in the areas of career counseling, job search, and outplacement assistance? Have I arranged for an outplacement firm or someone in human resources to assist them? Have I arranged an exit interview?
   - How soon will the person leave? (If feasible, allowing people some choice whether to leave right away, or at some later time as a gesture of respect.)
5. Is termination the only appropriate solution or is it my way of solving problems so that I will not have to face my deficiencies as a manager? What have I learned about my managerial skills as a result of this experience?

Adapted from Paula Michal-Johnson, *Saying good-bye: A manager's guide to employee dismissal*, 1985, and W. J. Morin and L. Yorks, *Outplacement techniques: A positive approach to terminating employees*, 1982.

time horizon. Since managers have been criticized for their overemphasis on short-term payoffs (Peters and Waterman 1981), human resource managers stand to make a major contribution to long-term organizational effectiveness by prompting consideration of these creative alternatives. Examples of these alternatives are discussed later in this chapter.

OUTPLACEMENT STRATEGIES

Definition and Scope

One manager dubbed it "the modern response to today's cutthroat corporate jungle—the product of a guilty conscience." Another quipped that it amounted to "refloating torpedoed executives." Outplacement refers to a systematic program for assisting excess, marginal, or nonproductive employees in finding suitable new employment. Although the emphasis was on minimizing unemployment (Scherba 1973), more recently there has been added emphasis on facilitating separation from the organization and providing counseling which helps employees deal with the stress of job loss and make career decisions that may involve retraining or career change (Brammer and Humberger 1984; Heistand 1986). In short, outplacement extends far beyond simplistic advice, often disputed by experts, such as "never fire on a Friday."

Initially, many organizations focused on higher-level executives but increasingly some form of outplacement assistance is being provided to all levels of employees. In addition, since organizations recognize that management bears some responsibility for unresolved performance problems, outplacement programs are including those employees terminated for reasons related to performance. They do, however, typically exclude employees fired in clear cases of ethical misconduct or violations of company policy.

The purpose of outplacement is to provide both economic and psychological support for the individual and insure minimum disruption to the organization. Outplacement programs may also be referred to as termination counseling or career continuation, and they are becoming an accepted part of corporate personnel policy in many firms (Greenberg and Zippo 1983).

Among progressive organizations, outplacement is often viewed as one dimension of a progressive career development program (Camden 1982). Such a program begins with the transition of newcomers into the organization, gives attention to a range of development and promotion opportunities during the person's organizational career, and concludes with a recognition of corporate responsibility for easing the transition out of the organization. This program acknowledges that the individual is still a valuable human resource who merits assistance in order to again be productive even though his or her services are no longer needed by the current employer. From an operational point of view, it is the other end of the pipeline from

Exhibit 20.2
Preparing and Conducting the Dismissal Meeting

1. Recognize that there is no easy way to fire someone, but the approach you take during the dismissal interview will have an impact on the employee and can help minimize potential negative consequences for the employee and the organization.

2. Commit yourself to making the process one that protects individual integrity. You, the supervisor, should conduct the meeting.

3. Consider timing, being respectful about the employee's life outside of work.

4. Assemble the facts and documentation.

5. Check with company physician to determine whether there are health considerations that should be taken into account in assessing whether the termination is likely to be exceptionally traumatic.

6. Plan what you will say and make an outline. Discuss it and role play the interview with the human resource staff or a trusted colleague.

7. Get to the point within the first five minutes:
   a. The employee has been dismissed and the decision is final.
   b. The organization values past service; outline severance agreement.
   c. Develop a consistent story to tell people in-house and agree on the contents of a letter of recommendation for prospective employers.
   d. Tell the employee that his/her duties are reduced or eliminated and that s/he is to focus on the job search.

8. Identify next steps and advise against immediate or hasty action; turn the employee over to an outplacement counselor or personnel representative.

Sources: Kaufman, *Professionals in search of work*, 1982; Morin and Yorks, *Outplacement Techniques: A positive approach to terminating employees*, 1982; Stybel, Cooper and Peabody, "Planning Executive Dismissals," 1982.

recruitment and should be incorporated into the human resource planning and utilization process (Rendero 1980).

Saying Goodbye: The Dismissal Interview

Although firing an employee is bound to be uncomfortable for the manager, there are guidelines for how to prepare and conduct a dismissal interview. These guidelines are summarized in Exhibit 20.2. We will highlight some of them here.

The first step is to commit yourself to making the process one that protects individual integrity. Choose a private place, your office or a conference room, where visibility to other employees will be minimized. Although the timing of the interview is a factor, experts disagree as to the best time to fire an employee. Some outplacement consultants will recommend against firing on a Friday, fearing that over the weekend the employee will brood and become depressed. They argue for firing early in the week so the person can begin thinking about the job search.

Our earlier discussion of stages of reactions would suggest, however, that it is unrealistic to expect an employee to immediately begin to focus on the job search when they may be going through a process of loss that includes considerable anger. In fact, employees who job hunt before they have reached some kind of resolution for the grief and anger may take a job just like the previous job, in an effort to "show those S.O.B.'s" that they made a mistake. Obviously, this could be the wrong career move.

If an employee has a strong family and friendship network for support, however, conducting the dismissal interview on a Friday may, in fact, be a good strategy. If the dismissal interview is conducted early in the day, the employee could have an opportunity to meet with an outplacement counselor who can assure him or her that support and help is available and who can help deal with some of the psychological effects. After the weekend and some time to absorb the shock, the person can begin working with an outplacement counselor the next week.

Experts also disagree concerning how long the dismissal interview should be allowed to continue. Some will argue that it should be brief (about ten minutes) and that nothing is served by elaborating on the reasons for the termination by allowing the employee to ventilate and express reaction to the manager who is doing the firing (Stybel, Cooper, and Peabody 1982). Others will argue that it is important to get the employee talking, find out his or her reaction, and deal with some of the rebuttals (Michal-Johnson, 1985).

If there is an outplacement counselor or personnel representative standing by, the manager may elect to keep the interview short and let the counselor deal with emotional reactions. On the other hand, if the employee is ushered out of the manager's office too quickly, this may be seen by the employee as further humiliation that the boss would not even take time to listen and answer questions. It is clear that the manager cannot allow employee rebuttals to drag on, but being willing to listen, making some supportive statements, and reiterating that the company will be providing help may assist the employee in moving ahead. Ultimately, the manager must balance his or her comfort and skill level with personal knowledge of the employee and whether or not the outplacement program includes counseling aimed at resolving the emotional impact.

Outplacement Programs: Components and Policy Issues

A comprehensive outplacement program provides a range of services. As indicated in Exhibit 20.3, outplacement programs include support for the terminated employees as well as organizational support systems which reflect top management human resource policy decisions and an integration of

Exhibit 20.3
Outplacement Program Components

Support for Dismissed Employees

1. Severance package—including severance pay and continuation of benefits for some time period beyond termination date; released time while still on the payroll for job search.

2. Counseling—dealing with psychological and social consequences of job loss; assessment of skills and job interests, career planning, stress management, financial management, personal counseling, ongoing support groups, family counseling.

3. Job search assistance—e.g., telephone, office space, stationery, resumé preparation and letter-writing, training in interviewing skills (including videotaped practice sessions and interview debriefings, negotiation, body language, grooming and dress), networking.

4. Career and job search resource information—employer contacts, directories, self-help manuals, referral to community information sources.

5. Clerical support—taking phone calls, typing and word processing, printing resumes, mailing privileges.

Organizational Support System

1. Top management support and commitment.

2. Exit and termination interviews.

3. Performance appraisal, coaching and development plans.

4. Training for managers—performance appraisal, coaching and career counseling, discipline, managing dismissals, and termination interviews.

5. Training for human resource staff—benefits, incentives, ERISA, UCC, EEO, developing case law related to employment-at-will, career and job loss counseling.

6. Human resource planning, budgeting, and cost containment.

---

outplacement with career development strategy. Outplacement as we have defined it here takes into account that when employees are terminated, they need more than job search assistance.

In the case of large-scale terminations in unionized settings, some employers develop programs jointly with union leaders and local government and community organizations including the Private Industry Councils established under the Job Training Partnership Act. A model program, drawn from a plant closing at the Stroh's brewery in Detroit, is outlined in Figure 20.1. The program is termed a transition program to underscore that it deals with all needs that employees might experience during the job loss transition—not just finding a job. Several examples of outplacement pro-

Figure 20.1
Stroh Transition Services Program Activity Flowchart

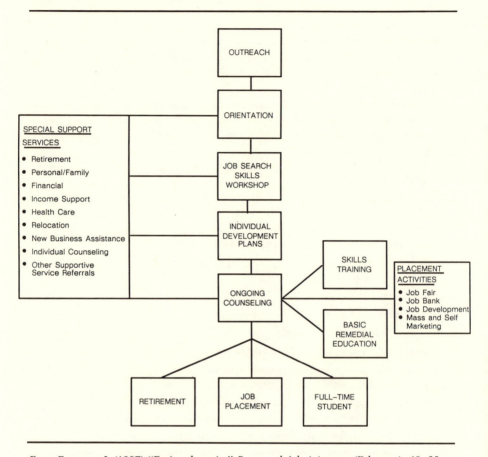

From Franzem, J. (1987) "Easing the pain," *Personnel Administrator* (February): 48–55.

grams are described in the case studies referenced in the Resources and Further Reading section at the end of this chapter.

The scope of outplacement assistance offered varies depending on corporate financial resources and job level. In the case of mass layoffs, financial constraints may dictate the scope of services offered. In most firms, individualized counseling and job search help may be offered only to middle management and above with other employees handled through group workshops.

Thus, initial policy decisions deal with a range of issues related to who gets what kind of assistance and for how long. Some representative examples from a recent survey by an outplacement firm (Drake, Beam, and Morin, no date) are summarized in Exhibit 20.4. Drake, Beam, and Morin reported that their average client was an exempt employee, forty-six years old, earning $42,000 with twelve years of service to the company. Severance payments ranged from twelve weeks' to twelve months' salary, with the average being 6.4 months' salary. Ultimately, managers must make the decision based on corporate financial resources and conscience, bearing in mind that it can take from four to six months for employees in middle management and above to find suitable employment.

Another policy decision revolves around whether outplacement will be handled internally or whether an outplacement consultant will be hired. The growth in the number of outplacement consultants reflects that many organizations contract externally for these programs. Fees range from 15 to 25 percent of the dismissed individual's salary plus bonus, and this fee is paid by the sponsoring organization. The charge for group workshops is typically $500 per employee. Most outplacement firms do not accept "retail" clients—that is, a dismissed employee cannot contract individually with an outplacement consultant. The organization must sponsor him or her and pay the fees.

If an outplacement firm is retained, internal human resource staff may handle determination and communication of severance benefits, with an external consultant providing all other assistance. Alternatively, internal staff may handle nonexempt employees, including job search contacts and workshops, with exempt employees being turned over to an outplacement consulting firm.

There are several advantages of using external outplacement consultants. The most important advantage is that they are specialists in providing the kinds of services needed. In addition, they provide office space for dismissed employees to use on a regular basis for job search activities. This may be more comfortable for the organization than providing office space on the premises. It may also help dismissed employees to make the transition and focus on the future if they are physically removed from the place of employment that is tied to the past. Furthermore, the outplacement firm does not function as an employment agency, so the individual takes responsibility for conducting his or her job search. Thus, dismissed employees receive

Exhibit 20.4
A Sample of Severance Pay Agreements

- One month's salary per year of service; maximum of two years
- Exempt: Below $31,100—two week's pay per year of service

  Exempt: Above $31,100—1 month's pay per year of service

  Non-exempt: Up to one week's pay per year of service
- Executive level—Six months to one year depending upon circumstances and level; upper management—normally six months
- Two weeks' salary for each completed year of service; maximum of fifty-two weeks
- Half month of salary for employee under one year of service; three months' salary for employee with more than one year of service
- A guideline of one to two weeks' pay per year of service with a two-month minimum. The executive group's policy is based on three to four weeks' pay per year of service. Notice, or pay in lieu of notice, and accrued vacation pay are provided for both groups. If outplacement is provided, the employee forgoes accrued vacation pay.
- One and a half times number of years of service = number of weeks severance
- One week per year of service in excess of five years (twenty-week maximum), plus one week per year of service in excess of forty years of age (twenty-week maximum), plus one week per $5,000 compensation in excess of $10,000 (twelve-week maximum)

| | *Years of Service* | | | |
Age	*0–5*	*5–10*	*10+*	
Up to 40	3 months	5 months	7 months	Full salary
40–49	4 months	6 months	8 months	for months
50+	5 months	7 months	9 months	shown

- For exempts: $\dfrac{Salary}{2,500}$ x Service Kicker = number of weeks severance pay

  Service Kicker: 5–9   yrs. = 1.25

  10–14 yrs. = 1.50

  15–19 yrs. = 1.75

  20+   yrs. = 2.00

Source: Drake, Beam, and Morin.

valuable training in job search skills. The expertise for this in-depth training is not available internally in many organizations. In addition, some organizational human resource staffs may take on too much of the responsibility (e.g., calling other employers) trying to get the person placed, which may add to feelings of helplessness and incompetence.

Criteria for selecting an outplacement firm can be identified by reviewing

Exhibit 20.3. A qualified outplacement firm should provide all or most of the components listed under support for dismissed employees. Some companies provide a list of outplacement firms and allow employees to choose the outplacement consultant with whom they wish to work (Fowler 1986). This is a questionable practice, however, since many people are in a state of shock following job loss and may not be qualified to make a considered decision. Instead, the human resource staff of the organization should evaluate several outplacement firms and select a qualified consultant. Important considerations are counseling and job market expertise, references from previous clients, facilities and resource materials, the degree to which the program is personalized, attention to resume preparation, and pretermination consultation and training.

To provide qualified counseling and job market expertise, the consultant should have staff available with graduate training or experience in career and employment counseling, as well as sufficient maturity and corporate experience to help a wide range of employees. In some cases, psychologists work for the firm on a full-time or consulting basis to provide personal and career assessment. Outplacement firms often use retired executives, with experience in specified areas (e.g., banking, restaurant and hotel management) to aid the outplaced employee in targeting his or her job search. If the person marketing the service is not directly involved in the outplacement counseling process, ask to meet with the staff who will be actually working with outplaced employees.

Contacting references is important as is considering the facilities and job search resources the firm provides. Contact other organizations who have retained the consultant and ask for their evaluation. Any reputable outplacement consultant will, with permission, provide names of client organizations. In addition, the firm should provide desks and telephones, preferably in semi-private cubicles and should have at least one private office for use by top executives. Appropriate job search resources (e.g., *The Wall Street Journal*, directories of employers) and how-to books should be available in the office, but an extensive career library is not usually needed. The consultant should be knowledgeable about where in the community career resource libraries and materials are available, however.

The program should be personalized, providing one-on-one counseling and consultation for outplaced employees. Considerable time, from twenty to thirty hours, should be devoted up front to assessment of experience, skills, preferences, and values, even for those individuals who are certain about the type of work they wish to do. This may involve testing and self-assessment exercises, as well as counseling interviews, and should be tailored to the individual.

Resume preparation should also be an individualized process. Ask to review the resumes prepared by the firm. Does each one appear unique, or do they have a canned appearance?

Finally, consider whether or not the firm provides pretermination consultation and training of managers. Ideally, you will be entering an ongoing relationship with the firm. Therefore, it is important that they be able to provide expertise on how to dismiss employees fairly and humanely, appropriate severance packages, strategies for legal protection and training for managers on how to communicate the termination decision. In addition, since an exploration of alternatives to termination is crucial, the firm should also be available to assist employees in a thorough self-assessment and to assist managers in identifying possible internal opportunities for people who are not working out in their present assignment. These services provide an important preventive approach and aid in building a comprehensive career development program.

INNOVATIONS: OUTPLACEMENT AND INPLACEMENT

Creative Variations in Outplacement

In addition to the typical outplacement services we have discussed, there are many exciting innovations being proposed: job hotlines, support groups, transition management, and outplacement avoidance.

One idea is a job hotline (Zelvin 1987) which would enable entrepreneurs to have access to qualified, experienced people. After obtaining employees' agreement in order to protect privacy rights, corporations who were terminating individuals could provide a computerized list of former employees organized by job description, location, and other pertinent information. This data could be made available to small business employers through a toll-free number. This relatively inexpensive aspect of outplacement has not generally been widely adopted but could go a long way toward easing the trauma of termination for many employees.

Another important innovation in outplacement is the use of support groups. This may involve regular group meetings during which dismissed employees discuss problems and generate the support and encouragement which is helpful to continued, effective job search. Group support can also come about when outplacement programs provide seminars and speakers brought in to provide information and motivation. Research on job loss has suggested that support from others is critical to successful job search and to buffering people from some of the negative effects of job loss (Kaufman 1982; Latack and Dozier 1986). Ongoing group meetings provide individuals an opportunity to help each other and promote goal setting and maintenance of initiative.

Furthermore, some group support initiatives should be focused on family members. The family is a key source of support for the unemployed, so they need to understand the outplacement process that the dismissed person is experiencing and how to be supportive during this time. In addition, the family itself is at risk during this time. Job loss can bring tensions to the family, and family members may worry and even express anger at the person who has lost his or her job. Involving family members in group outplacement workshops can reassure them that the employee is receiving assistance and help them cope with the stress of this experience.

Although not formally part of an outplacement program, transition management is being tried in some firms (Bridges 1986). Transition management acknowledges that during downsizing and reorganization, there is negative fallout for the employees who remain. Suspicion, distrust, and lowered commitment can be the result. Once a downsizing has occurred, and people have been let go, management's attention turns to managing the transition in a manner designed to reassure remaining employees and get them focused in a new direction.

In the first phase, a key factor initially is reasonable explanation as to why the changes, including the terminations, were necessary. This helps employees cope with the impact of seeing others fired, as well as with lateral moves, demotions, or other readjustments that can be viewed negatively, or at least ambivalently by employees who have been affected.

The second phase, often referred to as a neutral zone, is where doubts or worries may be most prevalent. During this phase, management must monitor employee reactions and take steps that acknowledge the changes, sometimes through rituals. Some firms have used teams of employees to communicate with upper management; others have hosted dinners which highlight those transferred or demoted, along with information about the company's outplacement support for those dismissed or taking early retirement.

In the final phase, "a new beginning" which offers people an opportunity to plug into the leaner organization is needed. In addition to communicating vision, top management should establish career development and training programs.

Finally, outplacement consultants have coined the term *outplacement avoidance* to refer to instances where they are brought in to assist individuals who have not been fired in the traditional sense. Although they have been asked to leave, they are still on the payroll of the organization and have been given a specified period of time (typically three months to one year) in which to find employment elsewhere. During that time, their regular duties are suspended and their assignment becomes working with the outplacement consultant to find another job. This is helpful to employees because they can job hunt while still on the payroll and avoid the stigma associated with being fired and unemployed. Under this arrangement, prospective employers may not even be aware that the individual is working with an outplacement firm.

Alternatives to Termination: Inplacement Strategies

As noted earlier, some organizations have found that the best approach to dealing with surplus employees is not termination but some other alternative. Typical alternatives have been normal attrition, early retirement, shorter workweeks, and reducing or postponing salary or benefits.

Recently, some companies are focusing on some form of inplacement or career rescue (Schuster 1987). These strategies emphasize comprehensive and creative efforts to absorb surplus employees and to salvage employees who are simply not working out well in their current jobs. This may involve reassignment elsewhere in the organization, retraining or some form of organizational restructuring that accommodates employees in new roles and job responsibilities. Top management and some outplacement consultants recognize that this approach may provide cost savings in the long run, including the hidden costs of terminating employees, such as reduced loyalty and commitment among remaining employees. A few innovative examples are renewal strategies for plateaued managers, downward moves, and "cycling" managers.

In the case of some managerial employees, those who are slated for termination have often been labeled as plateaued (see Hall and Rabinowitz, Chapter 5, in this volume)—that is, having little likelihood of upward movement within the organization. Although Hall and Rabinowitz discuss strategies relative to plateaued managers, a brief review will be provided here because these strategies generate creative alternatives to termination. Bardwick (1983) lists the following strategies for "renewing" plateaued employees: (1) exchanging people laterally between existing jobs for varying time periods; (2) designing positions so that new jobs require both old and new knowledge and skills; (3) creating temporary work units to solve specific problems, particularly complex problems that require deep study or long-range planning; (4) reappraising those contributions to the organization that are supplementary rather than directly contributory (for example, mentoring and major activities in community or government relations); (5) moving technically expert people into supervisory positions to manage other technical employees; and (6) using some individuals as internal consultants in different parts of the organization (p. 71).

Another strategy that is gaining acceptance in some organizations is downward movement. Although the stigma attached to demotions remains strong, the organizational reality in many firms dictates that the developmental aspects of downward moves be explored. For example, a divisional marketing manager who has become obsolete may still make a contribution and become updated by shifting back to a sales manager position. A senior corporate vice president might capitalize on years of organizational knowledge and industry contacts by heading up the public relations department (see Hall and Isabella 1985).

Another innovative idea is "cycling" managers—creating positions where senior managers who may be close to retirement are used as consultants and counselors to give a "big picture" and longer range view to supervisors (Tack 1986). Cycling provides for a role model and teacher role that allows the wisdom and experience of senior managers to cross departmental boundaries while opening up positions to those lower in the organization who are ready to move up.

SUMMARY

Although human resource managers confront considerable dilemmas as they develop termination and outplacement programs, systematic attention to this area of career development can have substantial payoffs for employees and for organizations. Like many organizational changes, the need to terminate creates both stress and opportunities for individual and organizational development. This chapter has reviewed managerial pressures related to terminations and the benefits of providing outplacement programs. The trauma that job loss and unemployment can inflict was discussed because an understanding of the psychological impact is the cornerstone of effective outplacement. Types of terminations and considerations in making termination decisions were summarized. Outplacement strategies and innovations were presented, along with examples of creative alternatives to termination.

The information in this chapter is intended to aid human resource professionals in managing the stress as well as taking advantage of, and expanding the opportunities for, development that outplacement can provide.

RESOURCES AND FURTHER READING

For a discussion of legal aspects of firing decisions, see David A. Bradshaw and Linda Van Winkle Deacon, "Wrongful discharge: The tip of the iceberg?" *Personnel Administrator* (November, 1985, 74–76; T. J. Condon and R. H. Wolff, "Procedures that safeguard your right to fire," *Harvard Business Review* (November-December, 1985, 16–19).

See H. J. Kaufman, 1982; C. R. Leana and J. M. Ivancevich, 1987; W. F. Leff and M. G. Haft, 1983; P. G. Leventman, 1981; H. Mauer, 1979 and Michal-Johnson, 1985 for a more detailed discussion of employee reactions to job loss and unemployment.

For details on the Stroh's program illustrated in Figure 20.1, see Joseph Franzem, "Easing the pain," *Personnel Administrator* (February, 1987, 48–55) and Joseph Janotta, "Stroh's outplacement success," *Management Review* (January, 1987, 52–53).

Sources for additional case study examples of outplacement programs see: "A happy ending in Connecticut," *ASPA Resource* (August, 1985, 2, 10–11); William L. Batt, Jr., "Canada's good example with displaced workers," *Harvard Business Review* (61, July/August, 1983, 6–7); "Company help for the laid-off," *Business Week* (February 4, 1980, p. 88); Philip D. Johnston, "Personnel planning for a plant shutdown," *Personnel Administrator* (26, August, 1981, 53); "Outplacement training: A case history,"

Training (*21*, May, 1984, 106–107); Thomasine Rendero, "Outplacement practices," *Personnel* (July-August 1980, 4–11); Nadeem Shahzad, "Outplacement services at Interfaith Medical Center," *Personnel Administrator* (*29*, June, 1984, 59–60); Joseph Tirpak and J. Richard Wible, "Even small organizations can provide job search assistance for their employees," *Personnel Administrator* (*29*, April, 1984, 71–72).

For further information on selecting an outplacement consultant, see F. Leigh Branham, "How to evaluate executive outplacement services," *Personnel Journal* (April, 1983, 323–26); John D. Erdlen, "Guidelines for retaining an outplacement consultant," *Personnel Administrator* (January, 1978, 27–28); Loretta D. Foxman and Walter L. Polsky, "How to select a good outplacement firm," *Personnel Journal*, September, 94–107, 1984.

For a directory of outplacement firms, contact the Association of Outplacement Consulting Firms, Inc., 364 Parsippany Rd., Parsippany, NJ 07054.

For additional discussion of making and communicating termination decisions, see L. M. Brammer and F. E. Humberger, 1984, *Outplacement and inplacement counseling* (Englewood Cliffs, NJ: Prentice-Hall); J. P. Bucalo, Jr., "Administering a salaried reduction in force... effectively," *Personnel Administrator* (April, 1982, 79–89); P. Michal-Johnson, 1985, *Saying goodbye: A manager's guide to employee dismissal* (Scott, Foresman & Co., Glenview, IL).

Additional ideas on downsizing and transition management can be found in William Bridges, "Managing organizational transitions," *Organizational Dynamics* (Summer, 1986); Bucalo, 1982; Elizabeth M. Fowler, "When a staff is cut," *New York Times*, March 16, 1987; Robert I. Sutton, Kathleen M. Eisenhardt, and James V. Jucker, "Managing organizational decline: Lessons from Atari," *Organizational Dynamics* (Spring, 1986, 17–29).

For a discussion of alternatives to termination, see Brammer and Humberger, 1984; R. Dean and D. W. Prior, 1986, "Your company could benefit from a no-layoff policy," *Training and Development Journal* (August, 38–41); Douglas T. Hall and Lynn A. Isabella, "Downward movement and career development," *Organizational Dynamics* (Summer, 1985, 5–23); Harold G. Kaufman, 1982, *Professionals in search of work: Coping with the stress of job loss and underemployment* (New York: John Wiley & Sons, pp. 257–60); K. Ropp, 1987, "Downsizing strategies," *Personnel Administrator* (February, 61–64); B. Saporito, 1987, "Cutting costs without cutting people," *Fortune* (May, 26–32).

REFERENCES

American Society for Personnel Administration. 1985. A happy ending in Connecticut. *Resource*, August, 2, 6, 11.

Bardwick, J. M. 1983. Plateauing and productivity. *Sloan Management Review*, Spring, 67–73.

Bennett, A. 1987. How a manager manages in wake of big staff cuts. *The Wall Street Journal*, May 4.

Bradshaw, D. A., and L. Van Winkle Deacon. 1985. Wrongful discharge: The tip of the iceberg? *Personnel Administrator*, November, 74–76.

Brammer, L. M., and F. E. Humberger. 1984. *Outplacement and Inplacement counseling*. Englewood Cliffs, NJ: Prentice-Hall.

Branham, F. L. 1983. How to evaluate executive outplacement services. *Personnel Journal*, April, 323–26.

Bridges, W. 1986. Managing organizational transitions. *Organizational Dynamics*, Summer, 24–33.

Brockner, J. In press. The effects of work layoffs on survivors: Research, theory and practice. In B. M. Staw and L. L. Cummings (eds.), *Research in organizational behavior* (vol. 10). Greenwich, CT: JAI Press.

Bucalo, J. P. 1982. Administering a salaried reduction-in-force... effectively. *Personnel Administrator*, April, 79–89.

Camden, T. 1982. Using outplacement as a career development tool. *Personnel Administrator*, 27, 35–37.

Condon, T. J. 1985. *Fire me and I'll sue! A manager's survival guide to employee rights*, Alexander Hamilton Institute.

Condon, T. J. and R. H. Wolff, Procedures that safeguard your right to fire. *Harvard Business Review*, November-December, 16–19.

Dean, R., and Pryor, D. W. 1986. Your company could benefit from a no-layoff policy. *Training and Development Journal*, August, 38–41.

Dobrzynski, J. H., and J. Berger. 1987. For better or for worse. *Business Week*, January, 38–40.

Drake, J. D., J. Beam, and W. J. Morin. No date. *Termination policies and practices: Survey results and analysis*. (100 Park Avenue, 4th Floor, New York, NY 10017, (212) 303–7900).

Erdlen, J. D. 1978. Guidelines for retaining an outplacement consultant. *Personnel Administrator*, January, 27–28.

Fowler, E. M. 1986. Placing dismissed employees. *New York Times*, January 22.

Fowler, E. M. 1987. When a staff is cut. *New York Times*, March 16.

Foxman, L. D., and W. L. Polsky. 1984. How to select a good outplacement firm. *Personnel Journal*, September, 94–107.

Franzem, J. 1987. Easing the pain. *Personnel Administrator*, February, 48–55.

Greenberg, K., and M. Zippo. 1983. How companies feel about outplacement services. *Personnel*, January-February, 55–57.

Hall, D. T., and L. A. Isabella. 1985. Downward movement and career development. *Organizational Dynamics*, Summer, 5–23.

Heistand, D. L. 1986. Outplacement counseling: A review of the literature. Center for Career Research and Human Resource Management, Graduate School of Business, Columbia University.

Henriksen, D. 1982. Outplacement: Program guidelines that ensure success. *Personnel Journal*, August, 583–89.

Hoban, R. 1987. The outplacement option: Everyone wins! *Personnel Administrator*, June, 184–93.

Hymomitz, C., and T. D. Schellhardt. 1986. Merged firms often fire workers the easy way—Not the best way. *The Wall Street Journal*, February 24.

Janotta, J. 1987. Stroh's outplacement success. *Management Review*, January, 52–53.

Kaufman, H. G. 1982. *Professionals in search of work: Coping with the stress of job loss and underemployment*. New York: Wiley-Interscience.

Kaufman, H. J. 1974. *Obsolescence and professional career development*. New York: IEEE Press/Wiley-Interscience.

Kaufman, H. J. 1975. *Career management: A guide to combatting obsolescence*. New York: IEEE Press/Wiley-Interscience.

Kessler, F. 1985. Managers without a company. *Fortune*, October, 51–56.

Kramer, A. M. 1987. The hazards of firing at will. *The Wall Street Journal*, March 9.

Kubler-Ross, E. 1969. *On death and dying*. New York: Macmillan.

Latack, J. C., and J. D. Dozier. 1986. After the ax falls: Job loss as a career transition. *Academy of Management Review*, April, 375–92.

Leana, C. R., and J. M. Ivancevich. 1987. Involuntary job loss: Institutional interventions and a research agenda. *Academy of Management Review 12* April, 301–12.

Leff, W. F., and M. G. Haft. 1983. *Time without work*. Boston: South End Press.

Leventman, P. G. 1981. *Professionals out of work*. New York: The Free Press.

Lynch, M. C. 1981. As recession deepens, white-collar workers join the jobless ranks. *The Wall Street Journal*, December 7.

Mauer, H. 1979. *Not working: An oral history of the unemployed*. New York: Holt, Rinehart & Winston.

Mellow, C. 1986. Outplacement passages. *Across the Board*, November, 39–44.

Michal-Johnson, P. 1985. *Saying good-bye: A manager's guide to employee dismissal*. Glenview, IL: Scott, Foresman & Co.

Morin, W., and L. Yorks, 1982. *Outplacement techniques: A positive approach to terminating employees*. New York: Harcourt, Brace, Jovanovich.

Nelson, B. 1983. Despair among jobless is on rise, studies find. *New York Times*, April 2.

Peters, T., and R. H. Waterman. 1981. *In search of excellence*. New York: Harper and Row.

Rendero, T. 1980. Consensus: Outplacement practices. *Personnel*, July-August, 4–11.

Ropp, K. 1987. Downsizing strategies. *Personnel Administrator*, February, 61–64.

Sadler, J. 1987. Labor letter. *The Wall Street Journal*, January 6.

Saporito, B. 1987. Cutting costs without cutting people. *Fortune*, May, 26–32.

Scherba, J. 1973. Outplacement as a personnel responsibility. *Personnel, 50*, 40–44.

Schuster, R. 1987. Schonberg Associates, Columbus, OH. Personal conversation, June 26.

Schweiger, D. L. and J. M. Ivancevich. 1985. Human resources: The forgotten factor in mergers and acquisitions. *Personnel Administrator*, November, 47–61.

Shad, J. 1987. Insider trading caveat: In the end, only ethics pays. *The Wall Street Journal*, February 6.

Stybel, L. J. 1987. Stybel, Peabody & Associates, Boston, MA: Personal conversation, May 15.

Stybel, L. J., R. Cooper and M. Peabody. 1982. Planning executive dismissals: How to fire a friend. *California Management Review, 24,* 73–80.

Sutton, R. I., K. M. Eisenhardt, and J. V. Jucker. 1986. Managing organizational decline: Lessons from Atari. *Organizational Dynamics,* Spring, 17–29.

Tack, W. L. 1986. Don't ignore seasoned managers—The case for management cycling. *Sloan Management Review,* Summer, 63–70.

The Wall Street Journal, Labor Letter, January 6, 1987.

The Wall Street Journal, Labor Letter, March 24, 1987.

Yao, M. 1982. Manager's miseries, middle-aged officials find new group hit by slump: Themselves. *The Wall Street Journal,* September 1.

Zelvin, A. 1987. A job hot line can help the pink-slip blues. *The Wall Street Journal,* February 2.

Part V

Multiple Roles of Human Resource Professionals

The themes in this book are evident in the human resource manager's roles of promoting individual growth and organizational effectiveness. In this concluding chapter, Manuel London considers the future of the human resource professional in career development—a future that recognizes the human resource professional's multiple roles as educator, facilitator, innovator, evaluator, experimenter, leader, and strategist.

London explains why individuals need to be flexible in their career goals and why organizations need to be flexible in their policies and programs. He predicts that human resources will be recognized by corporate leaders as being critical to accomplishing business goals, and that employee development will be viewed by corporate leaders as being essential to meeting both individual and organizational needs. Consequently, the human resource professional will become an integral part of the business, and employee development will become an investment in the future, not merely an overhead expense.

CHAPTER 21

THE FUTURE ROLE OF HR PROFESSIONALS IN EMPLOYEE CAREER DEVELOPMENT

MANUEL LONDON

This chapter examines issues and directions for future career management policies and programs. The linkages between business conditions, human resource strategies, and career development are explored. The human resource (HR) professional's role in articulating and communicating the organization's needs is outlined. Alternative roles for the HR manager are considered, including the HR manager as educator, facilitator, innovator, evaluator, and leader. The goal is to show how human resource management can be effective in meeting the objectives of employees and the organization.

LINKING CAREER DEVELOPMENT TO BUSINESS STRATEGY

The condition of a business and the general goals of its top management for the future of the business will affect what HR strategies are needed. Stated another way, HR strategies will increasingly be necessary to support the organization's business objectives. For instance, a growing organization needs to be concerned about hiring the right people, training them, and developing them to assume new and increasing responsibilities as the organization expands. A business start-up suggests the need to select people very carefully because the initial talent is likely to determine the direction and success of the new enterprise. A declining organization focuses on ways to cut costs, often by reducing force size. The reward for good performance is keeping your job. There are few opportunities for promotion, and the company is unlikely to spend money on training and development. An organization that is trying to redirect its mission to increase its profitability in light of changing market conditions will need a new mix of talent. One strategy might be to retrain employees who are capable and interested in staying with the organization.

While business conditions will influence human resource strategies, these strategies will also influence business conditions. The types of people hired by the organization and the employee development programs used will determine the creativity and ability of employees, which in turn is channeled into achieving organizational success. The extent to which top executives value employees will determine the executives' acceptance of new ideas and rewards for productivity.

Organizations that value employees' contributions will engender higher levels of motivation and commitment that translate into higher productivity and lower absenteeism and turnover than corporations which do not value employees' contributions. Organizations that value employees consider their development and motivation to be part and parcel of the way the company does business. Managers in these organizations recognize their role as human resource managers, and they are rewarded for developing people just as they are rewarded for financial and customer service performance.

Organizations that do not value employees' contributions treat people as meeting immediate business needs, not as resources to be developed for the future. Top managers do not recognize a relationship between bottom-line financial performance and morale, and they fail to see how leadership influences morale. High-performing employees will stay with the organization only as long as they are monetarily rewarded. Managers do not spend resources developing subordinates. Any efforts to improve morale are viewed as separate from operating the business.

Human resource strategies influence business conditions in that the values implicit in managing employees translate into ways of involving them in enhancing organizational effectiveness. Valuing employee participation in decisions affecting them may lead to a quality circle or a quality of worklife program to identify ways to enhance productivity. Or it may lead to self-managing work groups which schedule their own work assignments and work hours and solve problems on their own without constant supervision. Valuing learning may lead to new development programs which allow employees to learn new skills that increase their value to the organization for today and the future.

THE NEED FOR INDIVIDUAL AND ORGANIZATIONAL FLEXIBILITY

Organizations will require employees to adapt to changing business needs by learning new skills, taking on more responsibility, and perhaps changing their area of specialization. The organization must also be flexible in responding to the needs of individuals. Managers must learn to assess the skills and career goals of each employee. Each employee should have a personal development plan that is revised over time as the individual's needs change and as opportunities in the organization change. The supervisor's role is to work with subordinates in developing their career plans. Supervisors can provide information about opportunities and feedback about the individual's performance and developmental needs. Over time, perhaps after a series of positions in the organization, the individual develops an accurate self-concept and a meaningful career identity. This identity may include commitment to one's organization, profession, and family.

People go through cycles of stability and transition. Employees at different career stages face a variety of phenomena: the first job, learning the ropes in the organization, the decision to follow a particular career track (e.g., specialist versus generalist), reaching a level in the organization from which additional advancement is unlikely (plateauing), changing professions in mid-career, being part of a dual career couple, coping with the stress of organizational change (e.g., downsizing or merger), and retirement. These transitions have a variety of causes: not feeling challenged, losing support from higher-level managers, being in an industry that is declining, or having family problems, as examples.

Organizations respond to individuals in a variety of ways. Career management refers to the resources organizations make available to employees to help them accomplish their career goals. These resources include courses, workshops, counseling, career information, tools for supervisor and self-assessments, assessment centers, career paths, succession plans, staffing systems that match individuals to job vacancies, and programs for women and minorities to advance in the company.

The extent to which organizations invest in these programs will depend on the organization's goals and the extent to which top executives perceive and value employees' contributions to achieving these goals. Career management programs and systems need to fit together in a comprehensive way to match the needs of the business. Human resource managers must be aware of business needs to design appropriate development programs. For example, human resource managers must understand the skills required to manage the business if they are to design a management development program that meets the company's needs. The program must provide young managers with experiences that will prepare them to run the business in the future. HR managers must identify the key learning experiences. For example, having experience with starting a new venture will be important to an organization likely to diversify. The same young manager may also need experience running a stable unit and perhaps closing down a unit if the organization is likely to be in a variety of changing businesses.

MANAGING DIVERSITY

Corporate managers will have to learn to value the diversity of contribution if they are to make maximum use of the corporation's human resources. Valuing differences means understanding the different contributions people make to an organization. These differences come in many forms: cultural, gender, race, and age. The organization's HR strategies and goals must take advantage of this diversity. Such goals include commitment to opportunities for minorities and women. They may also include ensuring job security for a permanent work force by hiring temporary workers who can be added to the corporation during peak periods and dropped during slack periods. Temporary workers are likely to have lower commitment to the business than permanent workers. In general, managers will need to vary their management style to meet the needs of these different employees for structure and development.

THE ROLE OF THE HR PROFESSIONAL

Given the diversity and change in people, leaders' values, and business conditions, there is no one role for the human resource professional. The response of a human resource department to its clients internal to the organization will depend on the needs of the client departments. For instance, how much should the HR manager control line managers' ability to make decisions about employees? This depends on the importance of the issue, the willingness of the leadership to hold line managers accountable for HR management, and the knowledge and ability of line managers to perform the task (e.g., hiring minorities, giving subordinates feedback, allocating merit increases in pay, and so forth).

In general, HR professionals should be able to analyze the corporation's needs, anticipate and communicate these needs, and raise them for discussion in the corporation. In the process, HR professionals generate consensus on solutions to the issues and action strategies. They establish accountability and provide the necessary support to managers who are accountable for carrying out the solutions or recording actions. Sometimes the solutions necessitate central control and uniformity, and the HR department will be accountable for the outcome or for monitoring the outcome. Other times, the solution must be close to the line department, and the line manager retains accountability and the freedom to act. Consequently, the responses will vary from department to department and will vary within departments. HR professionals add value to the situations by helping managers share ideas and experiences and by consulting with line managers in tailoring programs to meet their needs.

An example of an area requiring uniformity is equal employment opportunity. Some observers say that corporations are lax in this area because the current federal administration is deemphasizing the importance of opportunities for minorities. Many major corporations still see equal employment opportunity as an essential social commitment and as a key to being competitive in a global marketplace. HR professionals may be called on to monitor the corporation's profile of women and minorities. However, the accountability should rest with line department leaders. The HR function helps the line departments track their programs. The HR department may also police the function by having veto power over selection or promotion decisions.

An example of an area requiring line accountability in management may be career development for young managers. The line department is in the best position to forecast its human resource requirements, select the people with the needed skills (perhaps with the help of HR professionals in recruiting and selection methods), and establishing career paths. HR professionals may help by developing appropriate performance appraisal procedures, potential assessment techniques, and career planning methods. These procedures may be shared by departments or tailored to a particular department's needs. The HR staff may also help by sponsoring interdepartmental groups to share information about career development activities and identify needs for generic programs. The HR staff may retain accountability for tracking and developing high-potential managers as they reach middle management and become corporate resources. Interdepartmental transfers are important for development as the high-potential manager learns the business. Consequently, the human resource department may maintain central control over executive staffing to ensure that top-rated managers have optimal development opportunities and experiences.

The extent to which line managers will adopt the role of human resource manager will depend on the extent to which this role is valued (rewarded) by the corporation. As mentioned before, this depends on the value the company's leaders place on employees, treating them as resources for the future or instruments to accomplishing immediate business goals. A role for the human resource professional may be to educate corporate leaders and line managers in the importance of valuing people and to educate managers in the tools, programs, and policies that support employee career development.

THE HR PROFESSIONAL AS EDUCATOR

HR professionals design and deliver training programs to help managers understand their role as developers. Again, the developer role is an important part of each manager's job. Yet it is a role the manager is likely to ignore, given heavy job demands. Also, many managers do not feel as comfortable developing people as they do with other aspects of management, such as providing direction and control. Giving subordinates performance feedback and working with them to improve their skills and offer them broader experiences takes time and may seem to be at the expense of accomplishing short-term departmental objectives. The organization can make the development role salient by rewarding managers for developing subordinates.

Courses may be necessary to help managers understand the meaning of developing subordinates and allow them to acquire and practice related supervisory skills. One company developed a day-long seminar to remind managers of their responsibilities as developers. The seminar gave participants an opportunity to discuss the barriers in the company to developing subordinates and ways to overcome these barriers. Corporate resources for improving managerial skills associated with developing people were highlighted, such as training programs, the staffing system, and career planning forms and procedures.

The HR professional needs to understand the educational value of key job experiences. After all, employee development is more likely to take place on the job than in the classroom. Each job assignment has the potential for teaching the employee new skills. For example, one young manager who had been with the company in a staff job for nearly one year was transferred to a line position in a customer service department. The manager was a twenty-three-year-old white female. Seven of her new subordinates were black females with an average of fifteen years' experience. Three additional subordinates were white males, each with over thirty years' experience. The unit was the lowest performing group in the department when the manager took over. The young manager overcame internal conflicts in the group by standing her ground and letting her subordinates know she was the boss. But she also wanted to learn from each of them, and she made that clear. After fifteen months, the group was number one in the department on the major performance indexes. This was an important learning experience for the manager. The HR professionals in charge of staffing worked with this manager's supervisor to find her next job assignment and then a series of subsequent positions that prepared the manager for early promotion to middle management.

Some companies want managers to have a variety of job experiences so they can handle any situation. Other companies want managers to specialize in particular situations. The HR staff must understand the needs of the business and individual career needs. Also, the staff must recognize the educational value of different job experiences, such as spearheading a new venture, managing a fast-growing unit, maintaining the profitability of a stable unit, coordinating the merger of two departments or the acquisition of a subsidiary, or overseeing the dissolution of a department.

The future will require human resource managers to understand and support a continuous learning environment where employees have opportunities to acquire and apply new skills. Corporations may support career changes by sponsoring courses and degree programs for retraining to meet the changing needs of the business. Also, periodic refresher courses may be crucial to ensure that managers have the latest technical and managerial skills.

THE HR PROFESSIONAL AS FACILITATOR

The HR professional can facilitate employee development by helping managers share ideas and by helping departments coordinate their objectives for HR development. Departments are likely to vary in what they feel is necessary for development of their people. Marketing departments may want to develop marketing experts. Finance departments may want to develop financial experts. Other departments may prefer generalist managers who have a broad base of experience in the company and who can pick up needed technical information quickly as they move from job to job. The human resource professional can work with each department to design appropriate development programs. Also, the human resource professional can bring departmental representatives together to discuss their common needs and how they can work on joint programs.

In one company, the human resource department was responsible for the policy guiding the development of high-potential lower- and middle-level managers. The policy specified the number of people in each department who should be in the program based on forecasted openings at higher organizational levels. The policy also indicated the general qualifications and the nomination and selection procedures. The operation of the program was up to each department. That is, each department determined who would be selected, what their job assignments would be, and the content of special programs to become acquainted with the company's officers and learn about business trends.

The human resource department also sponsored meetings of departmental representatives to discuss career development procedures and objectives, share ideas for programs, and commission the human resource department to develop general programs. The company also had a management development committee of senior vice presidents whose responsibilities included moving high-level managers between departments, overseeing internal management training programs, and selecting the most valued high-potential managers for special executive development sessions at universities such as Harvard and MIT.

HR professionals will find themselves assisting departments in planning and implementing unique employee development programs. An example of this occurred when a company's vice president of consumer marketing wanted his organization to be known as having the best consumer marketing department in American industry. This meant enhancing the professionalism of the managers in the department and those who would be selected in the future. He assigned a middle manager to develop a process to make that happen. Working with a task force of departmental managers, the managers decided to develop mastery paths for each job family in the department for occupational employees through middle management. The mastery path would specify the skills needed to be expert on the job, selection criteria for hiring people into the positions, the training available to build needed skills, the expectations for employees on the job as they develop their expertise, and a certification process for evaluating employees' job mastery. Current employees would have to be certified as would new employees who were hired after the program began. This process emphasized that development meant improving on the present job rather than preparing for the next job given that the company was reducing force to cut costs and there were few opportunities for promotion and transfer.

The human resource department was asked to help in this effort by bringing together personnel experts to design selection requirements and procedures, develop appropriate appraisal systems, approve new reward and compensation systems, and create and deliver needed training. The goal of the HR department was to facilitate the process by finding a way for the marketing department to accomplish its goal, rather than saying no to what had not been done before.

A similar effort was initiated in a technical operations department. Here the concern was that managers were not keeping up-to-date with technological developments and new management strategies. Human resource experts were asked to help develop standards, training courses, tests, career planning workshops, seminars on managers as developers, and leadership forums for higher-level managers.

THE HR PROFESSIONAL AS INNOVATOR

Just as any organization is concerned with meeting customer needs, an HR department must anticipate its clients' employee development objectives and provide innovative policies and programs in relationship to those objectives. The HR professional must stay abreast of developments in such fields as personnel psychology, career development, organizational behavior, and management. The HR professional must also study competitors and other companies thought to have excellent management. In doing so, HR professionals maintain their own expertise and are able to make timely, creative contributions to their organizations.

A number of valuable contributions to employee development have stemmed from behavioral science theory and research. One is behavior modeling training based on concepts of behavior modification, performance feedback, and role modeling. Trainees are presented with a set of learning points about management topics such as handling performance problems. The trainees watch a videotape of good ways to handle the problem. Then they have a chance to role play the behavior in the classroom with feedback and reinforcement from the trainer. Supervisors are instructed how to observe and reward the desired behavior on the job.

Assessment centers are another innovation for identifying high-potential managers early in their careers and providing information on strengths and weaknesses that have implications for future development. The assessment center is a series of behavioral exercises, tasks, and interviews pertinent to management development. Trained observers evaluate participants on dimensions of managerial performance. The results may be used to select individuals for high-potential programs, or they may be used to provide direction for strengths that need to be enhanced and weaknesses that need to be corrected.

Behavioral simulations of corporate life are another innovation. The participants play roles of people at different levels in the organization. The simulation may last six hours and be conducted in an office setting. Participants experience making important decisions in taking actions that influence the course of the organization. One version of such a simulation asks managers to design a new organization in hopes that they will experience what it's like to manage in an ambiguous environment.

The future will require human resource professionals to integrate programs such as simulations, assessment centers, and training in ways that meet the organization's human resource objectives. A large organization is likely to require different types of managers and so will have different directions for management development. The desirability of a policy of promotion from within and the opportunities for learning and applying new skills will depend on the business conditions and strategies. For instance, a rapidly growing organization may require hiring people into all organizational levels to ensure that the right talent is available to meet changing marketplace demands. A stable organization may be concerned about career development for all managers to attract bright people and keep them motivated with challenging jobs and opportunities for growth.

THE HR PROFESSIONAL AS EVALUATOR AND EXPERIMENTER

I believe that top management will increasingly expect HR professionals to evaluate their policies and programs to provide evidence for their effectiveness before they are implemented. HR professionals will have to show that employee development programs meet the strategic directions of the business. They will also have to establish criteria for the success of their programs—criteria which are ultimately associated with bottom-line financial performance. Utility analyses can estimate the incremental cost-benefit of new selection and new training programs. Experimental research designs can compare groups attending various versions of a program against control groups that are withheld from the program. Satisfaction measures can assess participants' attitudes about a career planning workshop or other training programs. Employee attitude surveys can be used to tap feelings about career opportunities, the company's support for women and minorities, and beliefs about the company as a good place to work.

The HR professional may have to demonstrate the relationship between such indexes and bottom-line results. This is particularly a problem with data on employee morale. Several studies indicate that employees are happier in companies that have better financial performance. Whether such results indicate that high morale encourages good financial results is difficult to say. However, the HR professional can build a cogent argument that enhancing employee morale is an integral part of the way top-performing companies do business. Other evaluation indexes include frequency counts of the number and types of people hired, transferred, and promoted. The HR professional may also be asked to compare the company with other corporations in the same industry to assess competitive advantage, for instance, on executive compensation and ability to attract top talent.

THE HR PROFESSIONAL AS BUSINESS LEADER AND STRATEGIST

Earlier I discussed the dialectic between the HR professional as the conscience of the corporation, the advocate of the employee, and the ensurer of equitable treatment versus the HR professional as provider of resources to the line manager who has the ultimate responsibility for HR management and the freedom to act to carry out this responsibility. This dialectic is resolved by a delicate balancing act in which HR professionals vary their stance (control versus facilitation) depending on the issues. (For example, equal employment opportunity probably requires more central control than employee development, although admittedly these two areas are related.)

The HR professional faces another dialectic: providing staff support that is responsive to client needs versus providing strategic initiatives and directions for the corporation's leaders and managers to follow. This leadership role treats HR management as a major business function and uses human resources as a competitive advantage. In this sense, the HR department is responsible for integrating HR management activities in all parts of the business. It is responsible for identifying and educating managers on better ways of managing, such as designing self-managing work teams, promoting quality of work life programs, and instituting an employee development ethic in the business. This requires proving the value of these programs to the corporation. It also demands an acute awareness of the business as a whole, which can only occur if HR professionals work as part of a team with leaders and managers in other departments as the strategic direction for the organization is established and implemented.

CONCLUSION

There are exciting possibilities for people in the human resource field. Rather than just providing services to meet client demands, the HR manager helps clients understand their needs and educates them about appropriate ways to use human resources. In this sense, HR professionals enact multiple roles in the organization: educator, facilitator, innovator, evaluator, and leader. The HR professional must be a monitor of behavior and actions and the source of empowering managers with the freedom to act in managing and developing the corporation's human resources. Therefore, in the future, HR professionals will become an integral part of the business—not overhead but a critical, value-added resource to enhanced financial performance.

INDEX

The Achieving Society, 86
Adult learning, 195
Advanced Management Potential Assessment (AMPA) Program, 183–88; discussion groups, 187–88; preprogram assignments, 186–87
Advancement motivation, 6–7, 14; decline in, 9–10
Advertisement of positions, 244–45
Ambition, 6–7
Analyzer firms, 140–41; and career plateaus, 145; and job attitudes, 146–48
Anthony, R., 157
Anticipatory socialization, 32–34
Application review, 245
Assessment. *See* Self-assessment
Assessment centers, 324–25; and administrative procedures, 178–79; design of, 173–81; exercises for, 177–78; goals of, 174; and high-potential career development, 183–93. *See also* Advanced Management Potential Assessment (AMPA) Program
Assessors, training of, 179–80
AT&T: Advanced Management Potential Assessment (AMPA) Program, 183–88; Basic Human Resources Research Section, 7; managerial career studies at, 6–13; self-assessment experience at, 157–59, 168; shift in careers at, 105; terminations at, 291
Attitude surveys, 8

Banas, Paul, 115–16
Bartoleme, F., 92
Basic Human Resources Research section, at AT&T, 7
Battlefield commissions, 112
Bolles, Richard, 162
Boss-subordinate relationships, 54; and executive development, 259
Boston Consulting Group, 140
Boudreau, J. W., 13
Business simulations, 195–206; benefits of, 204–5; computer-based, 199–200; diagnosis and development, 202–4; and human resource activities, 196–97; large-scale behavioral, 197–99; program design, 200–202
Business strategy, 135–50; of analyzers, 140–41; and career paths, 143–45, 317–18; of defenders, 136, 140; and human resource practices, 141–43; job attitudes and, 146–48; of prospectors, 150 n.1

Career and Life Planning Guide, 165
Career cycle, transition points in, 104–6
Career development, 131–33
Career-enhancing relationships: cross-race and cross-gender, 57–60; education and training, 61–63; factors shaping, 56–57; organizational change approach to, 63–65; peer, 55–56; superior-subordinate, 51–54; typology of, 52–54
Career exploration, 17–30; and career life cycle, 23–26; focus of, 20–21; human resource system support for, 29; obstacles to, 26–27; promotion of, 28; types of, 21–23
Career life cycle, 23–26; early, 25; late, 26, 83–89; mid-career, 25–26, 83–89
Career Management, 18–20, 319
Career paths: business strategy and, 143–45; professional organizational, 273–74. See also Self-assessment
Career plateau, 67–80; and business strategy, 143–45; early signs of, 68–69; effects of, 69–71; options for, 72–73; projects as antidotes, 75–79
Careers: goals, 189–90; helping subordinates manage, 190; two-path model, 73–75
Career success/personal failure (CS/PF), 81–83; explanatory framework for, 83–89
Center for Creative Leadership, 202, 262, 266
College recruiting, 13–14
Computer-based organizational simulations, 199–200
Conformity, 43
Corporate ladder, changes in, 67
CS/PF, See Career Success/ personal failure

Debasement experiences, 38–39
Defender firms, 136, 140, 141; and career plateaus, 145; human resource strategies for, 148–49; and job attitudes, 146–48

Developer role, 208–9, 214–21; institutionalization of, 209–10; programs and resources for, 213; support of, 210–13
Development needs and plans, 120–21
Diagnosis: and business simulation, 202–4; and organizational change 63–65
Discussion groups, 187–88
Diversity, value of, 101
Dobbins, G. H., 246
Double bind, of high income levels, 87
Dual ladder systems, 279

Education, 61–63
Employee development. *See* Philosophy of employee development
Entrepreneurship, 284–85
Equal opportunity, 238–39, 320–21
Ethical responsibility, 285–87
Executive development, 257–62; and course work, 261; future of, 265–66; and hardship, 260; and leadership challenge, 269; and the learning environment, 266–67; success of, 262–65; transition points in, 267–68
Expectations, 35–36

Feedback, in assessment process, 180
Feelings, and self-assessment, 163–64
Figler, H., 160
Fine, Sidney, 162–63
Flexibility, and the organization, 318–19
Ford, 115

Gabarro, Jack, 268
Gatekeeping, 282
Gender, and career-enhancing relationships, 57–60
General Electric, 268
Goals, 189–90; of business simulations, 201–2; definition of, 174; for development of a subordinate, 210–13
The Grapes of Wrath, 163
Guiding principles, 102
Guilt, from surpassing parents, 86–88

Hall, D. T., 75, 77
Hardee's, 112
Hardships, 260
Harvard Business Review, 247
Harvard Business School, 268
Hennig, M., 243
High income levels, effects of, 85–86
High Involvement Management, 71
High-potential career development pro-
   gram, 186–90
Holland, J., 192; *Making Vocational
   Choices*, 161
Horner, M., 88
Human Resources departments, and
   people philosophies, 106–7
Human Resources professionals: and
   business simulations, 196–206; and
   business strategy, 141–43, 326; and
   CS/PF, 89–92; as educators, 321–22;
   as evaluators and experimenters,
   325–26; as facilitators, 323–24; future role of, 317–27; as innovators,
   324–25; and managerial motivation,
   13–15; managing salaried professionals, 271–87; and minorities,
   236–38; and philosophies of development, 99–100; role(s) of, 49–65,
   106–7, 132–33; and socialization
   process, 44–45; and women's advancement, 252–53; and work force
   variety, 35
Human Resource systems: and career
   exploration, 29; for defender firms,
   148–49; self-assessment and, 167–70
Hymowitz, C., 67

IBM, 76
Income, high levels of, 85–86
Information management, 130
Inplacement, 308–9
Interests, and self-assessment, 161–62
Internal labor market policy, 277–78
Interviews, 7–8; bias at, 245; dis-
   missal, 299–300; and socialization,
   35

Jardim, A., 243
Job assignments, 38–39

Job attitudes, and business strategy,
   146–48
Job descriptions, 244
Job expectations, 36
Job involvement, 71
Jobs, analysis of, 175

Kaplan, Robert, 202
Kennedy, M. M., 31
Kodak, 291

Labor, and values, 160
Lawler, E., 71
Leadership: challenges of, 258–59,
   269; feminine style of, 247; skills
   underlying, 118–19
Leadership motivation, 7, 10
Learning environment, 266–67
Learning International, 125
Lepsinger, Richard, 204
Levinson, H., 91
Life changes, 9–10
Linkage devices, 277
Loughary, J. W., 165

McClelland, D., *The Achieving Society*,
   86
Making Vocational Choices, 161
Management: of diversity, 319–20; by
   objectives (MBO), 281–82; women
   in, 241–53
Management development policies,
   111–23; aims of, 117–19; execution
   of, 119–21; problems of, 112–17
Management motivation, 5–16; factors
   effecting, 8–13; in the future, 15–16;
   measurement of, 7–8; types of, 6–7
Management system support, 210–13
Managerial effectiveness, 125–33
Managerial roles, 126–27; the influencer, 130–31; the information manager, 130; the investor, 129–30; the
   visionary, 128–29
The Managerial Woman, 243
Managers: as developers, 207–21; and
   professionals, 272–73; and terminations, 294–95
Manus Associates, 204

Maturation, 111–12
Mauer, H., 293
Mentoring, 38, 40, 50, 53, 57, 278;
  formal programs, 60–61; women
  and, 250
Merit badge infatuation, 114
Mid-life crisis, 84–85
Minorities, problems faced by, 227–39
Motivation. *See* Management motiva-
  tion
Motorola, 73, 75
Mullen, Tom, 204

Neugarten, Bernice, 164–65
Newcomers: debasement of, 38–39;
  expectations of, 36; informal sociali-
  zation of, 39–41
New York City, 75
New York University, 204, 262
No-road-map syndrome, 113–14

Organizations: commitment to, 42;
  high-involvement, 71–72
Orientation programs, 37
Outplacement, 289–90; benefits of,
  291–93; creative variations in, 306–
  7; strategies for, 298–306
Overspecialization, 275–79

Parents: and achievement motivation,
  86; guilt from surpassing, 86–88
Peer relationships, 55–56
People, as critical resource, 101–2
Personality types, 161
Personnel Accreditation Institute (PAI),
  275
Philosophy of employee development,
  99–109; people as critical resource,
  101–2; roles and responsibilities in,
  102–3; strategies of, 103–4; values,
  101; and work environment, 102
Planned development, 112
Plateaued career. *See* Career plateau
Platz, S. J., 246
Political shyness, 116–17
Preparation for work, 25
Professionals, 271–87; autonomy of,
  279–81; ethical responsibility of,

285–87; and formalization, 283–84;
  overspecialization of, 275–79; and
  real world practice, 284–85; supervision of, 281–83
Programs: with business simulation,
  200–202; career exploration/man-
  agement, 28–29; for developer role,
  213; high-potential career development, 186–90; mentoring, 60–61;
  orientation, 37; training and development, 37–38
Project work, 75–77
Prospector firms, 150 n.1
Psychologists: in assessment programs,
  184, 187; and outplacement strategies, 305

Race, and career-enhancing relation-
  ships, 57–60
Racism, 227–28, 231–32; perceptions
  of, 228–30; and stereotypes, 232–33
Realistic job previews (RJPs), 35
Recruitment, 13–14; and selection, 34–
  36
Relationships. *See* Career-enhancing re-
  lationships
Relocation, 43
Research, on managerial effectiveness,
  125–28
Responsibility, delineation of, 115–16
Resume preparation, 305
Ripley, T. M., 165
Role modeling, 41
Role strain, 42
Rynes, S. L., 13

Sale, K., 238
Scanlon Plan, 71
Schoonmaker, A. N., 236
Selection process, 34–36
Self-assessment, 157–70; and decision-
  making, 165–66; and education,
  166; and feelings, 163–64; and the
  human resource system, 167–70;
  and interests, 161–62; and personal
  resources, 164; and skills, 162–63;
  timing and, 164–65; and values, 160
Sexism, 227–28, 247

Skills, 162–63; determination of, 175–77, 203–4
Social change, 10–13
Socialization, 31–46, 104–5; advantages of, 43–44; anticipatory, 32–34; disadvantages of, 42–43; formal, 37–39; and human resource professionals, 44–45, 278; informal, 39–41; outcomes, 41–44
Steinbeck, John, 163
STEP process (select, target, evaluate, prepare), 131–32
Stereotypes, racist, 232–33
Strategy: for employee development, 103–4. *See also* Business strategy
Success, costs of, 88–89
Sumner, H. L., 241
Super, D. E., 157
Superior-subordinate relationships, 51–54
Sustained career support relationships, 53

Temporary instrumental relations, 53
Termination, 289–309; decision-making, 296–98; trauma of, 293–95; types of, 295–96
Texas Instruments Corporation, 37

Timing, 164–65
Training and development, 61–63; and assessment centers, 178–80; motivation and, 14–15; scenario of, 121–23; self-assessment and, 166; and socialization, 37–38. *See also* Business simulations
Training, 195
Transition management, 307
Two-path career model, 73–75

Values, 101; and self-assessment, 160
Van Maanen, J., 32

Wall, Stephen, 204
The Wall Street Journal, 290–91
Wang Laboratories, 291
What Color Is Your Parachute?, 162
Women: and costs of success, 88–89; entry into management, 242–46; problems faced by, 227–39; strategies for success, 249–50; treatment of, 246–50; work versus nonwork conflicts, 250–52
Work, value and, 160
Work environment, 102
Work involvement, 7
Workshops, self-assessment, 169

ABOUT THE CONTRIBUTORS

VIRGINIA R. BOEHM is the owner of Assessment and Development Associates, a human resource consulting firm. Her research interests include assessment centers, job analysis, and organizational design. She has written a number of professional articles and chapters for books in the human resource area and serves on the editorial review board of *Personnel Psychology*. Dr. Boehm received her B.A. in psychology from Hanover College and her Ph.D. in social psychology from Columbia University.

DOUGLAS W. BRAY is chairman of the board of Development Dimensions International. His responsibilities include developing selection and training programs and consulting with organizations relative to selection, training, and development. Dr. Bray's research interests include adult human development and assessment centers. He is the author of *Formative Years in Business: A Long-Term AT&T Study of Managerial Lives* and co-author of *Managerial Lives in Transition: Advancing Age and Changing Times*. He has also written several chapters for books and articles appearing in publications such as the *Journal of Applied Psychology*, *Atlanta Economic Review*, the *American Psychologist*, *Professional Psychology*, and *The Wharton Magazine*. He serves on the editorial board of the *Academy of Management Executive*. Dr. Bray has received several honors including the Distinguished Contributions to Applied Psychology as a Professional Practice Award from the American Psychological Association, and the Professional Practice Award of the Society for Industrial and Organizational Psychology. Dr. Bray received his B.A. in sociology from American International College, his M.A. in psychology from Clark University, and his Ph.D. in psychology from Yale University.

PETER CAIRO is associate professor in psychology and education at Teachers College, Columbia University. His research interests include career development in organizations, counseling in business and industry, and computer-based adult career planning. He was consultant and staff psychologist for the AMPA Program at AT&T. His publications have appeared in the *Journal of Vocational Behavior, Personnel Psychology,* and *The Counseling Psychologist.* Dr. Cairo received his B.A. from Harvard University and his Ph.D. in counseling psychology from Columbia University.

GEORGIA T. CHAO is an assistant professor in the Department of Management at Michigan State University. Her current research interests include organizational socialization and career development. Her articles have appeared in such journals as *Personnel Psychology* and the *Journal of Applied Psychology.* Dr. Chao received her master's degree and Ph.D. in industrial and organizational psychology from Pennsylvania State University.

WILLIAM L. CRON is associate professor in the marketing department of the Edwin L. Cox School of Business, Southern Methodist University, Dallas, Texas. His research interests include marketing management and sales management. He has written for the *Journal of Marketing,* the *Journal of Marketing Research,* the *Academy of Management Journal,* the *Journal of Vocational Behavior,* and the *Journal of Personal Selling and Sales Management.* He serves on the editorial board of the *Journal of Personal Selling and Sales Management.* Dr. Cron received his B.S.B.A. from Xavier University and his M.B.A. and D.B.A. in marketing from Indiana University.

EDWARD R. DEL GAIZO is organizational effectiveness research manager at Learning International. His current research interest is management and sales research as it applies to overall organizational effectiveness. His articles have been published in the *Training and Development Journal* and *Behavioral Science Laboratory Research Report.* Dr. Del Gaizo received his B.A. in psychology from the State University of New York at Stony Brook, his M.A. in industrial and organizational psychology from the Ohio State University, and his Ph.D. in educational psychology from Fordham University.

RONALD G. DOWNEY is a professor in the Department of Psychology and Office of Planning and Evaluation at Kansas State University. His research interests include women in management, performance evaluation, part-time employment, and salary equity. Recent publications include articles in the *Psychological Bulletin, Journal of Applied Psychology, Research in Higher Education, Journal of Business and Psychology,* and *Educational and Psychological Measurement.* He is consulting editor to the *Journal of Applied Psychology* and *Psychological Bulletin.* Dr. Downey received his

B.S. in psychology from the University of Texas (Austin), and his M.S. and Ph.D. in psychology from Temple University.

JOHN P. FERNANDEZ is the division manager of Human Resource Forecasting and Planning at AT&T. His research interests are in racism and sexism in corporate life, child care, and upward mobility of managers. He has taught at the University of Pennsylvania, Antioch University, and Yale University. Dr. Fernandez's books include *Survival in the Corporate Fish Bowl: Moving into Upper and Middle Management* and *Child Care and Corporate Productivity: Resolving Family/Work Conflicts*. He received his B.A. in government from Harvard University and his M.A. and Ph.D. in sociology from the University of California, Berkeley.

MIRIAN M. GRADDICK is a division manager of Human Resource Strategy and Systems at AT&T. Her responsibilities include strategic business planning and leadership development programs. Dr. Graddick's research and development interests are in the areas of assessment centers, analysis of critical jobs, women in management, and the selection and development of expatriated managers. She has published in the *Journal of Applied Psychology*. Dr. Graddick received her B.A. in psychology from Hampton Institute and her M.S. and Ph.D. in industrial and organizational psychology from Pennsylvania State University.

JEFFREY H. GREENHAUS is professor in the Department of Management at Drexel University. His research interests include career planning and development, career decision making, and the interaction between work and family roles. His publications have appeared in journals such as the *Academy of Management Review*, the *Journal of Applied Psychology*, the *Journal of Vocational Behavior*, and *Human Resource Planning*. He serves on the editorial review boards of the *Journal of Applied Psychology* and the *Journal of Vocational Behavior*. Dr. Greenhaus received his B.A. in psychology from Hofstra University and his Ph.D. in industrial and organizational psychology from New York University.

DOUGLAS T. HALL is professor of organizational behavior in the School of Management, Boston University. His research interests include career development, executive succession, career plateauing, and work-family balance. Among other publications, he is author of *Careers in Organizations*, co-author of *Human Resources Management: Strategy, Design, and Implementation*, and editor of *Career Development in Organizations*. Dr. Hall is a fellow of the American Psychological Association and the Academy of Management. He is co-recipient of the Ghiselli Award from Division 14 of the American Psychological Association. Dr. Hall received his B.A. in industrial administration from Yale University and his M.S. and Ph.D. in management from M.I.T.

ANN HOWARD is president of Leadership Research Institute. Her research interests include leadership, career development, and managerial behavior. She is senior author of *Managerial Lives in Transition: Advancing Age and Changing Times*. She has written numerous book chapters and many articles appearing in publications such as the *Journal of Applied Psychology*, *Personnel Psychology*, the *Journal of Vocational Behavior*, the *Academy of Management Journal*, the *American Psychologist*, and *Professional Psychology*. Dr. Howard is president-elect of the Society for Industrial and Organizational Psychology and is former editor of *The Industrial and Organizational Psychologist*. She is recipient of an award for distinguished achievements in the sciences from Goucher College. Dr. Howard received her B.A. in psychology from Goucher College, her M.S. in industrial psychology from San Francisco State University, and her Ph.D. in industrial and organizational psychology from the University of Maryland.

HAROLD G. KAUFMAN is professor of management, director of the organizational behavior program and director of the research program in science, technology, and human resources in the Division of Management at Polytechnic University, Brooklyn, New York. His research interests include career management of organizational professionals, and utilization and obsolescence of knowledge and skills. He is the author of *Obsolescence and Professional Career Development*. His articles have appeared in a variety of publications including the *Journal of Applied Psychology* and the *Journal of Engineering Education*. Dr. Kaufman received the Outstanding Paper Award from the Continuing Professional Development Division of the American Society for Engineering Education. Dr. Kaufman received his B.M.E. in mechanical engineering from Cooper Union, his M.S. in industrial engineering from New York University, and his Ph.D. in industrial and organizational psychology, also from New York University.

ABRAHAM K. KORMAN is the Wollman Distinguished Professor of Management in the Department of Management at Baruch College. His research interests include success and alienation, irrationality in organizations, and the psychology of outsider groups. He is the author of *The Outsiders: Jews in Corporate America* and senior author of *Career Success/ Personal Failure*. He has lectured on management topics in Great Britain, the Netherlands, Egypt, Israel, and the People's Republic of China. Dr. Korman received his B.A. in economics from Brooklyn College, his M.A. in labor and industrial relations from the University of Illinois, and his Ph.D. in industrial and organizational psychology from the University of Minnesota.

KATHY E. KRAM is associate professor of organizational behavior in the School of Management at Boston University. Her research interests include adult development, career development, management of values and ethics in organizations, and gender dynamics at work. She is the author of *Mentoring at Work* and has written many articles appearing in publications such as the *Academy of Management Journal, Organizational Dynamics,* and *Organizational Behavior and Human Performance.* She serves on the editorial board of the *Academy of Management Executive* and is a staff member of the National Training Laboratories (NTL). Dr. Kram received her B.S. and M.S. in management from M.I.T. and her Ph.D. in organizational behavior from Yale University.

MARY ANNE LAHEY is a personnel management consultant. Previously, she was staff psychologist in the Center for Business and Economic Development at Auburn University in Montgomery. Her research interests include job security and performance appraisal. She has had articles in the *Journal of Applied Psychology, Psychological Bulletin,* and *Public Personnel Management.* Dr. Lahey received her B.S. in psychology from Illinois State University and her M.S. and Ph.D. in industrial and organizational psychology from Kansas State University.

JANINA C. LATACK is associate professor on the Faculty of Management and Human Resources at the Ohio State University. Her research interests include coping with job stress, career development, and job loss and outplacement. Her articles have appeared in the *Academy of Management Review, Organizational Behavior and Human Decision Processes,* and the *Journal of Applied Psychology.* Dr. Latack received her B.A. in advertising, her M.A. in higher education administration, and her Ph.D. in organizational behavior, all from Michigan State University.

MICHAEL M. LOMBARDO is director of research on leadership development at the Center for Creative Leadership in Greensboro, North Carolina. His research interests are in how people become successful in leadership positions. He is co-author of *The Lessons of Experience* and senior author of *Looking Glass: An Organizational Simulation.* Dr. Lombardo received his B.A. in political science and his M.Ed. and Ed.D. in educational administration, all from the University of North Carolina.

MANUEL LONDON is a district manager of Planning and Management Systems for AT&T's Network Operations Education and Training Group. His research interests include career development, personnel decisions, the relationship between work and nonwork, and the human resource professional as change agent. His books include *Developing Managers, Managing*

Careers (with Stephen Stumpf), and *Career Management and Survival in the Work Place* (with Edward Mone). Dr. London has been consulting editor for the *Academy of Management Journal* and currently serves on the editorial boards of *Personnel Psychology*, the *Journal of Applied Psychology*, and *Administrative Science Quarterly*. He is a fellow of the American Psychological Association. Dr. London received his A.B. in philosophy and psychology from Case Western Reserve University and his M.A. and Ph.D. in industrial and organizational psychology from the Ohio State University.

KAREN S. LYNESS is manager of Personnel and Field Management Research at Avon Products, Inc. Her projects focus on the key management positions in the field sales force. Her research interests also include how managers deal with ambiguity and change, the socialization of new managers, and job analysis of management positions. Her publications have appeared in the *Journal of Applied Psychology* and *Organizational Behavior and Human Decision Processes*. Before joining Avon Products, Inc., in 1987, Dr. Lyness was Director of Operations for the AMPA Program at AT&T Corporate Headquarters. Also, since 1983, she has been a member of the adjunct faculty for the graduate-level organizational psychology program at Columbia University. Dr. Lyness received her M.A. and Ph.D. in industrial and organizational psychology from the Ohio State University.

EDWARD M. MONE is a staff manager in the Network Operations Management Development Operations Group at AT&T. His responsibilities include generic management training, leadership training, and technical training for middle managers. His research interests are in management development and career development. He is co-author of *Career Management and Survival in the Work Place*. Mr. Mone received his A.B. in economics from Hunter College where he also received his M.A. in college counseling and student development. He is currently studying for his Ph.D. in organizational psychology at Teachers College, Columbia University.

SAMUEL RABINOWITZ is associate professor of management with the Faculty of Business Studies at Rutgers University. His research interests include job involvement and career dynamics. He has published in *Psychological Bulletin*, the *Journal of Applied Psychology*, and the *Journal of Occupational Behavior*. He serves on the editorial board of the *Journal of Vocational Behavior*. Dr. Rabinowitz received his B.B.A. in industrial psychology from Bernard Baruch College of the City University of New York. He received his M.A. and Ph.D. in industrial and organizational psychology from Michigan State University.

JOSEPH A. RAELIN is professor of administrative sciences in the School of Management, Boston College. His research interests concentrate on management and career concerns of salaried professionals. He is the author of *The Clash of Cultures: Managers and Professionals, The Salaried Professional: How to Make the Most of Your Career*, and *Building a Career*. His articles have appeared in such journals as the *Academy of Management Executive*, the *Academy of Management Review*, and the *Journal of Vocational Behavior*. Dr. Raelin received his M.Ed. in counseling from Tufts University, his C.A.G.S. in organizational development from Boston University, and his Ph.D. in policy studies from the State University of New York, Buffalo.

JOHN W. SLOCUM, JR., is the O. Paul Corby Professor of Organizational Behavior at the Edwin L. Cox School of Business at Southern Methodist University. His research interests include reward systems, corporate strategy, and mobility patterns of employees. He is co-author of *Management and Organizational Behavior*. His publications have appeared in the *Academy of Management Journal*, the *Academy of Management Executive*, the *Journal of Vocational Behavior*, and the *Journal of Applied Psychology*. Dr. Slocum is a fellow in the Academy of Management and the Decision Science Institute. He is past president of the Academy of Management and past editor of the *Academy of Management Journal*. Dr. Slocum received his B.A. in liberal arts from Westminster College, his M.B.A. in industrial relations from Kent State University, and his Ph.D. in organizational behavior from the University of Washington.

CYNTHIA B. SMITH is a staff manager of Consumer Markets and Services—Operator Services at AT&T, responsible for human resource development. Her research interests include hiring decisions, career management decisions, and diagnostic assessment. She has published in the *American Association of Counseling and Development Journal* and the *Journal of Employment Counseling*. Dr. Smith received her B.S. in sociology and psychology from West Virginia University, her M.A. in industrial sociology from Marshall University, and her Ph.D. in human development from the University of Maryland.

STEPHEN A. STUMPF is associate professor of management and director of the Management Simulation Projects Group in the Graduate School of Business Administration at New York University. His research interests include executive development, strategic decision making, strategic management, and career development. He is author of *Choosing a Career in Business* and co-author of *Managing Careers*. His articles have appeared in the *Academy of Management Journal*, the *Journal of Vocational Behavior*, *Personnel Psychology*, and the *Journal of Business Strategy*. Dr. Stumpf is a Fulbright Scholar and has won trwo awards for research, the S. Rains Wallace Dissertation Award and the Herman E. Krooss Award for Outstanding Dissertation. Dr. Stumpf received his B.S. in chemical engineering from the Rensselaer Polytechnic Institute, his M.B.A. in behavioral science from the University of Rochester, and his Ph.D. in management/organizational behavior and industrial and organizational psychology from New York University.

LYNN SUMMERS is vice president of training and management development at Hardee's Food Systems, Inc. His responsibilities include developing training and management development programs. He has published in the *Training and Development Journal*. He was a summer fellow at the Center for Creative Leadership and was a recent participant in the Executive Program at the University of North Carolina. Dr. Summers received his A.B. in psychology from Kenyon College and his M.A. and Ph.D. in industrial and organizational psychology from the University of South Florida.

DAVID A. THOMAS is assistant professor of management at the Wharton School of the University of Pennsylvania. His research interests include career dynamics, intergroup relations, and organizational change. He has written a chapter for the *Handbook of Career Theory* and for the *International Review of Industrial and Organizational Psychology*. Dr. Thomas received his B.A. in administrative science from Yale University, his M.A. in psychology from Columbia University, and his Ph.D. in organizational behavior from Yale University.

DATE DUE

AP 21 '92			
OC 15 00			

DEMCO 38-297